For mum,

with much lo

Mauuu

LEADERSHIP IN CONFLICT
1914–1918

LEADERSHIP IN CONFLICT
1914–1918

Edited by Matthew Hughes
and Matthew Seligmann

LEO COOPER

First published in Great Britain in 2000
by
LEO COOPER
an imprint of
Pen & Sword Books Ltd,
47 Church Street,
Barnsley, South Yorkshire S70 2AS

© Matthew Hughes and Matthew Seligmann

A CIP record for this book is available from the British Library

ISBN 0 85052 751 1

Typeset in Sabon by Phoenix Typesetting, Ilkley, West Yorkshire.

Printed in Great Britain by Redwood Books Ltd,
Trowbridge, Wilts

Contents

Notes on Contributors

Ian Beckett is Professor of Modern History at the University of Luton. A Fellow of the Royal Historical Society, he was formerly Senior Lecturer in War Studies at the Royal Military Academy, Sandhurst and has been Visiting Professor at the US Naval War College, Newport, Rhode Island. His study of the Great War in the Longman 'Modern Wars in Perspective' series was published in 2000.

J.M. Bourne is Senior Lecturer in Modern History at the University of Birmingham. He is the author of *Britain and the Great War* (London: Edward Arnold, 1989, 1991) and a contributor to *Facing Armageddon* (Barnsley: Pen & Sword, 1996), *Passchendaele in Perspective* (Barnsley: Pen & Sword, 1997) and *At the Eleventh Hour* (Barnsley: Pen & Sword, 1998). He is currently working on a multi-biography of British generals on the Western Front, which is due for publication in 2001.

Robert T. Foley is Lecturer in Defence Studies at the Joint Services Command and Staff College, Watchfield. He has been editor of *The War Studies Journal* and is the author of a number of articles on German strategic thought. His book *Schlieffen's Military Writings* is being published by Frank Cass in 2000.

James F. Gensch obtained his doctorate from King's College London with a thesis entitled 'Italy, Geography and the First World War'. He is currently working as a freelance military historian and is conducting research on the American Civil War with a particular emphasis on the battle of Shiloh.

Matthew Hughes is Lecturer in History at University College Northampton. He is author of *Allenby and British Strategy in the Middle East, 1917–1919* (London: Frank Cass, 1999) and a contributor to *Military Power: Land Warfare in Theory and Practice* (London: Frank Cass, 1997). He has written articles on the Spanish Civil War for the *Journal of the Royal United Services Institute* and *The International Journal of Iberian Studies* and on the Second World War for the *Imperial War Museum Review*.

David Jordan was educated at the Universities of Oxford and Birmingham. He is Lecturer in Defence Studies at the Joint Services Command and Staff College, Watchfield, where he is currently undertaking research into the British occupation of Indonesia, 1945–46. His book *Tactical Airpower in the First World War* is being published by Frank Cass in 2000.

Annika Mombauer, who studied at the Universities of Münster and Sussex, is Lecturer in European History at the Open University in Milton Keynes. Her research interests include Wilhelmine Germany, the origins of the First World War, and postwar Germany. Her publications include *Helmuth von Moltke and the Origins of the First World War* (CUP, 2001) and *The Debate on the Origins of the First World War* (Longman, 2000).

William Philpott is Senior Lecturer in Modern History at London Guildhall University. He is the author of a study of Allied strategic policy in the First World War, *Anglo-French Relations and Strategy on the Western Front, 1914–1918* (Basingstoke: Macmillan, 1996), and a number of journal articles and book chapters on aspects of alliance relations and military command in the First World War. He is currently editing the command diaries of Sir John French for publication by the Army Records Society, and co-editing a collection of essays on Anglo-French defence relations between the wars.

Denise Poynter is a part-time research student at the University of Luton. She is currently working on her PhD thesis, which is entitled 'Shell Shocked Women: A Study of the Incidence and Experience of War Neurosis and Other Psychological Disorders Occurring Amongst British Women who Served Alongside the British Expeditionary Forces during the First World War.'

Matthew S. Seligmann is Senior Lecturer in History at University College Northampton. Recent publications include *Rivalry in Southern Africa: The Transformation of German Colonial Policy* (Basingstoke: Macmillan, 1998), *Germany from Reich to Republic, 1871–1918: Politics, Hierarchy and Elites* (Basingstoke: Macmillan, 2000) and articles in *German History, Imperial War Museum Review* and *Imago*

Mundi. His current research is on external perceptions of German military intentions before the First World War.

Peter Simkins served for more than thirty-five years on the staff of the Imperial War Museum, where he was Senior Historian from 1976 until his retirement in 1999. He was Visiting Fellow at the Australian War Memorial in 1993 and the Douglas Haig Fellow in 1999. He is now Honorary Professor in Modern History at the University of Birmingham. His book *Kitchener's Army* (1998) was awarded the Templer Medal by the Society for Army Historical Research.

Matthew Stibbe was born in London in 1969 and educated at the Universities of Bristol and Sussex. He has previously taught at the University of Wales, Bangor, and is currently Lecturer in History at Liverpool Hope University College. He has recently completed a book on German Anglophobia during the First World War for Cambridge University Press and is now working on a new project on women in Nazi Germany.

Keith M. Wilson is Reader in International History at the University of Leeds. Among his publications are *The Policy of the Entente: The Determinants of British Foreign Policy 1904–1914* (1985); *The Rasp of War: The Letters of H.A. Gwynne to the Countess of Bathurst 1914–1918* (1988); *Channel Tunnel Visions 1850–1945: Dreams and Nightmares* (1994).

David R. Woodward is Professor of History at Marshall University in Huntington, West Virginia. He has been a student of the First World War for over thirty years. His publications include *Lloyd George and the Generals* (Newark NJ: University of Delaware Press, 1983), *Trial by Friendship: Anglo-American Relations, 1917–1918* (Lexington, KT: University of Kentucky Press, 1993), *The Military Correspondence of Field Marshal Sir William Robertson: Chief Imperial General Staff, December 1915–February 1918* (London: Army Records Society, 1989), and *Field Marshal Sir William Robertson: Chief of the Imperial General Staff in the Great War* (Westport CT: Praeger, 1998).

Foreword

Having edited collections of essays on the First World War and contributed to other volumes, I am all too well aware of the difficulties and possible pitfalls involved. Quite apart from the inevitable problems of deadlines and wordage, there are the more serious challenges of achieving a coherent structure and presenting fresh, original work to a readership which, though keen in principle, may suspect that the subject matter is already familiar to them.

The editors of *Leadership in Conflict 1914–1918* emerge with a good deal of credit on these criteria. True, some of the Western Front commanders re-assessed here, notably Foch and Rawlinson, have been much studied recently, but the worthwhile contributions on these controversial figures are complemented by two on the less well-known Sir William Heneker and on Trenchard as commander of the Royal Flying Corps. There are original – and critical – reappraisals, both based on doctoral research, of Moltke the Younger and Falkenhayn, but an opportunity has been missed to re-assess German commanders in the latter part of the war, or in other theatres.

Two essays are devoted both to the United States and Italy which all admirably sustain the volume's focus on civil-military relations and domestic politics as distinct from operations. It is again a matter of regret that space permits only one representative commander from each country to be studied (Pershing and Cadorna). One would have welcomed more than two contributions devoted to the 'Home Front', stimulating though these are. The volume concludes strongly with two excellent reappraisals of the roles and influence of the monarchs of Britain and Germany. Ian Beckett, in particular, has drawn on a wide range of sources, notably the royal archives at Windsor Castle, for a judicious reappraisal of the role of King George V.

Thus, so far from leaving the impression that this is just another canter over well-trodden battlefields, this lively collection which is mostly a showcase for a new generation of historians, opens up exciting possibilities for further research and publications along the lines developed here.

Brian Bond
(Professor of Military History at King's College London and President of the British Commission for Military History)

Introduction

People and the Tides of History: Does Personality Matter in the First World War?

Matthew Hughes and Matthew Seligmann

'The death of one person is a tragedy. The death of a million people is a statistic.'

(Joseph Stalin)

'Millions of individuals,' to cite the words of Professor Derek Beales, 'have found no defence against the juggernauts of history: the Cathars of Montaillou, the American Indians, or in the twentieth century those who fought in the trenches . . .'[1] That the First World War was one of these so-called 'juggernauts', a movement so powerful that no one single soul could hope to influence, let alone deflect, its course single-handedly, seems at first glance self-evident. It entailed such a massive array of force and forces that clearly no one person could be its master. It was such an overwhelming combination of the dislocative and destructive that it could not help but engulf the participants in their millions. Those caught up in the grasp of this colossal cataclysm were the masses and not the singular or the solitary.

Making sense of so vast a movement has led some historians to seek explanatory devices of comparable scope and grandeur. The bigger picture, it seems, when it is on the scale of the First World War, has required a gazetteer no less massive. As we will see, masculinity, agriculture, modernity and capitalism have all been wheeled out to serve as the base for a comprehensive explanatory model of the conflict. In this sense, the complaint of the nineteenth-century French historian, Monod, that 'historians are too much in the habit of paying attention only to the brilliant, clamorous and ephemeral manifestations of human activity, to great events and great men, instead of depicting the great and slow changes of economic and social institutions . . .'[2] does not apply to current historical treatment of the Great War. Historians have long viewed the war as one of history's 'juggernauts' and have all too often reached out for broad generalizations.

Is this situation satisfactory? To some historians this answer is clearly in the negative. If we return, for example, to the quotation from Derek Beales, it is clear that it is just such assumptions about the explanatory power of trends – 'the mythology of trends' he calls it – that he is trying to resist. As he perceptively comments: 'It must be remembered on the other side that the juggernauts are powered and directed by men . . .'[3] In other words, excluding acts of God, many, if not most, of the events of history are the product of some form of human agency. The First World War, we would argue, is no exception to this rule. In saying this, we recognize that we are going against the currents of contemporary historical opinion, the tide of which is to stress the sweeping overview and, thereby, deliberately to marginalize individual experience.

An example of a book that develops a broad theoretical approach, incorporating gender and the primal instinct to kill, and in so doing has raised much interest and controversy, is Joanna Bourke's recent *Intimate History of Killing: Face-to-Face Killing in Twentieth-Century Warfare* (1999). This volume builds upon ideas from her earlier work *Dismembering the Male: Men's Bodies, Britain and the Great War* (1996) to suggest that men (and women) like killing, that institutional structures channel this aggressive urge, and that war – including the First World War – is a logical outcome of a society that emphasizes such macho virtues. This emphasis, which is also discussed in Niall Ferguson's much noted *The Pity of War*, provides valuable insights into understanding conflict: in particular, it offers a psychological framework for explaining why soldiers fight.[4] As a result, in this interpretation, the Great War becomes a testing ground of masculine virtues and identities.

Another recent example of the way in which the First World War can be rendered subordinate to a single overarching historical principle is Avner Offer's *The First World War: An Agrarian Interpretation* (1989). Focusing on agricultural production and distribution, it examines the war in the light of food supplies. For Offer, the First World War was 'not only a war of steel and gold, but a war of bread and potatoes.'[5] In particular, the way in which these could be interdicted by enemy action and/or increased by domestic regulation and control is used as an explanatory device for the war in general.

Also germane to any discussion of overarching approaches to the First World War are those interpretations that focus on the issue of modernity and the war's role in ushering in a new era. This is an exciting area of inquiry that has produced some substantial scholarly advances.

Works by Modris Eksteins, Volker Berghahn and Stephen Kern, for example, have done much to alter our understanding of the extent to which the First World War represented a caesura in modern history.[6] However, best known in this context – perhaps because of his role in the well-received television documentary series '1914–18' – is Jay Winter. In his work *Sites of Memory, Sites of Mourning* he looks at popular reactions to the tragedy of the Great War, and examines how ordinary people expressed grief through various mourning processes. He shows that 'the universality of bereavement in the Europe of the Great War' was such that these grieving processes had the effect of changing societies irrespective of national frontiers. This approach challenges Paul Fussell's classic *The Great War and Modern Memory* (1975) which approaches changes in postwar society through the wartime experience of the educated class and their use of the ironic style in their later literary output.[7]

Not all of the impersonal interpretations of the First World War are recent. Lenin, for instance, provided the classic Marxist analysis of the First World War in his 1916 polemic *Imperialism: the Highest Stage of Capitalism*. Lenin's paradigm reduces the war to a clash between the capitalist monopoly conglomerates of the various protagonists, which use nations and peoples to wage their struggle for control of markets, raw materials and capital outlets. The Leninist approach focuses on industrial monoliths fighting across national borders. Therefore, people vanish from the picture.

Taken together, the above examples illustrate a variety of ways in which broad historical generalizations have been used to make the Great War more explicable. By subordinating the role of the individual and focusing on the more massive forces of historical change, all of the above-mentioned works have contributed a new understanding to the place of the First World War in the historical development of the modern period. Given the success these approaches have enjoyed, the question might be asked: why advocate a return to a methodology based upon examining personal traits and determining the role of the individual? There are, in fact, a number of reasons for so doing.

First of all, there are questions that can be raised with respect to the impersonal approach to history. As Otto Pflanze, editor of the *American Historical Review*, has observed, albeit in the context of modern German history, there is a danger in constructing a comprehensive explanatory model of major human events. It can lead to history that is 'frequently determinist and thoroughly depersonalised'. This can create circumstances in which the models become more important than the historical events that they purport to explain. As Pflanze put it, for some historians the models 'have ceased to be merely heuristic instruments but have themselves developed into fictitious historical reality.'[8]

While we do not believe that Bourke, Offer or Winter have fallen into this trap, few (non-Marxists) would deny that this has been a problem for Marxist historical interpretations in general, and for Lenin's view of the First World War in particular. Likewise, many 'post-modern' views suffer from this problem. One is reminded of the current joke among academics: 'Okay, so it works in *reality*, but does it work in *theory*?'

Another reason for adopting an approach that focuses on individuals and their personalities is that many of the people who read history find this to be both interesting and revealing and regret the passing of such ideas from the pages of history. The manner in which the removal of these foci from the history books might diminish popular appreciation of the historian's art has been examined by Robert Birley. He saw the matter thus:

> Should we tell these stories today? At least, I feel, we should realize how we cut ourselves off from the past if we do not. . . . More and more the historian has to concern himself with what is regarded as the essential substructure of society. . . . And yet Life, the actual life of individuals, goes on in the despised superstructure. Its twists and turns produce dramatic episodes, tragic or comic, pathetic or just plain exciting, and moments which test men and women so that their true character is displayed. These make good stories, which men feel instinctively to be significant, and much of the significance of History will be lost if they are ignored.[9]

A number of contemporary historians have demonstrated the validity of this point by writing acclaimed historical works with the stories about people not only left in, but given a prominent dimension. Orlando Figes, for example, makes substantial use of personal reminiscences in his *A People's Tragedy*, and in doing so brings alive the fact that Russia's part in the First World War involved a series of individuals interacting and competing at a time of great crisis.[10] In so doing, Figes' penmanship brings the war to life and keeps the reader's attention from beginning to end. There is perhaps an ironic contrast here in the fact that many Post-Modernists and Neo-Marxists, themselves uninterested in personalities, produce impenetrable general theories on history aimed at the initiated and inaccessible to the ordinary reader. Yet it is precisely these ordinary people that Post-Modernists are so keen to rescue from elite history. In failing to do so, they give substance to Disraeli's quip 'read not history, nothing but biography for that is life without theory. . . .'[11]

On top of this, many historians regard a focus on the individual as a useful explanatory tool. The American historian, Barbara Tuchman, whose book *The Guns of August* about the outset of the First World

War won a Pulitzer Prize, is among their number.[12] As she observed: 'Biography is useful because it encompasses the universal in the particular. It is a focus that allows both the writer to narrow his field to manageable dimensions and the reader to more easily comprehend the subject.'[13] Complementing this judgement from the other side is J.S. Mill's timeless comment that 'Men are not, when brought together, converted into another kind of substance.'[14] One must still look at the individual to understand the masses and the past.

*   *   *

The essays in this volume provide a coherent analysis of the many different roles that could be played by individuals in a range of fields during the First World War. For ease of access and to encourage ready comparison, they have been organized into six different sections, each of which reflects a different theatre of conflict or point of authority. Thus, Part One looks at the Western Front from the perspective of key figures who served on the Entente side. It opens with two essays, one by Peter Simkins and the other by William Philpott, that take as their theme inter-Allied interaction and interchange. As is well known, although successful coalition warfare requires close co-operation, relations between Allied military leaders were often fraught. This was partly a reflection of national chauvinism, but also reflected the temperament and personality of those involved. Some generals, as Peter Simkins shows with the example of Sir Henry Rawlinson, handled the diplomacy of alliance warfare better than others. Yet, there were other aspects to the relationship. When the British formed a minority proportion of the Allied army in France, they were more amenable to French direction of operations. By 1918, when the British formed a qualitative and quantitative majority on the Western Front they were more insistent on fighting the war the way they wanted. Moreover, as Philpott demonstrates, Foch as Allied generalissimo was able, by force of personality, to smooth over these differences and co-ordinate the British and French forces and take them to victory in November 1918. The following chapter moves from inter-Allied relations to the difficulties that could occur within particular armies. Through a study of the operational level of war, as illustrated by the career of Major General Sir William Heneker, John Bourne illustrates the impact a determined colonial soldier, with reasonable relations with his superiors, could make on the performance of a division. This is complemented by a chapter on inter-service rivalry by David Jordan. The First World War witnessed the advent of three-dimensional warfare as combat began to fill the skies as well as the land and sea. Some people recognized the importance of air power. As Jordan shows, Sir Hugh Trenchard figured large in the development of British air power. He had to fight to achieve this, as other commanders had different visions of future patterns of the war in the air.

Part Two takes a similar approach but this time looks at the Germans on the Western Front by way of two key commanders: Helmuth von Moltke the Younger and Erich von Falkenhayn. Both of these men were in charge of German strategy and war planning: Moltke was in command during the crucial days up to the failure at the Marne in 1914, Falkenhayn until his dismissal in late 1916. Both were found wanting as they struggled not only with a determined enemy but also with internecine conflicts within the German decision-making elite. Moltke, as Annika Mombauer convincingly shows, broke down under the strain of interference from the Kaiser, his military entourage and other generals hungry for his job. As Robert Foley goes on to argue, Falkenhayn suffered similarly from intrigues and backstabbing from those envious of his position and from those who opposed his war strategy. In particular, Falkenhayn was under pressure from Erich Ludendorff and Paul von Hindenburg, the men who would eventually take Germany to defeat in 1918 (and then claim it was not their fault). The role of these two influential figures is discussed in more depth in a chapter by Matthew Stibbe in Part Six.

America is the subject of Part Three. The entry of the United States into the war was a decisive factor in the eventual Allied victory, as the arrival of the doughboys gave the flagging Entente powers an immense psychological and material boost. Yet if morale increased at the popular level, at the top things were different. The forces of the United States were led by the imposing 'Black Jack' Pershing. An ardent American patriot, Pershing wanted the 'American' contribution to the war to be distinctly and unambiguously independent. As a result, he was determined to keep his troops together as a single force, against British and French pressure to dilute the American army in France. This led to a series of increasingly acrimonious personal exchanges as the British and French tried to dominate Pershing and use his men in penny packets with their own forces. Pershing would have none of this and, thus, fully deserves Woodward's sobriquet of 'Proconsul'. The next chapter switches the focus from American forces on the Western Front to American propaganda on their Home Front by looking at the activities of James Watson Gerard, America's ambassador to Berlin up to 1917. In this essay, Matthew Seligmann explores Gerard's portrayal of the German enemy to the American people. Looking at the spoken and written word as well as the motion picture, it details the way that Gerard's abrasive personality, not always useful as a diplomat, came into its own as Gerard toured the country detailing the wickedness of the 'Hun'.

Part Four moves the emphasis to Italy. This oft-neglected area of study is the subject of two essays. Firstly, James Gentsch examines the Italian army and its commander, Luigi Cadorna, in the period up the battle of Caporetto in 1917. The Italians were faced with fighting a war in the Alps: a war as much against the inhospitable terrain as the Austro-Hungarian army. Gentsch shows that this was not the only difficulty for Cadorna: struggles within the Italian military, in particular rivalry with the navy, as well as lack of co-ordination with politicians, hampered an already difficult position. Then Matthew Hughes takes up the story by looking at the period after Caporetto. Following this battle, an Anglo-French force was sent to stiffen the Italian line and Hughes examines the civil-military dispute within Britain over the deployment and objectives of the force. Hughes shows that Britain's generals did not attempt to usurp civilian control, unlike the situation in Germany described in Part Two. This was one of the reasons why Britain won the war.

In Part Five the Home Front comes under scrutiny. An in-depth essay by Keith Wilson examines the way in which a number of forceful personalities responded to the perceived inadequacies of a civilian administration fighting a total war, by forming a new party above politics dedicated to winning the war. Denise Poynter adds to our understanding of the Home Front at war by looking at the topical subject of shell shock victims and the treatment offered to them by the famous Dr Rivers. Rivers, along with some like-minded souls, were struggling with a medical establishment unfamiliar with the mental traumas of war and sceptical of the efficacy of new treatments for minds shattered by war in the trenches.

Finally, Part Six takes royalty as its theme. In 1914, the contribution of monarchs to military policy was still a substantial one, even in Britain. As Ian Beckett shows, King George V had many channels whereby he could have an input into British strategic planning. George V comes out of this as someone willing to interfere, but within constitutional limits; his cousin, Kaiser Wilhelm II, played a different role. Once seen as a weak-willed dilettante who was out of his depth when real fighting began, Matthew Stibbe shows that, while this was true, Wilhelm nevertheless resisted encroachments on his rights of appointment to command level positions. Hindenburg and Ludendorff challenged this. They were eventually able to marginalize the Kaiser and in so doing took away the restraining influence that had prevented foolish policies such as unrestricted U-boat warfare. As a consequence, the Germans moved from total war to absolute war to defeat.

As these essays make clear, both individually and collectively, in response to the question posed in the title of this introduction: personality did matter in the First World War. This was true not only in the clichéd sense that the war was a test of character, but also in respect to the fact that it produced situations in which successful co-operation and amicable interaction were vital for military success. In such scenarios some personalities meshed and others clashed – a true example of what we mean by leadership in conflict.

To conclude our summary of the role of the individual in this 'age of extremes', we would draw attention to the recent words of the eminent historian of Germany, Fritz Stern: 'These days my discipline and our culture like to deny the historic importance of individuals . . . an odd conclusion to reach at the end of a century that has had some terrifying and a few benign examples of people who by themselves shaped world history.'[15]

Notes

1   Derek Beales, 'History and Biography: An Inaugural Lecture', in T.C.W. Blanking and David Cannadine (eds), *History and Biography: Essays in Honour of Derek Beales* (Cambridge: CUP, 1996), p.282.
2   Quoted in G.V. Plekhanov, *The Role of the Individual in History* (London: Lawrence & Wishart, 1976), pp.23–4.
3   Beales, 'History and Biography', p.282.
4   Niall Ferguson, *The Pity of War* (London: Allen Lane, 1998), ch.12.
5   Avner Offer, *The First World War: An Agrarian Interpretation* (Oxford: Clarendon Press, 1991), p.1.
6   Modris Eksteins, *Rites of Spring: The Great War and the Birth of the Modern Age* (Boston: Houghton Mifflin, 1989); Stephen Kern, *The Culture of Time and Space, 1880–1918* (London: Weidenfeld and Nicolson, 1983); Volker R. Berghahn, *Sarajewo, 28. Juni 1914: Der Untergang des alten Europa* (Munich: Dt. Taschenbuch Verlag, 1997).
7   For a detailed look at the shortcomings of Fussell's work see Robin Prior & Trevor Wilson, 'Paul Fussell at War' in *War in History*, (1994) 1, 63–80.
8   Otto Pflanze, quoted in John C.G. Röhl, *The Kaiser and his Court: Wilhelm II and the Government of Germany* (Cambridge: CUP, 1994), p.109.
9   Robert Birley, *The Undergrowth of History* (London: Historical Association, 1955), pp.28–9
10 Orlando Figes, *A People's Tragedy: The Russian Revolution, 1891–1924* (London: Jonathan Cape, 1996).
11 Quoted in Karina Urbach, *Birmarck's favourite Englishman: Lord Odo Russell's Mission to Berlin* (London: I.B. Tauris, 1999), p.2.
12 Barbara Tuchman, *The Guns of August* (New York: The Macmillan Co, 1962).
13 Barbara Tuchman, *Practising History* (Basingstoke: Papermac, 1983), p.81.

14 J.S. Mill, *A System of Logic*, vii, 1. Quoted in E.H. Carr, *What is History?* (London: Penguin, 1978), p.31.

15 Fritz Stern, *Einstein's German World* (Princeton: Princeton UP, 1999). Quoted in the review by David Blackbourn in *London Review of Books*, 3 February 2000, p.32.

Part One
The Allied Powers on the Western Front

Chapter 1

For Better or For Worse: Sir Henry Rawlinson and his Allies in 1916 and 1918

Peter Simkins

The current upsurge of renewed interest in the First World War has been marked by the publication of several perceptive analyses by British, Commonwealth and American scholars, of inter-Allied relations from 1914 to 1918, particularly those between the British and Dominion forces and the armies of the other Entente powers on the Western Front.[1] However, as William Philpott, one of the leading specialists in this subject area, has observed, the primary focus of such studies has been 'the high political decision making which lay behind alliance military policy'.[2] At the other end of the scale, attention has also been paid by scholars to the many contacts between British and Dominion junior officers and other ranks and Belgian and French civilians behind the lines.[3] Rather less research has been devoted to inter-Allied command relationships at Army, corps and divisional level and the extent to which these influenced, or were affected by, the day-to-day conduct of operations on the Western Front. Like Philpott's own recent study of Britain, France and the Belgian Army, this essay seeks to fill another small part of that gap in the historiography of the Great War by examining how *one* of the British Army commanders – General Sir Henry Rawlinson – got on with his French and American counterparts at there crucial stages of the war in 1916 and 1918.

Rawlinson represents an interesting case study in this regard for a variety of reasons. As commander of the British Fourth Army, he was at the head of the principal formation which served directly alongside the French throughout the Somme offensive in 1916, in the defence of Amiens at Villers Bretonneux in April 1918, and finally in the victorious 'Hundred Days' offensive of August to November 1918. In each of the offensives in question, Rawlinson's Fourth Army was in the forefront of the battle and arguably constituted the cutting edge of the Allied effort. Moreover, in his very full daily diary entries, Rawlinson presents a substantial body of personal evidence about the events which he witnessed and influenced. Of the other army commanders who, under Douglas Haig, had the most prolonged and direct contacts with Allied units and leaders, Herbert Plumer, of the British Second Army, left no papers, while Henry Horne, of the First Army – whose daily letters to his wife do survive – dealt mainly with the Portuguese, a minor ally in comparison with the French, Belgians and Americans.[4] Fourth Army's operations in 1916 and 1918 were, of course, described in considerable detail in the British official history, but while the relevant volumes give extensive coverage to the discussions, agreements and occasional disputes between the Fourth Army and its allies, the official historians do not often deal with matters of temperament and personality and their record of inter-Allied relations is consequently rather flat and colourless in this respect.[5] Similarly, the excellent study by Robin Prior and Trevor Wilson of Rawlinson's period of command does contain frequent references to French operations and the problems of co-ordination between Fourth Army and the French Sixth and First Armies in 1916 and 1918, yet reveals relatively little of Rawlinson's private thoughts and feelings. Sir Frederick Maurice's life of Rawlinson only fleetingly touches upon these issues and hardly makes any mention at all of Rawlinson's recurrent difficulties with General Debeney of the French First Army in the spring, summer and autumn of 1918.[6] Even Rawlinson's Chief-of-Staff, Major General Sir Archibald Montgomery, diplomatically glosses over this controversial topic in his weighty account of the Fourth Army's operations and achievements in the 'Hundred Days'.[7] Rawlinson's own diary, therefore, offers us perhaps the best means of gaining a real insight into the personal aspects of inter-Allied relations at Army command level.

One should emphasize that, as a rule, Rawlinson's dealings with his allies – and especially the French – were rarely tinged with the mixture of prickly intolerance, contempt, suspicion and chauvinism which all too often characterized the attitudes of his Commander-in-Chief, Sir Douglas Haig. As early as November 1914, shortly after the First Battle of Ypres, Haig – then still commanding I Corps – was complaining of the French failure to relieve his hard-pressed and weakened formations. This, Haig commented, was because 'ever since we landed in France they seem ready to drain the last drop of blood out of the British force'.[8] In March 1916, he wrote that 'there are not many officers in the French staff with gentlemanly ideas. They are out to get as much from the British as they possibly can'.[9] Haig was no less acerbic in his remarks about individual Allied military leaders or officers from nations other than France. Of Joffre, the French Commander-in-Chief, Haig observed in April 1916: '. . . I gather that he signs anything which is put in front of him and is really past his work, if indeed he ever knew anything practical about tactics as distinct from strategy'. General Wielemans, the Belgian Chief-of-Staff, was judged to be 'a nice kindly old man, but quite stupid and I should say very lazy', and officers of the first Portuguese contingent were seen as 'conceited wretches'.[10] All would be much easier. Haig reflected, 'if I only had to deal with the Germans'.[11]

In Haig's defence, he found Foch's command style more agreeable than that of Joffre and, though sometimes fractious, his relations with the former were, according to Philpott, generally 'based on mutual understanding and respect', a factor of great importance in the crises and in the final offensive of 1918.[12] Haig also formed a good opinion of a few Allied senior officers, such as General Rosada, who took over the Portuguese forces on the Western Front in the autumn of 1918, and General Degoutte, of the French Sixth Army, who was appointed Chief of Staff to the King of the Belgians in September that year. Degoutte, he remarked, 'has a Mongolian type of head, but I think him a first rate soldier, apparently honest and very keen. I think his selection to help the King of the Belgians is a very good one'.[13]

Although not totally free of the kind of prejudices revealed by Haig, Rawlinson – in his own diary entries – is, on the whole, less acid or patronizing than his superior when commenting upon Allied generals and politicians. For much of the time, Rawlinson seems to have been on genuinely good terms with the French and American soldiers and statesmen with whom he came into repeated contact. When, in February 1918, Rawlinson began his brief period of service on the Executive War Board of the Supreme War council at Versailles, the *National News* reported that 'it is understood that General Foch particularly likes him' and the *Manchester Guardian* stated that his relations with the French had always been 'cordial'.[14] During both the planning and operational phases of the Somme offensive between mid-February and mid-November 1916, Rawlinson recorded some twenty-three personal meetings with Foch, then commanding the French Northern Army Group, and seventeen with General Fayolle, commander of the neighbouring French Sixth Army.[15] There were also, of course, many other written exchanges or telephone contacts, as well as reciprocal visits by staff and liaison officers, between their respective headquarters. After a fair proportion of these meetings, Rawlinson noted, for example, that Foch had been 'very affable', was 'in his best form and . . . most cordial in every way' or that they had been 'entirely in accord'.[16] Following a lunch with Fayolle on 26 April, Rawlinson wrote that the French Sixth Army commander 'has sound ideas and is very wide awake for a man of 67'. When Foch and Fayolle came together to see Rawlinson on 7 May to discuss the thorny problem of the boundary between the two armies, Rawlinson felt that 'it is something to have come to an agreement without a squabble. They were both very nice about it and we parted the best of friends'.[17] General Balfourier, whose XX Corps was deployed on the immediate right flank of Fourth Army, was deemed by Rawlinson to be a 'charming old gentleman'.[18] In April 1918, the critical month in the defence of Amiens, Georges Clemenceau, the French Prime Minister, visited Rawlinson's headquarters on at least three occasions, obviously seeking reassurance but also full of goodwill, and on 6 April – just after the First Battle of Villers Bretonneux – he brought Rawlinson a gift of chocolates.[19] Later in 1918, as it was becoming clear that the Allies were within sight of victory, Rawlinson was generous in his praise of Foch's strategy of mounting successive, rolling attacks at different points along the front to keep the Germans off balance. 'Foch deserves all possible credit for the combination of these attacks. . . . It is good war . . .', Rawlinson commented on 12 September that year.[20]

Rawlinson's mainly cordial relations with his allies stemmed, in part, from his moderate temperament. 'Rawly had a way of floating over and away from his troubles', wrote Edward Spears. Rawlinson himself confessed at the height of the Battle of the Somme: 'There are many worries and troubles in fighting a battle like this but I sleep like a top so am always fresh again the next day'.[21] Sometimes the intense demands of operational command caused him to show signs of strain. He admitted, on 22 July and 19 October 1916, that he had experienced a 'worrying' day and, at the end of October, complained that it was 'the constant interviews and decisions that take it out of one, and most of all the people who will multiply their little worries till they look as if the future of the Empire depended on them'. Even then he added: 'Thank God, I have a sense of humour and can see the funny side of most of them'.[22] Given Rawlinson's overall equability, his criticisms of his French and American allies, when they do occur, are therefore all the more significant.

Many of Rawlinson's initial problems in planning Fourth Army's role in the Somme offensive centred around the junction between the French and British forces in the Maricourt-Montauban area. He was especially concerned about the tactical and logistical difficulties created by the Maricourt salient. It would have made better administrative and logistical sense if the dividing line between the British and the French had been formed by the River Somme itself, but Foch insisted that Fayolle's Sixth Army should attack astride the Somme with Balfourier's XX Corps north of the river. The actual dividing line was settled in meetings between Foch, Fayolle and Rawlinson at the end of April and in May

1916, and, since the French needed access to Bray as a railhead, the boundary – as eventually agreed – ran through the middle of Bray and Maricourt. In the words of the British official historian, this was 'a most awkward arrangement for both parties. . . . The Maricourt salient was too small, as the Fourth Army had pointed out, to be shared by two corps, particularly corps belonging to two different Armies of two different nations, with different ammunition and equipment, and with separate communications'.[23] Rawlinson felt it advisable to establish a defensive flank from Maricourt to Mametz and to oppose the inclusion of Montauban as part of the first objective.[24] He anticipated some trouble with the French on this question, noting in his diary on 18 April: 'I know it will make the negotiations with the French more difficult but I am responsible for the attack of the Army and must deprecate taking in too much'.[25] In fact, Rawlinson appears to have discovered some common ground with Fayolle. After meeting Fayolle and Foch on 30 April, Rawlinson wrote: 'I did not find Genl.Fayolles [sic] anxious to do much from the Maricourt Salient'. Two days later he was told that 'Fayolles [sic] has put in a strong letter protesting against attacking from the Maricourt Salient and I am inclined to agree with him'.[26] However, Haig had already made it quite clear to Rawlinson that he was anxious to secure Montauban in the first attack and to develop subsequent operations 'with due regard to the need to assist the French Army', confirming his wishes regarding Montauban in writing on 16 May. As Rawlinson had confided in his diary over a week before: '. . . I am prepared to undertake it if D.H. so decides'.[27] Rawlinson's preference for 'bite and hold' tactics rather than an attempted breakthrough again seems to have been shared by the French – notably Foch – but was similarly overruled by Haig.[28]

The settlement of the inter-Army boundary did not completely allay Rawlinson's fears about possible congestion in the Maricourt salient. 'We shall be able to fix up the gun positions but it will be the hell of a squash', he wrote on 30 April, and on 7 May he still thought it would be 'a very tight fit'.[29] However, if, to date, his views had sometimes coincided more with those of the French than with the wishes of Haig, Rawlinson, from this point, encountered increasing difficulty with his allies on such issues as the timing and co-ordination of the assault – a problem which was to recur frequently throughout the Somme offensive and which would beset the Fourth Army again in 1918. Indeed, as the start of the offensive drew near, there were distinct signs of strain and reciprocal criticism between the various British and French headquarters. The choice of a mutually acceptable zero hour was one potential source of dispute. On 16 June Rawlinson took his chief of staff, Archie Montgomery, with him to discuss 'several intricate points' with Foch and Fayolle. Rawlinson recorded that the boundaries for the planned advance, as well as behind the line, were fixed without a great deal of trouble although the time of the assault proved harder to settle: 'I tried 7 a.m. but finally had to agree to 7.30. Fayolles[sic] would have preferred 9 a.m. but that I considered too late as it would keep the Infy. waiting in the trenches for 6 hours and more'. Fayolle was obviously still unhappy about this as late as 26 June, less than a week before the start of the offensive. 'He said some of his Corps Comrs. did not want to attack till the afternoon'. Rawlinson replied that 7.30 'was the latest hour I would deliver the assault. He left to talk it over with Foch . . .'[30] Edward Spears, the British liaison officer with the French Sixth Army, had written two days earlier that the French tended to look upon the British 'as a kind of enemy or rival at the least provocation'.[31] Rawlinson remained anxious to give Foch room to bring through as many divisions as he could collect but was determined that 'he must do his fair share of the fighting. I cannot pull the chestnuts out of the fire for him'. On 30 June, the eve of the offensive, Rawlinson was convinced that the French admired the way Fourth Army's part in the attack had been prepared. Nevertheless, he could not refrain from adding: 'If we do bring off a great success they will be jealous. If we do not they will say it is hopeless to try and break the line and will begin again to talk of making terms. This makes one's relations with them very difficult for they are like children in many ways'.[32]

Haig's insistence on including Montauban among the first objectives was, in some respects, justified on 1 July. The disasters elsewhere on the British front notwithstanding, a combination of more imaginative tactics by two good-quality divisions – the 18th and 30th – and substantial support from the heavy artillery of the French XX Corps made this the only sector where Fourth Army achieved any real success on the opening day of the offensive.[33] Now it had to be decided where the attack should be renewed. Once more Rawlinson found himself more in tune with the views of Joffre and the French than with Haig. Rawlinson opted to make the next major effort in the centre and north of his front and Joffre too asked the British Army to attack in the north to secure Pozières and Thiepval. Haig, on the other hand, wanted to exploit the success on the right at Montauban. Matters came to a head on 3 July when Haig felt compelled to remind Joffre that, as the British Commander-in-Chief, he was solely responsible to his own Government for the actions of the British Army and must therefore refuse to follow a tactical plan with which he did not concur. The official historian remarks that Haig 'emphasized his readiness to conform, as he had always done, to General Joffre's strategy, to this extent treating him as generalissimo of the Allied forces; but he could go no further'.[34]

The irony of this situation, as Elizabeth Greenhalgh rightly suggests, was that 'Haig was proposing to maintain and exploit contact with the French while Joffre intended to break the connection which had been the linchpin of his 1916 strategy . . .'[35] The fact that, on this occasion, Haig's view prevailed had a number of important implications. First, the incident drove Haig into a 'statement of independence which was to intensify in the coming weeks'.[36] Secondly, Joffre became less willing, for some time, to meet Haig in person and resigned himself to allowing the British greater freedom of action north of the Somme.[37] Thirdly, because Britain, in mid-1916, was still essentially the junior partner in the alliance, Haig was obliged to follow Joffre's overall strategic directives although he was equally resolved to determine for himself the best tactical means of fulfilling them. Consequently, as Philpott succinctly puts it: '. . . for the next two-and-a-half months the Allied armies were effectively conducting separate offensive operations side by side, rather than the co-ordinated strategic operation they had prepared'.[38] The outcome for Rawlinson was a summer and autumn of preoccupation with operations alongside the French – initially at Trones Wood, then around Guillemont and Ginchy, and finally in the Lesboeufs-Morval and Le Transloy sectors. Joffre's desire, after 3 July, to leave the tactical details of the offensive to his subordinates had some benefits in this regard, as Rawlinson continued to get on reasonably well with Fayolle and Foch. The negative aspect for Rawlinson was that, as the pressure for him to succeed on the right grew with every passing week, so his relationship with his own Commander-in-Chief temporarily deteriorated while the possibility of problems with his French allies over matters of tactical detail likewise increased.

Rawlinson's difficulties were exacerbated by French criticism of, and doubts about, British operational methods, and by a divergence between the two armies, in some areas of tactics, as the offensive progressed. Advancing in small groups rather than long lines, and making good use of cover, the French infantry had performed well on 1 July and Fayolle's Sixth Army had gained all of its objectives and more on the first day of the battle, with the I Colonial Corps, south of the Somme, establishing itself within assaulting distance of the German Second Position by nightfall.[39] In contrast to the deliberate advance of the British infantry, the French 'swarmed forward . . . illusive as quicksilver', Spears recalled.[40] French officers compared the British Expeditionary Force (BEF) to 'a second rate Italian force perpetually on the point of giving trouble'.[41] Although much research needs to be undertaken on the subject of tactical cross-fertilization between the Allied armies, it is known that some French tactical manuals and pamphlets were translated and issued to the BEF. It is also apparent that Spears submitted frequent reports on French tactics and that Haig

himself tried to ensure that Rawlinson and the other Army commanders were made aware of the lessons of the fighting at Verdun. On 19
July, Haig urged Fourth Army to 'follow the example of the French,
who were pushing forward small detachments and making good such
ground as was possible without heavy fighting'.[42] However, there is no
real evidence in Rawlinson's diary for 1916 that he made any significant attempt to disseminate such lessons. On the contrary, Rawlinson
seems to have studiously ignored French doubts and fears about his
projected night assembly and dawn assault on the German Second
Position between Longueval and Bazentin le Petit on 14 July, even
though Balfourier sent Spears, on the eve of the attack, to point out
that the operation was quite impossible for inexperienced troops.[43]
Rawlinson did not give due credit to the support provided by French
artillery for the attack, but the outstanding success of the operation
served to intensify the BEF's burgeoning tactical independence.
Again, an advance on Fourth Army's right made it inevitable that
Rawlinson's future operations would continue to be inextricably linked
with those of the French yet, at the same time, this growing British
tactical independence henceforth caused joint planning to degenerate
'into often bitter arguments about lines of demarcation and matters of
detail'.[44]

Rawlinson's own reactions to criticism on tactical matters were
somewhat inconsistent. On 21 September, he discussed the varying
methods of the French and British with John Du Cane, who was shortly
to take command of XV Corps and who had, in turn, recently been
talking to Spears. 'The French', noted Rawlinson, 'say we do not study
the ground sufficiently and are not so precise in our preparations as they
are. Our Infy. is better than theirs, our guns are not so good'. Rawlinson
went on to assert that: 'Our Arty. organisation differs in that we use the
Corps to control the Arty. while they use the Divn. Who is right time
can alone decide'.[45] However, on 29 September – following criticisms
of British generals and methods reported to have been made to Foch by
David Lloyd George, the Secretary of State for War – Rawlinson told
Lord Derby, the Under-Secretary of State for War, that he did not think
the BEF had much to learn from the French, particularly in artillery
tactics. 'In this connection', he urged, 'it is interesting to note that the
principle we have always adopted in the British Army of the establishment of a time-table for an attack, and the imposition of stationary and
creeping barrages to cover the infantry advance, has been adopted by
the French Sixth Army . . .' Even so, he reassured Derby about the health
of the alliance: 'The French and British armies now fighting in France
are one', he declared. 'The intimate relationship which exists between
us is of the most cordial and confidential nature. There are no secrets,
and each is out to help the other to the utmost of its powers, . . .'[46]

The Fourth Army commander's claims on behalf of British tactics may have been a trifle premature but, nonetheless, had some substance as, by late 1916, the BEF had undeniably begun the process of tactical and technological improvement which was to earn it the leading role in the final Allied offensive of 1918.[47] By the same token, his remarks on Franco-British relations on the Western Front were, perhaps, more than a little disingenuous, since his own day-to-day dealings with the French in the summer and autumn of 1916 were not entirely straight-forward. As at the start of the offensive, many of the minor squabbles were caused by problems over the timing and co-ordination of attacks, and such difficulties were not eased by Rawlinson's inability to secure Guillemont until the first week of September – a perceived failure which prompted Haig, in August, to criticize Rawlinson's repeated attacks with limited forces on narrow frontages and to send him a stern reminder of an Army commander's duties.[48] Postponement of attacks by either the French or the British, often for seemingly valid operational reasons, were possibly the most common cause of mutual irritation. A typical incident of this type occurred on 22 July, when the French – whose XX Corps was to have co-operated with an attack by the British XIII Corps against the German Second Position between Falfemont Farm and Longueval, including Guillemont – announced that they would not be ready until 24 July. After telephoning GHQ to bring some pressure to bear on Foch, Rawlinson wrote tersely in his diary: 'The postponement is very disgusting and it is most wrong of the French not to have given us more warning. It has much annoyed me'.[49] Sometimes – as on 5 August, when XIII Corps asked for the postponement of an attack on Guillemont – the boot was on the other foot. The French 'were by no means pleased at the alteration', Rawlinson admitted.[50] Four days later Rawlinson informed sub-ordinate commanders, including Congreve of XIII Corps, that the attack on Guillemont must be renewed 'when we are ready but not before. We will not be pushed into a premature attack by the French'.[51] On 25 August, after Rawlinson had been forced to cancel a XIV Corps operation near Guillemont, Haig told Rawlinson in person that 'the French are saying nasty things about us for not attacking yesterday on their left'.[52] However, it should be acknowledged too that, in mid-August, Foch and Fayolle incurred the displeasure of Joffre as a result of their readiness to co-operate with the British in subsidiary operations. Joffre tried twice – in August and October – to re-impose the original strategy based upon combined attacks on a broad front rather than the succession of intermediate, narrow-front attacks with shallow objectives which had become the norm during much of July, August and September.[53] On the latter occasion, the implied criticism stung Haig – on 19 October – into another sharp reminder that he, not Joffre, 'was the sole judge of what the British Armies could undertake and when they could undertake it'.[54] It should equally be emphasized, though, that the bulk of these disputes were settled quickly and amicably and, even as late as 3 November, towards the end of the offensive – during operations near Le Transloy – Rawlinson lunched with Fayolle and found him 'most amenable to all our arrangements'.[55] For all the stresses and strains which the Somme battle had placed upon them by November 1916, a strong residue of goodwill clearly remained between Rawlinson, Foch and Fayolle and would prove an asset not only to them individually but also to the alliance in general in 1918.

After a frustrating 1917 and a brief spell as British Military Representative on the Executive War Board of the Supreme War Council, Rawlinson began his second prolonged period of operations alongside the French on 28 March 1918, when he succeeded General Sir Hubert Gough in command of the Fifth Army in the midst of the crisis precipitated by the German *Michael* offensive in Picardy. The Fifth Army was redesignated as the Fourth Army on 2 April and, thereafter, Rawlinson's tenure of command was unbroken until the end of the war.[56] The decision reached at Doullens on 26 March – making Foch responsible for the co-ordination of Allied operations on the Western Front – unquestionably helped to boost Allied morale and Foch acted promptly to secure the link between the French and British armies, giving priority to the defence of the vital railhead of Amiens.[57] There was, however, very little that Foch could do, in practical terms, to influence the current tactical situation in front of Amiens, which was Rawlinson's immediate problem. Foch was anxious to build up a strong reserve in the Amiens area for a future counterstroke but, with the French then under pressure near Montdidier, he could not yet fulfil his promise to relieve the British forces up to the Somme. For the time being, therefore, Rawlinson would have to struggle on making the best use he could of dwindling resources and reorganizing his existing formations where they stood.[58] The gloomy prospects on 28 March impelled Rawlinson to write urgently to Foch that evening. Unless fresh troops were sent to him in the next two days, Rawlinson doubted 'whether the remnants of the British XIX Corps which now held the line to the east of Villers Bretonneux can maintain their positions'. Expressing his fears for the safety of Amiens and seeking to impress upon Foch the seriousness of the threat to it, if the Germans renewed their attacks from the east before the requested reinforcements arrived, he also predicted that the British XIX Corps was no longer capable of executing a counter-offensive.[59] Rawlinson did his best to reassure Clemenceau that he 'would accomplish the impossible' in the defence of Amiens but he was becoming increasingly critical of the French on his right. On 31 March he gave his views on the situation to Fayolle, now commanding the French Reserve Army Group, which included the French First and Third Armies: 'He said he could not send any help to us and I remained with the impression that we could expect nothing from the French'.[60] Next day, Clemenceau met Haig at Rawlinson's headquarters and Foch was sent for to settle details of the boundary between the French and British armies. 'Tavish' Davidson, Haig's Director of Military Operations at GHQ, drew up a proposal which Rawlinson felt 'will greatly help me with the future if only the French will hold their ground. If they don't there will be trouble'.[61]

As it transpired, Rawlinson's worst fears proved unfounded. Over the next two or three days more units *did* arrive to bolster the defences around Villers Bretonneux. They included the 2nd and 3rd Cavalry Divisions, which had previously been operating with the French, principally in a mounted infantry role. A series of actions between Moreuil and Hamel at the end of March and the beginning of April delayed the Germans sufficiently to allow time for further French reinforcements to reach the area and to take over, by 3 April, the sector from Moreuil to Hangard. Thanks largely to elements of the 9th Australian Brigade and the British 18th Division, 58th Division and 3rd Cavalry Division, Fourth Army was able to repel the first major German assault on Villers Bretonneux on 4 April, although it had been driven back along its whole front and up to two miles at some points. The French XXXVI Corps, on the right, had similarly been pushed back two miles beyond the Avre, to the west of Moreuil, and the Germans were in part of the Bois de Sénécat, from the eastern edge of which the outskirts of Amiens could be seen.[62] The successful defence of Villers Bretonneux and the presence of increasing numbers of Australians gave fresh heart to Rawlinson, who wrote in his diary on 5 April that he thought 'we ought to keep the Boche out of Amiens'.[63]

Whatever his private thoughts, Rawlinson continued to impress upon Foch and Haig his worries about the right flank. Lieutenant General Sir Richard Butler's III Corps had now taken over tactical responsibility for Fourth Army's front at Villers Bretonneux and, having discussed the matter with Butler and his divisional commanders, Rawlinson informed Haig that 'they are all agreed that unless something is done by the French to resolve the situation on the right it may become serious and the safety of Amiens compromised'. Haig duly wrote to Foch in much the same vein two days later.[64] Even before the first German attack on Villers Bretonneux, Foch, on 3 April, had issued a general directive for combined Franco-British operations to free Amiens by driving the Germans further away from the rail centre. The forces available would only permit this to be attempted in two stages. First, the French would try to push the Germans from part of the west side of the Avre while Fourth Army sought to clear up the messy tactical situation near its junction with the French First Army to the north and north-east of Hangard. When these preliminary steps had been taken, a joint attack would be launched to reach a line stretching from Moreuil to Warfusée on the Amiens-St Quentin road. The combined attack was scheduled for 9 April but the French were not ready and it was postponed until 13 April. 'The French do not seem out to do v[ery] much fighting', Rawlinson commented on 8 April. He was also unhappy about Foch's decision to place reserve divisions immediately west of Amiens in the Fourth Army area: 'It is an infernal nuisance as it blocks all the roads and I feel sure they will be too far off there to be of much real value.' However, Rawlinson grudgingly acknowledged that Foch was now 'Generalissimo and has issued the order in writing so it had to be obeyed'.[65]

German attacks on Hangard on 9 and 12 April caused further cancellations of the joint operation and did nothing to assuage Rawlinson's concerns about his right flank. At this point Rawlinson became increasingly critical of General Debeney, the commander of the French First Army. When Du Cane – now head of a British Military Mission to Foch's headquarters – had tea at Fourth Army headquarters on 15 April, Rawlinson said that he 'could get nothing satisfactory out of Debeney. He has not fallen in line with Foch and I predict there will be a row before very long'.[66] At last, on 18 April, Debeney's First Army delivered an attack without British assistance. As the British official historian sourly remarks, this was 'the first offensive action taken by the French to relieve the British since the fighting began on the 21st March'.[67] Debeney's operations were only partly successful and made no progress east of the Avre but the French did drive the Germans out of the Bois de Sénécat and the ridge north of it, thus depriving the Germans of their observation over the rear areas of the British III Corps. Rawlinson was disappointed that Debeney could not pursue his attacks the next day 'as Foch refuses to give him more Divns.'[68]

The next crisis occurred on 24 April when the Germans, using tanks, made their second major attack in the sector and actually succeeded in seizing Villers Bretonneux for several hours until a brilliant night counter-attack led by the 13th and 15th Australian Brigades drove them back again. It has to be said that the French did not offer a great deal of help when it mattered most. Debeney was informed of the plan and promised to co-operate if the counter-attack were postponed until 25 April. This, of course, did not suit Rawlinson, who wanted the counter-attack to take place before the Germans consolidated their gains. Debeney's only immediate measure was to order the Moroccan Division forward to a position behind the British right, where it occupied part of the reserve line near Gentelles and thereby freed some of the British 58th Division's reserves. Nevertheless, Debeney told Butler during the morning that the Moroccan Division must not, under any circumstances, be used piecemeal to counter-attack or to reinforce the front and could only be employed, in a counter-attack, as a complete formation. When Haig came to Rawlinson's headquarters at 12.30 p.m., he directed that a telephone message be sent to Du Cane asking for the Moroccan Division to join in the counter-attack rather than remain in reserve. It was therefore with some irritation that, in mid-afternoon, Haig received a written message from Foch – delivered by Du Cane – which stated patronizingly that the importance of recapturing Villers Bretonneux would not have escaped Rawlinson and urged the British to make a powerful counter-attack *'comme celle que le général Debeney a montée dès ce matin 10 heures . . .'* Haig wasted little time in making it clear to Foch that Debeney had not attacked at all and at 6.30 in the evening he asked Foch to direct the Moroccan Division, or another French Division, 'to co-operate energetically and without delay' with III Corps so that Villers Bretonneux might be retaken. By this time most of the key decisions concerning the counter-attack had been made and it was too late for the French to make a real contribution to it, though Foch *did* order Debeney to co-operate more actively on 25 April.[69]

Rawlinson was highly critical of Debeney's conduct during the crisis. 'I have found Debeney v[ery] difficult', Rawlinson complained in his diary on 24 April, accusing the French First Army commander of having 'misrepresented his ability to use the Moroccan Div. to Foch saying he was ready to attack with it'.[70] The Moroccans finally went into action in the early morning of 26 April, attempting to restore and straighten the line near Cachy and to the south by recapturing ground between Monument Wood and Hangard Wood. Given the vagueness of the British line in this sector, and the lack of detailed knowledge on the part of the British troops regarding their own positions, the French commanders, who were reluctant to advance from an imprecise line without a barrage, unwisely rejected advice from Butler and Rawlinson that they should not launch the Moroccan Division in daylight across ground registered by German gunners. In the event, the Moroccans lost their own barrage, suffered heavy casualties and were forced back by a German counter-attack. Rawlinson laid the blame squarely on Debeney, asserting that the latter 'has no knowledge of tactics and to my mind is a bad commander. His arrangements for taking over the line were bad'.[71] Relations did not improve over the next few days or weeks. On 29 April, Rawlinson was disappointed that he could not induce Debeney to take any further offensive action at Hangard and, on 11 May, he observed that the French First Army had 'got the wind up about being attacked and Debeney is fussing a good deal'. In June, Rawlinson had grave doubts about the state of French defences in the Amiens area, especially in comparison with the work put in by the Australians. On 19 June, Rawlinson went to see Debeney and pointed out that the French line was not ready and did not join up with that of Fourth Army. Eleven days later, Debeney told Rawlinson of his fears of an attack against the French First Army front. 'I personally think it is likely', Rawlinson conjectured, 'for he has made no back lines as he does not believe in them!! His reserves are not large and I am none too sure that his troops will fight well if they are surprised'.[72]

New allies had now begun to occupy Rawlinson's attention as various American units were attached to Fourth Army for training. Rawlinson's initial impressions were mixed. Having inspected the US 82nd Division on 28 May, he was 'much struck by the excellent material of which it is composed. The men are quite first class but the officers are far from good. . . . the senior ones are poor stuff . . .' He subsequently described the men of the US 27th and 33rd Divisions as 'magnificent' and felt that some of the regimental and battalion commanders were 'leaders and men of character', though he thought 'there was room for much improvement in the staff work'. In the light of future operations, it was also fortunate that Rawlinson swiftly struck up a good relationship with Major General G W Read for the US II Corps – a 'nice calm gentlemanly man who will not get rattled'.[73] Rawlinson and Lieutenant General Sir John Monash, the commander of the Australian Corps, planned to use ten companies from Major General Bell's US 33rd Division in their carefully-orchestrated set-piece attack at Hamel on 4 July – America's Independence Day – but on the evening of 2 July, to Rawlinson's considerable consternation, Read informed him that General J.J. 'Black Jack' Pershing, the Commander-in-Chief of the American Expeditionary Force and the subject of a later chapter in this volume, had refused to sanction their employment. Rawlinson told Read that he could withdraw the six rearmost companies but not the four 'which had already gone up into the trenches as we could not get at them'. Rawlinson then made a telephone call to Lieutenant General Sir Herbert Lawrence, Haig's chief of staff, who was in Paris, asking him to persuade Pershing to agree to this modification. 'I cannot postpone', Rawlinson wrote in his diary, 'and I cannot withdraw so am inclined to let the thing go on. Read can't get at them to stop them'. The next day, while Rawlinson was visiting units of the Australian Corps, Archie Montgomery informed him that formal orders had been received from Lawrence that no Americans were to take part. Monash, however, stood his ground and bluntly advised Rawlinson that, if the Americans did not participate, the attack must be abandoned – a view which Rawlinson entirely shared. On contacting Lawrence again, Rawlinson discovered that the orders had not come from Haig but 'only from

Pers[h]ing through Read who had been to see him'. Following Monash's advice, Rawlinson pointed out to Lawrence that, unless he received orders from Haig himself by 7 p.m. – when the infantry were beginning their final move to the start line – he could not postpone the attack. Fortunately for Rawlinson and Monash, Lawrence responded, shortly before the deadline, that Haig had returned from Paris and decided that not only was the operation to proceed but also that – in Rawlinson's words – 'if I could not withdraw the Yankees they must take part. I have therefore changed nothing and trust to the attack being a success'. Rawlinson need not have worried on the latter score for the Australians and Americans took all their objectives in just over ninety minutes and the superb operation at Hamel became the prototype for future larger-scale attacks by the BEF. 'What a mercy it was not postponed!!!', wrote Rawlinson, though shortly before the attack he had commented tartly: 'If Persing [sic] goes on like this we will never win the War'.[74]

The problems Rawlinson experienced with Pershing over the Hamel attack were only a temporary distraction from his ongoing difficulties with Debeney – which now related to preliminary operations aimed at improving Allied positions east and south-east of Amiens prior to the projected August offensive. Having let Lawrence know, on 9 July, that he was unhappy with the French First Army on his right, Rawlinson lamented two days later that it 'is unsatisfactory to have a man like Debeney to work with, he requires driving every yard and is afraid of responsibility in these matters'. On 14 July he failed to persuade Debeney to undertake an attack at Hangard Wood: 'He flatly refused saying that all his troops had been taken away'. None of this deterred Haig and Rawlinson from lending Debeney more than forty Mark V tanks for a French attack south of Moreuil on 23 July, an operation which Rawlinson believed would help his planned offensive at Amiens. The French First Army's attack succeeded and thereby gained valuable observation over the Avre valley, but fourteen British tanks were knocked out and Rawlinson could not resist criticizing some aspects of French tactics, particularly a delay of ninety minutes on one of the objectives.[75]

In his planning for the attack at Amiens, Rawlinson wished to take over the front as far south as Moreuil so that Fourth Army alone could carry out the operation, thus avoiding the problems of co-ordination experienced in many previous Franco-British efforts. Foch, however, decreed that Debeney should be given a role on the right between the Avre and the Amiens-Roye road, even though the whole French First Army would be placed under Haig's orders. 'I strongly deprecated the employment of the two armies side by side', a discontented Rawlinson remarked, 'but Foch insisted and it must therefore be done but it will be very difficult to keep it secret . . .' After a planning conference on

5 August, he was slightly less anxious: 'I think the French will be all right but they will be slow', he predicted.[76] Rawlinson's forecast was accurate. The sluggish performance of the French First Army at the opening of the offensive drew criticism from both Haig and Foch and, although Debeney's formations did better on 10 August, Rawlinson attributed this mainly to the fact that 'we have attracted all the hostile fresh Divns. to the British front'.[77] Once again he was not far from the truth. Rawlinson and Lieutenant General Sir Arthur Currie, the commander of the Canadian Corps, recognized the stiffening German resistance and persuaded Haig of the wisdom of shifting the weight of the BEF's offensive operations to another part of the front. Foch's desire for the BEF to prolong the increasingly difficult and potentially costly operations east of Amiens impelled Haig, not for the first time, to remind Foch that he alone was responsible to the British Government and people for the handling of his troops. Foch's acceptance of Haig's stand was, in essence, an acknowledgement that the BEF was setting the pace of Allied operations and, as Robin Prior and Trevor Wilson point out, it was 'the last time that Foch would ever try to issue orders to the British Commander-in-Chief', though the French First Army was now removed from Haig's control.[78]

Neither the Fourth Army's success at Amiens nor the removal of the French First Army from Haig's control did anything to warm the chilly atmosphere between Rawlinson and Debeney. On 17 August, the latter asked Rawlinson by telegram to attack and take Fresnoy, north of Roye – a request which Rawlinson was not yet ready to meet, partly because the French were about to relieve the Canadian Corps as far north as Lihons. 'He [Debeney] is a most difficult fellow to get on with and I fear I shall have a row with him if I am not very careful', wrote Rawlinson on 18 August. Next day he noted that Debeney was still 'very stuffy' with him for not attacking Fresnoy, but Rawlinson was unmoved, adding: 'I do not intend to waste valuable Canadian lives to pull chestnuts out of the fire for him'.[79]

By this time, in view of the imminent Franco-American operation at St Mihiel and also as a result of Pershing's desire to keep his units together as a distinct national entity, three of the five American divisions training with the BEF were in the process of being withdrawn. Rawlinson was particularly sorry to lose the US 33rd Division and its commander George Bell but was relieved to hear from Haig on 5 September that the US II Corps was likely to be made available to him for the forthcoming assault on the Hindenburg Line. This welcome accretion of strength made Rawlinson more optimistic that he would be able to 'do the trick' and he now believed that 'if the Allies will not fight amongst one another we shall finish the war next year and dictate our own terms . . .'[80] As Fourth Army approached the outlying defences of the main Hindenburg Position, however, Rawlinson's relations with Debeney again deteriorated with the news that weaknesses in infantry and artillery would render the French First Army incapable of offering substantial support in operations planned for 18 September. 'He[Debeney] is difficult as usual', a frustrated Rawlinson wrote on 13 September. At a meeting two days later, Rawlinson failed to persuade Debeney to co-operate with him on 18 September and protect the Fourth Army's right flank by pushing on as far as Fayet. According to Rawlinson, Debeney 'flatly refused saying [that he] had no troops or Arty. to do it with'. Since the French XV and XVIII Corps had been transferred from the French Third Army to Debeney, the reason for the latter's reluctance to co-operate was not readily apparent to Rawlinson, who at once asked Haig and Du Cane to press Foch to intervene. 'Debeney is really quite exasperating', Rawlinson commented. Though Davidson too 'could get nothing' out of Debeney on 16 September, a solution of sorts was reached on 17 September when Foch adjusted the inter-Army boundary so as to include Fayet within the zone of the British IX Corps. 'This is satisfactory in so far as it enables us to protect our right flank but it widens our front and I have no troops to spare', wrote Rawlinson, and he was still disappointed that, on 18 September, the French 'did little or nothing' and obliged him to throw back Fourth Army's right flank to face St Quentin.[81]

The employment of the American 27th and 30th Divisions with Monash's Australian Corps in the attack on the Hindenburg Position was not without risks and Rawlinson realized that both he and Monash would have to exercise tact in offering help and advice to Read's US II Corps. The French also remained a worry. At a conference attended by Foch, Haig, Fayolle, Debeney, Du Cane and Lawrence on 23 September, Rawlinson stressed that Debeney must be given enough guns to suppress German artillery in and around St Quentin. Fayolle promised to arrange this. On a visit to the US 27th and 30th Divisions on 25 September, Rawlinson tried to impress upon them the importance of mopping up the defences of the St Quentin Canal tunnel at Bellicourt but was disturbed to find their plans and arrangements 'backward'. Rawlinson's mood seems to have been subject to swings for, on 26 September, he expressed 'full confidence in the Yankees' and felt that all was 'shaping well', only to confess, on the day before the main attack, that the use of new troops like the Americans was 'a bit of a lottery'. He also observed that 'old Read' was 'somewhat fussed this being his first battle'.[82]

Rawlinson was right to temper his overall optimism with some degree of caution, as the failure of a preliminary operation by the US 27th Division on 27 September complicated the main assault and caused considerable difficulties on the northern flank of the attack near

Guillemont Farm and Bony. 'The Americans appear to be in a state of hopeless confusion . . .', Rawlinson remarked during the afternoon of 29 September: '[The] Yankees are short of officers and know nothing about fighting so they get hopelessly scattered and mixed up'. Happily for Rawlinson, the attack went much better further south, particularly at Bellenglise and Riqueval Bridge, where the British 46th (North Midland) Division crossed the canal and breached the Hindenburg Line in one of the outstanding operations of the war.[83] As at Villers Bretonneux in April, Debeney gave Rawlinson little assistance at the critical stage of the action, providing only fire support and a demonstration on a frontage of less than four miles, south of St Quentin, on 29 September. Foch ordered Debeney to capture Thorigny, on the inter-Army boundary, to guard the right of the British IX Corps but it was, in fact, IX Corps itself which captured the village on 30 September in the absence of the French XV Corps. The slow progress of Debeney's troops was now hampering Rawlinson's offensive and Haig urged Foch to make the left wing of the French First Army act with greater vigour. When, on 2 October, another French failure to come up on the British right contributed to a setback for IX Corps at Sequehart, Rawlinson voiced his dissatisfaction with the French First Army and let it be known that he could no longer accept excuses for Debeney, repeating this message to officers from Foch's headquarters the following day. Even Foch appears to have been mystified by Debeney's inaction, and orders were sent to the French First Army, through Fayolle, emphasizing the importance of supporting the British right 'at all costs'. By 9 October, Rawlinson was able to note that the French were 'gradually coming up into line' but he added that 'it was the devil getting them to start'.[84]

In contrast to the French, the Americans won praise from Rawlinson during the advance beyond the Hindenburg Line, though on 18 October he recognized that they were at last becoming tired and weak.[85] His impatience with Debeney, however, continued almost to the end. On 26 October, as the Battle of the Selle drew to a close, he was complaining that he could not force the crossings of the Sambre Canal until Debeney protected his right 'and he is very very slow'. As late as 2 November, he recorded that the zero hour for the Sambre operations had only been agreed with Debeney 'after a wrangle'.[86] In truth, Rawlinson's problems with the French First Army were now of little real importance, for the German Army was near to defeat. It is significant, nevertheless, that, whereas in 1916 – particularly at the beginning of the Somme offensive – the French had some cause to criticize Rawlinson's performance and tactics, the tables had completely turned by the 'Hundred Days', when it was the British who were forcing the pace. In this respect, Rawlinson's relations with Debeney in 1918 provide us with a good illustration of just how much both the balance of the alliance and the relative operational efficiency of the two armies had changed by the Armistice.

Notes

1   See, for instance, William Philpott, *Anglo-French Relations and Strategy on the Western Front, 1914–18*, Macmillan, London, 1996; 'Haig and Britain's European Allies' in Brian Bond and Nigel Cave (eds), *Haig: A Reappraisal 70 Years On*, Leo Cooper/Pen and Sword, Barnsley, 1999, pp.128–44; and 'Britain, France and the Belgian Army' in Brian Bond (ed.), *'Look to your Front': Studies in the First World War by the British Commission for Military History*, Spellmount, Staplehurst, 1999, pp.121–35; see also David French, *The Strategy of the Lloyd George Coalition, 1916–1918*, Oxford, 1986; Elizabeth Greenhalgh, 'Why the British Were on the Somme in 1916', in *War in History*, Vol.6, No.2, 1999, pp.146–73; Frank Vandiver, 'Haig and Pershing', in Hugh Cecil and Peter H Liddle (eds), *Facing Armageddon: The First World War Experienced*, Leo Cooper, London, 1996, pp.67–78.

2   Philpott, 'Britain, France and the Belgian Army', p.121.

3   See Peter H Liddle, *The Soldier's War, 1914–1918*, Blandford Press, London, 1988, pp.73–84; J G Fuller, *Troop Morale and Popular Culture in the British and Dominion Armies, 1914–1918*, Clarendon Press, Oxford, 1990, pp.72–80; Peter Simkins, 'Soldiers and Civilians: Billeting in Britain and France', in Ian F W Beckett and Keith Simpson (eds), *A Nation in Arms: A Social Study of the British Army in the First World War*, Manchester University Press, 1985, pp.166–191; Desmond Morton, *When Your Numbers Up: The Canadian Soldier in the First World War*, Random House, Toronto, 1993, pp.239–41.

4   Rawlinson's Diary can be examined at the Churchill College Archives Centre, Cambridge. The Horne papers are held by the Department of Documents at the Imperial War Museum, London.

5   Brigadier General Sir James Edmonds, *Military Operations: France and Belgium, 1916, Vol.I*, Macmillan, London, 1932; Captain Wilfrid Miles, *Military Operations: France and Belgium, 1916, Vol.II*, Macmillan, London, 1938; Edmonds, *Military Operations, France and Belgium, 1918, Vol.II*, Macmillan, London, 1937; *1918, Vol.IV*, HMSO, London, 1947; and *1918, Vol.V*, HMSO, London, 1947 (hereafter OH).

6   Robin Prior and Trevor Wilson, *Command on the Western Front: The Military Career of Sir Henry Rawlinson, 1914–18*, Blackwell, Oxford, 1992; Major General Sir Frederick Maurice, *The Life of General Lord Rawlinson of Trent: From his Journal and Letters*, Cassell, London, 1928.

7   Major General Sir Archibald Montgomery, *The Story of the Fourth Army in the Battles of the Hundred Days, August 8th to November 11th, 1918*, Hodder and Stoughton, London, 1919.

8   Haig Diary, 18 November 1914, Public Record Office (hereafter PRO), WO 256/2; Gerard J. De Groot, *Douglas Haig, 1861–1928*, Unwin Hyman, London, 1988, p.168.

9   Haig Diary, 28 March 1916, PRO WO 256/9.

10   Ibid., 12 March and 7 April 1916, PRO WO 256/9 and 20 September 1918, PRO WO 256/36.

11   Ibid., 8 March 1917, PRO WO 256/16.

12   Philpott, 'Haig and Britain's European Allies', op cit., pp.136–7; see also his *Anglo-French Relations and Strategy*, pp.156–60, and 'Britain and France Go to War: Anglo-French Relations on the Western Front, 1914–1918', *War in History*, II, 1995, pp.59–60.

13   Haig Diary, 14 and 20 September 1918, PRO WO 256/36.

14   *National News*, 24 February 1918, and *Manchester Guardian*, 24 February 1918; see also Rawlinson papers, National Army Museum (NAM) 5201/33–39; Prior and Wilson, *Command on the Western Front*, pp.276–7.

15   Rawlinson Diary, Churchill College, Cambridge (hereafter CC), 5 February–26 September 1916, CC1/5, and 27 September 1916–4 August 1917, CC1/7.

16   Rawlinson Diary, 2 March, 9 April, 20 June, 25 June and 19 July 1916, CC 1/5.

17   Ibid., 26 April and 7 May 1916, CC 1/5.

18   Ibid., 16 May 1916, CC 1/5.

19   Ibid., 1 April, 6 April and 21 April 1918, CC 1/9.

20   Ibid., 12 and 28 September 1918, CC 1/11.

21   Major General Sir Edward Spears, quoted in David R. Woodward, *The Military Correspondence of Field-Marshal Sir William Robertson, Chief of the Imperial General Staff, December 1915–February 1918*, Bodley Head for the Army Records Society, London, 1989, see 'Biographical Notes', p.343; Rawlinson Diary, 20 July 1916, CC 1/5.

22   Rawlinson Diary, 22 July 1916, CC 1/5 and 19 October 1916, CC 1/7; Maurice, *Life of General Lord Rawlinson*, p.177.

23   *OH, 1916*, I, pp.254, 256–7, 263–4; General Sir James Marshall-Cornwall, *Foch as Military Commander*, Batsford, London, 1972, p.156; Rawlinson Diary, 4 March, 6 April, 15 April, 16 April, 20 April and 7 May 1916, CC 1/5.

24   'Plan for Offensive by Fourth Army', 3 April 1916, in Fourth Army Summary of Operations, PRO WO 158/233; Prior and Wilson, op cit., p.146; *OH, 1916 I*, pp.250–1; Rawlinson Diary, 18 April 1916, CC 1/5.

25   Rawlinson Diary, 18 April 1916, CC 1/5.

26   Ibid., 30 April and 2 May 1916, CC 1/5. Rawlinson invariably misspells Fayolle's name in his diary entries. Whether this was deliberate or simply careless is not clear. The American commander General Pershing was treated similarly in 1918.

27 Rawlinson Diary, 15 April and 5 May 1916, CC 1/5; *OH, 1916, 1*, pp.251–9; Haig Diary, 5 April 1916, PRO WO 256/9; Haig to Rawlinson, 10 April 1916, in 'Battle of the Somme: Preparations by the Fourth Army', Fourth Army papers, Imperial War Museum (IWM), Vol.1; Kiggell to Rawlinson, 12 April 1916 (OAD 710), copy attached to Haig Diary, PRO WO 256/9; GHQ to Rawlinson, 16 May 1916, quoted in *OH, 1916, 1, Appendices*, p.89.

28 Marshall-Cornwall, *Foch as Military Commander*, p.188; Prior and Wilson, op cit., pp.139–53.

29 Rawlinson Diary, 30 April and 7 May 1916, CC 1/5

30 Ibid., 16 and 26 June 1916, CC 1/5; *OH, 1916, 1*, p.265.

31 Spears Journal, 24 June 1916, Spears papers, Churchill College, Cambridge, Acc.545, Box 59; see also Max Egremont, *Under Two Flags: The Life of Major General Sir Edward Spears*, Weidenfeld and Nicolson, London, 1997, p.47.

32 Rawlinson Diary, 29 and 30 June 1916, CC 1/5.

33 Captain G H F Nichols, *The 18th Division in the Great War*, Blackwood, Edinburgh and London, 1922, pp.35–50; John Baynes, *Far from a Donkey: The Life of General Sir Ivor Maxse*, Brassey's, London, 1995, pp.135–44; Peter Simkins, 'The War Experience of a Typical Kitchener Division: The 18th Division, 1914–1918', in Hugh Cecil and Peter H Liddle (eds), *Facing Armageddon*, pp.299–301; Brigadier General F C Stanley, *The History of the 89th Brigade, 1914–1918*, *Liverpool Daily Post*, 1919, pp.120–37; *OH, 1916,I*, pp.320–45.

34 Rawlinson Diary, 1 and 2 July 1916, CC 1/5; Fourth Army Operation Order No.3, 1 July 1916, Fourth Army papers, IWM Vol.7; 'Visit of Commander-in-Chief to Fourth Army Headquarters at 10.30 a.m. July 2 1916', Fourth Army War Diary, Fourth Army papers, IWM Vol.1; Kiggell to Rawlinson (OAD 37), 2 July 1916, quoted in Fourth Army War Diary; Haig Diary, 3 July 1916, PRO WO 256/11; *OH, 1916, II*, pp.18–19; Elizabeth Greenhalgh, 'Why the British Were on the Somme in 1916', pp.164–5; Prior and Wilson, op.cit., pp.185–7; Joffre Journal, 2, 3 and 4 July 1916, see G Pedroncini (ed.), *Journal de Marche de Joffre, 1916–1919*, Service Historique de I'Armée de Terre, Vincennes, 1990, pp.31–8.

35 Greenhalgh, op. cit., p.165.

36 Ibid., p.166.

37 Joffre Journal, 2 and 4 July 1916, op. cit., pp.36–8; Greenhalgh, op. cit., p.166.

38 Philpott, 'Haig and Britain's European Allies', p.135.

39 *OH, 1916, II*, pp.342–3, 489.

40 Major General Sir Edward Spears, *Liaison 1914: A Narrative of the Great Retreat*, Second Edition, Eyre and Spottiswoode, London, 1968, p.109.

41 Egremont, *Under Two Flags*, p.49; Spears Journal, 7 July 1916, CC Acc.545 Box 59.

42 Paddy Griffith, *Battle Tactics of the Western Front: The British Army's Art of Attack, 1916–18*, Yale University Press, New Haven and London, 1994, pp.53–6, 230–1; Greenhalgh, op. cit., pp.157–8, particularly fn.42; Major General Sir Edward Spears, *Prelude to Victory*, Cape, London, 1939, pp.91, 95; Egremont, op. cit., p.48; Tim Travers, 'July 1, 1916: The Reason Why', *MHQ: The Quarterly Journal of Military History*, VII, 1995, pp.62–73; Haig Diary, 4 March and 14 March 1916, PRO WO 256/9; *OH, 1916, II*, p.103.

43 *OH, 1916, II*, pp.82–3; Greenhalgh, op. cit., pp.166–7.

44 Greenhalgh, op. cit., p.158.

45 Rawlinson Diary, 21 September 1916, CC 1/5; Egremont, op. cit., p.48. General de Fonclare, a French Divisional commander, made similar remarks to Spears about the lack of thoroughness in British preparations for attacks.

46 Rawlinson to Derby, 29 September 1916, quoted in Maurice, op. cit., pp.172–3, For the alleged indiscretions of Lloyd George in a conversation with Foch, see also Randolph S Churchill, *Lord Derby: 'King of Lancashire'*, Heinemann, London, 1959, pp.222–4; John Grigg, *Lloyd George: From Peace to War, 1912–1916*, Methuen, London, 1985, pp.381–3; David R. Woodward, *Lloyd George and the Generals*, Associated University Presses, East Brunswick, New Jersey, 1983, pp.105–6.

47 For recent analyses of the nature and extent of the BEF's 'learning curve' from 1916 to 1918, see, for example, Paddy Griffith, *Battle Tactics of the Western Front*; Bill Rawling, *Surviving Trench Warfare: Technology and the Canadian Corps, 1914–1918*, University of Toronto Press, 1992; Peter Simkins, 'Co-Stars or Supporting Cast? British Divisions in the 'Hundred Days', 1918', in Paddy Griffith (ed.), *British Fighting Methods in the Great War*, Frank Cass, London, 1996, pp.50–69; Ian Passingham, *Pillars of Fire: The Battle of Messines Ridge, June 1917*, Sutton Publishing, Stroud, 1998; J P Harris with Niall Barr, *Amiens to the Armistice: The BEF in the Hundred Days Campaign, 8 August–11 November 1918*, Brassey's, London, 1998; G D Sheffield, 'The Indispensable Factor: The Performance of British Troops in 1918', in Peter Dennis and Jeffrey Grey (eds), *1918: Defining Victory* (Proceedings of the Chief of Army History's Conference, 1998), Army History Unit, Canberra, 1999, pp. 72–95; Richard Bryson, 'The Once and Future Army', John Lee, 'Some Lessons of the Somme: The British Infantry in 1917', and Peter Simkins, 'Somme Reprise: Reflections on the Fighting for Albert and Bapaume, August 1918', in Brian Bond (ed.), *Look to your Front*, op.cit., pp. 25–62, 79–88, 149–62.

48 Rawlinson Diary, 9 and 22 August 1916, CC 1/5; GHQ to Fourth Army (OAD 123), 24 August 1916, Fourth Army papers, IWM Vol.5; Peter

Simkins, 'Haig and the Army Commanders', in Brian Bond and Nigel Cave (eds), *Haig: A Reappraisal 70 Years On*, p.86.

49 Rawlinson Diary, 22 July 1916, CC 1/5; *OH, 1916, II*, p.113.

50 Rawlinson Diary, 5 August 1916, CC 1/5.

51 Ibid., 9 August 1916, CC 1/5.

52 Ibid., 25 August 1916, CC 1/5.

53 *OH, 1916, II*, pp.182, 184, 459, 563.

54 Ibid., p.459

55 Rawlinson Diary, 3 November 1916, CC 1/7.

56 *OH, 1918, I*, Macmillan, London, 1935, pp.115 and *OH, 1918, II*, pp.19, 27–8, 51; Prior and Wilson, op. cit., pp.276–80; Maurice, op. cit., pp.206–14; Rawlinson Diary, 26 and 28 March 1918, CC 1/9.

57 *OH, 1918, I*, pp.539–44; *OH, 1918, II*, pp.6–8; C E W Bean, *The Official History of Australia in the War of 1914–1918, Volume V : The Australian Imperial Force during the Main German Offensive, 1918*, Angus and Robertson, Sydney, 1937, pp.276–7; Marshall-Cornwall, op.cit., pp.219–20.

58 *OH, 1918, II*, pp.8, 83; Bean, V, pp.288, 295.

59 Rawlinson to Foch, 28 March 1918, Rawlinson papers, CC 1/10; see also *OH, 1918, II*, pp.51–2.

60 Rawlinson Diary, 31 March 1918, CC 1/9.

61 Rawlinson Diary, 1 April 1918, CC 1/9; *OH, 1918, II*, pp.111–113.

62 *OH, 1918, II*, pp.123–8; Bean, V, pp.298–355.

63 Rawlinson Diary, 5 April 1918, CC 1/9.

64 Rawlinson to GHQ, 15 April 1918, PRO WO 158/252; Haig to Foch (OAD 821), 17 April 1918, PRO WO 158/252; see also Rawlinson 'An Appreciation: 18/4/18', PRO WO 158/252.

65 *OH, 1918, II*, pp.114–117; GHQ to Byng and Rawlinson (OAD 806), 4 April 1918, PRO WO 158/252; Directive from Foch concerning the junction of the Franco-British Armies, 6 April 1918, PRO WO 158/252; Copy of Agreement made on 8 April at midday between the Commander of the Group of Armies of Reserve (GAR) and Rawlinson, PRO WO 158/252; Rawlinson Diary, 8 and 9 April 1918, CC 1/9.

66 Rawlinson Diary, 15 April 1918, CC 1/9.

67 OH, 1918, II, p.366.

68 Rawlinson Diary, 18 and 19 April 1918, CC 1/9; 'Report on the Operations of the III Corps from 5 April to 27 April 1918', Butler papers, IWM 69/10/1.

69 *OH, 1918, II*, pp.395–403; Haig to Foch at 6.30 p.m., 24 April 1918, PRO WO 158/252; Rawlinson Diary, 24 April 1918, CC 1/9; III Corps, 'Report on Operations', Butler papers, IWM 69/10/1.

70 Rawlinson Diary, 24 April 1918, CC 1/9.

71 *OH, 1918, II*, pp.404–5; Bean, V, pp.629–632; III Corps, 'Report on

Operations', Butler papers, IWM 69/10/1; Rawlinson Diary, 26 April 1918, CC 1/9.

72 Rawlinson Diary, 29 April 1918, CC 1/9; 11 May, 19 and 30 June 1918, CC 1/11.

73 *OH, 1918, III*, Macmillan, London, 1939, p.9; Rawlinson Diary, 28 and 30 May, 21, 24 and 25 June 1918, CC 1/11.

74 Rawlinson Diary, 2, 3 and 4 July 1918, CC 1/11; Rawlinson, 'Operations by the Australian Corps against Hamel, Bois de Hamel and Bois de Vaire July 4 1918', Rawlinson papers, NAM 5201/33/77; P. A. Pedersen, *Monash as Military Commander*, Melbourne University Press, 1985, pp.230–32; Lieutenant General Sir John Monash, *The Australian Victories in France in 1918*, Hutchinson, London, 1920, pp.52–4; Maurice, op. cit., pp.222–4.

75 Rawlinson Diary, 9, 11, 14 and 23 July 1918, CC 1/11; *OH, 1918, III*, pp.317–8.

76 Rawlinson Diary, 26 July and 5 August 1918, CC 1/11; *OH, 1918, III*, pp.315–320; *OH, 1918, IV*, pp.1–35; Haig Diary, 5 August 1918, PRO WO 256/34.

77 *OH, 1918, IV*, pp.59–60, 114–6; Rawlinson Diary, 10 August 1918, CC 1/22.

78 Rawlinson Diary, 13, 14 and 15 August 1918, CC 1/11; Haig Diary, 14 and 15 August 1918, PRO WO 256/34; Haig to Foch, 14 August 1918 (OAD 900/25), PRO WO 256/34; Haig to Foch, 15 August 1918 (OAD 900/27), PRO WO 256/34; *OH, 1918, IV*, pp.168–71; Prior and Wilson, op. cit., pp.334–6.

79 *OH, 1918, IV*, p.164; Rawlinson Diary, 17, 18 and 19 August 1918, CC 1/11.

80 Rawlinson Diary, 19 August, 5 and 6 September 1918, CC 1/11; *OH, 1918, IV*, p.166.

81 Rawlinson Diary, 13, 14, 15, 16 and 19 September 1918, CC 1/11; Haig Diary, 14, 15 and 16 September 1918, PRO WO 256/36; Dill to Du Cane, 15 September 1918 (OAD 920/1) PRO WO 256/36; *OH, 1918, IV*, pp.473–4.

82 Rawlinson Diary, 19, 20, 23, 25, 26 and 28 September 1918, CC 1/11; Haig Diary, 23 September 1918, PRO WO 256/36.

83 Rawlinson Diary, 29 September 1918, CC 1/11; *OH, 1918, V*, pp.95–113; Prior and Wilson, op. cit., pp.367–75; 'Offensive Operations undertaken by IX Corps from 18 September to 11 November 1918', Fourth Army papers, IWM Vol. 63; Montgomery, *The Story of the Fourth Army*, op. cit., pp.147–69.

84 Rawlinson Diary, 1, 2, 3 and 9 October 1918, CC 1/11; *OH, 1918, V*, pp.111, 132, 137, 132, 159, 180–1.

85 Rawlinson Diary, 8, 9, 15, 16, 17 and 18 October 1918, CC 1/11.

86 Ibid., 25 October and 2 November 1918, CC 1/11.

I am extremely grateful to Colonel A.J. Aylmer, Earl Haig, and Mr M.A.F. Rawlinson for permission to quote from material for which they hold the copyright. I am also deeply indebted to the Trustees of the Public Record Office and the Controller of HM Stationery Office; the Trustees of the Imperial War Museum; and the Archivist and staff of the Churchill College Archives Centre.

Chapter 2

Marshal Ferdinand Foch and Allied Victory

William Philpott

If any one man can be said to have won the First World War, it would be Marshal Ferdinand Foch. In recognition of his contribution to what was essentially an Allied victory, after four years of indecisive and often acrimonious coalition warfare on the Western Front, Foch is the only Frenchman to have been accorded the honour of a statue in London for his military deeds, and the dignity of Field Marshal of the British Empire.[1] Foch's contribution to victory was a strategic vision that looked beyond the particular military and political concerns of the individual Allied nations, an ability to see the 'big picture'; and equally importantly the qualities of leadership and motivation which allowed him to show this big picture to subordinate commanders of diverse nationalities, and to co-ordinate the particular efforts of individual Allied armies, French, British, American and Belgian, in the series of successive offensive blows that drove the German armies from occupied France and forced the enemy to sue for peace. Foch's task was not an easy one, for the management of Allied commanders was fraught with tensions and difficulties. Field Marshal Sir Douglas Haig, Commander in Chief of the British Armies in France and Flanders, had in particular to be managed carefully.[2] Towards the end of the campaign Haig's resentment at Foch's success showed through: 'Foch is suffering from a swollen head, and thinks himself another Napoleon'.[3] Although a private put down, Haig was indirectly paying Foch a great compliment, for he alone among the senior generals of the Great War deserved to be compared with the great captains of history.

There was indeed a marked difference between Foch and the other Allied military leaders. Although Haig was a determined fighting man, able to shoulder the burdens of command and stolid enough to see things through, he lacked the vision to see how to end things. General

Philippe Pétain, commanding the French army, was a soldier's general, who had saved France in the difficult year 1917, but he remained cautious and defensively minded, and preferred to look after number one than to serve the higher Allied cause. It was Pétain's slowness to support the hard pressed British forces in front of Amiens in March 1918 which was to be the catalyst for Foch's appointment to co-ordinate the Allied armies. The American General John Pershing was, as we shall see in a later chapter, assertive; yet, he was also inexperienced, as was his fresh but unblooded army.[4] King Albert I of the Belgians, uniquely on the Western Front a sovereign as well as an Allied commander, had proved from the start to be a weak link in the military alliance, and had to be managed carefully.[5] Although at heart a Frenchman, Foch rose above these petty national considerations to offer a single Allied strategy, and the personality and authority to translate his ideas into action.

At the beginning of 1918 the prospects of Allied victory before the end of 1918 looked remote. The year 1917 had been a difficult one for the Allied cause. One principal member of the alliance, Russia, had been knocked out, and the other Allies were showing signs of strain. The French army had mutinied, the Italians had suffered a major reverse and had had to be shored up by British and French reinforcements, and the British, after a year of sustained effort, were in the grip of a manpower crisis and riven by civil-military conflicts. Away from the battlefield, the German submarine campaign had strained the Allies' economic lifelines almost to breaking-point. There were some glimmers of hope. Pétain had managed to restore the morale of the French army which delivered two successful limited offensive blows, with considerable tactical sophistication and relatively light casualties, in the autumn of 1917 at Verdun and Malmaison. The British too, after the indecisive slogging match at Passchendaele, demonstrated for the first time the potential of combined arms operations with their initial success at Cambrai in November. The dynamic leadership of Lloyd George and Clemenceau in London and Paris had focused national energies on the total war effort, and munitions' production was at an unprecedented level. Moreover, they had belatedly tried to initiate a more dynamic management of the coalition war effort through the creation of a new Allied politico-military co-ordinating body, the Versailles Supreme War Council. Most significantly, there was the prospect of a decisive reinforcement for the Allied armies as American troops arrived in France over the coming year. Yet this was a long term benefit. The American formations had to be trained, equipped and initiated into the methods of modern warfare, which was anticipated to be the work of a year or more. Allied planners, including Foch, at the time chief of the French army staff, still expected the war to last into 1919, if not 1920. The immediate prospects for 1918 were grim. The battle hardened but war weary Allied armies were preparing for a gruelling defensive campaign as the enemy, victorious in the east, gathered their last reserves for a decisive offensive; and, following the failed experiment in unity of command in the spring of 1917, the Allies lacked clear military leadership on the principal front.

Into this decisive confrontation stepped Foch. Foch's star, which had waned along with that of his mentor Joffre after the indecisive 1916 Somme offensive, was in the ascendant again by the end of 1917. Recalled to boost the strategic authority of the French War Ministry in the spring of 1917, by the autumn he was once again at the heart of Allied decision making as French military representative on the Allied Supreme War Council. Foch's strategic appreciation at the turn of the new year gave a clear outline of his perception of the Allied position. While accepting that the Allies would have to fight a defensive battle in 1918, Foch, always a believer in the moral value of the offensive, appreciated that it would undermine Allied morale if the initiative were left entirely to the enemy. So in his plan for the coming year Foch contemplated a flexible response to the expected German offensive, an early indication of the strategic principles Foch was to follow in the 1918 campaign. Counter-attacks against the enemy's attacks, and prepared 'limited' counter-strikes on other parts of the Allied front to destabilize the enemy's strategic plan would be mounted; and if these proved effective a decisive Allied counter-offensive would follow.[6]

For this strategy to succeed, Foch felt that the Allies needed a strategic reserve and more effective 'unity of command' to co-ordinate the operations of the various Allied armies; in his own words: 'There must be a higher organ of command, which can at all times defend the general plan adopted as against personal inclinations and individual interests, and take rapid decisions and get them carried out without any loss of time.'[7] Foch was fond of quoting Machiavelli's dictum, 'never have more than one chief in war, because several wills enfeeble an army'.[8] It was this deficiency which had undermined the coalition war effort from the start,[9] and even in the face of adversity it appeared an insurmountable obstacle. The principle behind Allied military operations to date, Lloyd George had recently commented to Foch, had been: 'each general was interested mainly in his own front. Consequently, the Commanders-in-Chief and leading military authorities of the alliance did not draw up a plan in which the war was treated as a whole, but they each approved each other's plans and arranged for a certain amount of coincidence in point of time.[10] Yet the proposed remedy, an Executive War Board of the Allied Supreme War Council headed by Foch commanding an Allied General Reserve, only suggested a further multiplication of competing Allied military authorities. Not surprisingly, when faced with the united protestations of Haig and Pétain, who felt their executive authority to be threatened, Clemenceau set aside the Executive War Board scheme and placed his trust in the Allied army commanders' arrangements for mutual support.[11]

It was soon apparent once the German spring offensive opened on 21 March that this trust was misplaced. Haig and Pétain's arrangements quickly proved inadequate, and Pétain himself proved faint-hearted and unreliable. A hastily convened Allied conference, at Doullens on 26 March, assigned Foch the task of plugging the gap that was rapidly opening between the British and French armies. Foch responded to the challenge with gusto, injecting much needed energy into the French army. Within a week the gap was plugged with French divisions and the German advance on Amiens checked. Foch was rapidly given far greater authority than was envisaged under the Executive War Board scheme. Charged initially with the narrow responsibility of co-ordinating the operations of the Allied armies on the Western Front, a fortnight later at a second conference in Beauvais, Foch was appointed to direct the operations of the Allied armies on the Western Front, which would allow him to plan and prepare strategic operations.[12]

*   *   *

Foch had arrived at the pinnacle of the Allied military hierarchy after four years of hard campaigning. Although his record during the war was not one of unqualified success, Foch was the only man among the senior Allied commanders who possessed the character and experience for such a responsible and sensitive post. An artillery officer by training, he had served on the teaching staff of the French *École de Guerre* and gained an international reputation as a military theorist. Foch's particular belief, elaborated in his pre-war works of military theory, *Des Principes de la Guerre* and *De la Conduite de la Guerre*, was that morale was decisive in warfare, and that a successful offensive was the best way to raise an army's morale and lower that of the enemy. Among pre-1914 military theory books, these works were best-sellers, although the roots of the reverses sustained by the French army in the early battles of 1914 have been traced back to the misapplication of Foch's principles by the French high command. The 'cult of the offensive' failed the French army badly in 1914 and 1915, and ultimately led to Foch's own temporary fall from grace after the costly and indecisive Somme offensive of 1916. Foch was astute enough to temper military theory in response to his practical experiences in the offensive battles of the early years of the war. Like the other leaders of the French army he came to realize that a poorly prepared offensive, or one which was pressed once the chance of further significant success had been lost, leading to unnecessary casualties, was harmful to morale. In 1918 he was given the opportunity to translate this theory into practice on the battlefield.

As well as practical experience of the particular conditions of static trench warfare, Foch had lengthy experience of co-ordinating Allied operations. Nominated as Joffre's deputy in 1914, he had been charged with co-ordinating the operations of the French, British and Belgian armies in Flanders to block the German thrust to the Channel ports. In this job he gained an insight into the problems of military operations when Allied armies preserved their military independence, an experience reinforced when he directed the French armies in the joint battle on the Somme. This experience convinced Foch that a body needed to be created to co-ordinate Allied military strategy.[13] Foch's co-ordinating experience meant that he was one of the few Allied generals who saw the Allied front as a whole, and whose strategic vision extended beyond the Western Front. He was prepared to contemplate an offensive on the Italian Front in 1917, and arranged the deployment of British and French troops to the Italian Front after the Italian defeat at Caporetto.[14]

Foch brought to his new role a long acquaintance, and generally good relations, with other senior Allied political and military leaders. Lloyd George had grown close to Foch in 1917 as he looked to use him as a lever to force the British army's high command to look for strategic opportunities beyond the Western Front. Although at times they had their differences over practical matters, Lloyd George respected a man who he felt he had a broader and more sound strategic conception than Haig and the other British military leaders. Foch was singled out as a 'genius' in Lloyd George's controversial war memoirs, a word Lloyd George would not use lightly of a soldier.[15] His close relationship with the new Chief of the Imperial General Staff, Henry Wilson, dated back to their pre-war co-operation on the logistical arrangements for the deployment of the British Expeditionary force in France. He had worked on and off with Haig since 1914, and while their relations had always remained formal, they had come to develop a mutual respect for each other that survived intermittent disagreements over military details. Foch and Pétain were less congenial collaborators, and in time Foch had to fall back on the French military chain of command to ensure the full co-operation of the French army commander. More importantly, Foch had the unreserved support of Clemenceau, who despite their political differences, saw him as the only man able to win the war for the Allies, and was therefore willing to compromise. Although a confirmed anti-clerical, the French premier came to respect Foch's faith as fundamental to his ability to sustain the heavy responsibilities placed upon him. If he found Foch at Mass when he came to call,

Clemenceau would wait patiently for him to finish communing with God.[16]

Finally, Foch brought personal qualities to the role of generalissimo which enabled him to bear the heavy burdens of responsibility, and to execute his functions effectively. Although sixty-six when he assumed the supreme command, Foch was generally reckoned by contemporaries to have the constitution of a man half his age.[17] He had a strong Catholic faith from childhood, which sustained him in difficult times, as well as determination, a deep personal belief and a sense of mission.[18]

His style of command was unorthodox, but effective, according to the accounts of those who served close to him. As well as being a military theorist, Foch was a leader, for ultimately his job was to lead, not push. Foch knew how to persuade both subordinates and allies – to lead rather than to command, as he termed it himself.[19] Foch 'knows what he wants and gets it done', his British liaison officer Sir John Du Cane recorded in a postwar memoir. From his prior experience he knew that it was inappropriate to give Allied army commanders orders. Instead plans were developed by close liaison facilitated by regular written instructions and frequent personal meetings.[20] Foch was relatively unconcerned with the detail of operations, and unencumbered by having a large administrative organization to run. He saw his principal responsibilities to be to think and then to act; to develop broad strategic conceptions and ideas to be interpreted by his loyal and efficient Chief of Staff, General Maxime Weygand, and put into practice by subordinate Allied commanders. It is clear from reading Foch's directives that he thought in terms of armies and strategic objectives, rather than divisions and tactical successes like Pétain. Rather than draw up detailed orders, he would outline his broad strategic conception, then allow the national army commanders to reflect and comment upon it, and to make suggestions as to the individual operations which would go towards fulfilling that conception. Having apportioned responsibilities in the general plan, he would allow subordinates, who had a better knowledge of the tactical situation on their fronts, discretion as to the practical execution of the schemes he proposed. Only if he felt that the general conception of the combined battle plan was compromised would he overrule the proposals of Allied commanders for individual offensive operations. As Foch's judgements in the defensive battle proved astute, in time the Allied commanders came to respect his leadership style and strategic sense, and Foch found his authority was rarely challenged. As far as tactics went, it was enough to urge in flamboyant but vague language that subordinate commanders act with vigour on their own initiative. His 27 September directive, after the Allies had launched their decisive offensive, is typical of his style:

the progress of the battle depends upon the spirit of decision evinced by Corps Commanders and the initiative and energy shown by Divisional Commanders. The issue once more hinges upon the activity of the Commanders and the endurance of the troops: the latter is never found wanting whenever an appeal is made to it.[21]

On 7 August 1918 Foch was appointed a Marshal of France, the nation's highest military honour. Although the honour had been revived at the end of 1916 as a token recompense for the discredited General Joffre, for Foch the honour meant something else – the rank and dignity to go with his authority as generalissimo of the Allied forces on the Western Front.[22] It was also a reward for checking the German spring offensives that had come close to separating and defeating the Allied armies. Yet Foch's job was only half finished; while the war had not been lost, it had still to be won. The next day the battle of Amiens, the first of an uninterrupted string of offensives which were to sweep the Allies to victory over the next 100 days, opened. Amiens, the 'black day of the German army' which convinced Ludendorff that the war was lost,[23] is remembered as a great British victory although it was an Allied offensive, of the British Fourth and French First armies; Foch had insisted on French participation in the battle.[24] This was the key to the Allied victory in 1918. The British like to think that it was predominantly the effort of Haig's army which defeated the German army,'[25] while the French like to think that their army finally liberated occupied France. Americans have claimed that without the large reinforcement of American manpower sent to France in 1918 victory would not have been possible. In reality, all three Allied armies had their part to play, and whatever the postwar one-upmanship of national historians of the conflict, without the proper co-ordination of three armies, working to a single strategic plan, the successive blows that defeated the German army in the field would not have been possible.

Foch had at his disposal four Allied armies.[26] The French army had been the mainstay of the coalition since 1914, but by 1918 was exhausted by four years of constant effort. Although past its peak, it was a well equipped, well led and vastly experienced army. Its Commander-in-chief, Pétain, was idolized by his troops. Methodical in his tactical thinking, and the master of the limited offensive, Pétain did not share Foch's bold vision. After clashing with Foch over moving French troops from the French to the British sector of the front during the defensive battle, Pétain was to be formally subordinated to Foch by the French government.[27] This ensured that he could not challenge the generalissimo's authority during the Allied advance, although still on occasion he had to be urged to pursue his offensive operations with greater vigour.[28]

The British army was by 1918 a powerful fighting force which had mastered the art of the combined arms battle after two years of practice. But its cutting edge had been blunted by a manpower crisis in Britain and heavy casualties in the defensive battle, which meant that its ranks were increasingly filled by comb-outs and youths. Its commander, Haig, could not be formally subordinated to Foch in the way that Pétain could. However, Foch and Haig had long experience of working with each other, dating back to the first defensive battle around Ypres in 1914. While their relations remained formal, Foch and Haig worked well enough together. Foch's job was to ensure that the British army's operations were co-ordinated with other Allied offensive operations and contributed to his general strategic conception. Therefore he could allow Haig considerable latitude when it came to their execution. Foch always allowed Haig to have his say when it came to operations on the British front, and as often as not would accept Haig's recommendations as to the conduct of these operations.[29]

The American army was the only Allied army growing in strength, but it lacked equipment, especially heavy artillery, and experience. Foch greatly admired the *élan* of the American divisions, but felt that this lack of experience would lead them to disaster unless they were operating closely with experienced Allied formations. This appreciation of American strengths and weaknesses had to be factored into the general Allied plan. Foch wished to give the American troops the opportunity to develop battle experience, while at the same time struggling to check Pershing's overconfidence and sense of independence.[30] The Belgian army, in contrast, was relatively intact after four years of defensive warfare, but it had no experience of the offensive, and its commander, King Albert, was unwilling to allow its limited manpower to be squandered for no appreciable military result.[31]

Foch's first task had been to weld these four separate national armies into a single fighting machine. The defensive battle between March and June 1918 had given the new system of unified command time to develop into a smooth and relatively effective mechanism for co-ordinating Allied operations and forces. During the defensive battle it also became standard practice to unite multi-national forces under a single commander for the duration of individual operations. Foch's practice of *roulement*, resting tired divisions on quiet parts of the Allied front, established the principle that all Allied forces (except the Belgians) were available to be used along the whole length of the Western Front. In General Magnin's counter-stroke on the Marne in July, which gave the first indication that the battle was turning in the Allies' favour, an American Corps was placed directly under Magnin's orders.[32] At Amiens Foch placed Debeney's First French Army under Haig's orders for the duration of the battle. For the first time the Allies had a single force, whose troops were available for use anywhere along the front, albeit still composed of the separate national armies that comprised the coalition. By the time the counter-offensive opened, British General Headquarters acknowledged that 'Foch uses the divisions as he pleases and dictates our strategy'.[33]

As well as having all the resources of the Allied armies at his disposal, Foch also had a clear strategic plan. His 1 January memorandum had set out his broad conception for the 1918 campaign. Therefore, throughout the defensive battle Foch was always seeking opportunities for striking back at the enemy, either through small local counter-attacks or a larger counter-offensive. Through careful study of the enemy's successive offensives it became clear to Foch that, while it was possible using new offensive tactics to break through the enemy's defensive position and penetrate to a certain depth, eventually, as the retiring defenders consolidated their positions and the attackers' lines of supply were extended, the momentum of an attack would stall. Foch likened this pattern to the successive diminution of the power of waves as they hit the shore. Foch judged that the time to hit back was when the energy of the advancing wave had been dissipated, and the enemy was de-stabilized. Foch carefully chose his point of counter-attack. He appreciated that the enemy now had two armies, a 'storm-troop' shock army and a mass of second class defensive divisions, and he judged that the Allies would get better results retaliating against the latter.[34] This careful appreciation of the enemy's weaknesses bore fruit in July 1918, when General Mangin's attack against the weak flanks of the salient the Germans had created on the Marne recaptured all the ground gained by the enemy in their final major offensive of the year.

Success in the Second Battle of the Marne convinced Foch that the initiative had returned to the Allied side, and he was determined to keep it.[35] Foch's perception of the nature of the offensive was to be turned on its head and applied to drive back and defeat the German army. Since offensives eventually lost momentum, Foch determined on lateral exploitation of success once an offensive had stalled, to push the enemy back in a series of co-ordinated and concentric blows.

As perceived in the summer of 1918, Foch's plan was not one for winning the war in 1918, but a scheme for improving the Allied tactical and economic position to facilitate their success in the coming year. He set out his thoughts in a memorandum which he prepared for a meeting with the three Allied army commanders on 24 July (incidentally the only time Foch met all three Allied army commanders together). This memorandum is the clearest exposition of Foch's plan for Allied victory. He judged that German offensive potential was now exhausted, and that the Allies had 'arrived at the turning point of the road'. His acute strategic perception indicated that the balance of material forces was now tilting in the Allies' favour. As the enemy used up their reserves in a succession of costly indecisive offensives, American manpower and Allied munitions' production were both on the increase. Allied superiority in aircraft and artillery was pronounced, and artillery superiority was on the increase. Moreover Allied morale, which had remained high during the defensive battle, would be raised further by continuing a successful counter-offensive. The time had come to proceed to the second stage of Foch's plan for the year – a counter-offensive 'not only to pursue tactical success but to seek results such as might increase our resources and facilitate their employment'. A succession of offensive operations with the objective of disengaging strategic railway lines, securing economic resources and, equally importantly, preserving the initiative which the Allies had recently regained, were laid before the Allied commanders. Once the advancing wave of one offensive movement came up against hardening resistance, Foch contemplated shifting the attack to another sector of the front, or extending it to the previously static armies on the flanks of the attack, for success elsewhere would outflank the resistance on the earlier front of attack and facilitate the further forward movement of stalled Allied armies.[36] In practice Foch intended a succession of limited but carefully co-ordinated operations rather than a decisive breakthrough – repeated body blows to a tiring adversary rather than a single knockout blow to the head, demonstrated to the British Foreign Secretary, Arthur Balfour, on one memorable occasion in the gardens at Versailles in Foch's characteristic animated fashion, by 'violent pugilistic gestures first with his fists and then with his feet'.[37]

By the end of 1917 both the British and French armies had mastered the 'bite and hold' limited offensive battle.[38] However, the best tactical method of exploiting a successful forward movement still eluded Allied planners. After Malmaison in October 1917 the successful commander of the French Sixth Army, General Maistre, had suggested two possible solutions to this problem: forward exploitation with armoured and mobile forces (light tanks and cavalry with air support and self-propelled guns) beyond the range of the guns; or lateral exploitation to extend the front of attack with prepared assaults on either flank.[39] Whether Foch had studied Maistre's memorandum is not clear, although it is probable that it would have passed across his desk at the Ministry of War. Foch himself had certainly been struggling with the problem of tactical exploitation since he had failed to secure a decisive breakthrough on the Somme, and had concluded that armoured formation would be the means of exploitation in future.[40] In the early months of 1918 Foch was perfecting the methods which Maistre had suggested,[41] and both were to be employed in the Allied offensives in the second half of 1918. Mobile formations broke into the enemy's front position and then extended the penetration beyond the range of the guns; and lateral exploitation was used to outflank enemy resistance and force the enemy to withdraw. Much of the ground gained was not won at the point of a bayonet, but renounced by the enemy when their position became untenable. The principles of mobile warfare had been rediscovered.

*　　*　　*

The Allied commanders' initial reaction to Foch's 24 July memorandum was not promising. Both Haig and Pétain complained that their armies were exhausted by the defensive battle and unable to begin a counter-offensive, while Pershing stated that the American army was not yet ready to fight. Foch urged the practicability of the plan if the Allied forces were properly co-ordinated, and gave the Allied Commanders-in-Chief forty-eight hours to respond. All accepted the proposals the next day.[42]

The consequence was a series of successful offensives beginning on 8 August at Amiens and continuing until the middle of September, culminating in the American capture of the St Mihiel salient. While the most effective Allied offensives of the war so far, they were by no means decisive, and had done no more than to force the enemy back to their strong prepared defensive positions on the Hindenburg Line, restoring the situation to that which had existed at the start of the year. But an effective counter-offensive had regained for the Allies the military initiative and moral ascendancy over the enemy, Foch's keys to decisive operations. Foch was convinced that he had found the tactical key to breaking the enemy's resistance, lateral exploitation; and, moreover, that it was necessary to keep attacking to exploit the disorganization of the enemy's forces that the recent operations had induced.

In early September Foch made the decision to switch to the final phase of his plan, the decisive offensive. Foch had to choose whether to shift the offensive to the flanks or break through the enemy's fortified position. Boldly, Foch decided that with proper co-ordination of operations he could do both. It was time to throw all Allied resources into the ring – 'tout-le-monde à la bataille', as Foch was fond of declaiming.[43] Foch's decisive offensive was to consist of four co-ordinated Allied operations directed at strategically significant points in the enemy's line, together comprising a 'general offensive from the Meuse to the North Sea'.

Between 26 and 28 September Franco-American forces were to attack on the right flank, between the rivers Suippe and Meuse, the Americans in the Meuse-Argonne sector and the French further west. After this offensive had started the British were to attack the Hindenburg line at Cambrai on 27 September. The next day a Belgian, French and British army group was to attack on the left flank in Flanders to break out of the Ypres salient and capture the Passchendaele ridge. Finally on 29 September British and French armies were to attack the southern sector of the Hindenburg line. If these attacks were successful the French were to mount a follow-up operation in the centre to liberate the Chemin-des-Dames.[44]

Foch's bold vision proved astute. With the exception of the American attack in the Argonne, which bogged down due to logistical difficulties, these co-ordinated offensives were decisive. After their principal defensive position was ruptured, the enemy was forced to begin a strategic withdrawal, and sued for an armistice in early October. While negotiating the terms of the armistice Foch did not relax the pressure on the enemy, who were closely pursued by triumphant Allied forces. He recognized the importance of not allowing a disorganized and retiring enemy, who still had considerable strength and fighting potential, the opportunity to rest and reorganize. The German army could still organize effective pockets of resistance, if not a single defensive front, and Foch feared that they could still retire to the strategic barrier of the Rhine if not constantly pressed. The Allies themselves were suffering from manpower and munitions shortages and communications difficulties as they advanced over ground devastated by the retreating enemy. When the momentum of the late September offensives stalled and a new line of resistance threatened to coalesce in mid-October, Foch launched another series of co-ordinated offensives, his so called – 'general offensive' – forcing the Germans into headlong retreat. To ensure that his and his armies' efforts were not in vain, Foch insisted in the armistice negotiations that the Allies secure bridgeheads over the Rhine, to ensure that the enemy could not consolidate a new defensive position over the winter and renew hostilities in the spring.

*   *   *

On 21 October Clemenceau wrote to Foch; 'What matters is the immense battle now going on, a battle which you have conducted in such a way as to place you in the front rank of great captains.'[45] Although his contemporaries judged Foch to be the greatest strategist of the war, his reputation has attracted little interest among modern historians.[46] An early biographer of Foch, Basil Liddell Hart, ever the enemy of the great captains, ascribed Allied victory in 1918 to superior material force.[47] Even here Foch deserves considerable credit for his foresight, for while Chief of Staff in the summer of 1917 he had drawn up the munitions programme for the French army that was to furnish them with the wherewithal for military victory in the summer of 1918. In a total war this is one of the keys to victory, and undoubtedly superior

Allied material force would eventually have secured victory, even without Foch. But as well as having the means to victory, the Allies needed the will. This, according to Sir James Marshall-Cornwall, is what Foch, 'the keystone in the arch of Allied victory', provided,[48] for the unanticipated victory of the autumn of 1918 was the result of Foch's vigorous application of superior Allied strength.

Victory in 1918 resulted from a combination of three factors: operational sophistication; strategic vision; and effective co-ordination. By the second half of 1918 the Allied forces had mastered the means of tactical and strategic offensive on the Western Front. The combined arms battle of 1918 was a long way from the offensive methods that had served the French army so poorly in 1915 and 1916, for which Foch will always have considerable responsibility. Foch's careful study of the offensive in early 1918 enabled him to understand the nature of battle on the Western Front, and to develop an operational theory, which capitalized upon the Allied armies' ability to break into the enemy's position and exploit that break-in. Credit for developing the tactics of break-in must go predominantly to Pétain and Haig, and their subordinate army commanders who managed the successful offensives of 1917.[49] Foch's contribution was to be the operational principle of lateral exploitation, which enabled individual tactical successes on different sectors of the front to be combined into a coherent strategic offensive. Foch correctly perceived that successive destabilizing blows – advancing waves as he termed them – were the means by which the Allies could seize and retain the initiative. Consequently,

> instead of hammering away at a single point, we had made a series of successive attacks, all more or less surprises and all profitable, but not carried further than the circumstances justified in each case. The very reverse, in fact, of what we did last autumn which [Foch] characterized as "abominable".[50]

In 1918 there was never the decisive breakthrough that Allied generals had striven for in vain from 1915 to 1917, but the rolling back of the enemy's line, and the successive outflanking of the enemy's prepared defensive positions,[51] to liberate occupied France and Belgium.

This co-ordinated series of operations along the whole length of the Allied front would not have been possible without a supreme Allied commander who not only possessed the strategic vision which the individual army commanders had lacked before, but also had the authority to direct and the personality to lead. General Sir Henry Rawlinson, commander of the British Fourth Army and subject of the last chapter, acknowledged Foch's contribution in this vital respect as the decisive offensive opened: 'Today has been a record in the way of Allied successes on the Western Front. Under Foch's tuition and the lessons of over four years war (sic) we are really learning and the synchronization of the various attacks had been admirable.'[52] While it took time for Foch's authority to become firmly established,[53] by the time the campaign drew to a close Foch had welded four separate Allied armies into a single force through the strength of his personality.[54] The enemy recognized the importance of this contribution: 'The Entente has to thank general Foch for successfully subordinating the divergent interests of the Allies to a higher, united purpose.'[55] This was his supreme achievement, the result of the force of his personality. Liddell Hart wrote: 'The indefinable effect of Foch's spirit endowed his actions with more effect than the facts convey.'[56] Perhaps this is the mark of a great captain.

Notes

The author would like to thank the Clerk of the House of Lords Record Office and the Trustees of the Beaverbrook Foundation (Lloyd George); Mr M.A.F. Rawlinson (Rawlinson); Lord Esher (Esher); and the Masters and Fellows of Churchill College Cambridge.

1   Ironically the latter dignity had before the war been bestowed on the German Kaiser.

2   See W.J. Philpott, 'Haig and Britain's European Allies' in *Haig, A Reappraisal 70 Years On*, ed. B.J. Bond & N. Cave (Barnsley: Leo Cooper, 1999), pp.128–44.

3   Haig diary, 27 October 1918, *The Private Papers of Sir Douglas Haig*, ed. R. Blake, (London: Eyre and Spottiswoode, 1952), p. 207.

4   For details of Foch's difficulties in managing the American military effort see F. Foch, *The Memoirs of Marshal Foch* (Trans. T. Bentley Mott: London: William Heinemann, 1931), pp.268–9, 352–3, 397–8 and 504–5.

5   For details see W.J. Philpott, 'Britain, France and the Belgian Army'. in B.J. Bond et al, *Look to Your Front: Studies in the First World War by the British Commission for Military History* (Staplehurst: Spellmount, 1999), pp.121–36.

6   Memorandum for the Supreme War Council, 1 January 1918, quoted in Foch, *Memoirs*, pp.270–1.

7   Ibid., p. 272.

8   Major General Sir G. Aston, *The Biography of the Late Marshal Foch* (London, Hutchinson & Co., n.d.), p. 182.

9   Foch had appreciated this from early in the war. See his note of 16 November 1915 in 'Cahiers du Marechal Foch', Fonds Weygand, *Service Historique de l'Armée de Terre*, Vincennes, 1K130/9/6. For a detailed analysis see W.J. Philpott, *Anglo-French Relations and Strategy on the Western Front, 1914–18* (Basingstoke: Macmillan, 1996).

10 'Secretary's notes of a conversation at Chequers Court', 14 October 1917, Lloyd George Papers, House of Lords Record Office, F23/1/24.

11 Philpott, *op. cit.*, p. 153.

12 Ibid., pp.154–6.

13 Foch, *Memoirs*, p.257.

14 Ibid., pp.256 & 261–6.

15 D. Lloyd George, *War Memoirs* (London: Odhams Press, 2 vols, 1938 edn), ii, 1688.

16 Lieutenant Colonel M. Hunter, *Foch: A Study in Leadership* (Ottawa: Director of Military Training, Army Headquarters, 1961), pp.182–3

17 Ashton, *Foch*, p.174.

18 Ibid., p.56.

19 Ibid., p.227.

20 Lieutenant General Sir J. P. Du Cane, *Marshal Foch* (privately printed, 1920), Imperial War Museum, 71/48/1, pp.2–5.

21 Foch, *Memoirs*, p.477.

22 Foch was given the task of co-ordinating Allied operations on the Western Front on 26 March, and received the official title of Commander-in-Chief of the Allied Armies in France on 3 April.

23 J. Terraine, *To Win a War: 1918, The Year of Victory* (London: Papermac, 1986), pp.106–14.

24 R. Prior and T. Wilson, *Command on the Western Front* (Oxford Blackwell, 1992), p.305.

25 For example T. Wilson, *The Myriad Faces of War* (Oxford: Blackwell, 1986), pp.593–4, even attributes the broader strategic conception to Haig.

26 For Foch's assessment of the Allied armies see note of 2 September 1917, 'Cahiers du Marechal Foch', Fonds Weygand, 1K130/9/6.

27 Foch, *Memoirs*, pp.384–6.

28 Ibid., pp.511–13.

29 For example, see Ibid., pp.446–7. See also Philpott, 'Haig and Britain's European Allies', pp.136–7.

30 See for example, Hankey diary, 31 August and 8 October 1918, Hankey papers, Churchill College Cambridge, HNKY 1/5 and 1/6.

31 Philpott, 'Britain, France and the Belgian Army', pp.122–3.

32 Foch, *Memoirs*, p.415.

33 Esher journal, 15 April 1918, Esher papers, Churchill College Cambridge, ESHR 2/21.

34 Foch, *Memoirs*, p.426.

35 Note of 24 July 1918, 'Cahiers du Marechal Foch', Fonds Weygand, 1K130/9/6.

36 This memorandum is reproduced Ibid., pp.425–9.

37 Lloyd George, *War Memoirs*, ii, 1844.

38 The British army had achieved notable successes at Vimy Ridge (April), Messines (July) and on the Menin Road Ridge (September); the

French had had similar success at Verdun (August) and Malmaison (October).

39 'Rapport sur la bataille de Malmaison', by Maistre, 25 November 1917, *Service Historique de l'Armée de Terre*, Vincennes, 16N1992/1.
40 Note of 24 November 1916, 'Cahiers du Marechal Foch', Fonds Weygand, 1K130/9/6.
41 Notes of 16 and 19 February 1918, Ibid.
42 Foch, *Memoirs*, p.430.
43 J. Marshall-Cornwall, *Foch as Military Commander* (London: Batsford, 1972), p.235.
44 Ibid., pp.467–75.
45 Ibid., pp.504–5.
46 'One of the ablest commanders of the war, Foch remains one of the least known', D. Winter, *Haig's Command* (London: Viking, 1991), p.275. There have been three English language studies of Foch, two biographies shortly after his death, by Aston (see note 8) and B.H. Liddell Hart, *Foch: The Man of Orleans* (London: Eyre and Spottiswoode, 1931), and a study of his leadership by Marshall Cornwall (see note 43).
47 Liddell Hart, *op. cit.,* p.333.
48 Marshall-Cornwall, *Foch as Military Commander*, p.234.
49 For a study of the development of battlefield operations on the Western Front see Prior and Wilson, *Command on the Western Front*.
50 Milner to Lloyd George, 17 September 1918, reporting a conversation with Foch, Lloyd George Papers, House of Lords Record Office, London, F38/4/17.
51 Marshall-Cornwall, *Foch as Military Commander*, p.240.
52 Rawlinson diary, 28 September 1918, Rawlinson papers, Churchill College Cambridge, RWLN 1/12.
53 For an uncensored account of the practical day to day problems of co-ordination see the entries for April to July 1918 in the diary of the Major General Sidney Clive, head of the British liaison mission at French army headquarters, in 'Correspondence Used in the Compilation of the Official History', Public Record Office, Kew (CAB 45): Cab 45/201.
54 Epitomized in the Flanders army group, commanded by King Albert, managed by a French Chief-of-Staff, and comprising the Belgian army, the French Sixth Army and the British Second Army.
55 Quoted in Lloyd George, *War Memoirs*, ii, 1836.
56 B. Liddell Hart, *Foch*, vii.

Chapter 3

Major General W.C.G. Heneker: A Divisional Commander of the Great War[1]

J.M. Bourne

Studies of the British Army during the Great War have traditionally focused either on the activities of GHQ and its relationships with a handful of senior commanders or on the life of the ordinary soldier in the front line trench. In recent years, however, there has been a growing realization among scholars of the need for greater knowledge and understanding of the army's intervening levels of command, especially corps and division.[2] Despite this, there is as yet no modern study of corps level command and only one modern divisional history.[3] Only three corps commanders, two of whom were Dominion officers, have found biographers and no divisional commander.[4] Except for the Canadian and – eventually – the Australian Corps, division was the highest level of homogeneous command in the British Expeditionary Force (BEF).[5] It was where operations and tactics met. In the peculiar conditions of the Western Front, division was also, perhaps, the highest level of command at which personal leadership could make itself felt. Commanded by a major general, each infantry division was a 'mini-army' with its own infantry, artillery, sappers, transport, medical and veterinary facilities, machine guns, trench mortars and, occasionally in 1918, its own tanks and ground attack aircraft. At full strength an infantry division consisted of approximately 18,000 officers and men, nearly as many British troops as Wellington commanded at Waterloo. It represented the key level of 'middle management' in an increasingly large, complicated organization.

One hundred and seventy-nine men commanded an infantry division on the Western Front during the Great War. Most commanded only one division before being promoted or replaced. This represents a significant turnover in an army that had sixty divisions at its maximum strength. Finding competent divisional commanders at the start of the war was not easy. When the war broke out only one man in the British Army, Sir Horace Smith-Dorrien, had commanded an infantry division in action and fewer than forty had commanded one at all. There were 110 major generals on the active list in August 1914. Many of these were considered too old for field command. Others, such as Allenby, Byng, Monro and Rawlinson, were destined for rapid promotion to corps and army command. Only one major general in August 1914, Sir George Gorringe (GOC 47th Division, 1916–18) was a divisional commander when the war ended. Of the rest, only Sir Percival Wilkinson (GOC 50th Division, 1915–18) and Sir Thompson Capper (killed in action at Loos while GOC 7th Division) made much impact as divisional commanders during the war. The bulk of the 179 men who commanded an infantry division on the Western Front were regimental officers in 1914, some of them quite junior, who were promoted during the war. This is the story of one of them.

William Charles Giffard Heneker was descended from an old Staffordshire family, but his immediate antecedents were to be found in Ireland and Canada. His father, Richard William Heneker, was an architect who emigrated in the mid-nineteenth century from Dublin to Canada, then very much a pioneer society, where he was one of the principal founders of the town of Sherbrooke, Ontario. William Heneker was born on 22 August 1867, the year in which Canada achieved Dominion status. He was educated in Canada, at the Bishop's College School, Lennoxville, Ontario. Bishop's College was an elite institution in the Canadian context, educating some famous Canadian soldiers, including H.E. Burstall, F.O.W. Loomis and Andy McNaughton, but it meant that Heneker missed the English public school education, common to many of his contemporaries in the British Army. He missed Sandhurst, too. His preliminary military training was undertaken at the Royal Military College of Canada, Kingston, Ontario, from which he graduated on 28 June 1888, twenty-six years to the day before the assassination of the Archduke Franz Ferdinand in Sarajevo changed Heneker's life and the world he grew up in forever.

Graduates of the Royal Military College of Canada were low in the pecking order of the British Army. Heneker was not in a position to pick and choose his regiment, but given his Irish connections his commission in the 1st Battalion Connaught Rangers on 5 September 1888 was, perhaps, not uncongenial. Heneker was no dilettante, concerned only with polo and pig sticking. He was serious about his profession from the start. As a 'colonial' with limited means, he doubtless had small choice. He paid assiduous attention to his work, took and passed courses in gymnastics, signalling and musketry, and early in his military career displayed the high sense of duty that was the foundation of his character.

The British Army that Heneker joined was ill equipped to fight a continental war. At every level of military command, except the tactical, the army's institutional inheritance bequeathed a legacy of weakness. A long service, volunteer force, generally recruited from among the least well educated sections of British society, the urban and rural poor, it was designed, trained and equipped as a colonial *gendarmerie* and spread across the Empire on garrison and policing duties. There was a sense in which the British Army did not exist at all. The focus of officers' and soldiers' loyalties was not the army but the regiment and, in practice, the battalion. The army's regimental ethos and its deployment in 'penny packets' produced an institution weak in trained staff officers, lacking heavy artillery and with scant opportunity for senior officers to command large all-arms formations or to 'think big'. However, at the lowest level of military command, tactics, the situation was different. The British Army was an active service army. It presented numerous opportunities for ambitious officers to experience the realities of command in combat conditions. The wars of empire produced, by 1914, a reserve of officers at regimental level with combat experience, often achieved in demanding climatic, geographical and political conditions in which physical courage, moral resilience, independent judgement, resourcefulness, tactical flexibility and good small-unit administration were paramount. This helped to ensure that the pace of change at the tactical level in the BEF was more dynamic than at the strategic and operational levels.

Heneker was certainly a member of this combat experienced group. He had an early introduction to the realities of British soldiering when his battalion proceeded to India as part of the Sikkim Expeditionary Force within a few weeks of his joining the unit. But it was his secondment to the Niger Coast Protectorate in 1897 and then to the West African Frontier Force that did most to shape his pre-war career. West Africa was one of the principal theatres in which ambitious young officers could find a route to professional distinction. It was a particularly demanding one. Many officers, including Sir Thomas Morland (GOC X Corps on the Western Front), had their health ruined through service there. Heneker himself succumbed to a fever during the Igara expedition in 1903. But he also saw a great deal of combat. As second-in-command of the Southern Nigeria Regiment, he commanded the Ubium, Ishan, Ibeku-Oloku, Afikpo and Igara expeditions, winning the DSO. He also commanded columns in the Benin Territories and Aro expeditions and served as a Travelling District Commissioner. In 1906 he made the benefit of his experience available to a wider audience by publishing a book, *Bush Warfare*. Between 1906 and 1910 he added staff work to his combat experience as Deputy Assistant Adjutant and Quartermaster-General, Orange River Colony.

From a career perspective, Heneker's *cv*, perhaps, lacked two things. He had not served in the South African War. This was not only the biggest and most important contemporary war fought by the British Army, but also a splendid opportunity to develop helpful contacts and relationships. And he had not passed staff college. Nevertheless, there were clear signs that Heneker was a 'coming man'. He received a brevet majority in 1901 and a brevet lieutenant-colonelcy in 1905. In 1907 he was made brevet colonel and appointed Aide-de-Camp to King Edward VII. (He later rode in the funeral procession of Edward VII and the Coronation procession of George V.) And, in 1912, he got his own battalion. It was not, however, a battalion of the Connaught Rangers. The highest aspiration of most pre-war regimental officers was to command the battalion in which their careers began, or at least a sister battalion. But the Connaughts had no vacancies in 1912. Instead, Heneker was 'fast-tracked' to the 2nd Battalion North Staffordshire Regiment, following the retirement of its commanding officer, Lieutenant Colonel E.G. Snow, halfway through the normal four-year tour as battalion commander. Intruding an outsider as Commanding Officer was always difficult, not least in a regiment with a number of talented majors, including T.A. Andrus, V.W. de Falbe, A.R. Hoskins, F.E. Johnston and L.J. Wyatt, all of whom reached general officer rank during the Great War, and may have felt themselves to have superior claims to the new CO. Heneker, however, seems to have had no difficulty adjusting to his new command or his new command to him. He must have been extremely pleased by his good fortune, but within two years the appointment seemed like a curse.

The reason for this was simple. The 2nd North Staffords were stationed in India, at Peshawar. They were still there when war broke out.[6] The Great War probably represents the greatest professional challenge in the British Army's history. For its Regular officers, however, it also represented an unprecedented professional opportunity. It was an opportunity that Heneker feared would pass him by. 'What a thing for me if there is war and we are dragged in while I am out here,' he confided to his diary on 30 July 1914. 'My career will be finished.'[7] He was in despair at the thought of being 'marooned' in India. He did everything he could to get back home. Major General C.V.F. Townshend included Heneker's name in his petition to Sir John French for a place in the expeditionary force. Although the petition was delivered by Townshend's wife, which shows a fine understanding of French's character, it was unavailing. Heneker then offered his services to the assembling Canadian contingents and was again refused. A petition to the King was also unsuccessful.

Heneker was partially correct in believing that, from a career point of view, the BEF was the place to be. Four of the six corps commanders who served in the BEF in 1914 (Allenby, Haig, Rawlinson and Smith-Dorrien) became army commanders and two (Allenby and Haig) became Commanders-in-Chief; eight of the twelve infantry division commanders (Fergusson, Haldane, Keir, Monro, Morland, Rawlinson, Snow and H.F.M. Wilson) went on to command corps, two (Monro and Rawlinson) to command armies and one (Monro) to become a Commander-in-Chief; twenty-five of the thirty-three infantry brigade commanders (Bulfin, Cavan, Congreve, Cuthbert, R.H. Davies, B.J.C. Doran, Douglas Smith, R. Fanshawe, Gleichen, Gordon, Haking, Haldane, Hickie, Hull, Hunter-Weston, Ingouville-Williams, Landon, Lawford, Maude, Maxse, McCracken, Ruggles-Brise, Shaw, Watts, H.F.M. Wilson) went on to command a division, eleven to command a corps (Bulfin, Cavan, Congreve, Haking, Haldane, Hunter-Weston, Maude, Maxse, McCracken, Watts, H.F.M. Wilson) and two (Cavan and Maude) to become Commanders-in-Chief. But at battalion command level in the BEF, which was Heneker's alternative to being 'marooned' in India, it was a different story.

Fifty-nine of the 196 infantry battalion commanders who served in the BEF in 1914 became brigade commanders, but only thirteen went on to command a division. Twenty-five were killed in action, three died of wounds, eleven became prisoners of war and twenty-five were wounded, many seriously. The 2nd Battalion Connaught Rangers suffered particularly badly. Its CO, Lieutenant Colonel A.W. Abercrombie, was one of six officers to be captured. Another seventeen were killed. Heneker's frustrations were understandable, but his apparent isolation in India, in keeping him out of the 1914 fighting, almost certainly preserved his life and made his subsequent career possible.

It was not until 25 November 1914 that Heneker received orders to proceed to England and not until March 1915, six months into the war, that he was offered command of 54th Infantry Brigade at Colchester. 54th Brigade was part of 18th (Eastern) Division, a new army unit, mostly recruited from the east and south-east of England. The Military Secretary stressed that Heneker's appointment was provisional and dependent upon a favourable report from the divisional commander. The divisional commander was Major General Ivor Maxse. If avoiding the fighting of 1914 was Heneker's first piece of luck during the war, having Maxse as divisional commander was his second. Maxse's expertise as a trainer of troops made his reputation in the army and he turned 18th Division into one of the best in the BEF. As GOC 1st (Guards) Brigade in the original BEF he also had experience of the recent fighting. Above all, he was an excellent judge of men and immediately recognized Heneker's qualities. Heneker shared Maxse's commitment to training, especially a high level of rifle skills, ordering his battalions to train for at least two hours a day, practising rapid fire and fire discipline by sections.[8]

18th Division was deployed to France at the end of July 1915, taking over the Fricourt sector in mid-August. For the rest of 1915, 54th Brigade gradually acclimatized itself to the Western Front. But on 10 December, while visiting trenches on the Somme, its GOC was wounded in the left thigh by a German machine gun firing at long range. Thigh wounds are often portrayed as 'minor', and Heneker's never seems to have been life threatening, but they are slow to heal owing to the amount of tissue and arterial damage they can inflict. Heneker's wound put him out of action for ten months. He missed 18th Division's auspicious debut on the Somme, when it was one of the few units to capture all its objectives on 1 July, and was not passed fit again for general service until 12 September 1916.[9] He was ordered to France on 10 October and told to report to HQ Reserve (later Fifth) Army, commanded by General Sir Hubert Gough, where he was to wait for a brigade command vacancy. Heneker was not a man for waiting. Three days after joining Reserve Army he drove to see Ivor Maxse at HQ 18th Division, quizzing him about the division's five attacks on the Somme and taking away papers and notes about attack formations.[10] He also began to badger the Military Secretary, Major General Walter Peyton, for a command. This soon had the desired effect. On 29 October he was made GOC 190th Brigade, 63rd (Royal Naval) Division, in succession to Brigadier General Hon. C.J. Sackville-West, who had been wounded. Heneker's luck had come full circle.

Heneker commanded 190th Brigade for less than two months. On Gough's advice, he put his claims forward to the Military Secretary to command a division. On 8 December 1916 he got his wish. Despite his complete absence of experience as a battalion commander on the Western Front and after only eight months in command of a brigade (mostly occupied in line holding), Heneker was made GOC 8th Division. He had risen from Lieutenant Colonel to Temporary Major General in twenty-nine months of war, during ten of which he had been *hors de combat*. His appointment was symptomatic of the army's difficulties in finding suitably qualified commanders at this stage of the war.

The 8th Division was a Regular Army formation, which Heneker himself described as consisting of 'All Old Regiments'.[11] He made his first inspection on 12 December 1916. He was not impressed with what he saw. 8th Division's condition was also symptomatic of the BEF as a whole. The BEF's rapid and haphazard expansion from six infantry divisions to nearly sixty in a little over two years had resulted in widespread 'de-skilling' at all levels. 8th Division was 'Regular' in name only. It had lost many of its outstanding early officers, including

Hastings Anderson (GSO1), Arthur Hoskins (AA&QMG), Percy Radcliffe (AA&QMG), Arthur Holland (BGRA), Gordon Guggisberg (CRE), Reginald Pinney (GOC 23rd Brigade), Travers Clarke (GOC 23rd Brigade) and Reginald Stephens (GOC 25th Brigade), all to promotion. The proportion of soldiers trained to peacetime standards of musketry and discipline was tiny. 8th Division had suffered heavily in the fighting of 1915, at Neuve Chapelle, Aubers Ridge, Fromelles and Bois Grenier, and had done badly on 1 July at Ovillers, where it had lost half its strength and failed to capture its objectives.

Heneker was the division's third, and last, commander. His predecessor, Major General Havelock Hudson, was an Indian Army cavalry officer with some expertise as an administrative staff officer. He was returning to India, memorably described by Paddy Griffith as the 'sin bin of the First World War', as Adjutant General. By common consent, he was neither stupid nor lazy. He simply lacked the force of personality to command a division in the trying conditions of the Western Front. Hudson was 54. Like his division, he was tired and somewhat demoralized. Under his leadership 8th Division had dropped from the first or second class into the third or fourth. It is difficult not to conclude that Heneker was brought in to 'kick ass'. This he did. He was forty-nine.

Douglas Haig was among those who believed that divisions were a true reflection of their commanders, who had to be 'able to inspire the unit with their own personal energy and fighting spirit'.[12] Heneker set about doing this, beginning at the top. He quickly concluded that many of his senior officers would have to be replaced. Lieutenant Colonel E.H.L. Beddington, the new GSO1 appointed only days before Heneker, came to the same independent conclusion. Like most dedicated pre-war Regular officers Heneker could not abide 'slackness'. The surest indicator of slackness was dirt. Dirty rifles, dirty uniform and webbing, dirty trenches, and unshaven chins indicated poor discipline, lack of spirit and bad leadership. He inspected 23rd and 25th Brigades on Boxing Day, 1916, and found them both 'dirty'. The following day he had lunch with XV Corps commander, Sir John Du Cane, and asked for the removal of Brigadier General G.H.W. Nicholson (BGRA), Brigadier General A.J.F. Eden (GOC 24th Brigade), Brigadier General J.W.H. Pollard (GOC 25th Brigade) and Major J.C. Freeland (GSO2).[13] Neither Heneker nor Du Cane had the power to sack anyone, but Du Cane promised to bring Heneker's concerns to the attention of the Fourth Army commander, General Sir Henry Rawlinson. When a divisional commander expressed lack of confidence in his subordinates, higher authority had only two choices. Either the divisional commander or his subordinates had to go. The situation could not be allowed to fester. The subordinates duly went, to be followed within less than three months by the surviving brigade commander, Brigadier General E.A. Fagan (GOC 23rd Brigade). 'Sad news greets me on returning to the Battalion,' Lieutenant Colonel J.L. Jack (CO 2nd Battalion West Yorkshire Regiment) confided to his diary on 11 March 1917. 'General Fagan, our popular brigade commander has left owing to a difference with the divisional general, a fine but exacting chief. General Fagan is the third brigadier to quit the Division within a few months; other commanders and staff officers have also felt the blast.'[14]

It was one thing to 'blast' but it was another to find suitable replacements. Although the process of firing commanders on the Western Front is now well documented and understood, the process of hiring is not. The loss of all the Military Secretary's papers in a German air raid on 8 September 1940 is a great handicap. The operation of the Military Secretary's office has rarely been scrutinized. As Heneker's experience shows, lists of candidates for promotion were kept. But how these lists were compiled, other than through personal solicitation, and what criteria the Assistant Military Secretaries applied as they went round the armies to identify candidates for promotion is not known. Heneker was not in a position to dispose of the vacancies he had created but he could propose and his proposals seem often to have been acted upon.

As GOC 23rd Brigade Heneker got Brigadier General G.W.St G. Grogan, aged 41, latterly CO 1st Battalion Worcestershire Regiment. 1st Worcestershires were part of 24th Brigade, so Grogan's was an internal divisional appointment, in which Heneker must have had a hand. Significantly, perhaps, Grogan, like Heneker, had served in West Africa. He remained in command of 23rd Brigade for the rest of the war, winning a Victoria Cross in the desperate fighting on the Aisne in May 1918, rallying his men by riding up and down the line on horseback under artillery, trench mortar, rifle and machine-gun fire.[15] Grogan was the second of Heneker's brigade commanders to win the VC. The first was Clifford Coffin (GOC 25th Brigade), a 46 year-old sapper, latterly CRE of David Campbell's 21st Division, well described by Philip Ledward, a staff captain in 8th Division, as 'hard and sphinx like'.[16] Coffin commanded 25th Brigade until 4 May 1918 when he was promoted GOC 26th (Ulster) Division, a command he retained until the end of the war. Coffin's replacement was a remarkable one, the 36 year-old Ralph Husey, a Territorial officer, latterly CO 5th Battalion London Regiment (London Rifle Brigade). Husey began the war as a Territorial Captain, after a remarkably unsuccessful career in the City that had yet to see him qualify as a chartered accountant. His tenure was brief, a mere nineteen days, before he died in enemy captivity on the Aisne. He was last seen armed with a rifle, manning a front-line trench in the face of overwhelming odds. He hated Germans. Brigadier General H.W. Cobham, Eden's replacement as GOC 24th Brigade, was less successful.

Cobham was a fifty year-old Indian Army cavalryman who had retired in 1910. His appointment was in marked contrast to those of Grogan and Coffin. Cobham did well to last until November 1917 when Heneker triumphantly replaced him under the '6 months rest rule' with the CO 2nd Battalion Royal Berkshire Regiment (23rd Brigade) Lieutenant Colonel Roland Haig, another internal appointment.[17] Haig, like Cobham, was also a 'dugout', having retired from the army in 1903 following a serious hunting accident. But he was only forty-four and a man of great courage and leadership. He commanded 24th Brigade until his replacement in the aftermath of the Aisne fighting in June 1918. Heneker's new BGRA was Brigadier General H.G. Lloyd. He was the division's artillery commander until the eve of the German spring offensive in 1918, when he transferred to 24th Division. Lloyd does not seem to have been a very impressive commander. One observer claimed that he 'did not function on the broader aspect of artillery tactics' and undertook no training for mobile warfare.[18] His replacement was Brigadier General J.W.F. Lamont, a forty-five year-old Scot. 8th Division's artillery in the March battles has been criticized, together with the rest of the artillery of Fifth Army for being either so far forward that it got knocked out or so far back that it could not aid the infantry, but Heneker was generous in his praise for the divisional artillery's 'boldness and close support of the infantry'.[19] Later in 1918, Lamont proved to be a resilient, innovative and resourceful gunner.[20]

Heneker was also generally well served by his GSO1s, the chief staff officers of a division upon whom rested responsibility for much of a division's efficient operation. Heneker was fortunate to inherit 'Moses' Beddington, a clever, 34 year-old cavalryman who suffered fools no better than his GOC. Beddington was promoted GSO1 Fifth Army on 1 December 1917. He remembered his time at 8th Division with affection and retained a high regard for Heneker. Beddington had three successors: Lieutenant Colonel H.S. Adair (Cheshire Regiment); Lieutenant Colonel C.C. 'Clem' Armitage (Royal Artillery), who came from GHQ; and Lieutenant Colonel A.G.B. Bourne (Royal Marine Artillery), who had spent the first three years of the war serving with the Grand Fleet! All four were staff college graduates. Armitage and Bourne were both able men who became full generals after the war.

One of the main duties of a divisional commander was to identify, encourage and promote able subordinates. Heneker must be given high marks on this score. Many of the appointments and promotions in the division bear his personal stamp. His concern to maintain professional standards of duty and leadership among his subordinates was unrelenting. He never ceased to prize 'smartness' and outward appearance as indicators of morale and efficiency. But he also valued training and kept a careful eye on it, as he did on everything else in his division.

'General Heneker has seen us training several times,' noted Colonel Jack, 'and has expressed his high satisfaction with the companies' work.' 'His compliments,' Jack added, 'are the more valued since he is sparing of them.'[21] Heneker did not prize popularity and made no compromises with the 'amateur' nature of the expanded BEF, with its essentially civilian volunteers and conscripts, something that they did not always appreciate. Amateurism would not win the war. His leadership style was that of the 'auditor'. His job was to expose faults and to make sure they were put right. He could not do this unless he made himself known in the division. He was, therefore, not a remote figure, but a striking personality and a real commander. What kind of general he was 1918 would discover.

The year 1918 was a cruel time for 8th Division. Three times it found itself in the path of major German offensives, first on the Somme, then at Villers-Bretonneux and finally on the Aisne. The division's casualties were catastrophic. It lost 250 officers and 4,693 men on the Somme, 133 officers and 3,240 men at Villers-Bretonneux and 366 officers and 7,496 men on the Aisne.[22] Together, these were the equivalent of its total strength prior to the German offensive. Every battalion commander became a casualty: some battalions got through three. A brigade commander was also killed. Only the 50th (Northumbrian) Division suffered higher casualties in the whole of the BEF. During the summer 8th Division had to be completely reconstituted. Heneker has received little praise and some blame for his role in these events.

On the Somme, in nine days of savage fighting, 8th Division was used to hold the Somme crossings. Fed piecemeal into the battle, it held the Somme line on a nine-mile front for nearly two days, despite being attacked by nine German divisions, until its right flank was turned. Fifth Army, in general, and XIX Corps, in particular, insisted on fighting a linear defence. After a disciplined withdrawal, 8th Division then made a second stand at Rosières. Sir Henry Rawlinson's hope that the situation would permit the 8th Division to have a 'well earned rest' proved hollow. Within less than a month, and now part of III Corps, Fourth Army, the Division found itself six miles in front of the vital rail junction of Amiens, at Villers-Bretonneux. The successful defence of Villers-Bretonneux was undoubtedly one of the decisive moments in the eventual defeat of the German spring offensive. Credit for it has been granted almost entirely to the Australians and, especially, to the 13th and 15th (Australian) Brigades for their brilliant night counter-attack on 24–25 April, an attack in which supporting units of 8th Division were conspicuously less successful. This counter-attack was necessary because 8th Division had lost Villers-Bretonneux, though not the important high ground surrounding the town, in the face of the first major tank attack inflicted on the BEF. The 8th Division's defence, hampered by the loss of its own artillery and its own CRA on 29 March, was less resolute than on the Somme. Casualties included a large number of prisoners. Heneker was later criticized for not launching an immediate counter-attack after the town fell. One was planned, but Heneker rightly cancelled it after representations from Coffin (GOC 25th Brigade) and two of his battalion commanders that such an attack, in broad daylight, over open ground would be both suicidal and doomed to failure. He did this despite pressure from III Corps and Fourth Army to proceed with the attack. It was also Heneker who vetoed a midday attack by H.E. 'Pompey' Elliott's 13th (Australian) Brigade.[23] But he is usually portrayed as having been browbeaten by Bill Glasgow into changing the actual evening attack time from 8.00 p.m. to 10.00 p.m. Although it is possible to imagine the fire-eating, pom-bashing Elliott in the role of browbeater, it is less easy to imagine the subtle, intelligent and gentlemanly Glasgow. In neither case is it easy to imagine Heneker, who had several times in the proceeding hours stood up to higher authority, being browbeaten. Beddington was in no doubt that credit lay with his old chief.[24]

The 8th Division's final torment lay on the Aisne, a 'quiet sector' whence it was sent with other British divisions to rest and recuperate under the command of French Sixth Army (General Denis Duchêne). There, on 27 May, the Germans achieved one of the greatest strategic surprises of the war. Three armies, enjoying a numerical advantage of 6:1, advanced twelve miles in three days, sweeping across the Chemin des Dames and crossing the Aisne on an eighteen-mile front as far as the river Vesle, capturing Soissons and threatening Paris. The French were unaware of an impending attack until it was too late to do anything about it. The Sixth Army commander acted as though the fighting on the Somme and the Lys had never happened. Once more, it was to be a linear defence, shoulder-to-shoulder. Not only Heneker but also the other British divisional commanders, David Campbell (21st Division) and Henry Jackson (50th Division) protested to Duchêne, demanding that the British divisions should be removed from the salient that they occupied in front of the Aisne. Duchêne was unmoved. His decision was predictably disastrous. Troops north of the Aisne were shattered by the German bombardment and ceased to exist as organized fighting units.

Much of the fighting in the great spring battles was disorganized and confused. They were soldiers' battles. The performance of 8th Division steadily degraded after the Somme fighting, where it performed a disciplined and heroic withdrawal against great odds, to Villers-Bretonneux where its raw reinforcements panicked in the face of German tanks, to the Aisne where the division disintegrated during a leaderless rout. Heneker performed no great acts of generalship. The successive events in which he found himself were exceptionally demanding, physically, mentally and morally. It was very difficult to find out what was happening, even after personal reconnaissance. Support from corps and army was often exiguous and unhelpful. Heneker's ability to effect the course of battle quickly became limited, something he recognized by twice devolving command of the divisions' infantry, first to Coffin (on the Somme) and then to Grogan (on the Aisne). His subordinate commanders served him well, but even they were eventually exhausted by the experience and Roland Haig had to be replaced. With the drafts of inexperienced troops, after the Somme, too much of the Division's effectiveness came to depend on the actions of senior officers. When they failed to act or were removed by death or wounds command paralysis set in. But throughout these traumatic months Heneker never lost his nerve or his judgement. The casualties suffered by the Division could not be laid at his door. He must, nevertheless, have felt them grievously.

During the summer, while 8th Division was refitting, Heneker sat down to consider the events of the past few months. He put his thoughts down on paper and sent them to his old mentor, Ivor Maxse, now Inspector General of Training for the whole of the BEF. They make very interesting reading, particularly in the light of the BEF's supposed 'defence-in-depth' tactics in March. It is clear from Heneker's six-page critique that no such tactics were actually employed. Heneker attributed the BEF's shattering casualties to this failure. Someone on Maxse's staff underlined Heneker's key point:

> . . . it is better to lose a 1,000 yards of ground and suffer no casualties, than for a division to be overrun and lose a half to three-quarters of its infantry and all its guns because it is stout hearted and obeyed orders to hold out to the last man in an impossible situation.[25]

This was the comment of a courageous, tactically astute and humane commander. After the war, he became an advocate of wholesale mechanization as a way of avoiding the scale of infantry losses suffered on the Western Front.

During the summer of 1918 Heneker rebuilt his division. Captain (later Major General) Hubert Essame, adjutant of 2nd Battalion Northamptonshire Regiment (24th Brigade), who had a high regard for Heneker, not least for his 'kindness', believed that this was the general's finest hour. Heneker set about his task by applying his normal pre-war Regular Army standards. 'He expected to be saluted by everyone within eye range,' recalled Essame, 'his eagle eye could detect an unshaven chin, the need for a haircut, a grease stain or an unpolished button at a considerable distance. His comments were unequivocally clear, vividly expressed and long remembered.'[26] But this was not all. Heneker also brought his experience of the war to bear. Training was intensive. Rifle practice was constant. Great stress was laid on manoeuvre and co-operation with the artillery. Night operations were also practised. Great attention was paid to the physical and mental wellbeing of troops who had endured much. By the end of August 8th Division was ready to take its place in the Great Advance.

Notes

1   This essay is based on work undertaken by the Abbots Way Research Group, as part of its multi-biography of the British Army's Western Front generals during the First World War. I should like to thank, in particular, the following members of the Group: the late Peter Lawrence (for work on the Haig Diary) and Alun Thomas (Heneker Diary, Beddington Papers and private information from the Heneker family).

2   Much work is currently being undertaken at postgraduate level, including studies by Andy Simpson (Corps), Helen McCartney (55th Division), Simon Peaple (46th Division), Alun Thomas (8th Division) and Kathryn Snowden (21st Division). See also, John Lee, 'The SHLM project – Assessing the Battle Performance of British Divisions', in Paddy Griffith (ed.) *British Fighting Methods in the Great War* (London: Frank Cass, 1996), pp.175–81.

3   Terence Denman, *Ireland's Unknown Soldiers. The 16th (Irish) Division in the Great War, 1914–1918* (Dublin: Irish Academic Press, 1992). There are modern histories of some Dominion divisions.

4   Sir John Baynes, *Far From a Donkey. The Life of General Sir Ivor Maxse* (London: Brassey's 1995); Daniel Dancocks, *Sir Arthur Currie. A Biography* (Toronto: Methuen, 1985); and A.G. Serle, *Sir John Monash. A Biography* (Melbourne: Melbourne University Press, 1982). See also, Christopher Page, *Command in the Royal Naval Division. A Military Biography of Brigadier A.M. Asquith DSO* (Staplehurst: Spellmount, 1999).

5   British Corps, until the very late stages of the war, did not control the same divisions. Instead, divisions were rotated through them, often quite rapidly. The Canadian Corps had an homogeneous organization, including all four Canadian divisions from an early stage, to the great benefit of its fighting efficiency.

6   2nd Battalion North Staffordshire Regiment remained in India throughout the First World War.

7   Heneker Diary, 30 July 1914. Manuscript copy in the possession of the Heneker family.

8   Department of Documents, Imperial War Museum: Heneker Diary, 3, 5 August 1915.

9   1 July 1916 was also notable for the death, in action, of Heneker's younger

brother, Major F.C. Heneker (Leinster Regiment), attached to 20th Battalion Northumberland Fusiliers (Tyneside Scottish). Heneker, like many other senior commanders, experienced the personal and family costs of war.

10 Department of Documents, Imperial War Museum; Heneker Diary, 18 October 1916.

11 Department of Documents, Imperial War Museum: Heneker Diary, 25 December 1916.

12 Public Record Office, Kew: WO 256/6 Field Marshal Earl Haig Diary, 7 November 1915.

13 Heneker clearly found his subordinates more wanting than did the army. Nicholson found re-employment as BGRA 40th Division and 30th Division. Eden became GOC 52nd Brigade and 57th Brigade. Pollard, after a brief spell at home, was given 106th Brigade. All three were in post at the Armistice. Heneker palmed Freeland off on his old GOC Royal Naval Division, Cameron Shute.

14 John Terraine (ed.), *General Jack's Diary 1914–1918. The Trench Diary of Brigadier General J.L. Jack DSO* (London: Eyre & Spottiswoode, 1964), p.197.

15 *The Register of the Victoria Cross* (Cheltenham: This England Books, 1988), p.132.

16 Quoted in Malcolm Brown, *The Imperial War Museum Book of 1918 Year of Victory* (London: Sidgwick & Jackson, 1998), p.57.

17 Department of Documents, Imperial War Museum: Heneker Diary, 16–31 October 1917.

18 Tim Travers, *How the War was Won. Command and Technology in the British Army on the Western Front, 1917–1918* (London: Routledge, 1992), p.86.

19 Lieutenant Colonel J.H. Boraston and Captain Cyril E.O. Bax, *The Eighth Division 1914–1918* (London: Medici Society, 1926), p.197.

20 Boraston and Bax, *Eighth Division*, p.257.

21 Terraine, *General Jack's Diary*, p.217.

22 Boraston and Bax, *Eighth Division*, p.296.

23 C.E.W. Bean, *Official History of Australia in the War of 1914–1918. Volume V: AIF in France 1918* (Sydney: Angus & Robertson, 6th edition, 1939), p.639.

24 Liddell Hart Centre for Military Archives, King's College, London: Beddington Papers, p.153.

25 Department of Documents, Imperial War Museum: Maxse Papers, 69/53/13, File 53/2. I owe this reference to Sarah Cade.

26 H. Essame, *The Battle for Europe 1918* (London: Batsford, 1972), p.109.

Chapter 4

The Battle for the Skies:
Sir Hugh Trenchard as Commander of
the Royal Flying Corps

David Jordan

On 10 February 1956, Marshal of the Royal Air Force Viscount Trenchard died. He was buried in Westminster Abbey, the mourners led by Sir Winston Churchill. All had gone to remember the 'Father of the Royal Air Force'. In 1961, Trenchard was memorialized in bronze. At the statue's unveiling, Prime Minister Harold Macmillan said Britain owed Trenchard 'a debt beyond measure.'[1] In 1962, Trenchard's biography appeared.[2] This account secured the image of Trenchard as a far-sighted leader of men, worshipped by his subordinates and not guilty of the alleged blunders of his fellow First World War commanders. Others were less sure. Reviewing the biography, Oliver Stewart, formerly of the Royal Flying Corps (RFC), noted the work's partiality, but praised its valuable insight into 'one of the strangest personalities this country has produced'.[3] Stewart's description was not a compliment. He rejected the image of Trenchard as a universally loved figure. To junior officers, Trenchard seemed more concerned with driving them harder than with 'guarding his men from danger as much as is possible within the framework of their duty', as other great leaders had done.[4] Stewart's ambivalence was supported by another veteran, Arthur Gould Lee, who criticized Trenchard for wasting men and aircraft.[5]

This is not unfair. Although Trenchard's contribution to the Royal Air Force was immense, he was not alone. He himself felt the title of 'Father of the Royal Air Force' (RAF) belonged to the almost-unknown Sir David Henderson, who was General Officer Commanding (GOC) of the RFC from its inception in 1912 until 1917. Trenchard bitterly opposed the creation of a separate air service, while Henderson advised

General Smuts' committee on Britain's air services that a separate force was needed. Trenchard ignored his other notable colleague, Major General Sir Frederick Sykes. The two did not get on, and Sykes' reputation suffered as a result. The RAF's official history, *The War in the Air*, commissioned by Trenchard when he was Chief of the Air Staff (CAS), rarely mentions Sykes.[6] Trenchard himself was a complex character, an inflexible leader who listened to his juniors and followed their advice. He could be incoherent, was nicknamed 'Boom' for his clumsy speaking style, could not express himself on paper, yet produced a clear and coherent vision of air power; he drove his men hard, but nonetheless had deep concern for them. These contradictions, though, might never have come to prominence, had it not been for the invention of the aeroplane. Without this, it is unlikely that Trenchard would have risen to greatness.

As Trenchard cheerfully admitted, he was not especially intellectual. He tried to enter the Royal Naval College, but failed the examination. In the dictation paper, he spelt 'why' as 'yi', and bizarrely transcribed 'misdemeanour' as 'Mister Demeanour', even though there could be little doubt that this was wrong given the context of the dictated passage.[7] This hints at Trenchard's individualistic thought processes. Failing to join the Navy, Trenchard went to an Army 'crammer' to prepare for entrance to Woolwich. He avoided work, and failed the exam three times. He passed the mathematics paper each time, but failed *every* other subject (each time), so there was little hope of success.[8] Eventually, in 1893, Trenchard secured a commission through the easier route of the Militia (this was after two further failures). He was gazetted to the 2nd Battalion of the Royal Scots Fusiliers in India, where he 'did no work' and life consisted of 'rifle shooting, game shooting and polo'.[9] This was not uncommon in the British Army of the late nineteenth century, and Trenchard was typical of his generation of officers. When required to practise his profession, first in South Africa, and then in Nigeria, Trenchard did not shirk from his duty. On 9 October 1900, he was shot through the chest by a Boer sniper. There was some doubt as to whether he would survive the journey to hospital; he did.[10] When Trenchard returned to Britain in December 1900 to convalesce, he had only one functioning lung and was limping badly. His military career appeared to be over.[11]

Trenchard's determination transformed the situation. Taking doctor's advice, he went to St Moritz for the air. Trenchard became a tobogganing champion while there, and in the process, his health improved. Overcoming opposition from army doctors, he returned to South Africa in July 1901.[12] At the end of the war he returned to England, and then joined the West African Frontier Force. Trenchard stayed in Nigeria until 1910. His successful time there, including the award of a DSO, was ended by an abscess on the liver.[13] Although he made a swift recovery, by 1912 he was searching for a new challenge, but could not find one. A letter from a close friend, Captain Eustace Lorraine, then on the staff at the Central Flying School (CFS), arrived, urging Trenchard to join the RFC. Attempts to persuade Trenchard he was too old for pilot training failed miserably, and he gained his certificate from the Royal Aero Club.[14] Like all prospective RFC members, Trenchard then had to go to the CFS to learn the military aspects of his new skill. Two days after arriving, he was made the CFS's staff officer, and found himself setting his own exam papers. He was unsurprised when he passed.[15] Trenchard remained at the CFS for the next two years. When he became Assistant Commandant of the CFS in September 1913, Trenchard was a forty-year-old major, with few obvious prospects of advancement. Five years later, he was a major general and regarded as Britain's leading airman.

This transformation began slowly. When the RFC mobilized war in August 1914, the Director General of Military Aeronautics (DGMA) and GOC the RFC, Brigadier General Sir David Henderson, took personal command in France, leaving a subordinate, Major W. Sefton Brancker, to deal with matters at the War Office. This meant that Lieutenant Colonel Frederick Sykes, who had expected to command the RFC in the field, became Henderson's deputy.[16] Trenchard's chances of going to France were slim before this; with Henderson and Sykes there, he was not required overseas. Trenchard was most unhappy, even though he was given command of the RFC in Britain. His disappointment was not unconnected with the fact that Henderson and Sykes took most of the RFC with them to France. Trenchard claimed that he was abandoned, and left with one clerk and an orderly, plus a locked confidential box, said to contain plans for defending Britain against Zeppelin attack. Sykes gave Trenchard the key, but the following morning, Trenchard arrived in his office to find Major Robert Brooke-Popham on his hands and knees extracting a pair of old boots from the box.[17] Although entertaining, Trenchard's account is doubtful: how did Brooke-Popham open a locked box without a key and without forcing it?[18] The story owed more to Trenchard's bitter dislike of Sykes than to the facts; the chances are that Sykes left Trenchard a key, and that a box containing old boots also happened to be around. The distrust between Trenchard and Sykes destroyed the chance of combining Trenchard's drive with Sykes' cerebral considerations on air power. Sykes appreciated that air reconnaissance might be vital for tracking the German advance through Belgium and northern France, and took as much of the RFC's strength as he could; he can hardly be blamed for this. Trenchard resented being left at home, fearing he would miss the war. His claims to have been left with almost nothing are equally debatable.

He actually had about a third of the RFC's strength under his control, although most of the aircraft were unserviceable.[19] It is also notable that Trenchard lacked understanding of the size of air service that was needed. When the question of expanding the RFC was first raised, Brancker suggested thirty new squadrons should be formed. The proposals went to the Secretary of State for War. Typically, Lord Kitchener's response was brief. He magisterially minuted 'double this' in the margin, and the first expansion of the air service was settled.[20] Trenchard had proposed just twelve new squadrons.[21]

Displeasure notwithstanding, Trenchard exercised his command well. He had to overcome rules preventing direct enlistment of volunteers, a lack of accommodation, and no uniform or personal equipment for the recruits. He ignored the rules and enlisted all volunteers, decided upon their rates of pay, and then requisitioned the pub near Brooklands aerodrome, 'piano and all', to house them.[22] He was about to procure equipment when War Office staff expressed anger at his initiatives. Kitchener then fortuitously issued regulations which retrospectively authorized Trenchard's actions, and Trenchard heard nothing more about his unorthodox methods. He celebrated by ordering a batch of greatcoats and primus stoves from Harrods. Within a month, the nucleus of men for three or four new squadrons was in place.[23] This was typical of Trenchard. When faced with obstacles, he took the simplest route to overcome them. Trenchard continued this when in command of the RFC in France, but the most obvious option to Trenchard was not always the best course of action.

As the British Expeditionary Force (BEF) expanded, it became clear that central control of aviation by GHQ hampered flexibility. Consequently, the division of the BEF into Armies saw the formation of RFC Wings, with each army having a Wing to support it. Trenchard was given command of First Wing on 18 November. He was displeased to discover that Henderson had left to command 1st Division, giving Sykes control of the RFC. He was saved by Kitchener's decision that Henderson could not be spared from the air service. Henderson was sent back to RFC headquarters, resuming command in early December.[24] As commander of First Wing, Trenchard's squadrons supported Sir Douglas Haig's First Army. This was a happy coincidence. Shortly after assuming command, Trenchard was summoned by Haig. Trenchard was apprehensive, since he had heard that Haig was 'reserved, austere, severe and . . . did not believe a great deal in the air'.[25] Haig had made a number of disparaging remarks about the value of air power before the war, but swiftly became the most important supporter of aviation in the British Army once he had seen the RFC at work.[26] Trenchard found Haig willing to take expert advice; Haig found Trenchard an agreeable colleague.[27] The close relationship that developed between the two was of crucial importance to the RFC as the war progressed. First Wing supported the operation at Neuve Chapelle in March 1915. Within the Wing, 3 Squadron had begun to conduct the first meaningful photographic reconnaissances. By the end of February, Captains George Pretyman and C.C. Darley had mapped the German trench system opposite First Army. Three Squadron's commander, Major John Salmond, took the photographs to First Army HQ, where he was received with 'surprise and sincere congratulations'.[28] More importantly, the RFC had a vital role to play in directing artillery fire. Unfortunately, some battery commanders proved unwilling to use the RFC's information. At Neuve Chapelle, several artillery officers questioned the value of air observation. This irritated Haig, who summoned his senior artillerymen to a meeting, and informed them he would not tolerate any 'early Victorian methods'. Haig further added that 'he was going to use the air in this war, and they had to use it.'[29] Bolstered by this, Trenchard sought to improve photo-reconnaissance methods, deputing Captains J.T.B. Moore-Brabazon and Darley to oversee this. Trenchard took considerable interest in their work, but did not interfere. One of his commendable features was a willingness to listen to junior officers when they clearly knew more about a subject than he did. A number of official memoranda on photography from RFC headquarters bear the signature of senior officers, although it is quite clear from the drafts that they were written by Moore-Brabazon or Darley.[30]

Trenchard's advance continued in the aftermath of Neuve Chapelle. Henderson's health was poor, and he was often on sick-leave. When Henderson returned from such leave in May 1915, it is alleged that he discovered that Sykes had plotted against him, and had Sykes transferred to advise the Admiralty on air operations at Gallipoli. Eric Ash rightly disputes this interpretation, suggesting that Henderson intended to give Sykes command of a Wing – something Sykes wanted – replacing him as Chief-of-Staff with Trenchard.[31] The Admiralty then asked for an advisor, and Sykes was despatched. Bearing in mind Trenchard's apparent aversion to office work, it was fortunate that Henderson's plan had to be modified. This opened the way for Trenchard, since he was the most likely replacement for Henderson, should the latter leave before Sykes returned. His chance came when Henderson finally accepted Sefton Brancker's arguments that the RFC needed him at the War Office. As a Lieutenant Colonel, Brancker was junior to most of his colleagues in Whitehall and was often ignored; Henderson would not have this problem. Henderson returned to London, and chose Trenchard to replace him. On 25 August 1915, Trenchard was promoted to Temporary Brigadier General and given command of the RFC in France.

Between August 1915 and his departure to become Chief of the Air

Staff in January 1918, Trenchard established the policy by which the RFC (and the RAF) operated. Through a mixture of empirical observation and instinct, some of it not always sustained by facts, Trenchard moulded the RFC into an effective machine. Although some of Trenchard's actions merit criticism, it must be remembered that he did not have the benefit of hindsight to guide him. Historians can criticize Trenchard's policies and all too easily forget that Trenchard and his subordinates were the first to gain the practical experience of air warfare, and had nothing to fall back upon. To assist in forming policy in these conditions, Trenchard continued to listen to his men. Trenchard stressed the importance that he attached to taking soundings from his squadrons, since this provided the means to distil information and to prosecute operations more effectively.[32] Air warfare was in its early stages, and pilots came up with a number of ideas for making their aircraft better tools of war. To this end, Trenchard allowed each squadron to keep one aircraft for experimental purposes. Every three months, he would inspect the experimental machines from six different squadrons, so that modifications could be approved or rejected. Trenchard's role in this was minimal. Judgement was almost always passed by the assembled pilots; Trenchard estimated that 95 per cent of the modifications were criticized and rejected by the pilots, so that he 'never really had to decide.'[33] The other 5 per cent of suggestions were met with approval, and Trenchard was more than happy to have them incorporated. This contrasts with the popular image of Great War generals ignoring their subordinates. Trenchard made a statement that 'each of us talks unmitigated rot, but combine the talk and there was a thread of sound common sense . . . my particular job was to find that grain of common sense. . . .'[34]

The year 1915 had further significance for Trenchard: Sir Douglas Haig assumed supreme command of the BEF. This secured the RFC's role in the war. Although by late 1915 there were very few officers who thought that air power was a pointless diversion of resources, Haig's appointment gave Trenchard a remarkably free hand to formulate policy. The image of a technophobic Haig is destroyed by his support for Trenchard and the RFC, which extended to reading assiduously the RFC's daily reports and annotating them with favourable comments.[35] Haig left the running of the RFC to Trenchard, and never sought to interfere. He was resolute in his support for his air commander, and more than happy to complain on Trenchard's behalf when supplies from Britain were slow in arriving. Trenchard had already seen Haig's willingness to defer to him on aviation matters, and this continued. The relationship between the two was steadfast; Trenchard later wrote that Haig 'made me all I rose to in France.'[36] Since all that Trenchard became owed everything to his actions in France, there is a strong case for seeing Haig as the man who facilitated Trenchard's rise to greatness.

Trenchard had another enormous advantage in his formulation of policy. This was the presence of the Honourable Maurice Baring as his Aide-de-Camp. Baring was an unlikely soldier. He was a forty-year-old civilian at the outbreak of war, and was commissioned by Sir David Henderson.[37] Trenchard initially considered sacking Baring, but swiftly changed his mind. Trenchard's nickname of 'Boom' stemmed from his difficulty in stringing a coherent sentence together. Nor was he blessed with particularly strong literary skills, even if the image of him being barely capable of expression is rather unfair. Baring, on the other hand, was decidedly skilled in the use of words; he had been a journalist, was multi-lingual and a published author. Consequently, the elegant and erudite phraseology in many of Trenchard's memoranda owed much to Baring. It is not hard to imagine the impression that RFC memoranda had at GHQ; thanks to Baring, they were lucid and generally brief expositions of RFC policy and ideas. This would not have been unappreciated at headquarters, and seems to have confirmed Haig's impression that he had an excellent subordinate in Trenchard. This is not to say that Trenchard was incapable; the policies expressed were his. Trenchard knew that Baring could be relied upon to craft them into a persuasive whole, and used that facility to the full. This explains Trenchard's effusive praise for Baring, recognizing his importance to his command.[38]

These advantages made it possible for Trenchard to promote a view of air warfare that became accepted throughout the BEF's high command. While this gave air policy great consistency, it sidelined Sykes, whose input would have been valuable.[39] Trenchard based his policy around three key factors: unwavering co-operation with the ground forces, morale and the offensive. Sykes was critical of what he termed Trenchard's 'battering ram' tactics, and others have doubted the efficacy of the offensive policy. It has been further noted that Trenchard fought against the creation of an independent air service, condemned strategic bombing, and then went on to conduct an astounding volte-face in the 1920s, becoming a 'bomber baron'.[40] This has not helped Trenchard's image. There are clearly areas where he failed to frame policy properly, and did not appreciate some of the nuances that operational experience provided. Nonetheless, his rejection of the formation of a separate air service and his antipathy towards strategic bombing are far more complex matters than have been previously allowed for.

Trenchard was not untypical in his belief in the offensive spirit. Tim Travers notes widespread support in the British army for the morale value of offensive action.[41] Unlike other proponents of the offensive, Trenchard could point to clear evidence of the utility of offensive action. Two case studies supported his contention. The first was the 'Fokker Scourge' of late 1915 and early 1916. The Fokker Eindekker, an otherwise unremarkable monoplane, struck dread into the RFC by virtue of the fact that it carried the first operational synchronized machine gun. The ability to fire through the propeller ended the difficulties of mounting and aiming a machine gun, and handed the Germans a distinct advantage. The Eindekkers were relatively few in number, and their performance was mediocre. This was offset by the tactical advantage of the forward-firing machine gun, and by the lack of suitable British fighters to deal with the Eindekker. On 14 January 1916, Trenchard felt obliged to issue an order that all reconnaissance aircraft should be protected by at least three other fighting machines, and that the reconnaissance should not be continued if the formation broke up.[42] Trenchard was not unaware of the implications of this for operational efficiency. He also made the observation that the Fokkers were not operating in large numbers, but in small groups. This was curious, since it seemed that had the Eindekkers been used aggressively to gain air superiority across the front, the RFC would have been much less effective. Since artillery operations were almost totally reliant upon air observation, losing the ability to reconnoitre would have had profound implications. Trenchard was not happy with the need for close escort but persisted with it. The policy had the effect of making it more difficult for the Germans to score easy victories, buying time until the FE 2 and DH 2 fighter aircraft arrived in the last week of February 1916. Both types were more than a match for the Eindekker, thus allowing the limitations on reconnaissance to be relaxed.[43] At the same time as the new types arrived, the Germans launched their offensive at Verdun. As well as moving German aviation assets away from the RFC, permitting time for better aircraft to become fully operational, Verdun again suggested the value of offensive action. The French air service found that attacking the Germans dislocated enemy operations. When French ground troops demanded defensive patrols, the air service was forced to fly above its own lines, handing the advantage to the Germans. The reason for this was simple. The sheer volume of sky above the French lines meant that it was easy for attacking aircraft to evade the defenders, who could be seen flying over fixed points. Trenchard drew the obvious conclusion: to make life difficult for the enemy, the air services had to take the fight to him, otherwise the enemy would dictate matters.

This is not to say that the idea was Trenchard's alone. The notion of offensive action was widespread in the army, and as far as the RFC was concerned, Trenchard was following policy laid down by Sykes.[44] This point is often lost in understanding the RFC during the war. Trenchard's contribution was not to create an offensive policy, but to formulate the policy's fine points. The policy took the form of offensive action by fighter aircraft well over enemy lines. The logical complement to this was the use of bombers, both in the immediate area behind the battle and deep inside enemy held territory. Trenchard is frequently accused of having ignored the value of strategic air operations, but to him, the fighters were engaged in a strategic mission. They were to prevent enemy aircraft from arriving over the battlefield to interfere with the army co-operation aircraft. Between June and September 1916, Trenchard laid out the framework for both fighters and bombers.

On 3 June 1916, Trenchard tackled the use of bombers. As far as short-range bombing operations were concerned, Trenchard regarded these as inherently linked to the land battle. It is hard to disagree with this statement, or with Trenchard's belief that the choice of target should be left to GHQ rather than to the RFC.[45] As for bombing attacks far behind the lines, there were obstacles:

> The RFC in the field is not in a position at present to undertake bombing operations at any great distance behind the enemy's lines. To enable it to do so, it would be necessary to supply ten squadrons in two wings under one Brigadier for the sole purpose of long distance bombing. But before such an addition to the RFC for the special purpose of bombing can be contemplated, it is essential that our full requirements for artillery work and fighting should be complete.[46]

In June 1916, this was a perfectly reasonable position. The RFC was faced with increasing demands from GHQ for artillery observation and reconnaissance in preparation for the forthcoming offensive. The supply of aircraft and adequate aircraft engines from Britain was insufficient to allow the commencement of long-range bombing; this supply problem hindered any expansion of the RFC's tasks throughout the war, giving Trenchard little option but to give army co-operation first priority. This did not make Trenchard an opponent of strategic bombing, and he made clear that neither he nor Haig had any objection to the Royal Naval Air Service's efforts to bomb long-distance targets.[47] This was an understandable line of thinking. The army, of which the RFC was a part, was not regarded as being responsible for strategic missions or attacking the enemy's homeland. This had always been the job of the Navy; since it had its own bomber force, Trenchard viewed it as perfectly natural that the RNAS should have this role. The difficulties of co-operation between the RNAS and RFC that manifested themselves in 1916 had more to do with inadequate aircraft production than a conflict over doctrine. Indeed, Trenchard's later opposition to the creation of an independent air service was because, amongst other things, this might reduce resources for army co-operation missions, not because he opposed the notion of air attack against Germany itself.

These thoughts on bombing policy were followed by Trenchard's famous memorandum, 'Future Policy in the Air'.[48] This was despatched on 22 September 1916, and stated the doctrine that the RFC and then the RAF followed until the end of the war. Trenchard, aided by Baring's prose, made an elegant case. He recognized that ground troops often felt that they were not being adequately supported by the air service when they rarely saw their own aircraft and often saw those of the enemy. This had an effect on morale:

> The moral[e] effect produced by a hostile aeroplane is . . . out of all proportion to the damage which it can inflict.
>
> The mere presence of a hostile machine in the air inspires those on the ground with exaggerated forebodings with regard to what a machine is capable of doing.
>
> The sound policy then which should guide all warfare in the air would seem to be this: to exploit this moral[e] effect of the aeroplane, but not to let him exploit it on ourselves. Now this can only be done by attacking and continuing to attack.[49]

Trenchard used the example of the French at Verdun to sustain this contention, explaining that defensive methods failed since:

> An aeroplane is an offensive and not a defensive weapon. Owing to the unlimited space in the air . . . it is impossible for aeroplanes to prevent hostile aircraft from crossing the line if they have the initiative and determination to do so.[50]

Trenchard also noted that the presence of just one enemy aircraft led to reports of multiple aircraft; he was too politic to note that the standards of aircraft recognition were such that it was not unknown for returning RFC machines to be mistaken for the enemy. Trenchard remained unshakeable in believing that the offensive was the only sensible doctrine to be followed. The relationship between Haig and Trenchard meant that this became GHQ's belief too. Given Haig's belief in the value of the offensive, this was unsurprising; it also confirmed Haig's view of Trenchard as being a sound commander. Additionally, Trenchard and Sykes, although they appear not to have agreed on anything, were in fact in accord on this issue. Their disagreement was over the application of the policy and its efficiency.

The doctrine was reiterated in 'Short notes on the Battle of the Somme', Trenchard's report on the RFC's activities in that battle.[51] Between 1 July and 17 November 1916, the RFC lost 782 aircraft struck off charge or missing and 576 pilots from its strength.[52] When the battle began, there were 410 aircraft available, giving a loss rate of 190.7 per cent. The offensive policy was having an effect: of the 190 aircraft missing, only 45 were army co-operation machines. The percentage loss of aircrew was lower, but still worrying. Although the figure of 576 included those 'sick, worn out, etc', as there had only been 426 aircrew on charge at the start of the battle, this still meant that there had been a crude loss rate of 135.2 per cent. These figures are slightly misleading since the RFC's strength increased during the battle as new squadrons arrived; nonetheless, they demonstrate the intensity of air operations. The disparity in losses between fighters and army co-operation machines suggests that the offensive policy worked, since it protected the army co-operation types. It also suggests the offensive policy was extremely costly. Trenchard was quite clear that he was opposed to close escort of reconnaissance machines by fighters, and fighters were often sent on patrols when they did not encounter any enemy machines. This was a waste of effort, particularly when the fighters could and perhaps ought to have been protecting reconnaissance aircraft. This was particularly true at times when the Germans held air superiority. Part of the reason for the losses sustained towards the end of the Somme campaign was the arrival of superior German fighter aircraft, particularly the Albatros DIII. This rose to a peak in 1917, during 'Bloody April'. Between 4 April and 8 April (the first four days of the Battle of Arras), the RFC lost seventy-five aircraft.[53] In spite of this, Trenchard made clear his opposition to the provision of escorts for reconnaissance missions. Trenchard saw this as being an obstacle to fighters going out and engaging the enemy. Some RFC wing commanders disagreed, since there were instances of three reconnaissance machines being accompanied by up to fifteen fighter escorts. Where reconnaissance machines attempted self-escort, disaster often resulted. On 13 April, number 59 Squadron sent six RE 8s to reconnoitre the Drocourt-Quéant line. Four of the aircraft were sent as escorts to two with cameras. The RE 8s proved no match for German fighters and all six were shot down. Even the usually uncritical official historian suggested that a proper escort should have been provided. An escort would have been available, since fifteen Sopwith Triplanes of 1 (Naval) Squadron were simultaneously conducting a fruitless offensive patrol nearby.[54] The issue here, though, was not so much one of faulty doctrine as of faulty co-ordination. Trenchard was quickly aware of the problem, and on 15 April told Brigade commanders to consider co-ordination of fighter and reconnaissance missions.[55] The results were patchy, suggesting that the note lacked the firmness it required. When missions were co-ordinated, there was success: on 16 April, number 11 Squadron was tasked to photograph the Drocourt-Quéant line. Four

Nieuport fighters provided a close escort, while numbers 48, 60 and 1(Naval) squadrons were sent on a fighter sweep in conjunction with the reconnaissance flight.[56] The latter three units flew above Douai aerodrome, giving the Germans the uncomfortable options of taking off to engage the reconnaissance at a considerable disadvantage, or staying on the ground. They chose the latter option.[57] Although this did not lead to the engagement of the enemy, the reconnaissance mission was a complete success. Trenchard perhaps did not appreciate that preventing the Germans from fighting was as of much use as engaging them.

Arthur Gould Lee, a veteran of 1917, felt that Trenchard viewed the offensive with regard to gaining territory: 'To [Trenchard] as to his staff, and most of his senior commanders, for a British plane to be one mile across the trenches was offensive: for it to be ten miles across was more offensive.'[58] There is an element of truth in this criticism, although Trenchard's view must also have been based on the notion that the further over German lines that engagements took place, the less likely the Germans were to be able to get through to the artillery co-operation machines. Gould Lee noted two major problems with the distant offensive, namely a lack of incident and the likelihood of losses through engine failure and other non-combat causes.

> While we thus dissipated our strength, more often than not merely beating the empty air, the Germans . . . concentrated forces superior in numbers or equipment and engaged our scattered line patrols in turn, and our Distant Offensive Patrols as and when it suited them. The result was that in 1917, British air losses were at times nearly four times as great as the German.[59]

Furthermore, with German air superiority lasting from late 1916 through to late May 1917, the RFC suffered more losses by virtue of having inferior equipment. This is one of the great enigmas concerning Trenchard. While he was more than happy to show flexibility in allowing escorts in early 1916, and through consultation with his air crews on the matter of equipment, the offensive policy was ruthlessly inflexible. Even without air superiority in the early months of 1917, proper co-ordination, the use of large formations and focus upon key objectives would have had some effect on reducing RFC loss rates. As it was, small patrols were overwhelmed, and men and machines lost. Even with the restoration of parity and then superiority from summer 1917 as aircraft such as the Sopwith Camel, Bristol Fighter and SE 5a arrived in large numbers, patrols were unfocused. Fighters were sent out simply to engage the enemy, something which they often failed to do, since the enemy decided not to oblige. Trenchard apparently never realised that although the offensive was the right policy, clear objectives for attack (aerodromes, etc) would have helped. Trenchard's 'Review of Principles Adopted by the RFC since the Battle of the Somme' from August 1917 failed to make any distinctions or to set firm objectives for the offensive. Trenchard preferred declamatory statements instead:

> The battle in the air can only be won by taking the offensive and per-severing in it . . . victory over [enemy] low-flying aircraft [will come] through *offensive* superiority [emphasis in original] . . . The aeroplane is a weapon that has no exact counterpart. . . . but the principles which guide it in warfare, in order for it to be successful, are those which guide all other arms in all other elements of warfare, and the most important of these is the will and power to attack the enemy, to force him to fight, and to defeat him.[60]

This suggests that Trenchard wished to be more offensive than the enemy, hence the incessant driving on of his aircrew. The lack of focused objectives was a flaw in Trenchard's policy, and it was not unreasonable for Sykes to reflect that this was wasteful in effort, lives and machines. Trenchard helped to lay the foundations for the modern mission of offensive counter air (OCA), but was not unique in recognizing the principle that aircraft were far better weapons of attack than defence.

Trenchard's vision of air power did not extend to the creation of a separate air force. Trenchard's opposition was based on simple grounds.[61] Trenchard believed that the RFC should support the BEF, and saw no reason why it should compromise this position. He was not unaware of the difficulties caused by the RFC and RNAS competing for resources, but felt that efforts to create a separate air service would be dangerous. He pointed out that the new service would be another competitor for resources, and that the changes might dislocate production. Trenchard also argued:

> Uncontrolled by any outside naval and military opinion, exposed as it would inevitably be to popular and factional clamour, it would be very liable to lose its sense of proportion and be drawn towards the spectacular such as bombing and home defence, at the expense of providing the essential means of co-operation with our naval and military forces.[62]

On this latter point, Trenchard was not mistaken. In spite of this opposition, General Smuts' committee suggested the creation of a unified air service. This was unsurprising, as David Henderson was Smuts' key advisor. In a lengthy submission, Henderson made clear the reasons for creating a separate air service.[63] Smuts was unlikely to ignore such authoritative advice, particularly when it was in line with the hopes and expectations of the government which had commissioned his report.[64] Trenchard recognized at an early stage that the air service was to be separated from the army, and changed his tack. Having lost the battle to remain part of the army, Trenchard, with the co-operation of GHQ and the War Office, set about plotting to ensure that the RAF would continue to support the BEF.

By late August 1917, Whitehall was awash with rumours, including one that Henderson had engineered the situation so that he could become the military head of the air service.[65] Even if such a plan existed, it was unlikely to bear fruit. Henderson had slowly lost the confidence of his fellow officers and then of Lord Derby, the Secretary of State for War. Combined with his generally poor health, this meant that Henderson was unlikely to benefit from the creation of a new service. In fact, Whitehall opinion wanted Trenchard to lead the new service. Derby had attempted to bring Trenchard home to become DGMA in April 1917, but had been rebuffed by Haig, who argued that he needed Trenchard.[66] Trenchard was not eager to leave, either. With the battle to prevent a separate service lost, in October 1917 he embarked upon a bout of scheming to ensure that he maintained full control of the RFC in France. The extent of his personal ambition in this is not clear, but ambition was balanced by the constant notion of ensuring that the creation of an Air Ministry did nothing to change the role of the RFC in supporting the army.

Trenchard by this point realized that he was the leading contender to become the first Chief of the Air Staff, but still hoped he could stay in France, as he was 'not good in an office'. On the other hand, he felt that Henderson had allowed himself to be sidelined as DGMA, and that this had adversely affected the already labyrinthine method of supplying airframes and engines. Henderson was shortly to move from the Directorate of Military Aeronautics to help implement the plans for the separate air service. This meant that there was a serious danger of Henderson, who would still be the most senior officer connected with military aviation, becoming a loose cannon in the new air service. Trenchard feared that Henderson might give the government advice that was diametrically opposed to Trenchard's ideas or to those held by the new DGMA. Units in France might be diverted from army co-operation to strategic bombing. Trenchard saw this as a thoroughly bad idea. Additionally, the existing Deputy DGMA, Brancker, might prove an obstacle. Trenchard was clear that the new DGMA had to ensure that the RFC 'gets what it requires', but was equally clear that Brancker was not the man for the job.[67] By 6 October 1917, Trenchard had worked out the solution:

a) to leave me as GOC RFC in the field with responsibility for, and command of, all RFC units in France

b) to give General Henderson some other appointment not connected with the RFC or the air [service]

c) to give the DGMA sufficient control over design and supply to ensure that the RFC gets what it requires.[68]

This displayed clear disloyalty to Henderson, even if Trenchard believed that Henderson had become ineffectual. He followed this with a final point: suggestions for the new appointments. The commander of the RFC Training Division, Major General John Salmond, was proposed as the DGMA, while Brancker was to be sent to the Middle East as commander of the RFC Brigade out there. The extent of Trenchard's willingness to sacrifice colleagues is demonstrated by a letter he received on 12 October from a deeply unhappy Brancker, furious at having been effectively sacked. It began with the words 'They have got me at last', followed shortly by 'I don't know how far you have helped them indirectly.'[69] It is interesting to speculate how Brancker would have reacted had he known that 'they' included Trenchard, whose help had been most direct. Henderson was not removed from matters connected with military aviation, but without a clear post in the new structure, he was almost without influence. Ironically, the decision to follow up Trenchard's ideas meant that what he most wanted – command of all units in France – was not to be realized. With no other obvious candidates left, Trenchard was the only man for the job of Chief of the Air Staff (CAS).[70] He was informed that he would take this post with effect from the start of 1918, the RAF forming after the necessary administrative arrangements had been put in place. This demanded his return to London. If Trenchard thought this would ensure that the RAF supported the BEF before it considered any other options, he was to be sadly mistaken.

Trenchard began work as Chief of the Air Staff on 18 January 1918. He was succeeded in France by Salmond. Trenchard viewed Salmond as a protégé who would follow his master's original course, as the tone of their correspondence suggests.[71] This was about all that Trenchard was happy with. The new Secretary of State for Air, Lord Rothermere, was unprepared to take Haig's line of listening only to his chief advisor on aviation matters. Trenchard's contempt for political scheming – or perhaps scheming which he could not influence – increased. He became aware that the Air Ministry existed for more than just tactical reasons: Rothermere was clearly intent, at the behest of Lloyd George, on removing control of the RAF from Haig.[72] Less than a month after becoming CAS, Trenchard wrote to Salmond, expressing disillusionment. This owed much to his reduced influence, as he made clear:

I am still on the brink of stopping, but if I stop, I do not know if I shall be doing right to the Flying Corps . . . I am certain that I could get this show running perfectly if I only became a dictator at home, but of course this is impossible.[73]

Although Trenchard recognized that he could not run the Air Ministry in the same way he controlled virtually all aspects of air policy in France, his frustration with Rothermere's decision to seek other opinions mounted until he could control it no longer. As Malcolm Cooper suggests, Trenchard had 'single-minded ideas on the exercise of authority' which had come from his time in command in France. As Rothermere was unwilling to sit back and allow Trenchard to run the Ministry, disaster was inevitable.[74]

On 19 March 1918, Trenchard could take no more, and resigned. Rothermere asked him to reconsider, but he refused, only to change his mind when the Germans launched a massive offensive on 21 March. This should have been the end of the matter, at least until after the crisis was over, but on 13 April, Rothermere suddenly accepted the resignation, concluding his letter with the uncomplimentary 'for anything you have done since I have been here I wish most cordially to thank you.'[75] This suggests that Rothermere had a low opinion of Trenchard, but his letter to Lord Derby the following day suggests otherwise: 'As you know, he is a most highly efficient fighting general. He desires to return to the army and I think at this juncture every use should be made of his great qualities.'[76] Rothermere clearly agreed with Trenchard's self-assessment that he was much better in the field than an office. Trenchard's response to his departure was to ask for two weeks' leave, followed by a return to the army. This proved to be politically impossible, as questions were asked in Parliament, particularly by Lord Hugh Cecil, who as well as being an MP had been a junior officer on Trenchard's staff. It became clear that the matter would not rest; Rothermere resigned on 25 April. This created a serious problem for the government, namely what to do with Trenchard. He could not be returned to the role of CAS, since there had already been a new appointment: Major General Frederick Sykes. After two years in the wilderness, Sykes had returned to the air service, and was its undisputed titular head. David Henderson had resigned from the Air Council as he felt unable to work with Sykes, and it was clear that there would be major difficulties in persuading Trenchard to serve in the RAF in a position which would make him subordinate to his old rival. The matter exercised the new Air Minister, Sir William Weir, for some time, not helped by Trenchard. In spite of protestations that he was averse to scheming for personal advantage, this was exactly what Trenchard embarked upon. Weir found himself confronted with impossible demands as Trenchard attempted to create a job for himself, one which would effectively give him command over the RAF in France and bypass Sykes.

Weir knew that there were political demands to give Trenchard a suitable position in the RAF, but Trenchard – quite improperly – attempted to decide what that position was. Weir was quite clear in his own mind that Trenchard should command the Independent Air Force (IAF), an expansion of VIII Brigade, RAF. This Brigade had the task of bombing Germany, and did little in the way of army co-operation. The IAF would be separate from the RAF command structure, to prevent it from being diverted away from bombing Germany to participate in the land battle. Trenchard dug in his heels, seeking a position akin to 'GOC of the Air Force'. Since they were written by Trenchard, it is not absolutely clear from his letters to Weir what he meant by this, but it is obvious that he sought equal status with Sykes, leaving the latter in charge of administration, while Trenchard conducted the business of fighting in France. Weir would not capitulate. He finally offered Trenchard the choice of four posts: Inspector General of the RAF Overseas, GOC of the RAF in the Middle East, commander of the IAF and Inspector General of the RAF at Home.[77] Trenchard regarded the Middle East as a backwater, and had suggested Brancker be sent there to get him out of the way. Inspector General Overseas was unappealing, and Trenchard had already rejected it, as it had no real power. Finally, being Inspector General at home would place Trenchard under Sykes' command, something he could not accept. This effectively left Trenchard the IAF, in spite of his opposition to the force. Weir made it obvious that these options were all Trenchard was going to be given: 'I trust I have made it clear to you that I will not create a position specially for you. The above are positions requiring men and I want you to accept one of them so that your experience may contribute to the success of the RAF . . .'[78] Trenchard knew he had been outmanoeuvred, and accepted with ill-grace; he at least had the consolation of being totally independent of Sykes, communicating directly with Weir. Trenchard assumed command of the IAF on 15 June, and spent the rest of the war attempting to effect a policy he believed in under the auspices of a command he did not believe in.

Trenchard initially sent his forces against enemy aerodromes and rail targets behind the battle area, prompting criticism that he was misusing his forces. Trenchard explained that he attacked German airfields to prevent their being used to strike at his aerodromes; railways were justifiable targets since the Germans were very short of rolling stock.[79] These diversions did not prevent attacks being made on Germany itself, although these were hampered by bad weather, navigational problems, the unreliability of the DH 9 day bomber and the inaccuracy of bombing, particularly at night.[80] Trenchard had few illusions about the effectiveness of his organization, but examination of his diaries suggests that his greatest concerns were not so much with the effectiveness of operations, but with administrative inefficiency and his isolation from major operations at the front. He was acutely aware that the IAF was mistrusted by RAF headquarters, who saw the force as a rival for vital supplies, much as Trenchard had predicted. On 10 June 1918, he noted:

> The last two days has made me think more and more what a great mistake it has been to start this bombing force in such a war as this and in such a battle [German Spring Offensives] . . . it involves a large staff being here and less efficiency in bombing, resulting in a waste of manpower . . . I shall run this force efficiently and get it going, but at a great unnecessary waste of manpower, time and energy.[81]

This unease was repeated in further diary entries; on 26 June, Trenchard gloomily recorded that the only purpose of the IAF, as far as he could see, was

> to employ about forty officers on the staff, about 200 men, a large amount of transport besides building many huts for the HA, etc, in order to take the place of GHQ and HQ RAF and to carry on the work these organisations were quite capable of carrying out.[82]

Five days later, Trenchard complained that although the staff was continuing to expand, there was too much work for the existing staff officers to do, the result being 'nil to the effectiveness of the bombing of Germany.'[83] His greatest problem was one of perception: Trenchard felt that the army now regarded him as having lost all interest in helping them, while 'amongst the bombing people I am looked on as only a luke-warm bombing enthusiast, and only keen on the army.'[84] Trenchard in fact attempted to take a broader view. His objection to the IAF was not that it was bombing Germany, which was 'now a necessity', but on organizational grounds.[85] Trenchard regarded the IAF as an unnecessary structure, and would rather have seen the RAF and the IAF operating under one command – his – and employed where the need was greatest. This would have prevented an expansion of bombing forces from compromising tactical operations, which he saw as the most important. Trenchard wished to see both tactical and strategic forces increase in size, since he saw both as being important to the prosecution of the war.[86] Trenchard's final comment on the IAF came on 11 November: 'The Armistice was signed this morning. Thus the Independent Air Force comes to an end. A more gigantic waste of effort and personnel there has never been in any war.'[87] This comment was not a reflection on his force or its operations, but on the organization. The IAF had 'done splendidly', but

> It would have done just as splendidly had it remained under the command of the Expeditionary Force with half the number of officers and men. . . . An impossible organisation was set up by the politicians simply in order that they could say 'I am bombing Germany' . . . .It has undoubtedly caused unrest in Germany, but it would undoubtedly have caused the same unrest had it not been 'independent'.[88]

It is hard to disagree with this assessment, apart from noting that Trenchard would probably have been tempted to employ his forces in support of Haig more readily than in bombing Germany to keep the War Cabinet happy.

The end of the war saw serious danger to the future of a separate air service. The appointment of Winston Churchill to lead both the War Office and the Air Ministry gave Trenchard the opportunity to show his political skills. Aware that massive financial cutbacks would be forthcoming, he proposed a minimalist air service that appealed to Churchill. Sykes was moved to control civil aviation, and Trenchard returned as Chief of the Air Staff. Once there, he set about integrating strategic bombing into the modus operandi of the RAF to the extent that it came to dominate, with results that are well known. Trenchard retired in 1929, to be replaced by John Salmond. He saw a further spell of command, this time in charge of the Metropolitan Police, before returning to the RAF on the outbreak of the Second World War. He held no command positions, instead offering advice to his successors and visiting operational squadrons. It should be noted that his charisma was well received by the new generation of aircrew.

Trenchard's influence over the RAF remained strong until after the Second World War, and possibly longer still. There is no doubt that he was a great leader through sheer personality. Whether this makes him a great commander is less certain. He was too ready to make the offensive policy a sweeping statement of intent rather than focus on key areas for attack. This could cause heavy casualties, sometimes unnecessarily. On the other hand, the methods that cost so many lives in 1916 and 1917 were the same methods that helped to win the war in 1918. The difference was that by 1918, the RFC/RAF had matured into a force that could provide highly effective co-operation almost all of the time, rather than for just some of the time. Additionally, Trenchard (followed by Salmond) constructed a proper training organization to supersede the ramshackle system that existed until early 1916. On the matter of bombing, he was largely correct. The IAF was administratively inefficient, while the technology did not exist in 1918 (or, indeed, for much of the Second World War) for it to be decisive.[89] Trenchard never abandoned the idea of strategic bombing, as he showed in peacetime; his difficulty in the First World War was a lack of adequate technology and, more fundamentally, a lack of aircraft. Strategic bombardment was a logical progression of the offensive that Trenchard so valued, but without the means to bomb properly, he chose to co-operate with the army, and was right to do so.

Trenchard valued the offensive, and its role in establishing moral ascendancy over the enemy, like many of his colleagues. Unlike some, he had vision. He also had luck. He had the best connections possible – the C-in-C of the British Expeditionary Force and one of the most literate officers serving on the Western Front. This helped him to push his views to the highest levels. He was not the only visionary in the RAF – Sykes and Henderson were too, especially the former – but Trenchard's 'masterful imaginative touch of the natural leader' set him apart.[90] Although not the father of the RAF, he brought it up and educated it, and his efforts can still be seen today.

Notes

I am extremely grateful to Mr Peter Elliot and all the staff of the Records Department at the Royal Air Force Museum, Hendon, for access to the Trenchard and Salmond papers, and for their assistance.

1 Henry Probert, *High Commanders of the Royal Air Force* (HMSO, 1991), p.4.
2 Andrew Boyle, *Trenchard* (Collins, 1962).
3 Oliver Stewart, review of *Trenchard* in *The Journal of the Royal Aeronautical Society*, Volume 66 (1962), pp.595–596.
4 Ibid.
5 Norman MacMillan, *No Parachute: A fighter pilot in World War One* (Jarrolds, 1969), pp.217–218.
6 Incredibly, Ash's study of Sykes is the first to make serious efforts to redress the imbalance.
7 RAF Museum Hendon, Trenchard Papers, MFC 76/1/61, autobiographical notes. Boyle records that Trenchard went on spelling 'why' and 'yi' for many years afterwards.
8 Ibid.
9 Ibid.
10 Boyle, *Trenchard*, pp.16–17.
11 Ibid, p.29.
12 Trenchard returned to Britain with his trophies, only to find that the War Office disputed his fitness to return to duty. Trenchard was sent on leave while his case was considered. To help deliberations, Trenchard entered two tennis tournaments reaching the semi-finals of both. He was not well enough to complete either match, but used press reports of his matches to

suggest he was fit enough to resume duty. He did not wait for a reply from the doctors before departing for South Africa.

13 Ibid, pp.58–91.

14 His satisfaction was dulled by the fact that Lorraine had been killed in an accident at Larkhill.

15 RAF Museum, Trenchard Papers, MFC 76/1/61.

16 The RFC was theoretically divided into Military and Naval Wings, but the Royal Navy was unhappy with the arrangement. It staged a takeover of the Naval Wing, renaming it the Royal Naval Air Service. See S W Roskill, *The Royal Naval Air Service 1914–1918* (London: Naval Records society, 1969).

17 Ibid. Brooke-Popham had commanded Number 3 Squadron before the war and was one of the best staff officers the RFC had. The criticism later visited on him for the loss of Singapore in 1942, particularly that by Norman Dixon is not a true reflection on his contribution to the RAF (and a fair reflection on Duff Cooper's ability to deflect the blame).

18 See Eric Ash, *Sir Frederick Sykes and the Air Revolution, 1912–1918* (London, 1999), p.52.

19 Ash, *Sykes*, p.51.

20 Cited in various works, for example, Ralph Barker, *The Royal Flying Corps in France: From Mons to the Somme*, (London: Constable, 1994).

21 RAF Museum, Trenchard papers, MFC 76/1/61. In fairness to Trenchard, he freely admits this in his autobiographical notes.

22 Ibid.

23 Ibid.

24 As compensation for the disappointment of losing the Division (arguably the pinnacle of an officer's career at that time), Henderson was allowed to remain a Major General.

25 Ibid.

26 For the disparagement, see Sir Frederick Sykes, *From Many Angles: An Autobiography* (Harrap, 1942), p.105.

27 RAF Museum, Trenchard papers, MFC 76/1/61.

28 RAF Museum, Salmond Papers. Salmond draft autobiography, p.163.

29 RAF Museum, Trenchard Papers, MFC 76/1/61.

30 Public Record Office [PRO] AIR 1/539/16/14/2, notes on practice photography, 1 December 1915, from DA & QMG, RFC, Colonel Robert Brooke Popham.

31 Ash, *Sykes*, pp.64–65.

32 Unpublished autobiographical notes, RAF Museum, Trenchard Papers, MFC 76/1/61. These notes are not particularly extensive, but provide some helpful insights.

33 Ibid.

34 Ibid.

35 See PRO Air 1/520/16/11/2 and PRO WO 158/34.

36 RAF Museum, Trenchard Papers, MFC 76/1/61.

37 As Baring later recorded, this was in the days 'when a General's word was law'. Henderson had no idea of Baring's military qualities, but was a close friend, and considered that this was more than enough to make Baring an officer without further ado. He was proved to be correct.

38 RAF Museum, Trenchard Papers, MFC 76/1/61. As if to prove his lack of logic in written passages, Trenchard follows up three-quarters of a page of high praise with 'words fail me in describing this man', when they quite clearly did not.

39 See Ash, *Sykes*, particularly Chapters 3–7.

40 For examples of these criticisms, see Sykes, *From Many Angles*, Gould Lee, *No Parachute* and Cooper, *Independent Air Power*.

41 Tim Travers, *The Killing Ground: The British Army, the Western Front and the Emergence of Modern Warfare 1900–1918* (London: Unwin, 1987), especially Chapters 2 and 3.

42 Boyle, *Trenchard*, pp.162–163.

43 The FE 2 and DH 2 were both 'pusher' aircraft, that is to say that the engine was mounted behind the pilot. This enabled a machine gun to be mounted in the nose of the aeroplane without the need for interrupter gear.

44 See Ash, *Sykes*, p.42.

45 RAF Museum, Trenchard Papers, MFC 76/1/4.

46 Ibid.

47 Ibid.

48 Ibid; also H A Jones, *The War in the Air, Being the Story of the Part Played in the Great War by the Royal Air Force*, Volume II (Oxford: Clarendon Press, 1928), Appendix IX.

49 RAF Museum, Trenchard Papers, MFC 76/1/4

50 Ibid.

51 RAF Museum, Trenchard Papers, MFC 76/1/4, 'Short notes on the Battle of the Somme', 20 November 1916.

52 Ibid.

53 See D J Jordan, unpublished PhD Thesis *The Army Co-operation Missions of the Royal Flying Corps/Royal Air Force 1914–1918* (University of Birmingham, 1997), p.35.

54 Jones, *The War in the Air Being the Story of the Part Played in the Great War by the Royal Air Force*, Volume III (Oxford, Clarendon Press, 1931), p.351. The Sopwith Triplane was at least the equal of German fighter types; the presence of naval fighter squadrons alongside the RFC resulted from awareness that the Germans had superiority.

55 Jones, *War in the Air*, III, p.355.

56 11 Squadron flew the FE 2; 48 Squadron the Bristol F2B ('Bristol Fighter') two-seat fighter; 60 Squadron the Nieuport Scout and 1(Naval) the Sopwith Triplane. The FE 2 had, by 1917, become a multi-role aircraft, conducting reconnaissance and bombing operations as well as being

employed as a two-seat fighter. It was soon to be replaced in the latter role by the Bristol Fighter. Even in April 1917, it was arguably better equipped to defend itself than the RE 8.

57 Jones, *War in the Air*, III, p.355.

58 Arthur Gould Lee, *No Parachute: A Fighter Pilot in World War I* (London: Jarrolds, 1969), p.217.

59 Ibid, p.218.

60 RAF Museum, Trenchard Papers, MFC 76/1/4, 'A Review of Principles adopted by the RFC since the Battle of the Somme', 23 October 1917.

61 For the creation of the RAF, see Cooper, *Independent Air Power*, particularly Chapters 8–10.

62 PRO AIR 1/718/29/9, letter from Trenchard to CGS GHQ, 30 August 1917.

63 PRO AIR 8/2, Memorandum by Henderson on the organization of the air service, 19 July 1917.

64 For details of the Smuts report see Cooper, *Independent Air Power*, Chapter 8.

65 PRO AIR 1/718/29/9. Letter to Trenchard, 2 September 1917. The signature of the author is illegible. Whoever it was, he absolved Henderson of plotting for his own advancement.

66 See Cooper, *Independent Air Power*, pp.109–110.

67 PRO AIR 1/718/29/9, memorandum by Trenchard, recipient unnamed, but possibly Field Marshal Sir William Robertson, Chief of the Imperial General Staff, 6 October 1917. Trenchard, Haig and Robertson were all of the same mind with regard to the function of the air services being to support the army. Trenchard and Robertson corresponded occasionally.

68 Ibid.

69 Letter from Brancker to Trenchard, 12 October 1917, cited in Cooper, *Independent Air Power*, p.113.

70 Sykes was at this point working at the Allied mission at Versailles, where his ability was highly regarded. It seemed that he had moved on from any connection with air power.

71 See RAF Museum, Trenchard Papers, MFC 76/1/90–92.

72 This was in keeping with the policy of reducing the number of men available to Haig. This was particularly true in early 1918. See David Woodward, 'Did Lloyd George Starve the British Army of Men Prior to the German Offensive of 21 March 1918?', *Historical Journal*, XXVII (1984), pp.241–252.

73 RAF Museum, Trenchard Papers, MFC 76/1/92, private letter Trenchard to Salmond, 13 February 1918.

74 Cooper, *Independent Air Power*, p.122.

75 RAF Museum, Trenchard Papers, MFC 76/1/19, letter Rothermere to Trenchard, 13 April 1918.

76 Ibid, letter Rothermere to Derby 14 April 1918.

77 RAF Museum, Trenchard Papers, MFC 76/1/20, letter Weir to Trenchard 5 May 1918.

78 Ibid.

79 RAF Museum, Trenchard Papers, MFC 76/1/70, Despatch on operations of the IAF.

80 The DH 9 was derived from the far more successful DH 4. The DH 9 suffered from appalling engine problems. Fitted with a reliable engine and designated the DH 9a, the type went on to enjoy a long post-war career with the RAF.

81 RAF Museum, Trenchard Papers, MFC 76/1/32, Trenchard private diary, 10 June 1918.

82 Ibid., 26 June 1918.

83 Ibid., 1 July 1918.

84 Ibid., 13 July 1918.

85 Ibid.

86 Ibid., 13 July and 22 July 1918.

87 Ibid., 11 November 1918.

88 Ibid.

89 The debate over the decisive capacity of strategic bombardment in the Second World War has taken up millions of words. The best work on the RAF remains C F Webster and Noble Frankland, *The Strategic Air Offensive Against Germany*, 4 volumes (London: HMSO, 1961). Also see Sir Arthur Harris, *Despatch on War Operations* (London: Cass, 1995); The British Bombing Survey Unit, *The Strategic Air War Against Germany 1939–1945* (London: Cass, 1998), particularly the splendid and thought-provoking introduction by Sebastian Cox; R Cargill Hall (ed), *Case Studies in Strategic Bombardment* (Washington: Air Force History and Museums Program, 1998).

90 RAF Museum, Salmond Papers, B2621, Draft autobiography, p.138.

Part Two

Germany at War

Chapter 5

Helmuth von Moltke: A General in Crisis?

Annika Mombauer

When war began in August 1914, Helmuth von Moltke had been Chief of the German General Staff for over eight years. Despite the fact that he was in charge of Germany's war planning and led the German army into the First World War, he is today rarely remembered for his role in the outbreak and first months of war. He has been overshadowed by his more famous colleagues and successors, men such as Erich von Falkenhayn, Wilhelm Groener, Erich Ludendorff and Paul von Hindenburg, and of course, his more successful uncle, General-feldmarschall Helmuth von Moltke (the Elder). He is usually only remembered for his failings, his name being indelibly linked to the defeat of the Battle of the Marne. For many commentators, this was the beginning of the end of Germany's chances at victory in a two-front war. Moltke's decisions during the first weeks of the war are seen as having caused Germany's defeat, and the changes he had made to her deployment plan in the years prior to the outbreak of war are regarded as a direct cause of the country's military demise. The apologetic military history writing of the inter-war years, under the auspices of former General Staff officers, created the image of Moltke as an ineffectual and reluctant military leader whose inglorious role was at best either played down or ignored, at worst seen as directly responsible for Germany's defeat.[1]

This analysis investigates Moltke's role in the early weeks of war and examines how Moltke came to be a personality both in conflict with his surroundings and in conflict with himself, leading to a crisis from which he would never recover. He is often condemned for having taken wrong decisions at crucial junctures, but hindsight has informed his critics. How wrong were his decisions in the light of the knowledge Moltke had, given the problems of communications and the difficulties in co-ordinating a million-strong army in a war on two fronts? Before addressing this question, it is necessary briefly to go back further in time, in order to understand Moltke's state of mind when war began.

TROUBLED BEGINNINGS

Helmuth von Moltke's time in office, 1906–1914, spanned some of the most important years of Germany's preparation and planning of the war which would break out in 1914. Under Moltke's leadership of the General Staff, Germany ended up with a one-sided and narrowly conceived deployment plan which staked everything on a speedy initial success on Germany's western front. A separate 'Eastern Deployment Plan', which had existed for the (increasingly unlikely) event that France and Britain would remain neutral in a future conflict, was abandoned in April 1913. Henceforth, whatever the *casus belli*, wherever the source of international tension, Germany would have to begin hostilities in the west, by invading neutral Luxembourg and Belgium in order to conduct an offensive campaign against France, while avoiding the heavy fortifications along the Franco-German border. Success in the west came to depend on a risky *coup de main* on Liège, whose capture was essential for the deployment of German troops into Belgium. This difficult manoeuvre was necessitated by Moltke's change to his predecessor's deployment plan (the infamous Schlieffen Plan), which had envisaged a violation of neutral Holland in addition to that of Luxembourg and Belgium. Moltke considered it necessary for Holland to remain neutral in the coming war, because it was to be used as a 'windpipe' for Germany, allowing her vital access to foreign markets. By 1909, with heavy artillery available to render such an attack on a strong fortification a possibility, Moltke and Ludendorff planned the 'lightning strike' for which troops would first have to march into neutral Luxembourg before war was even declared, before taking Liège in a surprise attack.

Despite such tight and careful planning, Germany's success was far from assured, as Moltke realized. In private, he was far from confident that Germany's deployment plan would work. At their last personal meeting in Carlsbad on 12 May 1914, he replied to Conrad von Hötzendorf, his Austrian counterpart, who anxiously enquired what would happen if success in the west could not be achieved quickly: 'Yes, I will do what I can. We are not superior to the French.'[2] Yet, despite his doubts, he urged Germany's civilian decision-makers to embark on a war before time ran out for Germany's deployment plan – a nightmare scenario that would become reality once Russia's mobilization and deployment of troops to Germany's eastern border was speeded up following the extension of railway links. Moltke favoured and advocated a war 'the sooner the better' (as he put it in the famous 'war council meeting' of December 1912), because he had no alternative to the Schlieffen-Moltke plan that had been developed since 1906. Increasingly, Germany's future opponents were rising to the challenge that Germany posed. The Belgian army was increasing its numbers of troops, making it more difficult in the near future to implement the first part of Germany's deployment plan. Moreover, by 1916/17, Moltke predicted, Russia would be too strong to be defeated by Germany.

The assassination of Archduke Franz Ferdinand provided a golden opportunity for a European war with Austria on Germany's side before it was too late for her to embark on a war with any chance of success. As such, Moltke and his colleagues in the General Staff did their utmost to encourage an escalation of the July Crisis.[3] Military concerns and reasoning had become common currency, accepted without question by civilians and determining their decision-making. At the end of July, the dogmatic belief in the Schlieffen-Moltke Plan not only narrowed down the military and strategic options, but also significantly reduced the political room for manoeuvre. Moltke had deliberately painted an optimistic picture of Germany's chances at present, and conjured up images of a not-too-distant future in which the country would be unable to resist an attack from her eastern neighbour.

When the Kaiser returned from his North Sea cruise on 27 July, it appeared to the disappointed 'war party' in Berlin as if war would again be averted, as it had on so many occasions.[4] However, the Kaiser's mediation proposal to Vienna (the idea of a 'Halt in Belgrade') was deliberately delayed by the Chancellor, and in any case by the next day, following Austria's declaration of war to Serbia, the Kaiser had changed his mind again. This was not the only dithering that Moltke would have to endure from his 'Supreme War-Lord' at a time when the Chief of Staff was determined to see a war result from the current crisis, as the Bavarian military plenipotentiary in Berlin, Karl Ritter von Wenninger, noted:

[Moltke] uses his whole influence towards ensuring that this unusually favourable military situation be used in order to strike; he points out that France is almost in a military embarrassment[5], that militarily Russia feels anything but secure; in addition the favourable time of year, the harvest largely brought in, the annual training programme completed.[6]

The circumstances for a war at that time were considered favourable, as for example the Bavarian envoy Count Lerchenfeld noted on 31 July:

In military circles here one is feeling most confident. Months ago [sic!] the Chief of the General Staff, Herr von Moltke, had already expressed the opinion that the point in time was militarily as favourable as it would not be again in the foreseeable future.[7]

However, despite such bellicose statements, Moltke also feared the coming war, which he believed would be a long, drawn-out struggle which Germany could only *hope* to win, although she could not be certain of victory. Moltke's personal adjutant, Hans von Haeften, recorded his impressions that Moltke 'was suffering serious psychological turmoil'[8] under the pressure of having to advocate German mobilization against Russia. He made his fears plain to Haeften: 'This war will turn into a world war in which England will also intervene. Only few can have an idea of the extent, the duration and the outcome of this war. Nobody today can have a notion of how it is all going to end.'[9]

THE FIRST DEADLOCK

'I want to wage a war against the French and the Russians, but not against such a Kaiser.'

(Helmuth von Moltke, 1 August 1914)[10]

The desire of Germany's decision-makers to let the Russians appear as the aggressors resulted in an agonizing waiting game. The Kaiser and his Chancellor, Theobald von Bethmann Hollweg, advocated a delay of the declaration of Germany's mobilization until such measures had first been instigated by Russia, while Moltke, in the knowledge that every hour counted for the success of the surprise attack on Liège, pushed for immediate action. The Kaiser finally signed the mobilization order at 5 p.m. on 1 August, just after news of Russia's own mobilization had been received.[11] The first mobilization day was to be 2 August.

Moltke had already left the *Schloss* (the Kaiser's residence) when the arrival of a fateful telegram threatened to overthrow all the careful military arrangements for the first days of the war. Germany's ambassador, Prince Lichnowsky, reported from London that Britain would remain neutral, and that she would guarantee French neutrality in a forthcoming war, if Germany refrained from hostilities against France.[12] At this late moment in the crisis, this unexpected offer seemed to provide a real opportunity for avoiding the dreaded two-front war. In the words of Moritz Freiherr von Lyncker, the news hit him 'like a bomb':

Immediately the opinion was prevalent that this request could under no account be turned down, even if the offer was only a bluff, which was possible after all. For firstly this might be the opportunity perhaps to have to face only one rather than three opponents, that is Russia, against whom war has already been declared today, and secondly the Kaiser must grasp the hand that is offered and must not reject it out of loyalty for the [German] people.[13]

The Kaiser and the Chancellor were concerned to preserve British neutrality. In fact, a détente with Britain had always been the basic premise of Bethmann's policy. Now the Kaiser insisted on a change of deployment. Instead of heading west, he wanted 'his' troops to go east. He ordered that no German troops were to cross the border with France.

Moltke was immediately summoned back to the *Schloss*. As he recalled, 'there was a joyful mood. Now we only had to conduct the war against Russia. The Kaiser said to me: "So we simply deploy the whole army in the east!"' To everyone's astonishment, Moltke replied that 'the deployment in the west could no longer be stopped and that war would have to be forced onto France despite everything.'[14] Admiral von Müller, who was also present at the meeting, recorded similarly:

The Kaiser says: "Of course we must go along with this and therefore stop the deployment in the West for the time being." General v. Moltke: "We cannot do that, if that were to happen, we would disrupt the whole army and would give up any chance of success. Besides, our patrols have already entered Luxembourg and the Division from Trier is to follow immediately."[15]

To the shocked Moltke, the Kaiser's interference demonstrated that the monarch still wanted to preserve peace. Could it be that, at the last minute, the war that already seemed unavoidable would be averted? Outraged, he complained: 'The final straw would be if Russia now also fell away.'[16] He declared that he could not accept any responsibility for the war if the 16th Division was prevented from leaving Trier for Luxembourg. Bethmann's response was that for his part he would not accept responsibility if the British offer were declined.[17]

It was during these tense hours on 1 August that Moltke 'lost his nerve', as commentators put it, because he had no alternative to the deployment of troops in the west, and to the surprise attack on Liège before war was even declared. Railway timetables and mobilization plans had been worked out meticulously by the General Staff – what had taken months to perfect could not simply be changed at the last minute. No such painstaking attention had been devoted to an alternative plan. Moltke recalled explaining to the Kaiser. 'If His Majesty insists on leading the entire army to the east then you would not have an army that was ready to strike but a messy heap of disorderly, armed men without supplies.'[18] After all, on what basis would such a change be made? On a vague promise from Britain that could be revoked at any moment? German strategy could not be based on such an unreliable premise. Moltke explained that it was impossible for Germany to respect Belgium's neutrality. Even the prospect of British neutrality would not make this worthwhile, because an offensive against France was only possible via Belgium.[19]

Moltke's refusal to comply with the Kaiser's order led to the monarch snapping: 'Your uncle would have given me a different answer', and 'it must be possible, if I order it'. The 'Supreme War-Lord' ordered a stop to the advance of the 16th Division. Although Moltke tried to explain the strategic importance of the Luxembourg railways, which the 16th Division was to occupy on the first mobilization day, he was simply told that he would have to use different railway tracks instead.[20] Eventually, Moltke was able to achieve a compromise: deployment was allowed to continue as planned, but had to stop just before the French border. Depending on the nature of French assurances, an orderly move to the east could then be undertaken, rather than halting the deployment immediately and creating chaos. However, Moltke could not change the monarch's decision that the declaration of war against France and any hostilities were to be postponed.[21]

When Moltke returned to the General Staff building that evening, the excitement of the day had proved too much, and eyewitnesses recorded that the Chief of Staff might have suffered a slight stroke as a result of his confrontation with the Kaiser.[22] In the eyes of his critics, Moltke's failing health would become a frequently cited reason for his downfall. Certainly, he never quite recovered from the traumatic events of 1 August. Moltke complained bitterly to Haeften: 'I want to wage a war against the French and the Russians, but not against such a Kaiser'.[23] He feared that the monarch would not even have signed the mobilization order if Lichnowsky's telegram had arrived half an hour earlier.[24] One could at least speculate whether in such a case war might still have been averted.

It was only later that night that Moltke was finally given the go-ahead for the occupation of Luxembourg, after the Kaiser had discovered that Lichnowsky's telegram had been based on a misunderstanding.[25] Of course, the Kaiser's potentially disastrous intervention was not altogether unexpected. He had always been a risk factor in military planning, his interferences, although less frequent by the time Moltke was Chief of the General Staff, were still unpredictable and potentially dangerous. Even the most careful planning could not pre-empt the contingency of the Kaiser's meddling in military affairs. Before war had even begun, Moltke's confidence had been severely shaken.

MOBILIZATION AND DEPLOYMENT:
THE MOLTKE PLAN IN ACTION

When mobilization was finally declared, and war had become a reality, the details of the carefully guarded plans only needed to be distributed. Everything had been painstakingly prepared in anticipation of this important moment. Luxembourg was invaded on 2 August, an essential part of Germany's deployment plan in which speed and surprise were of the essence in advancing quickly towards Belgium and then on to France. Now the first major objective of the war, the *coup de main* on Liège, had to be achieved, clearing the way for the armies of the right wing to march into neutral Belgium. Moltke explained on 5 August, following the Chancellor's apologetic remarks in the Reichstag about 'the wrong that we inflicted with this measure', that it was impossible to spare Belgium because this was the only way 'to achieve a quick reckoning with France'. He announced that Liège was to be occupied the next day.

However, the first major objective of the war was threatening not to go according to plan. Liège, one of the strongest fortresses in Europe, proved more difficult to storm than anticipated, and the Belgians put up unexpectedly determined resistance. As a result, Moltke had a further confrontation with the Kaiser on 6 August, when he reported to him on the initial failure to capture Liège. The Kaiser severely reproached him, pointing out how he had always considered the plan of a *coup de main* nonsense and unworkable (when he had in fact not known about the details). When Moltke was able to bring better news about Liège later that day, the Kaiser could not find enough words of praise for his Chief of Staff.[26] Moltke was left feeling deeply disillusioned with his 'Supreme War-Lord'.

Following this first hitch in the plan, the last of Liège's concrete and iron forts was finally taken on 16 August, and the next day, two days later than planned, the German right wing could proceed with its enveloping move through Belgium and into France.[27] Moltke now considered it time to move the military headquarters (*Oberste Heeresleitung* – OHL) nearer to the main theatre of war, the Western Front. When the trains departed from Potsdam station for Koblenz, Müller recorded the mood of the departing officers: 'Excellently optimistic mood of the Chief of the General Staff, General v. Moltke and the Austrian General Count Stürck [sic]. Moltke says: "Today the last forts of Liège will be shot to pieces".'[28] Moltke even expressed confidence in the abilities of the Austrian army, telling Stürgkh: 'You have a good army. You will defeat the Russians.' Stürgkh, quite rightly, considered this wishful thinking. Moltke's parting words to Generaloberst von Kessel demonstrated, however, that he was partly relying on fate, for he declared 'if there is any justice left in this world, then *we* must win this war.'[29]

The serious repercussions for Moltke's health of the events of 1 August seem confirmed by the fact that a special allowance was made for the Chief of the General Staff when it was decided at the last minute that his wife Eliza was to accompany the military headquarters. According to Haeften's recollections, the permission to accompany her husband to the front had been requested by Eliza von Moltke in the light of his frail state of health following the confrontations with the Kaiser on 1 and 6 August. The Kaiser had initially refused such a request as 'completely impossible [. . .] The Generaloberst is not that ailing, surely.' It was when the Kaiserin suggested that Eliza von Moltke could make herself useful at a Red Cross hospital in Koblenz that the Kaiser finally conceded. Moltke's wife was allowed to board the royal train and accompanied her husband to the front.[30] Moltke's colleagues commented increasingly sarcastically on this over the next few weeks. Major Friedrich Mewes recalled: 'Already in Koblenz [Moltke's] wife arrived to care for him, during meals she sat at the table of the Chief of the General Staff, which caused much upset with the officers of the headquarters.'[31]

Now that war-time decision-making had to begin, Moltke was perhaps not in the best state of mind to conduct and co-ordinate decisions. He was under immense pressure in these first weeks of war, due to the need to win the first battles quickly, and due to his fear of the alternative scenario: a long, drawn-out war of attrition which Germany would be unlikely to win. One of the problems that Moltke faced was to anticipate and respond to enemy action. Following the *coup de main* on Liège, it was difficult to predict where the French would concentrate their troops. Would they send considerable numbers north to counter the German advance, or would they concentrate their forces in Lorraine to attempt an offensive in the south? From the middle of August onwards, Moltke expected a French offensive between Metz and the Vosges. Moltke's pre-war planning had always anticipated such a move and he was prepared to engage the French in the south, rather than concentrating solely on the right wing, as the original Schlieffen Plan had demanded.

It was assumed that the French had amassed about one fifth of their entire army between Metz and the Vosges.[32] The plan was to lure the French behind the Saar River and then launch a counter-attack. In three days of fighting the German Sixth and Seventh Armies managed to achieve a victory in the Battle of Lorraine (20–23 August). Although they had not managed to envelop and destroy their opponent, the hasty retreat of the French was considered a victory and reported as such to the military headquarters.[33] When the good news arrived at the headquarters on 22 August, the Kaiser's depressed mood lifted and he was immediately led to exaggerated expectations. 'The strategic hopes are very wide-ranging', Müller recorded.[34] Plessen remembered after the war: 'On 24 or 25 August Tappen literally said to me: "The whole thing will be over and done with in six weeks."'[35]

At the same time, the armies of Germany's right wing had begun their advance in accordance with the overall strategy of the Schlieffen/Moltke Plan. German troops were progressing rapidly into Belgium and France through the narrow corridor at Liège. They headed for Paris, reaching Brussels on 20 August, and engaging the French and British forces in the so-called Battles of the Frontiers between 14 and 25 August.[36] Tappen recalled that the movement of the armies that had begun on 18 August had been progressing inexorably. The ability of the armies to march and advance, particularly in the 'enveloping right army wing was of the kind that one had never considered possible in peacetime.'[37] For the French, the Battles of the Frontiers spelt the end of Plan XVII; for the Germans, the Schlieffen Plan seemed to be delivering its promise of speedy and decisive victory.

Following the victory in Lorraine, Moltke faced a difficult decision. Should troops from the south join the right wing to strengthen it for the intended enveloping move? Or should they press forward in Lorraine, in order to stop the French from bringing in reinforcements? Because Moltke expected a military decision on the right wing to be imminent, he decided to engage the French further in Lorraine, in an attempt to drive the French armies apart and to annihilate them. The right wing could then use its superiority to achieve an overall victory. Like many of Moltke's operational decisions, this plan was condemned by his critics after the war was lost. Moltke's decision to pursue the enemy with the armies on the left wing amounted in effect to a strategy of double envelopment, which has been interpreted as an adulteration of the Schlieffen Plan and as a serious misjudgement both by contemporary critics and some historians. Holger Herwig comments: 'Moltke's spur-of-the-moment decision to send the 16 divisions of the German Sixth and Seventh Armies not north via Metz to join Bülow and Kluck but east towards Épinal, constituted one of his gravest errors during the Marne campaign.'[38] According to Gerhard Tappen, however, this decision was based on the facts available at the time, such as the destruction of much of Belgium's railways which would have delayed the transport of troops from the south too long to make a significant impact on the ongoing fighting on the right wing. Moreover, he argues that adapting a plan to changing circumstances as the war developed, rather than sticking to one developed in peace time, was a courageous and difficult decision.[39] Clearly, it could not have been expected of Moltke to adhere to a plan that was developed years before the outbreak of war, rather than adapting it as the situation demanded.

An even greater, and potentially more dangerous, problem presented itself to Moltke on the Eastern Front. Moltke had anticipated a 'racial struggle' against the Slavs, and had feared Russia's increasing strength. Initially, of course, the numbers of troops deployed on the Eastern Front were woefully insufficient. The preoccupation with the Western theatre of war in the years of pre-war planning, and the importance attached to a quick victory in the west meant that the Eastern Front seemed only of minor importance. The orders given to the Eighth Army were to try to divert Russian forces away from the Austrian armies. This would easily be achieved if the Russian armies operated offensively against East Prussia. If they decided to remain waiting or on the defensive, then a German offensive would have to ensure that Russian troops would be engaged away from the Austrians.[40] Moltke's approach to the question of a two-front war differed from that of Schlieffen in that he was not prepared to allow the Russians to occupy East Prussian territory. He deployed more troops there than Schlieffen had planned; allegedly, another adulteration of a 'perfect' plan.

The campaign on the Eastern Front would always be difficult, owing to Germany's numerical inferiority. Generalleutnant Max Hoffmann, First General Staff officer of the Eighth Army, recorded in his diary on 7 August: 'We have a hard task before us, harder, almost, than any in history.'[41] After initial favourable news from East Prussia on 20 August, the OHL learnt a day later that Generaloberst Max von Prittwitz, leader of the Eighth Army, had discontinued the Battle at Gumbinnen, which had already seemed almost won, and was contemplating a retreat, perhaps even behind the Vistula. In three separate battles the Eighth Army had achieved only incomplete victories on the flanks and had been defeated in the centre.[42] The Russians were threatening to cross the border into East Prussia. In a telephone call the Eighth Army demanded urgent reinforcements if Prittwitz were to be able to defend the Vistula. Moltke ordered that a retreat behind the river had to be avoided at all cost.[43]

By 21 August it was beginning to look as if the only way to avoid a retreat and stop Prittwitz from dividing his forces was a replacement of the supreme command of the Eighth Army. Wenninger reported from the OHL to Munich: 'One hears here of the "worry of being cut off", of a "hurried retreat behind the Vistula", meaning giving up on East Prussia.'[44] Similarly, Müller learnt from Plessen that the situation in the east was a cause for concern. 'In Moltke's eyes Prittwitz had operated in a completely wrong way. The General Staff is alleged to be angry with him', he recorded in his diary.[45] On this important occasion, Moltke intervened forcefully, as even Groener, one of Moltke's fiercest critics, had to admit after the war: 'The only time that I have seen him in determined yet tearful excitement was at the moment when he found out that the Oberkommando VIII had stopped the battle at Gumbinnen and wanted to retreat behind the Vistula.'[46] Moltke had only authorized such a retreat in an extreme emergency, because its implications were that Russia would be free to turn on Posnan or Silesia, or even towards the Austrians. It was imperative that the Eighth Army stay east of the Vistula if at all possible.

Against this tense background, Moltke had to decide whether more troops should be sent east straight away, as the Eighth Army so urgently requested, or whether they should be kept to strengthen the right wing for the decisive battle in the west. The mood in the OHL, judging by contemporary accounts, was desperate, as Plessen's diary confirms:

> But East Prussia! Gumbinnen and Allenstein occupied by the enemy! The Russians burn and pillage everything! – We must make haste to finish up in the west as quickly as possible in order to come to the rescue of the east.[47]

News from the First and Second Armies on the Western Front gave the OHL the impression that victory in the west was almost achieved, and faced with the imminent threat of a Russian invasion of East Prussia, Moltke decided to move six corps from the Western to the Eastern Front. In the event, this number was reduced to only two corps (the Guard Reserve Corps and the XI Army Corps). In the meantime, Paul von Hindenburg and Erich Ludendorff had replaced Max von Prittwitz and Georg von Waldersee at the Eighth Army. Although Ludendorff had informed the OHL prior to the dispatch of the two corps that they would arrive too late to make any difference, they were sent anyway. Perhaps the OHL simply did not believe that Ludendorff would be able to turn around the situation which to them had seemed so desperate. Before the reinforcements arrived, Hindenburg and Ludendorff had managed to avert the threatening German defeat, eventually turning it into a victory at the Battle of Tannenberg (27–30 August). The two corps were, however, sorely missed in the decisive battle in the west. Not surprisingly, Moltke's critics have found in his decision to send troops east rather than keeping them on the right wing further reason for doubting his strategic competence. Again, however, this criticism benefits from hindsight because Moltke could not have predicted that the dire state of the Eighth Army would so quickly be turned around and a major defeat avoided.[48] Moreover, as Dennis Showalter points out in Moltke's defence, German military doctrine had emphasized for the previous twenty years that troops needed to be sent east following initial, decisive victories in the west.[49] On 25 and 26 August, this point in time seemed to have been reached. Based on 'exceedingly favourable news' from Lorraine, Moltke was under the impression that the French were virtually defeated.[50]

Contemporary accounts attest to the anxiety that was widely felt in the OHL about the precarious situation in the east, and Moltke's decision to move troops from the Western Front can only with hindsight be condemned as a mistake. Critics have maintained that the two army corps that were sent east would have made a decisive difference to the fate of the German armies in the battle of the Marne, events that are widely regarded as Moltke's greatest blunder, and that spelt the end of his time in office. However, a variety of reasons led to the fateful defeat in September 1914, and it could be argued that two additional army corps would not have made a decisive difference.[51]

THE BATTLE OF THE MARNE

By 22 August, the invasion of Belgium was nearly completed. The Battles of the Frontiers had been decided in Germany's favour, and France's Plan XVII had collapsed. By the beginning of September, the German right wing had almost reached Paris. However, the French were not yet beaten, but had managed an orderly retreat and were strengthening their left wing. The leadership of Germany's right wing, under the command of Generaloberst von Kluck (First Army) and Generaloberst von Bülow (Second Army) was divided, because the two generals differed in their views on operations.

Moltke ordered a rapid advance to stop the French from reorganizing, but Kluck felt that the First Army did not have the necessary strength to attempt to envelop Paris. When the German armies crossed the Marne to move towards Paris, on the extreme right wing, the balance of power had changed to Germany's disadvantage, with twenty German divisions facing thirty French and British ones. On 4 September, Joffre decided to attack the flank of the First Army. Although Kluck's army defended successfully against this attack, a wide gap developed as a result between the First and Second Armies, into which the enemy was able to advance. Bülow and Kluck lost touch, partly due to a lack of adequate communications. The news received in the OHL was scant and contradictory, making it difficult for Moltke in the military headquarters to issue orders to the army leaders.

On 9 September, the First and Second Armies retreated, even though they had so far been victorious in their campaigns.[52] In his diary entry of 10 September, Wenninger recorded the depressed mood in the headquarters following the retreat: 'It is as quiet as a mortuary in the school building in Luxembourg – one tiptoes around, the General Staff officers rush past me with their eyes down-cast – best not to address them, not to ask.'[53] There could be no starker contrast to the mood of elation he had described just after mobilization had been declared.

The retreat behind the Marne was the result of misunderstandings and communications so bad that they were at times non-existent. On 9 September, a day that in Lyncker's words was 'the most critical day of the war so far', Moltke suggested a retreat, while Stein and Plessen opposed such a measure. Resignedly, Lyncker concluded: 'All of this is however meaningless, because there is no communication with the First and Second Armies at the present time.'[54] The military headquarters in Luxembourg had only radio contact with the crucial right wing armies, which was becoming increasingly unreliable. With the First Army, communication was often only possible via the Second Army. Unfortunately (and inexplicably), no attempts were made to improve communication, for example by mending already existing wires.[55] Even on the left wing, where telephone connections existed, communications was not straightforward. No separate communication system for the army had been established, and civilian lines (including civilian operators) had to be used. No direct lines existed to the military headquarters, exposing any telephone calls to the risk of espionage. All conversations were to be conducted in code, which did not ease the communication difficulties.[56] Nor were the headquarters moved closer to the front, another measure which would have aided communication. According to Tappen, Moltke had wanted to move the headquarters, but 'technical difficulties' as well as a reluctance to separate a small *Operationsstaffel* from the headquarters as a way of leaving the Kaiser behind in safety, prevented this. Moltke had considered moving the headquarters to Namur, but had to change his mind due to considerations regarding the Kaiser's safety.[57] Although the Kaiser, too, demanded that the headquarters be moved, his wish was not granted on the pretext of 'technical grounds'.[58] Moltke later defended himself against criticism from the former Minister of War Karl von Einem: 'But my dear Einem, I couldn't have travelled through half of France with the Kaiser during the advance.'[59]

Another alleged mistake of Moltke's was that he did not travel to the front himself in order to establish the seriousness of the situation. On 8 September, Moltke wrote to his wife: 'The terrible tension of these days, the lack of news from the far away armies, the knowledge of what is at risk here, almost exceeds human strength.'[60] Moltke feared that the enemy might advance into the gap that had developed between Kluck's and Bülow's armies. Rather than go to the army headquarters himself, he chose Oberstleutnant Hentsch[61] as his envoy to report back on the situation at the front as no news had been received. It was he who ordered the First and Second Armies to retreat behind the Marne. It has never been firmly established whether Hentsch had been authorized by Moltke to order the retreat, or whether it was his own decision. Claims have even been made that Hentsch acted in defiance of clear instructions to avoid a retreat at all cost. An enquiry undertaken in April 1917 revealed that Hentsch's orders had been to direct and co-ordinate a retreat, if one had already been started by the First Army, in order to close the gap between the two armies. However, Hentsch ordered a full retreat of both armies, claiming that he had been authorized by Moltke to do so – an allegation that Moltke and other commentators denied. In the margin of the war-diary of the First Army, Moltke commented after the fateful mission (probably in February 1915):

> Oberstleutnant Hentsch only had the order to tell the First Army that – if its retreat became necessary – it should go back to the line Soissons-Fismes, in order to reconnect with the Second Army. He did not have the order to say that the retreat was *unavoidable*. [. . .] I did not give *an order* for the retreat of the First Army. Nor was an order for the retreat of the Second Army given.[62]

This is confirmed by Tappen, who recalled in 1925: 'During the discussion it was again and again being pointed out that the armies absolutely must hold their positions.'[63]

Unusually, Hentsch did not receive a written order, and we will never know what exactly Moltke had instructed him to do, or what exactly Hentsch thought he was authorized to do. In any case, the damage was done. Moltke finally travelled to the army headquarters of the right wing on 11 September, together with Tappen and Dommes, when it appeared as if the enemy would break through between the Second and Third Armies. Confronted with the situation as it presented itself, Moltke had to give the order to withdraw the Third, Fourth, and Fifth Armies to re-establish a united front. He wrote after the event: 'It was a difficult decision that I had to take without being able to get His Majesty's approval first. It was the hardest decision of my life, one that made my heart bleed.'[64] That night, he returned to the headquarters a broken man. Lyncker recorded in his diary on 12 September: 'Moltke returned, very depressed, came back with bad impressions. Should he fade away ('ausspannen'), Falkenhayn will have to take over.' The next day, his verdict was even more damning: 'Moltke is completely crushed by the events, his nerves are not up to this situation.'[65] During these tense days, 'Moltke was reported to have been terribly agitated and had been quite harsh in his excitement. His wife! [sic] had continually remained in the room next door in order to be able to calm him.'[66] The retreat on the Marne spelt the end of the Schlieffen/Moltke Plan, the end of Germany's hopes of a swift victory in the west. For Moltke, it indicated that his worst fear, a battle of attrition, in which Germany's chances of victory were only slim, had become reality.

MOLTKE'S PERSONAL CRISIS

The failure on the Marne also spelt the end of Moltke's military career and led to his physical and mental collapse. Both friends and foes of Moltke stress that he clearly suffered under the increasing burden of co-ordinating and leading the massive German army, especially once the strategic 'blueprint' for the first weeks of fighting had come to an end. After the Battle of the Marne, contemporaries witnessed a nervous man who was increasingly losing control over his actions, and over the leadership of the army. Major Mewes recalled a striking image of the Chief of Staff. The nervousness of the General was displayed outwardly particularly in that he walked ceaselessly up and down in the room and exhaled air with a whistling sound through the teeth. Within the General Staff there was the general point of view that General von Moltke was powerless vis-à-vis his great task on account of his physical condition, and that he let the chiefs of the departments do as they pleased.[67]

For Moltke, the Marne was more than a first setback of the so-far victorious German campaign – it was his personal defeat. Voices demanding his dismissal, which had made themselves heard in influential places even before this disaster, now found willing listeners, especially as it was easier to blame Moltke for the turn of events than address other possible shortcomings. Müller recorded on 14 September: 'Apparently the news has been received from the General Staff that things cannot go on with Moltke, while Moltke himself is of a different opinion. Lyncker should convince him.'[68] Lyncker had asked Minister of War Erich Falkenhayn as early as 10 August if he were willing to replace Moltke. It is a possibility that these intrigues were one of the reasons why Moltke did not leave the headquarters; knowing about them would certainly have added to his growing sense of insecurity.[69] When, in the aftermath of defeat, the Chief of the General Staff suffered a nervous breakdown, Lyncker's and Falkenhayn's time had come and they succeeded in convincing the Kaiser that Moltke should be replaced.

The lost battle of the Marne confirmed to Moltke's many critics that he had failed, that he had proved unable to stand up to the pressures of the war. Wenninger judged harshly in his diary: 'without doubt Falkenhayn has his own thoughts, whereas Moltke and his helpers were completely sterile. All they could do is turn the handle and roll Schlieffen's film, and they were clueless and beside themselves when the roll got stuck.'[70] Observers started to remember doubts they had had ever since Moltke had been appointed Chief of Staff. Moltke's break-down – both mental and physical – following these events confirmed their worst expectations. Wenninger was a particularly harsh critic: 'Shame, but one should not try to force it to elevate epigones to the names of the fathers and uncles – Napoleon III, Siegfried Wagner, Moltke II.'[71] It should, however, be noted that Moltke was not the only military official who could not take the strain of the first weeks of the war. The leader of the Third Army, General von Hausen, was replaced by General von Einem on 19 September, on account of 'nervousness'.[72] On 20 August, the Kaiser's *Oberstallmeister* Walter von Esebeck committed suicide 'in an attack of nervous collapse', in Müller's words. 'As Lyncker tells me, this was only one of many nervous breakdowns among officers, an occurrence that had also been observed in 1870 shortly after the outbreak of the war.'[73]

Moltke was told by the Kaiser to report sick, on account of his 'fragile state'.[74] After some debate, during which Moltke vehemently refused to do so, it was agreed that Moltke would stay at the headquarters, but he was in effect replaced by Falkenhayn on 14 September. The Kaiser's choice of successor, a general who was younger than most other commanding generals in the German army, was not widely popular, but, as eight years previously in the case of Moltke's appointment, the monarch's decision could not be overruled.[75] The replacement was initially secret, to avoid alerting the German public to the defeat, or to give the enemies opportunity for triumph, and was only made public in November when Moltke actually left the headquarters. Even the Austrian ally had not been informed.[76]

Moltke's position had been reduced to that of an onlooker who had to stand aside and let Falkenhayn, promoted to *Generalquartiermeister*, do his work. Already on 15 September, it was Falkenhayn who gave the daily General Staff talk. Plessen recorded: 'Moltke says almost nothing. Falkenhayn delivers the talk very well.'[77] A week later, Moltke complained to the Kaiser in front of a large group of officers: 'Majesty, one doesn't tell me anything anymore!', to which the Kaiser replied that he was in the same position. Wenninger commented: 'A sad ending!'[78] It is not difficult to imagine the humiliation this entailed for Moltke. In October, Moltke wrote to his wife from Mézières about his attempts 'to keep myself informed about everything that is being done and to keep up the relationship between Falkenhayn and myself, it is not easy but I am doing what I can. I believe that a more difficult test can hardly be imposed on a human being.'[79] Even the hostile Groener seemed to feel pity, describing the way Moltke was treated as 'humili-ating', especially as Falkenhayn lacked the necessary tact to ease the situation.

As is argued in the chapter by Robert Foley, for the rest of his life, a bitter and resentful Moltke would attempt to justify his actions, and to refute his numerous critics. He also tried in vain to regain his former position of influence by participating in intrigues against Falkenhayn.[80] In a letter to Plessen of 2 May 1915, he admitted having been nervous 'in the critical September days', blaming the events of the first mobilization days (the scene in the Kaiser's Schloss on 1 August) for this. Moltke contended that future commentators would agree with him that his decision to withdraw troops on the Marne had been the right one: 'I look forward with a clean conscience to the judgement of military history about this episode.'[81] Similarly, he wrote in May 1915 that it had come to his attention that the retreat on the Marne was being blamed on his nervousness, an allegation that he considered completely wrong. 'Given the situation, the retreat was a completely unavoidable necessity that I had to order after full consideration, – even if with a heavy heart – and I am certain that military history will one day prove me right.'[82]

For Moltke, the humiliation of his replacement and subsequent demotion to Chief of the Deputy General Staff in Berlin was the worst disgrace imaginable. He was tortured by these events, and thought that even the death of a son would have been preferable to the fate he had suffered, as he told the Austrian attaché Count Joseph Stürgkh:

> And yet I envy him [Conrad, who had just lost a son], when I compare myself to him. What is his loss compared to the blow that has struck me! Just consider from what position, from what field of influence a tragic fate has torn me; no one has ever experienced anything like that. [. . .] I will never get over it.[83]

He was wrong, of course, to think that history would prove him right. After his death in June 1916, and particularly after the war was lost, his critics became increasingly vociferous, often forgetting or glossing over their own mistakes in the process.[84] Moltke provided a convenient scapegoat. They argued that it was not German war planning, or the conduct of the German army during war, that had failed Germany, but rather the hapless successor to the great Chief of Staff Alfred von Schlieffen. It was they who wrote the history of the war, and thanks to their efforts, Moltke was marginalized and almost forgotten as an unsuccessful military leader.

Notes

1   For a more detailed account of Moltke in the pre-war years, and for the history-writing of the 'Schlieffen school', see Annika Mombauer, *Helmuth*

von Moltke and the Origins of the First World War, Cambridge 2001 (forthcoming).

2 Franz Conrad von Hötzendorf, *Aus meiner Dienstzeit 1906–1918*, 5 vols, Vienna, Leipzig, Munich 1921–25, III, pp.669 ff.

3 See A. Mombauer, 'A Reluctant Military Leader? Helmuth von Moltke and the July Crisis of 1914', *War in History*, vol.6, No.4, 1999.

4 Alfred Graf von Dohna, 'Der Feldzug in Ostpreußen 1914', 24 April 1920, in BA-MA, W-10/51032, pp.136 f.

5 On 13 July 1914, the French Senator Charles Humbert had publicly revealed serious shortcomings within the French army during a speech to the Senate. This knowledge made the current crisis appear even more of a golden opportunity for Germany. On Humbert's revelations, see Bundesarchiv-Militärarchiv Freiburg (BA-MA), PH3/629, pp.12 f.; Gerd Krumeich, *Armaments and Politics in France on the Eve of the First World War. The Introduction of the Three-Year Conscription 1913–1914*, London 1984, p.214; John Keiger, *France and the Origins of the First World War*, London 1983, p.149.

6 I. Geiss, (ed), *Julikrise und Kriegsausbruch*, 2 vols, Hanover 1963/4, II, doc.704, 29 July 1914.

7 Lerchenfeld to Hertling, 31 July 1914, in E. Deuerlein (ed), *Briefwechsel Hertling – Lerchenfeld 1912–1917*, Boppard/Rhein, 1973, doc.113, p.322. Moltke gave several reasons why Germany was still stronger than Russia and France, such as the superiority of German artillery and of the German infantry gun, as well as the inadequate training of French soldiers due to the recent change-over from two to three year service.

8 BA-MA, W-10/50897, Haeften to Reichsarchiv, 30 January 1926.

9 BA-MA, N35/1, Aufzeichnungen v. Haeften, p.27.

10 Haeften, 'Meine Erlebnisse aus den Mobilmachungstagen 1914', BA-MA, N35/1, p.34.

11 Geiss, *Julikrise*, II, doc.1000, Falkenhayn diary, 1 August 1914; A.v.Wegerer, *Der Ausbruch des Weltkrieges*, 2 vols, Hamburg 1939, II, p.187. See also Lerchenfeld to Hertling, 1 August 1914, in Deuerlein, *Briefwechsel*, doc.114,p.323. The events are described in detail in Mombauer, 'A reluctant military leader?', pp.440 ff.

12 Geiss, *Julikrise*, II, doc.983.

13 Lyncker's diary, Geiss, *Julikrise*, II, doc.1000b. There are several accounts of the events in the Schloss that day, collected in ibid, doc.1000 a-e; see also Wegerer, *Ausbruch*, II, pp.188 ff. Haeften's accounts are particularly important. See BA-MA, N35/1, also his article in *Deutsche Allgemeine Zeitung*, 11 October 1921.

14 Geiss, *Julikrise*, II, doc.1000b.

15 W. Görlitz (ed), *Regierte der Kaiser? Kriegstagebücher . . . des Chefs des Marinekabinetts Admiral Georg Alexander von Müller*, Göttingen, 2nd ed. 1959 (Müller, *Diary*,) pp.38 ff.; also in Geiss, *Julikrise*, II, doc.1000d.

16 Müller, *Diary*, p.39; Geiss, *Julikrise*, II, doc.1000d. Thomas Meyer, one of Moltke's apologists, credits the Chief of Staff with rather a lot of foresight: 'The first telegram had appeared unrealistic to Moltke's political astuteness, and thus he had to refuse to alter the entire deployment of the army.' In fact, Meyer tries to blame Britain for the outbreak of war. *Helmuth von Moltke, 1848–1916. Dokumente zu seinem Leben und Wirken*, 2 vols, Basel 1993, vol. I, pp.16 f.

17 Müller, *Diary*, p.39.

18 H.v.Moltke, *Erinnergungen, Briefe, Dokumente 1877–1916*, Stuttgart 1922, p.20; also in Geiss, *Julikrise* II, doc.1000c.

19 Lerchenfeld to Hertling, 4 August 1914, in Geiss, *Julikrise*, II, doc.1148.

20 Moltke, *Erinnerungen*, pp.20/21; also in Geiss, *Julikrise*, II, doc.1000c; Wegerer, *Ausbruch*, II, p.190.

21 Wegerer, *Ausbruch*, II, p.189.

22 BA-MA, W-10/51061, Dommes to Reichsarchiv, 14 January 1926. Haeften's memories of the event record that Eliza Moltke thought her husband had suffered a slight stroke.' Haeften, 'Meine Erlebnisse aus den Mobilmachungstagen 1914', BA-MA, N35/1, p.35. See also J.v.Grone, 'Zum Kriegsausbruch 1914', *Die Drei. Zeitschrift für Anthroposophie und Dreigliederung*, 1964/1, p.8.

23 Haeften, 'Meine Erlebnisse aus den Mobilmachungstagen 1914', BA-MA, N35/1, p.34.

24 Heisterkamp, 'Lebensskizze', in Meyer, *Moltke*, I, p.35.

25 Lichnowsky's telegram has usually been regarded as based on a misunderstanding (e.g. Geiss, *Julikrise*, II, p.530), but see H.Afflerbach, *Falkenhayn. Politisches Denken und Handeln im Kaiserreich*, Munich 1994, p.166, note 82, who argues it was in fact motivated by Grey's difficulty in getting an approval from the Cabinet for intervention on the continent. On the Kaiser's interference on 1 August see also Afflerbach, 'Wilhelm II as Supreme Warlord in the First World War', *War in History*, vol.5, 4, 1998, p.433.

26 Haeften, 'Meine Erlebnisse aus den Mobilmachungstagen 1914', BA-MA, N35/1, p.36.

27 For details on Liège, see John Keegan, *The First World War*, London, paperback ed. 1999, pp.87 ff.; Martin Gilbert, *The First World War*, London, paperback ed. 1995, pp.36/7, 43; Hans Herzfeld, *Der Erste Weltkrieg*, Munich 1968, p.55; Holger Herwig, *The First World War. Germany and Austria-Hungary 1914–1918*, London 1997, p.96. Schlieffen had preferred avoiding Liège in his planning by marching through Holland, because he had anticipated that the fortress town would be difficult to take. G.Ritter, *Staatskunst und Kriegshandwerk*, 4 vols, Munich 1954–1968, II, p.332.

28 Müller, *Diary*, p.48.

29 J.Stürgkh, *Im Deutschen Grossen Hauptquartier*, Leipzig 1921, p.23.

30 Haeften, 'Meine Erlebnisse aus den Mobilmachungstagen 1914', BA-MA, N35/1, p.37. According to Haeften, as a result of Eliza von Moltke's request, Lyncker approached Falkenhayn that day to enquire whether he would be willing to take over Moltke's duties if the Chief of Staff proved unable to take the strain.

31 BA-MA, W-10/51063. 'Charakteristik der massgebenden Persölich-keiten', p.1.

32 Reichsarchiv (ed), *Der Weltkrieg 1914–1918*, 14 vols, Berlin 1925 ff, 1, p.184.

33 Tappen, 'Vor zwanzig Jahren. Generaloberst v. Moltke', BA-MA, N56/5, pp.262 ff.; Reichsarchiv, *Weltkrieg*, I, pp.263 ff; p.302.

34 Müller, *Diary*, p.50.

35 BA-MA, W-10/50897, 'Mündliche Mitteilungen des Generalobersten von Plessen', 10 April 1923, p.148.

36 Herwig, *First World War*, p.97.

37 BA-MA, W-10/50661: Tappen, 'Kriegserinnerungen', p.27.

38 Herwig, *First World War*, p.99.

39 BA-MA, W-10/50661: Tappen, 'Kriegserinnerungen', p.27.

40 *Der Weltkrieg*, vol.II, p.43.

41 Hoffmann, *War Diaries*, vol.I, p.38.

42 See D.Showalter, *Tannenberg. Clash of Empires*, Hamden, Conn. 1991, pp.190 ff.

43 Count von Dohna to Waldersee, 28 August 1914, BA-MA, W-10/51032. See also Reichsarchiv, *Der Weltkrieg*, vol.I, p.431, See Robert B. Asprey, *The German High Command at War. Hindenburg and Ludendorff and the First World War*, London 1994; Martin Kitchen, *The Silent Dictatorship. The Politics of the German High Command under Hindenburg and Ludendorff, 1916–1918*, London 1976; Showalter, *Tannenberg*, p.194.

44 Schulte, 'Neue Dokumente', 21 August 1914, pp.154/5.

45 Müller, *Diary*, p.50. See also Showalter, *Tannenberg*, pp.195 ff.

46 Groener to Oberstleutnant von Strube, 7 January 1931, BA-MA, NL Groener, N46/39, pp.180 f.

47 Plessen diary, 24 August 1914, BA-MA, W-10/50676.

48 See Reichsarchiv, *Weltkrieg*, vol.I, pp.604 ff, vol.II, pp.206 ff.; Showalter, *Tannenberg*, pp.293 ff.

49 Ibid, p.294.

50 The diary of Crown Prince Rupprecht (Sixth Army) testifies to the delight with which the news of his victory were received by Moltke and Falkenhayn, who were 'moved to tears' and by the Kaiser, who was 'nearly ecstatic'. BA-MA, W-10/50659, p.19, 23 August 1914.

51 For a more favourable assessment of Moltke's impact on the events on the Marne, see Sebastian Haffner/Wolfgang Venohr, *Das Wunder an der Marne*, Bergisch Gladbach 1982, pp.13 ff.

52 Bericht der OHL zum Ende der Marne-Schlacht, 10 September 1914, in W. Bihl (ed), *Deutsche Quellen zur Geschichte des Ersten Weltkrieges*, Darmstadt 1991, p.63.

53 B.-F. Schulte, 'Neue Dokumente zum Kriegsausbruch und Kriegsverlauf 1914', *MGM*, 25, 1/1979, p.172.

54 BA-MA, W-10/50676, Lyncker diary, 9 September 1914, p.27.

55 Reichsarchiv, *Weltkrieg*, vol.IV, p.139; Ludendorff, *Das Marne-Drama. Der Fall Moltke-Hentsch*, Munich 1934, p.13.

56 BA-MA, W-10/50076, Krafft von Dellmensingen, 'Kommentar zum Weltkriegswerk', p.95. On the lack of adequate communication, see also Dieter Storz, *Kriegsbild und Rüstung vor 1914*, Herford 1992, p.321.

57 BA-MA. W-10/50897, 'Mündliche Mitteilungen des Generalobersten von Plessen', p.147. Dommes recalled in March 1921 that Moltke apparently wanted to move the HQ to Rethel, but then refrained from this because he did not want to separate the General Staff from the Kaiser. See J.v.Grone, *Wie es zur Marneschlacht 1914 kam*, Selbstverlag, Stuttgart 1971, p.16.

58 Reichsarchiv, *Weltkrieg*, vol.IV, p.129, also pp.138/9.

59 K.v.Einem, *Erinnerungen eines Soldaten*, Leipzig 1933, p.177.

60 Moltke, *Erinnerungen*, p.384.

61 He was Head of the *Nachrichtenabteilung* from 2 August 1914 until 28 May 1915. Oberst von Dommes had also volunteered himself for the trip, but Moltke chose Hentsch because the latter had already recently visited the First and Second Armies. Reichsarchiv, *Weltkrieg*, vol.IV, p.223.

62 Ibid, vol.IV, p.223; BA-MA, N56/2, NL Tappen, Reichsarchiv (v.Haeften) to Tappen, 29 February 1920.

63 Dommes to Reichsarchiv, quoted in BA-MA, N56/2, NL Tappen, Haeften to Tappen, 29 February 1920. Tappen's letter of 1925 quoted in Reichsarchiv, *Weltkrieg*, vol.IV, p.224.

64 Moltke, *Erinnerungen*, p.24.

65 BA-MA, W-10/50676, Lyncker diary, pp.29 ff.

66 Bayerisches Hauptstaatsarchiv-Kriegsarchiv, Munich (BayHSTA-KA), HS2642, Crown Prince Rupprecht, Diary 18 September 1914, p.1.

67 BA-MA, W-10/51063. 'Charakteristik der massgebenden Persönlichkeiten', p.1.

68 Müller, *Diary*, p.59.

69 J.Wallach, *The Dogma of the Battle of Annihilation: The Theories of Clausewitz and Schlieffen and their Impact on the German Conduct of Two World Wars*, Westport, CT, 1967.

70 BayHSTA-KA, HS2662, NL Wenninger, diary entry, 16 September 1914.

71 Ibid, 21 September 1914.

72 BayHSTA-KA, NL Krafft von Dellmensingen, vol. 48, diary entry 19 September 1914.

73 Müller, *Diary*, p.50. For Esebeck's suicide, see also Stürgkh, *Hauptquartier*, p.36. Not surprisingly, the cause of Esebeck's death was kept a secret in the headquarters. BayHSTA-KA, NL Krafft, Kriegstagebücher, vol.48, 19 September 1914.

74 BA-MA, W-10/50676, Plessen diary, 14 September 1914, p.68.

75 Stürgkh, *Hauptquartier*, p.26. It was because of the Kaiser's favour that Falkenhayn managed to stay in office as Chief of Staff until 1916, against widespread opposition, among others from Hindenburg and Ludendorff, the Chancellor and, of course, Moltke himself.

76 Stürgkh, *Hauptquartier*, p.45; Herwig, *First World War*, p.106.

77 BA-MA, W-10/50676, Plessen diary, 15 September 1914, p.68.

78 BayHSTA-KA, HS2662, NL Wenninger, diary entry, 21 September 1914.

79 Moltke, *Erinnergungen*, 11 October 1914, p.387/8.

80 Details in Afflerbach, *Falkenhayn*, p.307 ff; Mombauer, *Helmuth von Moltke*, Chapter 5.

81 BA-MA, NL Moltke, N78/6, p.13.

82 Moltke, *Erinnerungen*, 4 May 1915, p.424.

83 Stürgkh, *Hauptquartier*, p.89.

84 See e.g. Oberst von Mantey to Foerster, 30 June 1931: 'Kuhl [First Army] is complaining terribly about Moltke, but has himself made such severe mistakes that I would say *he has spoilt many an idea for Moltke* [. . .]'. BA-MA, RH61/v.68, pp.56 ff.

Warriors of the Skies

Right: Sir Hugh Trenchard, Commander of the Royal Fying Corps.

Below: Those he led. Men of the Royal Flying Corps with their machines – S.E.5 fighters.

Men at War

Some of those who decided to fight: Doughboys on parade in Chicago.

The men: British and French soldiers together behind the lines.

Some National Party Spirits

The Earl of Derby.   Viscount Milner.   Sir Edward Carson.   Sir Henry Wilson.

Allies or Rivals?

Sir William Robertson.   Sir Henry Rawlinson.

Philippe Pétain.   Robert Nivelle.

Germany: The Leaders and the Led

The First Army High Command: General Helmuth von Moltke.

The Second Army High Command: General Erich von Falkenhayn.

Kaiser Wilhelm II views the trenches.

German troops on the move through Belgium and France in the opening moves of the Great War.

America Prepares for War

James Watson Gerard:
diplomat and successful propagandist.

The politician: President Woodrow Wilson

Doughboys in France

'Black Jack' Pershing with Foch and Joffre.

Woodrow Wilson with Lloyd George and Clemenceau.

Allied Generals in Italy

Lord Cavan

Sir Hubert Plumer

Luigi Cadorna

Italy's General Garibaldi meets British Tommies.

King George V with President Raymond Poincaré (second from left) and their Generals (from left) Joffre, Foch and Sir Douglas Haig at GHQ during the Battle of the Somme, 9 August 191

Kaiser Wilhelm II being briefed by Third Army Commander, Paul von Hindenburg (left) and h Chief of Staff, Erich Ludendorff.

Chapter 6

East or West? Erich von Falkenhayn and German Strategy, 1914–15

Robert T. Foley

As has been seen in the previous chapter by Annika Mombauer, on 14 September 1914, to the surprise of most German soldiers, Generalleutnant Erich von Falkenhayn took over the direction of Germany's war effort from the shattered Helmuth von Moltke.[1] Falkenhayn inherited a difficult situation. The Battle of the Marne (5 to 10 September) had forced a German retreat and had seemingly brought an end to Germany's pre-war campaign plan. Having failed to defeat the French quickly, Germany was now faced with the very real prospect of having to fight a war on two fronts against enemies who were superior in numbers of men and material. To make matters worse, the German High Command (the *Oberste Heeresleitung*, or OHL) had become paralyzed in the wake of the completely un-expected defeat at the Marne. While Moltke had never been in close control over the operations of his higher commands, his physical and emotional collapse in September now left the officers of his staff with no direction as well.[2] Consequently, the OHL was increasingly unable to react effectively to the rapidly changing battlefield situation in the days after the Marne. In the sarcastic words of Falkenhayn, 'Schlieffen's notes [had] come to an end, and with this, Moltke's wits.'[3]

From the beginning of his tenure, Germany's new strategic leader was thus faced with a two-fold task: first, he had to impose his will upon the enemy and rescue Germany from an increasingly desperate strategic situation; second, the new chief was forced to impose his will upon the contumacious officers of his staff and higher commands and bring some central direction back to Germany's operations. However, in an attempt to find an answer to the first task, Falkenhayn's unique approach toward dealing with the enemy would counteract his efforts to impose his authority on the German army and would ultimately undermine his position within his own army. By late 1914–early 1915, his battle with his subordinates over strategy would reach a point where it looked likely to do more damage to the German army than the best efforts of the Entente forces.

*   *   *

Erich von Falkenhayn was an unexpected choice to take over from the younger Moltke. At fifty-three years old, he was younger than most of the army's corps and army commanders.[4] Falkenhayn had only risen to prominence in 1913 when the Kaiser surprised observers by appointing a relatively obscure and certainly junior Falkenhayn to the post of Prussian Minister of War.[5] In this capacity, he had accompanied the Imperial Headquarters into the field. Despite the best efforts of the General Staff to keep him in the dark concerning operations,[6] the Minister of War was able to keep in touch with units at the front and develop a dark picture of Moltke's conduct of the war.[7] Already tipped in early August to succeed Moltke in case of trouble, Falkenhayn was prepared to assume the responsibilities of the Chief of the General Staff following the Battle of the Marne.[8]

The new Chief of the General Staff quickly restored order in the OHL and moved the headquarters closer to the front to improve communications with the German armies.[9] Additionally, Falkenhayn, who kept his position as Minister of War even while taking up the duties of Chief of the General Staff, was able to improve relations between the rival General Staff and Ministry of War.[10] In terms of strategy, Falkenhayn chose initially to attempt to continue the pre-war plan, believing the French to be near exhaustion and unable to withstand a renewed German assault.[11] With the idea of building a new force to strike the enemy's vulnerable flank, on 17 September he ordered the transfer of the Sixth Army from the army's left wing to the right. However, the French were able to transfer troops as quickly as the Germans and the so-called 'race to the sea' (17 September to 18 October) resulted in the nearly exhausted two armies facing each other in improvised field positions along the entire front.[12] All movement had come to a halt. 'Position warfare' [Stellungskrieg], dreaded by the Germans, had seemingly set in.[13]

With no vulnerable flank to envelop, the Germans now faced a situation which they were doctrinally ill-equipped to face. German training before the war had heavily emphasized a 'war of movement' [Bewegungskrieg] that sought to exploit enemy weaknesses. Although the Russo-Japanese War and the Balkan Wars had demonstrated the likelihood and the nature of position warfare, German manuals stressed that field positions were a temporary expedient, and Germans had only trained to conduct breakthroughs on a limited scale. They were unprepared to conduct the breakthrough operations necessary on the scale now demanded by the position warfare that had engulfed the entire Western Front.[14]

Reckoning once again that the French were near exhaustion, Falkenhayn's response to this unwelcome occurrence was to hit the Allied line at Ypres with heavy artillery and infantry attacks in an attempt to break the enemy position and restore mobility once again to the battlefield. To lead this new assault, Falkenhayn brought together four reserve corps recently formed from recruits who, swept away in the wave of enthusiasm, had volunteered at the war's outbreak. Despite suffering extremely high casualties,[15] the assault force built by Falkenhayn failed to break through the improvised Entente line, and in mid-November, Falkenhayn ordered all attacks to cease.[16] Temporarily exhausted, both sides withdrew into field positions to rebuild their respective strengths and to create new plans to bring the war to a conclusion. Position warfare and a two-front war for Germany were now a reality.

The failure of all attempts to bring the war to a conclusion in the west and the advent of a two-front war caused the German strategic leadership to reassess their assumptions about warfare and their strategic ideas. The abject failure of the attempted breakthrough at Ypres, and the horrendous casualties suffered, demonstrated to the German leadership once and for all the strength of an entrenched enemy backed by artillery and machine guns. No longer did German officers believe that they could pierce an enemy position if their troops had sufficient élan.[17] It was clear to all observers that the German army would need many more men, much more heavy artillery, and perhaps new operational ideas if it were to break the deadlock of the trenches.[18]

The campaign's failure had a profound impact upon Falkenhayn. Indeed, the German official history speaks of the General Staff Chief experiencing an 'inner change'[19] and his close staff attested to the emotional blow caused by the high German casualties.[20] Whether or not he experienced an 'inner change,' the inability to breakthrough the Entente line and the high German casualties caused Falkenhayn to rethink his strategic approach fundamentally. Since the victories in the German Wars of Unification, German strategists had focused on fighting and winning wars with a few great battles of annihilation along the model of the battles that had won the Austro-Prussian War and the Franco-German War – Königgrätz and Sedan. Rapid, crushing military victories would enable Germany's political leaders to dictate whatever peace they saw fit.[21]

However, by mid-November 1914, Falkenhayn had come to a radical conclusion for a German soldier – he concluded that such 'decisive' victories were not possible with the forces at Germany's disposal and under the conditions prevailing in 1914. Falkenhayn had come to believe that military force could, at most, only hope to achieve local successes. Instead of seeking a purely military solution to Germany's strategic situation, he now turned to the Reich's political leadership. On 18 November he held a long meeting with the Chancellor, Theobald von Bethmann Hollweg, during which he outlined his new strategic assumptions and concluded by asking the Chancellor to negotiate a separate peace with one of Germany's enemies as soon as possible. Bethmann later communicated the content of this conversation to the Under Secretary of State for Foreign Affairs, Arthur Zimmermann:

> This is how General von Falkenhayn judges the situation:
> As long as Russia, France and England stay together it is impossible for us to defeat our opponents in such a way that we can make a decent peace. On the contrary we would run the risk of slowly exhausting ourselves. Either Russia or France must be detached. If we can succeed in causing Russia to make peace – and in first line this is what we should try to do – then we will be able to defeat France and England so decisively that we could dictate the peace. . . . It is, however, to be expected with certainty that if Russia should make peace, France would also sing a different tune. Then, if England were not completely acquiescent we would wear her down, starving her out by means of a blockade based in Belgium, even though some months would be necessary to do so.[22]

Falkenhayn's conversation with Bethmann revealed a further strategic assumption. It is clear from his conversation that, to Falkenhayn, Germany's main enemies lay in the west. He believed that between Russia and Germany there existed no real conflict of interests and that a peace between the two nations could be found with little difficulty. He hoped that local military success, particularly the then ongoing German offensive, would further the political agenda for peace.[23] Further, he felt that by following a policy of peace with only minimal annexations, peace could be negotiated with France after Russia was removed from the war. Great Britain was another story. Falkenhayn viewed Britain as Germany's main enemy, and believed that Britain's 'Vernichtungswille' (will to annihilate) and hatred for Germany would rule out any negotiated peace between the two nations.

Instead, Germany would have to fight a long war against Britain utilizing the resources of the whole Continent.[24] Indeed, as early as August 1914, he had written in his diary that '. . . without the defeat of England this war will be lost for us.'[25]

Not everyone in the German strategic leadership agreed with Falkenhayn's opinions, however. Not long after his conversation with the General Staff Chief, Bethmann travelled to the headquarters of Generalfeldmarshall Paul von Hindenburg and Generalleutnant Erich Ludendorff's *Oberbefehlshaber Ost* (OberOst) in Posen.[26] There, he found two highly capable and popular officers who maintained the traditional view that the military was capable of setting the conditions for peace on its own, without any assistance from the Foreign Office. These men believed that Russia could, and should, be defeated militarily, allowing Germany to dictate peace on her terms. This was to be accomplished in a time-tested manner. Despite the evidence of the war to date, Hindenburg still felt that the military overthrow of Russia was possible, if not through a single great battle, a 'Sedan' in his words, then '. . . through a series of such and similar battles.'[27] Already dissatisfied with Falkenhayn's handling of the war and offended by his lack of regard for their strategic ideas, Hindenburg and Ludendorff argued that OberOst should be reinforced and that Germany's main effort should shift from the west to the east, and only after Russia had been defeated should Germany concern herself with her western enemies.[28]

Indeed, the belief that Germany's main effort should now shift to the east was strong amongst German soldiers. On the Eastern Front, the conditions were very different to those on the Western Front. Rather than static, trench warfare, war in the east maintained a mobile character. The great distances and poor communications network did not permit a continuous trench line, and Germans excelled at fighting a war of movement. The battles of Tannenberg (26 to 31 August) and the Masurian Lakes (9 to 14 September) demonstrated this, and also ensured that the names of Hindenburg and Ludendorff would be on the lips of every German. Moreover, this victory reinforced the opinion traditionally held by Germans that the Russians were incompetent soldiers. Understandably, a war of movement in the east seemed preferable to trench warfare in the west to many German officers, and pressure grew on Falkenhayn to shift the German effort to the Eastern Front.[29]

Falkenhayn resisted strongly this shift of emphasis. In addition to his belief that Germany's main enemy was in the west, the General Staff Chief did not believe in OberOst's strategic approach. As we have seen, the failure in the west had convinced the General Staff Chief that 'decisive' battles on the model of Königgrätz or Sedan were no longer possible. Already in mid-November, Falkenhayn had rejected reinforcing OberOst on these grounds. On 18 November, he wrote to Hindenburg that he could only send reinforcements east when

> ... a well-found hope exists that within the realm of possibility the arrival of new forces in the east could bring about a final decision. However, at the moment this hope does not exist. In the best case, we would succeed in pushing the enemy back behind the Narew and Weichsel River lines and force him to abandon Galicia. However, this does not constitute a war-winning decision [*Kriegsentscheidung*], although I cannot dispute that such a result would be of wide-ranging political significance.[30]

The General Staff Chief clearly believed that the Russian forces could easily withdraw into the expanses of Russia and avoid any 'decisive' engagement.[31] Moreover, Falkenhayn feared that any withdrawal of units from the Western Front would dangerously weaken the German position there. He wrote that a transfer of troops to the east 'would certainly be without any value if in the meantime the western enemies were successful in crushing our western forces or only even in forcing us to give up the North Sea coast.'[32] Citing similar reasons, Falkenhayn refused the Austro-Hungarian Chief-of-Staff's request for reinforcements as well.[33]

Regardless of opinion, by the end of November the German army was incapable of any further offensive action. The war to date had exhausted the German army. Between the war's outbreak and the end of the Ypres offensive on 18 November, the German army had suffered 800,000 casualties, including 116,000 dead, or nearly half the strength of its field army.[34] German soldiers on the Western Front were so weary of battle that on some occasions during the Ypres offensive officers had driven their men at pistol point out of the trenches into the attack.[35] Further, there existed no appreciable reserve of artillery munitions.[36] Until sufficient reserves could be built and the German army rested, the question of where to place the emphasis of the German war effort remained merely a staff problem.

However, the question remained just under the surface, and Falkenhayn's refusal to seek a 'decisive' victory in the east threw into question once again Falkenhayn's competence to be Chief of the General Staff. While the German army was rebuilding in December 1914, those determined to see the main German effort in the east linked up with others within the army unsatisfied with Falkenhayn's leadership to form an anti-Falkenhayn cabal. Centred on OberOst, these men were determined to see the main German effort in the east and Falkenhayn's dismissal from his position as General Staff Chief. The situation was brought to a head by the creation of four new army corps during December 1914, which would be ready for employment by

20 January. During December and early January, OberOst increased their efforts to gain the new force for employment in the east and to bring down Falkenhayn. As the new force neared its completion, the power struggle between OberOst and Falkenhayn became ever more vicious and personal.

Appealing to differing motives, the energetic officers of the OberOst worked feverishly behind the scenes in December 1914 and January 1915 to reach their goals, and Falkenhayn soon developed powerful enemies. Finding members for this *Fronde* was not difficult for the 'easterners.' By December 1914, many within the army were clearly dissatisfied with the progress of the war, and they tended to blame Falkenhayn for some of the more spectacular failures. There was a general feeling that Falkenhayn was too junior and lacked the necessary experience and authority to lead the German army.[37] For years, the post of Chief of the General Staff had been filled by men of great stature within the German army: men such as Helmuth von Moltke the Elder and his nephew and Alfred Graf von Schlieffen. These men commanded great respect, something the junior Falkenhayn lacked. These fears seemed to be highlighted by the results of Falkenhayn's first strategic decisions.

In particular, Falkenhayn's conduct of the Ypres offensive, with its terrible casualties, had shaken several important army commanders. Already during the offensive, Bavarian Kronprinz Rupprecht, commander of the Sixth Army, had clashed with the General Staff Chief, and this mistrust continued into the new year.[38] Further, the commander of the Third Army, Karl von Einem, was also dissatisfied with Falkenhayn,[39] and Kronprinz Wilhelm, who commanded the Fifth Army, went so far as to write to his father advising that Falkenhayn should be replaced by Hindenburg.[40]

In addition to the army commanders, many in the political leadership began to doubt Falkenhayn's suitability to be Chief of the General Staff, most dangerously the Chancellor. Bethmann had been won over by the officers of OberOst at their meeting on 6 December. Already shaken by what he saw as Falkenhayn's undue pessimism and perhaps fearful of Falkenhayn's bureaucratic power, Bethmann came to believe that he should be removed from his position as Chief of the General Staff and restricted to his duties as Minister of War and that the emphasis in Germany's military effort should shift to the east.[41] Bethmann was supported in this belief by the Under Secretary of State, Zimmermann, who argued that Russia was a more dangerous enemy than Britain and should be dealt with first.[42]

Upon his return to Berlin, Bethmann began agitating for Falkenhayn's replacement as Chief of the General Staff. Generaloberst Hans von Plessen, the Kaiser's Adjutant General and commander of the Imperial Headquarters, recorded in his diary on 8 December: 'At his request, I travelled to see the Chancellor. He is very apprehensive about our future. Has no trust in Falkenhayn. Wants Ludendorff instead. Falkenhayn shall be only Minister of War.'[43] Again on 10 December, Bethmann pushed the matter with the army authorities. Plessen found him arguing with Generaloberst Moritz Freiherr von Lyncker, the head of the Kaiser's Military Cabinet.[44] The Chancellor again put forward the argument that 'Falkenhayn should be limited to the post of Minister of War and Ludendorff should become Chief of the General Staff.'[45]

Indeed, by attacking the unification of two important army bureaucracies under Falkenhayn, the Chancellor was playing a shrewd game. If Bethmann had criticized Falkenhayn directly on operational matters, the soldiers of the Kaiser's headquarters would certainly have resented the interference of a civilian in strictly army business. Instead, Bethmann attacked Falkenhayn at the political level and was able to awaken in soldiers a degree of unease about Falkenhayn's position. Since at least the Franco-German War, the Ministry of War and the General Staff had gradually grown apart and had become rivals, and their independence from one another had become a matter of convention if not law.[46] (Although the Chancellor probably did not know this, Falkenhayn harboured the desire to subordinate once again the General Staff to the Ministry of War.[47]) Now, the Chancellor was arguing '. . . the great increase in authority that the unification in one person of the offices of Minister of War and Chief of the General Staff means a great danger, especially in such a difficult man as Falkenhayn.'[48]

Having won over a number of key officers to his side, including Hans von Plessen, Bethmann finally broached the subject of dismissing Falkenhayn with the Kaiser on 3 January 1915.[49] The Chancellor marshalled his arguments and claimed that '. . . the objections to the office-accumulation are all the greater, as General v. Falkenhayn possesses no great trust in public opinion, in the important political circles, and, as I know definitely, in a greater part of the army.' As a successor, Bethmann recommended Ludendorff. The Kaiser, however, would not hear of dismissing Falkenhayn. While Kronprinz Wilhelm had made him aware of the objections to the unification of the two key offices in the army, the Kaiser '. . . claimed to know nothing of the mistrust of General von Falkenhayn.' Further, Wilhelm declared that Falkenhayn still possessed his full trust and confidence and that he could never countenance the appointment of Ludendorff, a 'dubious character, eaten away by personal ambition,' in the Kaiser's words, as Chief of the General Staff.[50] It looked as if the campaign to unseat Falkenhayn and to shift German strategy to the east had failed. Indeed, Bethmann's attack on what Wilhelm saw as his 'command authority' had actually done harm to the effort to remove Falkenhayn from one of his posts. According to Plessen's diary, the Kaiser had already decided to name Generalleutnant Adolph Wild von Hohenborn Minister of War and restrict Falkenhayn to his post of General Staff Chief.[51] After his meeting with Bethmann, Wilhelm determined to keep Falkenhayn in both his posts.

Despite the setback, the campaign against Falkenhayn was not yet dead. To co-ordinate their anti-Falkenhayn campaign, OberOst employed an energetic younger officer, Major Hans von Haeften, to work behind the scenes, and Haeften was able to keep the campaign alive even after the Kaiser's initial command. In addition to being an intelligence officer in OberOst, Haeften was also the personal adjutant to Helmuth von Moltke. His positions gave him access to the highest levels of the Reich's government and army and allowed him to travel relatively freely from front to front. Haeften was fanatically wedded to the concept of an eastern offensive and, like many in OberOst, carried a great deal of personal animosity towards Falkenhayn.[52] From 5 to 8 January, he travelled to the armies of the Western Front to brief them on the situation on the Eastern Front and to organize their opposition to Falkenhayn. Haeften was able to convince the leaders of the *Westheer*, particularly Kronprinz Rupprecht and Kronprinz Wilhelm, that the Eastern Front should be reinforced as soon as possible. After Haeften's briefing, these leaders acknowledged that '. . . it is obvious that the new corps should not be employed in the west, but rather in the east,' and the Sixth Army even put forward the opinion that they could make at least one additional corps available for service in the east.[53]

Also in early January, Haeften was able to bring Moltke into the fray against Falkenhayn. Now posted to Berlin with little meaningful to occupy his time, the former General Staff Chief was anxious to regain influence within the army.[54] Like Bethmann, Moltke decided to attack Falkenhayn on the political level. On 8 January 1915, he wrote to the Chancellor, providing him with much-needed military support:

There is no question . . . that the unification of the offices of Chief of the General Staff and Minister of War in one hand is judged as unfavourable by a wide circle of the nation. I personally hold the unification for unde-sirable. The General Staff and the Ministry of War are two authorities, which must form a balance to one another if they are to work in a useful way. Additionally, the Minister of War belongs in Berlin at the centre of his effectiveness. The unification of both offices is personally comfortable for the holder; when he meets opposition, he can decide dictatorially. This has recently been demonstrated in the question of the formation of the new corps. As I have heard, the Ministry of War, and Falkenhayn as Minister of War, was against their formation and for a reinforcement of our *Westheer*, while General v.Falkenhayn the Chief of the General Staff ordered their formation. In this case, I would have followed the Ministry of War's opinion.[55]

Moltke put forward Generaloberst Karl von Bülow to be Falkenhayn's successor, as he believed Ludendorff to be too young for the post. The fact that Moltke had held the position of Chief of the General Staff at once gave his arguments greater force and allowed him to go further in his criticisms of Falkenhayn. He was able to suggest that Falkenhayn's western strategy was incorrect and that Russia should first be defeated before the situation in the west was tackled.

Despite the intrigues against him, Falkenhayn stood firm in his strategic beliefs and, in keeping with the strategy he outlined to the Chancellor in November, the General Staff Chief declared in January 1915, 'the war will be decided here in the west at Calais.'[56] Falkenhayn continued to believe that conditions did not allow for a 'decisive' victory. Therefore, he still felt that the only way to bring the war to an end was through some sort of separate peace with one of Germany's enemies. He was under no illusions about what could be accomplished with only four and a half corps. Unlike OberOst, Falkenhayn was convinced that '. . . the nine divisions alone . . . would not lead to a decision in either the west or the east.'[57] However, the opposition to his western strategy and the weakness of Austria-Hungary made him pause to consider a *limited* eastern offensive. On 2 January, he now told Franz Conrad von Hötzendorf, the Austro-Hungarian Chief of Staff, that he would decide within three weeks whether or not he would deploy his new army corps in the east.[58]

Also in early January, the frustrated General Staff Chief finally struck back at his tormentors in an effort to silence his most violent critics. First, a number of German units, formed with a number of Austro-Hungarian units into the so-called *Südarmee*, were sent to the Austro-Hungarian section of the Eastern Front from OberOst as reinforcements.[59] Although he did not believe this force would accomplish much, it was intended to end his ally's cries for reinforcement and provide the Austrians with assistance for their forthcoming offensive in the Carpathians. Second, in an attempt to quell OberOst's insubordination once and for all, Falkenhayn ordered the separation of the Hindenburg-Ludendorff team. On 8 January 1915, Ludendorff was ordered to report to General Alexander von Linsingen's *Südarmee* as Chief-of-Staff. Further, on 11 January, the General Staff Chief travelled to Posen to meet Hindenburg and attempt to come to some form of understanding with OberOst.[60]

However, Hindenburg was in no mood to compromise with Falkenhayn after the latter had just transferred his Chief-of-Staff, and

Falkenhayn's attempt to sideline his most vocal critic – Ludendorff – was met with hefty opposition, which brought the power struggle between OberOst and Falkenhayn to a head. Ludendorff's first reaction to this transfer was to request to be relieved of his duties as Chief-of-Staff and given a division instead, and he immediately wrote to the Military Cabinet. However, at Hindenburg's request, Ludendorff withdrew this request.[61] Now Hindenburg took up the fight for his former Chief-of-Staff. At his meeting with Falkenhayn, Hindenburg demanded Ludendorff's return and a shift of strategy to the east. When Falkenhayn refused, Hindenburg informed him that the army no longer had confidence in him and the Field Marshal advised that he resign immediately. Additionally, Hindenburg informed Falkenhayn he had written to the Kaiser saying exactly the same thing. All Falkenhayn's attempts to mollify the Field Marshal and to get him to refrain from sending his letter were in vain.[62]

True to his word, in rapid succession, Hindenburg wrote first to the head of the Kaiser's Military Cabinet, Lyncker, and then to the Kaiser himself. The Field Marshal called for Falkenhayn's replacement, Ludendorff's return to OberOst, and the employment of the new corps in the east. Haeften recorded Hindenburg's words in his diary: Hindenburg felt that it was his duty as the oldest general in the army to inform the Kaiser that 'with a few strokes of the pen, [he] could bring calm, security, and trust to the nation again through the reinstatement of Moltke to his previous position as Chief of the General Staff, through the return of Ludendorff to his position as Chief-of-Staff in Posen, and through the employment of the new corps in the east.' He further declared that he could no longer work with Falkenhayn and gave the Kaiser an ultimatum – either Falkenhayn was dismissed or he would resign.[63]

Like Bethmann's intervention earlier in the month, Hindenburg's *démarche* only enraged the touchy Kaiser. To Wilhelm, Hindenburg's letter smacked of insubordination and even of a threat to the monarchy. The Kaiser and his headquarters maintained that a German field marshal could not resign in the face of the enemy; he could only be dismissed by his Kaiser.[64] Further, the Kaiser was very sensitive to Hindenburg's growing popularity with the German public, and in Hindenburg's letter was an implied threat to appeal to public opinion if the Kaiser did not do as Hindenburg desired.[65] The angry Wilhelm compared Hindenburg with Wallenstein, and his first response was to order Hindenburg's dismissal and court martial.[66] With difficulty, his staff dissuaded him from such a course. Moreover, Bethmann intervened once again and informed the Kaiser that he 'could no longer bear responsibility for the political situation if the Kaiser dismissed Hindenburg.'[67]

Hindenburg's letter brought forth a deluge of support. Once again, Haeften was able to bring Moltke into the fray. Moltke first wrote to Hindenburg encouraging him to stand fast in the face of the Kaiser's anger, promising that 'I stand or fall with you.'[68] Moltke then wrote the Kaiser two letters in which he used words as strong as Hindenburg's: 'General v. Falkenhayn is, in my firm opinion, neither in his character nor in qualifications suitable to be Your Majesty's principal advisor in military affairs in these difficult times. – His person constitutes a serious danger to the Fatherland.' Moltke went on to say that a western strategy, as advocated by Falkenhayn, could only lead to minor successes and that only an eastern strategy could result in any meaningful victory. Like Hindenburg, Moltke threatened resignation if Falkenhayn were not replaced.[69]

At the same time Moltke was writing to support Hindenburg, Haeften and OberOst were able to call upon a wide range of others, including many in the Imperial family. First, Kronprinz Wilhelm, who had spoken against Falkenhayn for some time, was consulted when Hindenburg's letter arrived. According to Plessen, although the Kronprinz sympathized with the Kaiser's anger, he 'blew the same horn as Hindenburg.'[70] A visit by another of the OberOst conspiracy, Elard von Oldenburg-Januschau, to Fifth Army headquarters on 16 January resulted in an additional letter of support for Hindenburg from the Kronprinz.[71] Further, another of the Kaiser's sons who had served on the staff of OberOst, Prince Joachim, paved the way for Haeften to meet Kaiserin Augusta Victoria on 18 January. At their meeting, Haeften informed the Kaiserin of the contents of Hindenburg's letter to the Kaiser and of the danger he believed Falkenhayn represented to Germany. The Kaiserin sent Haeften back to Berlin carrying a letter from her to her husband, in which she urged the Kaiser to acquiesce to Hindenburg's demands.[72]

While support for Hindenburg was coming in from all around the Reich, the Kaiser's staff were taking steps to resolve the leadership crisis. Wilhelm had been greatly taken aback by the actions of his subordinates. Yet at the same time, as offended as he was, he had to take seriously their opinions, and from this finally came a compromise that brought order once again to the German army. On 15 January, the Kaiser discussed the matter with his two closest aides, Plessen and Lyncker. Lyncker, who was Falkenhayn's firmest supporter, advised the Kaiser to defuse the situation by sending Hindenburg a 'soothing letter' and maintained that 'there existed no basis for relieving [Falkenhayn] of his position.' The three men determined, however, that Falkenhayn should give up his post of Minister of War and confine himself to the duties of Chief of the General Staff. On 16 January, the Kaiser met Falkenhayn alone and informed him of this. Falkenhayn's favourite candidate, Adolph Wild von Hohenborn, was named as his replacement. Further, the Kaiser and his General Staff Chief determined that three of the four reserve corps would be employed in the east and that these would be reinforced by a corps from the west. Almost as an afterthought, Ludendorff was transferred back to OberOst.[73]

This compromise seemed to defuse the situation. Yet, the perceived insubordination of his subordinates and the intervention of his family in the Kaiser's 'command authority' had angered Wilhelm greatly. Although he was dissuaded by his aides from cashiering Hindenburg, Wilhelm let his disfavour be known to the Field Marshal by issuing a Cabinet Order forbidding Hindenburg to resign even when Falkenhayn remained as Chief of the General Staff.[74] Additionally, he wrote a scathing letter to Moltke threatening him with dismissal, although at the last minute he ordered Plessen to ask Moltke not to open the letter.[75]

It was Haeften, however, who bore the brunt of Wilhelm's wrath. Haeften arrived in Imperial Headquarters carrying the Kaiserin's letter on 20 January, after the issue had been settled. Wilhelm complained that 'now the ladies room becomes involved in this issue also. The behaviour of Field Marshal v.Hindenburg is completely unheard of.'[76] The Kaiser ordered Haeften to submit to a questionnaire, the results of which would determine whether or not a court-martial was warranted. However, before the Kaiser could fully vent his rage, Plessen intervened and had Haeften transferred to an out-of-the-way position in Cologne.[77]

Both sides were able to claim victory in the 'leadership crisis.' On paper, at least, OberOst seemed to win most of their goals. Falkenhayn no longer held two high-level posts, Ludendorff was back again with OberOst, and four army corps were gained as reinforcement for the Eastern Front. Finally, OberOst could go ahead with their much anticipated offensive as soon as the reinforcements arrived.

However, their victory was at a great cost. Falkenhayn, who seemed to have lost a great deal, in fact had emerged from the crisis seemingly strengthened in his position. He retained the most important of his posts, Chief of the General Staff, and with it the strategic direction of the war. He had even been promoted to General der Infanterie. Further, his candidate, Wild von Hohenborn, was put into the position of Minister of War and was to remain in the headquarters with Falkenhayn rather than return to Berlin. Perhaps most importantly, however, Falkenhayn retained the favour of his Kaiser.[78] Throughout the crisis, Wilhelm had stood by his Chief of the General Staff. The conduct of the anti-Falkenhayn cabal had clearly filled him with distaste, and often angered him greatly. While he had never liked Ludendorff (a 'dubious character, eaten away by ambition'), he formed a very poor opinion of Hindenburg as well. It was only the vigorous intervention of his staff that prevented the Kaiser from cashiering the insubordinate Hindenburg. In his final tirade, Wilhelm had informed Haeften that Hindenburg '. . . sees mere figments of his imagination,' and that a close aide had found the Field Marshal 'a completely worn out, frail old man.'[79] Finally, the results of OberOsts's 'Winter Battle' (7 to 21 February) vindicated Falkenhayn. After some initial successes, the German forces were forced to give up their gains in the face of stiff Russian counter-attacks and the terrible eastern winter weather. While the Russians suffered high losses, so too did the Germans.[80]

*   *   *

The 'leadership crisis' that beset the German army in late 1914–early 1915 was perhaps unique in modern warfare. Hindenburg's challenge to Kaiser Wilhelm in January 1915 was certainly, in the words of the well-known historian Gerhard Ritter, 'unprecedented in Prussian military history.'[81] Never before had a German officer challenged his superior officer and his Kaiser in such a manner. However, never before had a German officer enjoyed so much popular support as did Hindenburg in early 1915, and he was prepared to appeal to this mass support to get his way if need be. This fact changed the relationship between the Kaiser and his generals fundamentally. For the rest of the war, Wilhelm knew that he risked becoming redundant (a 'shadow Kaiser') if ever a figure as popular as Hindenburg were to come to the High Command.

However, this unique command situation without a doubt fitted the unique military situation that Germany found herself in. While previous authors have largely seen this crisis in political terms, it in fact represents the playing out of an important split in German military thought which had begun even before the war's outbreak.[82] The failure of Germany's initial plans to win the war in a few rapid, decisive battles represented the failure of the 'traditional' German approach to warfare and left Germany in a precarious strategic position. Germany now found herself surrounded by enemies who possessed far greater resources, both in terms of manpower and material. Additionally, mass armies armed with rapid-fire weapons and artillery created an operational difficulty that further complicated the strategic picture.[83]

To Falkenhayn, these challenges called for a new way of thinking about warfare. The General Staff Chief believed that Germany did not have the resources necessary to win the war outright. Therefore, he abandoned the traditional German army approach of attempting to deal its enemy an annihilating blow and concentrated instead on trying to find a political solution to the war. In Falkenhayn's approach the military still played a role, yet it was subordinate to the political leadership. He envisioned limited military successes leading to political success. However, peace was not to be dictated to a prostrate foe and would as a consequence have to be moderate.

This approach, a 'strategy of attrition' as the military historian Hans Delbrück would term it, was rejected completely by the officers of OberOst.[84] These men remained wedded to the traditional German approach to warfare. Unlike Falkenhayn who did not believe a 'decisive' victory was possible after November 1914, OberOst still maintained that battles along the lines of a Königgrätz or a Sedan could be fought. Following a 'strategy of annihilation,' they hoped to win the war militarily before concluding peace, and they bent all their efforts toward accomplishing this strategy.

In a very real sense, the Chancellor was stuck in the middle of these two opposing approaches. Although Falkenhayn's approach gave the Reich's chief political leader more control over the outcome of the war, Bethmann shied away from such responsibility. While coming to an agreement with Russia was more difficult than Falkenhayn imagined, the Chancellor's attempts to separate Russia from the Entente in late 1914 were half-hearted at best. Instead, he pinned his hopes on OberOst and their promised military solution to Germany's strategic dilemma.[85]

The real outcome of the leadership crisis of late 1914–early 1915 was an unworkable command structure. Although Falkenhayn seemed to emerge victorious from the crisis, he was never able to implement his strategic approach properly. Germany clearly faced an extremely difficult strategic situation by November 1914. Falkenhayn's approach of linking the military with the political offered some chance for Germany to survive the war. However, the leadership crisis ensured that this collaboration would never come about. For his approach to work, there would have to be close co-operation between the Reich's military and political leadership, and his poor relations with Bethmann ensured that this did not occur. While Falkenhayn concentrated on achieving limited military success, and often succeeded, Bethmann and the Foreign Office did little to exploit these gains.[86] Further, OberOst still remained a potent force, and after two years of hard fighting under Falkenhayn's strategic approach, he was relieved of his position by his bitter rivals, Hindenburg and Ludendorff. In the end, Falkenhayn must truly have come to regret his words from the war's beginning: 'Even if we go under as a result of this [war], it was beautiful.'[87]

Notes

1 See also, Holger Afflerbach, *Falkenhayn: Politisches Denken und Handeln im Kaiserreich* (Munich: Oldenburg Verlag, 1996) pp.179–189.

2 On the chaos of the OHL after the Marne, see Friedrich Mewes to Reichsarchiv, 7 December 1920, BA/MA, W10/51063; and Wilhelm

Groener, *Lebenserinnerungen* (ed. Friedrich Frhr. Hiller von Gaertringen) (Göttingen: Vandenhoeck & Ruprecht, 1957) pp.188 ff.

3 Quoted in Hans von Zwehl, *Erich von Falkenhayn: Eine biographische Studie* (Berlin: ES Mittler, 1926) p.66.

4 Zwehl, *Falkenhayn*, p.71.

5 On Falkenhayn's early career, see Afflerbach, *Falkenhayn*, pp.9–190, passim.

6 Hermann Ritter Mertz von Quirnheim to Reichsarchiv, 4 January 1934, Bundesarchiv/Militärarchiv (BA/MA), W10/51523.

7 These are recorded in the diary of the Bavarian military plenipotentiary at the OHL, Karl Ritter von Wenninger, printed in Bernd F. Schulte, 'Neue Dokumente zu Kriegsausbruch und Kriegsverlauf 1914,' *Militärgeschichtliche Mitteilungen* 1/79 pp.123–185.

8 Although Falkenhayn took up the duties of Chief of the General Staff on 14 September, he was not officially appointed to the post until 3 November 1914.

9 Erich von Falkenhayn, *Die Oberste Heeresleitung in ihren wichtigsten Entschließungen* (Berlin: ES Mittler, 1920) p.9. Wenninger wrote to his wife on 10 October 1914 praising the new Chief's efforts, 'we all lost our heads a bit – with one exception – Falkenhayn. A practical man, a Gneisenau, who leads us from retreat to victory,' printed in Schulte, 'Neue Dokumente,' p.177.

10 Friedrich Mewes to Reichsarchiv, 7 December 1920, BA/MA, W10/51063.

11 Reichsarchiv, *Der Weltkrieg* Bd.V: *Der Herbst-Feldzug 1914 (I)* (Berlin: ES Mittler, 1929), p.21.

12 For details of the so-called 'race to the sea', see ibid., pp.69–118.

13 The advent of position warfare was greeted by shock among many German officers, Gerhard Tappen, the OHL's operations officer, recorded in his diary that the trenches across the whole front constituted a 'completely new form of warfare.' Gerhard Tappen, 'Kriegstagebuch,' 26 September 1914, BA/MA, Tappen Nachlass (N56)/1.

14 The operations to reduce the French forts at Camp des Romains are a good example of the German army's ability to fight 'position warfare' on a limited scale. See Reichsarchiv, *Von Nancy bis zum Camp des Romains, 1914 (Schlachten des Weltkrieges* BD.6) (Berlin: Stalling, 1925). For pre-war ideas about breakthrough operations, see Brückner, 'Der Durchbruchsangriff vor dem Weltkriege in Anwendung und Theorie,' *Militärwissenschaftliche Rundschau* Jg.3 H.5 (1938) pp.586–601.

15 Between 10 and 18 November, the armies leading the assault at Ypres (Fourth and Sixth suffered 23,500 casualties. Reichsarchiv, *Der Weltkrieg* BD.VI: *Der Herst-Feldzug 1914 (II)* (Berlin: ES Mittler, 1929) p.25.

16 Falkenhayn reached this decision against the advice of the General Staff Chiefs of Fourth and Sixth Armies. Konrad Krafft von Dellmensingen to

Reichsarchiv, 3 November 1926, BA/MA, W10/55176; and 'Die deutsche Oberste Heeresleitung im Westen von 2.–28. November 1914,' unpublished manuscript prepared by the Reichsarchiv in BA/MA, W10/51159, p.15. For the most recent analysis of the Ypres campaign (18 October to 18 November), see Karl Unruh, *Langemarck: Legende und Wircklichkeit* (Koblenz: Bernard & Graefe, 1986).

17 The German regulations instructed infantry to advance '. . . cost what it may.' Kriegsministerium, *Exerzier-Reglement für die Infanterie* (Berlin: ES Mittler, 1906) para.265. On the 'cult of the offensive,' see Jack Snyder, *The Ideology of the Offensive: Military Decision-Making and the Disasters of 1914* (Ithaca, NY: Cornell University Press, 1984).

18 See Tappen, 'Kriegstagebuch,' 26 September 1914; Plessen, 'Tagebuch,' 9 November 1914.

19 *Der Weltkrieg* VI, p.437. See also Afflerbach, *Falkenhayn*, p.21 f.

20 Adolph Wild von Hohenborn to his wife, 10 November 1914, BA/MA, Wild Nachlass (N44)4.

21 Jehuda L. Wallach, *The Dogma of the Battle of Annihilation: The Theories of Clausewitz and Schlieffen and Their Impact on the German Conduct of Two World Wars* (Westport, CT: Greenwood Press, 1986).

22 Bethmann to Zimmermann, 19 November 1914, Public Record Office, Kew, German Foreign Ministry Files (GFM) 34/2156 (*Weltkrieg geh*, Bd.2). Also printed in Paul R. Sweet, 'Leaders and Policies: Germany in the Winter of 1914–1915,' *Journal of Central European Affairs*, Vol.XVI Nr.3 (1956) p.232.

23 For details of OberOst's Lodz offensive (11 to 25 November), *Der Weltkrieg* VI, pp.104–226.

24 Afflerbach, *Falkenhayn*, pp.198–210

25 Quoted in Zwehl, *Falkenhayn*, p.211.

26 On 1 November 1914, the command of Eighth Army was redesignated '*Oberbefehlshaber über die gesamten Streitkräfte im Osten des Reiches*,' or 'Supreme Commander, German Forces, Eastern Empire,' OberOst for short. Under the command of Hindenburg were Eighth and Ninth Armies and various Landwehr and fortress units. *Der Weltkrieg* VI, p.37 f.

27 Paul von Hindenburg, *Out of My Life* (London: Cassell and Company, 1920) p.132.

28 *Der Weltkrieg* VI, p.415 f.

29 Even some of the officers of his own staff felt this way. See Wild's memorandum of late December 1915 recommending the employment of the four new corps in the east in BA/MA, W10/51151.

30 Falkenhayn to Hindenburg, 18 November 1914, quoted in *Der Weltkrieg* VI, p.95 f.

31 Falkenhayn, *Oberste Heeresleitung*, p.48.

32 Falkenhayn to Hindenburg, 18 November 1914, quoted in *Der Weltkrieg* VI, p.96.

33 Falkenhayn to Conrad, 18 November 1914, quoted in ibid., p.95.
34 Holger Herwig, *The First World War: Germany and Austria 1914–1918* (London: Arnold, 1997) p.119; Richard Bessel, *Germany After the First World War* (Oxford: Clarendon Press, 1993) p.6.
35 Mertz to Reichsarchiv, 24 January 1924, BA/MA, W10/51177.
36 On 12 November, the First General Staff Officer (Ia) of the Operations Section of the OHL recorded in his diary that there existed artillery ammunition for only six more days of fighting. Major von Redern, 'Tagebuch,' 12 November 1914, BA/MA, W10/50676.
37 See Groener, *Lebenerinnerungen*, p.205 f; Josef Stürgkh, *Im deutschen Grossen Hauptquartier* (Leipzig: Paul List, 1927) pp.81 ff.
38 Falkenhayn, not satisfied with the progress being made by Sixth Army, created a new army group outside of Rupprecht's command to continue the offensive. Rupprecht was so offended that he considered appealing Falkenhayn's decision directly with the Kaiser. Rupprecht, *Mein Kriegstagebuch* Bd.I (ed. Eugen von Frauenholz) (Berlin: ES Mittler, 1929) pp.232 ff.
39 Karl von Einem, 'Kriegstagebuch,' BA/MA, N324/12. A much edited version of Einem's diary was published after the war as *Ein Armeeführer erlebt den Weltkrieg* (ed. Junius Alter) (Leipzig: v.Hase and Koehler, 1938).
40 Paul Herre, *Kronprinz Wilhelm: Seine Rolle in der Deutschen Polittik* (Munich: C.H. Beck, 1954) p.55 f.
41 Falkenhayn did indeed have a tendency to interfere in areas more properly left to the Reich's political leadership. Karl-Heinz Janßen, Der Kanzler und der General: Die Führungskrise um Bethmann Hollweg und Falkenhayn (1914–1916) (Göttingen: Musterschmidt-Verlag, 1967) pp.21 ff.; Zwehl, *Falkenhayn*, p.166 f; Sweet, 'Leaders and Policies,' p.235.
42 Zimmermann to Bethmann, 27 November 1914, reprinted in Sweet, 'Leaders and Policies,' pp. 236–239. Zimmermann's memorandum was in response to Bethmann's letter of 19 November outlining Falkenhayn's strategic ideas. On Zimmermann's eastern ideas, see also Gerhard Ritter, *The Sword and the Scepter: The Problem of Militarism in Germany* Vol.III: *The Tragedy of Statesmanship – Bethmann Hollweg as War Chancellor (1914–1917)* (trans. Heinz Norden) (Coral Gables, FL: University of Miami Press, 1972) pp.45–48.
43 Hans von Plessen, 'Tagebuch,' 8 December 1914, BA/MA, W10/51063.
44 The Military Cabinet was responsible for officer assignments. See Rudolf Schmidt-Bückeburg, *Das Militäarkabinett der preußischen Könige und deutschen Kaiser* (Berlin: ES Mittler, 1933).
45 Plessen, 'Tagebuch,' 10 December 1914. Both Lyncker and Plessen defended Falkenhayn at this stage. Plessen gave him the credit for rebuilding the army, a task which he believed was accomplished so effi-

ciently because Falkenhayn was at once Minister of War and Chief of the General Staff.

46 On the tensions between the army's bureaucracies, see Heinrich Otto Meisner, *Der Kriegsminister 1814–1914* (Berlin: Hermann Reinshagen Verlag, 1940) passim; and Gordon Craig, *Politics of the Prussian Army* (New York: Oxford University Press, 1956) pp.219–299, passim.

47 Even before the war, Falkenhayn had expressed this desire and in October, he is reported to have said that one of the war's lessons was the necessity of the General Staff being subordinated to the Ministry of War. Falkenhayn said that this was one of the war's lessons. Zwehl, *Falkenhayn*, p.53 f.; Ernst von Wrisberg, *Heer und Heimat 1914–1918* (Leipzig: KF Koehler, 1921) p.21.

48 Quoted in Hans von Haeften's 'Tagebuch,' reprinted in Ekkehart P. Guth, 'Der Gegensatz zwischen dem Oberbefehlshaber Ost und dem Chef des Generalstabes des Feldherres: Die Rolle des Majors v.Haeften im Spannungsfeld zwischen Hindenburg, Ludendorff and Falkenhayn,' *Militärgeschichtliche Mitteilungen* 1/84, p.89.

49 As his diary clearly demonstrates, Plessen's opinion of Falkenhayn had varied considerably over time. Plessen at first did not like Falkenhayn, but then his handling of the army after the Marne won Plessen's grudging respect. However, the refusal to shift his focus to the east turned Plessen against Falkenhayn. By the end of December, he was supporting the Chancellor and OberOst. Plessen, 'Tagebuch,' 30 December 1914.

50 Bethmann to the Under State-Secretary of the Reich Chancellery, Arnold Wahnschaffe, 7 January 1915, quoted in Afflerbach, *Falkenhayn*, p.222 f.

51 Plessen, 'Tagebuch,' 2 January 1915.

52 See Guth, 'Gegensatz,' pp.75–111, passim, Max Hoffmann, OberOst's Ia, spoke of Falkenhayn as the 'evil angel of the Fatherland.' See his diary entry for 1 December 1914, in Max Hoffmann, *War Diaries and Other Papers* (tr. Eric Sutton) (London: Martin Secker, 1929) p.51. Also Ludendorff openly spoke of his hatred for Falkenhayn. See his letter to Moltke, 2 January 1915, printed in Egmont Zechlin, 'Ludendorff in Jahre 1915. Unveröffentlichte Briefe,' *Historische Zeitschrift* Bd.211 (1970) pp.324 ff.

53 Haeften, 'Tagebuch,' 8 January 1915, in ibid., p.93.

54 See Annika Mombauer, *Helmuth von Moltke and the Origins of the First World War* (Cambridge: Cambridge University Press, 2001).

55 Moltke to Bethmann, 8 January 1915, printed in Helmuth von Moltke, *Erinnerungen Briefe Dokumente, 1877–1916* (ed. Eliza von Moltke) Stuttgart: Der Kommende Tag, 1922) p.395 f.

56 Quoted in Janßen, *Der Kanzler und der General*, p.41.

57 Falkenhayn, *Oberste Heeresleitung*, p.36.

58 Tappen, 'Kriegstagebuch,' 2 January 1915; Janßen, *Der Kanzler und der General*, p.66; Afflerbach, *Falkenhayn*, p.231.

59 Reichsarchiv, *Der Weltkrieg* Bd.VII: *Die Operationen des Jahres 1915: Ereignisse im Winter und Frühjahr* (Berlin: ES Mittler, 1931) pp.10 ff.

60 Ibid., p.13 f; Tappen, 'Kriegstagebuch,' 12 January 1915.

61 Ludendorff to Moltke, 9 January 1915, in Zechlin, 'Ludendorff in Jahre 1915,' pp. 326 ff; Erich Ludendorff, *Meine Kriegserinnerungen* (Berlin: ES Mittler, 1919) p.89 f.

62 Afflerbach, *Falkenhayn*, p.226; Haeften, 'Tagebuch,' 12 January 1915, in Guth, 'Gegenstaz,' p.96 f.

63 Haeften, 'Tagebuch,' 12 January 1915, in Guth, 'Gegensatz,' pp.96 ff.

64 Plessen, 'Tagebuch,' 14 to 16 January 1915.

65 Janßen, *Der Kanzler und der General*, p.76.

66 Axel Freiherr Varnbüler von und zu Hemmingen to Carl von Weizsäcker, 29 May 1916, published in Janßen, *Der Kanzler und der General*, p.291 f.

67 Bethmann to Lyncker, 14 January 1915, in ibid., p.79.

68 Moltke to Hindenburg, 14 January 1915, printed in Moltke, *Erinnerungen*, p.409 f. Cf. Haeften, 'Tagebuch,' 17 January 1915, in Guth, 'Gegensatz,' p.99.

69 Moltke to Wilhelm, 15 and 17 January 1915, printed in Moltke, *Erinnerungen*, pp. 410–416.

70 Plessen, 'Tagebuch,' 14 January 1915.

71 Janßen, *Der Kanzler und der General*, p.77; Haeften, 'Tagebuch,' 16 January 1915, in Guth, 'Gegensatz,' p.99.

72 Haeften, 'Tagebuch,' 18 January 1915, in Guth, 'Gegensatz,' p.101 f.

73 Plessen, 'Tagebuch,' 15 and 16 January 1915; Afflerbach, *Falkenhayn*, p.227 f.

74 This was delivered to OberOst by Lyncker's deputy, Ulrich Freiherr von Marshall, on 18 January. Janßen, *Der Kanzler und der General*, p.79; Haeften, 'Tagebuch,' 18 January 1915, in Guth, 'Gegensatz,' p.100 f.

75 Plessen, 'Tagebuch,' 23 and 24 January 1915.

76 Quoted in Afflerbach, *Falkenhayn*, p.229.

77 Plessen, 'Tagebuch,' 21 January 1916; Guth, 'Gegensatz,' pp.105–107; Ritter, *Sword and the Scepter* III, p.55 f.

78 See Holger Afflerbach, 'Wilhelm II as Supreme Warlord in the First World War', *War in History* 5(4) (1998) pp.427–449.

79 Quoted in Afflerbach, *Falkenhayn*, p.230.

80 On the 'Winter Battle', see *Der Weltkrieg* VII, pp.260 ff; Herwig, *The First World War*, pp.135 ff.

81 Ritter, *Sword and the Scepter* III, p.52.

82 Cf. Janßen, *Der Kanzler und de General*; Ritter, *Sword and the Scepter* III: and Heinz Kraft, *Staatsräson und Kriegführung im kaiserlichen Deutschland 1914–1916* (Göttingen: Muster-Schmidt Verlag, 1980).

83 On the split within German strategic thought before 1914 and Falkenhayn's strategic and operational ideas throughout the war, see Robert T. Foley, 'Attrition: Its Theory and Application in German

Strategy, 1880–1916,' unpublished PhD thesis, University of London, 1999.

84 Hans Delbrück, 'Falkenhayn und Ludendorff,' *Preußische Jahrbücher* Bd.180 (1920) pp.249–281.

85 Bethmann was aware, however, of the risks of supporting OberOst. He said, 'with Falkenhayn, we risk losing the war strategically; with Ludendorff politically.' Quoted in Janßen, *Der Kanzler und der General*, p.253.

86 On Bethmann's diplomatic initiatives, see Rudolph Stadelmann, 'Die Freidensversuche im ersten Jahre des Weltkrieges, *Historische Zeitschrift* Bd.156 (1937); L.L. Farrar, *Divide and Conquer: German Efforts To Conclude a Separate Peace, 1914–1918* (New York: Columbia University Press, 1978) pp.13–34.

87 Falkenhayn to Bethmann, 4 August 1914, quoted in Herwig, *The First World War*, p.37.

Part Three

America at War

Chapter 7

'Black Jack' Pershing:
The American Proconsul in Europe

David Woodward

It was not a difficult choice. John J. Pershing was the man to build an army and lead it in the land war in Europe. Shortly after the United States declared war on Germany in April 1917, President Woodrow Wilson, on the recommendation of Secretary of War Newton D. Baker, selected Pershing to command the first contingent of American forces shipped to Europe, a skeleton force which grew to be the largest American force ever assembled, some 2,000,000 men.

A country boy from tiny Laclede, Missouri, Pershing entered West Point shortly after his twenty-second birthday. Having taught at a country school for three years, he was an unusually mature plebe and his leadership abilities outshone his academic achievements. Chosen president of his class, he graduated thirtieth out of seventy-seven. A fine horseman, he chose the cavalry, serving on the frontier in the Apache wars and during the final campaign against the Sioux. He subsequently fought in the Spanish-American War, had a tour of duty in the Philippines, and served as an observer in the Russo-Japanese War. When the First World War erupted he was stationed in the United States where in 1915 an unimaginable personal tragedy occurred: his beloved wife Frankie and their three daughters suffocated in a fire at the Presidio in San Francisco. His only son survived.

The European war initially seemed very remote to Pershing. Stationed in El Paso, the troubled Mexican-American border dominated his thoughts. In 1916–1917, he led the army's last great cavalry campaign, the Punitive Expedition, into northern Mexico. Although dwarfed by the clash of arms in Europe, this military venture represented the US Army's first real experience with industrialized warfare. Pershing employed airplanes, radios, trucks, and machine guns in his unsuccessful effort to capture the Mexican bandit Francisco (Pancho) Villa. Pershing also gained valuable experience in commanding a force which grew to almost 11,000 men. None of his contemporaries had ever commanded a force as large.[1]

Pershing, a Republican, needed to prove his loyalty to President Wilson if he hoped to command US forces in Europe. Rumours circulated that he resented the tight restrictions which Washington had placed upon the deployment of his forces in Mexico. In a letter to Hugh L. Scott, the Chief of the General Staff, Pershing denied these accusations and insisted that he sympathized with Wilson's Mexican policy which he described as being 'prompted by the very highest of motives.' He asked Scott to assure Baker and Wilson that they could count on him 'to the last extremity, both as to word and deed, for loyalty and fidelity, in any task that may be given me to perform.'[2] After Wilson delivered his war message to Congress, Pershing corresponded directly with his Commander-in-Chief. His 'soul-stirring patriotic address,' Pershing informed Wilson, had aroused 'in the breast of every soldier feelings of the deepest admiration for their leader.'[3] Pershing's professed loyalty to Wilson gave him a decisive edge over his only real rival for the command. General Leonard Wood, a former Chief of the General Staff, who had been openly critical of Wilson's leadership.

Fifty-seven years old when he got the command, Pershing – broad-shouldered, robust, and ram-rod straight – projected a powerful physical presence. His tailored uniforms (he never put anything in his pockets) fitted him perfectly. 'He was the perfect picture of the indomitable high commander,' writes S. L. A. Marshall, 'tailor-made for monuments.'[4] 'Pershing was all soldier – right-side-up – upside down, inside, outside, dead or alive – every day in the week and twice on Sunday,'[5] was the equally apt opinion of a member of the American Expeditionary Force (AEF).

Aloof, stubborn, single-minded, and impersonal, he inspired confidence rather than affection. His men would never call him 'Papa'. His nickname was 'Black Jack,' a derisive reference to his command of African-American troops on the frontier, given him by cadets who saw him as a fierce taskmaster when he taught tactics at West Point. The heavy responsibilities of higher command have made many a general a lonely and remote individual. Perhaps no American officer was better able to cope with this reality than Pershing. James G. Harbord, who served as his Chief-of-Staff in France and probably came closest to being a friend, makes this revealing comment: 'No intimate has ever captured his soul. . . . He has been militantly self-sufficient since he donned his Corporal's stripes in 1883.'[6]

No other First World War Commander-in-Chief held his position from the beginning of his country's participation in the war until the Armistice; and no Commander-in-Chief enjoyed greater control over his forces. 'Pershing was to be no less of an autocrat in France,' is the verdict of an early biographer, Frederick Palmer, 'than the commander of a western post under Indian attack in the old army in the west. He was to build his own kingdom in France as an absolute monarch.'[7] Although Pershing meticulously documented the contributions of the men and units under his command in *My Experiences in the World War*,[8] he failed to show the same appreciation for the contributions, sacrifices, and frustrations of those working beyond his sphere of control in France. The able Chief of the General Staff in the War department in 1918, Peyton C. March, who played a vital role in increasing the flow of US troops to France, thought that a more appropriate title for Pershing's account would have been *Alone in France*.[9]

No democracy has ever given a field commander such myriad responsibilities; unlike Allied generals such as Sir Douglas Haig, Joseph Joffre, and Robert Nivelle, Pershing also enjoyed extraordinary support from his political superiors. Baker is reputed to have told him: 'I will give you only two orders – one to go to France and the other to come home. In the meantime your authority in France will be supreme.'[10] What is especially striking about Pershing's position is that he acted as both ambassador and warrior, determining the extent of US co-operation in the coalition war. His formal instructions included the following language:

In military operations against the Imperial German Government, you are directed to cooperate with the forces of the other countries employed against that enemy; but in so doing the underlying idea must be kept in view that the forces of the United States are a separate and distinct component of the combined forces, the identity of which must be preserved. This fundamental rule is subject to such minor exceptions in particular circumstances as your judgment may approve. *The decision as to when your command, or any of its parts, is ready for action is confided to you, and you will exercise full discretion in determining the manner of cooperation.*[11]

These instructions were put in a safe at Pershing's headquarters in France and never revised.

What explains Pershing's extraordinary powers, especially in a country that was profoundly unmilitaristic when the Great War began? Wilson loathed militarism, was suspicious of soldiers, and sought to limit their influence on society. His secretaries of navy and of war were decidedly anti-war if not pacifistic. The armed services were seen as instruments of national policy which only civilians determined. No generals or admirals, for example, had been consulted when Wilson made his decision for war with Germany.[12] Yet he now made Pershing the virtual tsar of American participation.

Just prior to giving Pershing his instructions, Wilson had been informed of an alarmist assessment by Tasker H. Bliss, who served as acting Chief of General Staff when Scott was sent to Russia on the Root mission. Bliss argued 'that what both the English and French really wanted from us was not a large well-trained army but a large number of smaller *units* which they could feed promptly into their line as parts of their own organizations in order to maintain their manpower at full strength.' If the Americans fought only in battalions and regiments, there would be 'no American army and no American commander,' and the US role in the war would be obscured.[13] In these circumstances, Wilson feared he would have little influence at the peace table beyond economic and perhaps moral leverage. In his effort to repudiate power politics in world affairs, Wilson relied himself on the use of military force to achieve his political objectives. Pershing's subsequent role in inter-Allied negotiations, on both military and political questions, abundantly demonstrated that Wilson could not have found a more effective instrument for the use of American arms to further his 'new diplomacy'.

Wilson's tepid interest in most military questions and geography also played a part in Pershing's virtual independence. The capitals of Paris and London were in close proximity to the battlefield and civil-military relations were characterized by distrust and acrimony as political and military leaders in frequent contact haggled over tactics, strategy, and other matters pertaining to the war. Separated from Washington by an ocean, Pershing talked with Wilson only once during the war, just before he departed for France.

Protective of American neutrality, Wilson had kept the general staff from developing contingency plans for US participation in the war.[14] Military involvement in Europe after April 1917 was thus very much a work in progress. The forceful Pershing filled this void, and he did so without serious interference from the civilians, or for that matter, the Chief of the General Staff in Washington. He knew and almost always got what he wanted.

The American public was largely spared the heart-rending and bloody consequences of the killing fields on the Western Front. With the vast majority of US soldiers being withheld from combat until the last 110 days of the war, there seemed little to find fault with Pershing's dominant role. Once US forces began to participate in major operations, however, the dead and wounded paralleled the losses suffered by the European armies. If the war and these heavy casualties had continued into 1919, both the public and the President would have taken a much greater interest in Pershing's conduct of operations, especially in light of the losses and performance of American forces during the greatest battle the US Army had ever fought the Meuse-Argonne offensive.[15]

With his roots firmly in rural Missouri, Pershing was deeply patriotic and convinced of the superiority of the American people and their traditions. Correct and generally courteous with 'foreign' generals, he obviously believed that he could learn little from them and that his troops were superior to the soldiers under their command. In his view, America's history, opportunities, and political institutions produced a unique soldier, 'a type of manhood superior in initiative to that existing abroad, which given approximately equal training and discipline, developed a superior soldier to that existing abroad.'[16] He planned to show the French and British how to defeat Germany.

On 8 June 1917, the vanguard of the AEF arrived at Liverpool, the first foreign troops to arrive in England since 1688. Although destined to be a Commander-in-Chief without an army for many months, Pershing did not think small. He contemplated a war-winning American offensive in 1919. Rightly suspecting the British in Flanders and northeast France of trying to harness the emerging US military power to their own, he chose Lorraine, the area between the Argonne Forest and Vosges Mountains, as the American sector. In Lorraine he would have more secure supply lines and access to the ports on the south-western French coast. He also saw a front that could enable the Americans to win the war. His operations section prepared a memorandum, dated 25 September 1917, and titled 'A Strategical Study on the Employment of the AEF against the Imperial German Government,'[17] which influenced decisively Pershing's approach to coalition war-making.

Taking over a section of the British front, even if the BEF found itself in dire straits, was rejected. 'If the British cannot hold, etc., their own line, certainly our entrance therein cannot produce any decisive results.' Placing the AEF at the juncture of the French and British lines would also assign the Americans 'an indecisive part'. AEF planners were determined to husband American manpower in 1918, participating in minor attacks which might keep up Allied morale while at the same time preparing the way for decisive victory in 1919. 'Piecemeal waste of our forces will result from any other action and we will never have in France the power to accomplish our objective.'[18]

Pershing and his operations section thought the Lorraine front attractive for several reasons. A breakthrough in the sector facing and flanking Metz might prove decisive. If the eastern end of the vital railroad running from Metz to Maubeuge were cut, Germany's southern defences might collapse, with the enemy falling back beyond the Rhine or 'at least to the eastern part of Belgium'. Vital coal, salt, and iron deposits were located in this region and the German economy might collapse if these resources fell into American hands.

Once an American army was created, AEF planners hoped to eliminate in 1918 the salient of St Mihiel, south-west of Metz. Once this minor and preliminary operation straightened the front, the main American offensive would be launched in 1919. An army of five corps (or 1,272,858 men when lines-of-communications troops were included) was thought sufficient to rupture the German front.[19] Although Pershing eventually raised his requirements to an unrealizable 5,000,000 men, this September memorandum with its ambitious objectives continued to serve as the strategical bible for the AEF.

Allied generals soon despaired over Pershing's unwillingness to subordinate his plans for a war-winning offensive to their desperate need for US manpower, but Pershing's agenda greatly contributed to ultimate victory in one respect. He played a central role in accelerating America's commitment to the Western Front by asking his government in December 1917 to supply him with twenty-four divisions by June, with an additional six divisions by autumn. A single US division, with an authorized strength of some 28,000 men, was the equivalent of two French or British divisions. Not by accident, the thirty divisions (or five corps) fitted exactly the AEF's initial requirements for an offensive in Lorraine in 1919. Given the breakdowns in American mobilization and the lack of shipping, the French and British high commands did not think such an expansion of the American presence in Europe was possible, but they played along with Pershing and joined him in making this request. 'Is such a programme *possible*?' a stunned Wilson asked Baker.[20]

In making an army of these raw recruits, Pershing emphasized discipline and appearance. His attention to detail made his frequent inspection tours an ordeal for those involved. Baker once wondered aloud how a general so obsessed with buttons could have such broad vision. Vision he had in abundance, but it seems that Pershing did not always understand the citizen soldier he commanded. Once, for example, he thought of 'rewarding' especially productive members of the Services of Supply by handing them a rifle and sending them into combat.

When a sceptical reporter asked Pershing in the autumn of 1917 if he believed that the German front could be broken, he did not equivocate. 'Of course the western front can be broken. What are we here for?'[21] If the AEF succeeded, it promised to give Wilson a commanding position at the peace table. But Pershing's desire for overwhelming victory put him at odds with Wilson's peace programme in one respect. Wilson contemplated a balanced peace, a 'peace without victory'; Pershing sought a breakthrough and the annihilation of the enemy.

A question that is begging to be asked is, why did Pershing think that he could accomplish in 1919 what had been unobtainable for the

European and British generals in their massive and prolonged offensives? Before Pershing departed for France, the President had expressed some general concerns over the costly methods employed by Joffre and other Allied generals. In Wilson's view, 'never before in the world's history have two great armies been in effect so equally matched; never before have the losses and the slaughter been so great with as little gain in military advantage.' A war of movement, he wrote in a private note, had become 'almost a thing of the past,' replaced by a 'mechanical game of slaughter.'[22] Wilson hoped that Pershing could avoid the costly Allied tactics of 1914–1917 in what had become a war of attrition. Learn from past mistakes and explore new approaches, he advised the Commander-in-Chief of the AEF.[23]

Pershing's approach to the stalemated Western Front reflected the 'can do' attitude of Americans and their boundless optimism at the turn of the century. With some justification, Pershing believed that the French and British (if not such commanders as Haig and Nivelle) had lost faith in any assault which aimed at distant strategical objectives. It simply was not in the nature of Americans to fight a static war. As his Chief-of-Staff Harbord noted, 'the tradition of marksmanship still lingered in America, and pioneer history had not yet lost its influence. . . . Nor were Americans willing to sit down in trenches and permanently exchange "dirty looks" with an enemy in another trench but a few yards away.'[24] 'Victory could not be won by the costly process of attrition,' Pershing writes in his account of the war, 'but it must be won by driving the enemy out into the open and engaging him in a war of movement.'[25] He saw fresh and aggressive US infantrymen, relying on the rifle and bayonet and operating in the open field, as representing the key to victory. 'An aggressive spirit must be developed until the soldier feels himself, as a bayonet fighter, invincible in battle,' was the language employed in AEF training instructions. Pershing and some other American tacticians also expressed scepticism over Allied reliance on artillery. Employment of rolling barrages, it was argued, imposed a rigidity on attacking formations with 'fixed distances and intervals between units and individuals, voluminous orders, careful rehearsal, little initiative upon the part of the individual soldier.' AEF combat instructions emphasized the 'infantry's own fire power to enable it to get forward' and 'the greatest possible use of individual initiative by all troops engaged in the action.'[26]

Given the experiences of the European armies, this was surely a recipe for disaster. In his account of the war, Pershing asserts that ultimately he 'had the satisfaction of hearing the French admit that we were right, both in emphasizing training for open warfare and insisting upon proficiency in the use of the rifle.'[27] One of Pershing's research assistants, assigned to the task, however, was unable to discover any original

French statement to support this claim. Even more telling was the battle-field performance of the AEF. 'The AEF,' according to one harsh critique, 'succeeded not because of imaginative operations and tactics nor because of qualitative superiority, but by smothering German machine guns with American flesh.'[28] As US troops were marching to the front, a popular story goes, one Doughboy asserted, 'Pershing says he'll take Metz if it costs a hundred thousand lives.' The irreverent response by one of his comrades was: 'Ain't he a damned generous guy!'[29]

This sarcastic remark, of course, could have been made by other nationalities about their commanders. If indeed the AEF's losses were disproportionate to those suffered by the French and British in 1918, more than flawed tactics were responsible. The regular army prior to America's entry into the war consisted of little more than 100,000 men and officers. It has been described as 'a constabulary force whose principal missions included defending the coasts from seaborne attack and policing the Mexican border and America's insular possessions.'[30] As Pershing ruefully admitted, 'It was one thing to call one or two million men to the colors, and quite another thing to transform them into an organized, instructed army capable of meeting and holding its own in the battle against the best trained force in Europe with three years of actual war experience to its credit.'[31] The French and British offered a quick solution to this dilemma: amalgamation with their armies. It is possible that US infantry might have gone into action sooner and fought more effectively if they had become a part of the French and British war machines which had mature logistical systems, well-trained artillerymen, and experienced staff officers.

As long as Pershing remained Commander-in-Chief, however, there was almost no chance that American boys would be used to sustain the armies of other nations. Pershing argued that no great nation would accept such a demeaning blow to its national pride. And he had a point. Certainly the British would never have accepted the loss of the BEF's identify on the Western Front, even when it was small and incapable of decisively affecting the course of the war in 1914–1915. But Pershing had another motive in hoarding his growing manpower and preventing his forces from being distributed and tied down on the French or British sectors. He was assembling a force with which he expected to win the war in 1919.

The massive German assaults during the first half of 1918, however, placed his timetable in jeopardy. On 21 March the Germans launched an offensive that ruptured the British front, destroyed the British Fifth Army, and threatened to divide the British and French armies. This grave crisis forced the Allied leaders to accept unity of command, with Ferdinand Foch being granted 'co-ordinating power' over the forces on the Western Front. Foch's role on the Western Front is explored in more detail in William Philpott's chapter in this volume. Pershing immediately visited the Allied generalissimo at his headquarters and made a dramatic promise: 'Infantry, artillery, aviation, all that we have are yours; use them as you wish. More will come, in numbers equal to requirements.'[32] Unfortunately, Pershing did not yet have either the trained men or the equipment to back up his pledge, and no US combat divisions were involved in stopping this first German drive. Moreover, as we shall soon see, his deployment of US forces to assist the Allies was hardly unqualified.

Enormous pressures now existed to involve American troops at once in the fighting. On 7 April, a year and a day after America became a belligerent, Haig sent an alarmist cable to London. With no additional reinforcements forthcoming from Britain, he emphasized, the situation would 'become critical unless American troops fit for immediate incorporation in my Divisions arrive in France in the meantime.'[33] When the British War Cabinet discussed Haig's cable, the BEF's position was even more precarious. A second German offensive (9–10 April) had broken through another section of the British front.

US infantry and machine gunners incorporated in British units remained the only realistic way in which America might give immediate help. This Pershing continued to reject despite his dependence on British shipping to get his men to Europe. He was only prepared to reinforce the British and French by stationing newly arrived American forces behind their fronts to be trained and formed into US divisions as a preliminary to the creation of an American army, but he was not going to parcel out his battalions to keep British or French divisions up to strength. Major General Sir Charles Sackville-West, the British military representative on the Supreme War Council, expressed in earthy terms Allied outrage at Pershing's emphasis on building an American army without consideration for the increasingly desperate Allied situation: 'The man's an ass. I think – he doesn't mean business – what Bliss calls the God-damned American programme is going to f— up the whole show.'[34] In more diplomatic language, Clemenceau and especially Lloyd George made emotional appeals to Wilson over Pershing's head. The AEF commander, however, remained steadfast in his course no matter what the consequences to Allied fortunes.

On 1 May at a SWC meeting, when asked by Clemenceau if he were prepared to see the French forced behind the Loire, Pershing responded: 'Yes, I am willing to take the risk. Moreover, the time may come when the American Army will have to stand the brunt of this war, and it is not wise to fritter away our resources in this manner.' A month later, after the third German offensive had sent Parisians fleeing their city in panic, Pershing continued to stand his ground.[35]

As the fate of the Allies hung in the balance, Pershing took a tremendous risk in rejecting amalgamation. To his critics he seemed to justify the jibe that AEF stood for 'After Everything's Finished'. In the end, the Allied front withstood the violent German onslaught, but it was a close call.

Not surprisingly some Allied leaders were prepared to take desperate measures to get Pershing out of the way. The most astounding proposal to curb his powers came from the South African soldier-statesman, Jan Christian Smuts, who had joined the British War Cabinet. Smuts, who believed that Allied fortunes depended upon 'the incomparable resources in material and manpower of America,' thought that Pershing was 'overwhelmed by the initial difficulties of a job too big for him' and must be replaced. In a letter to Lloyd George, he suggested that he become the 'fighting' commander of the AEF, with Pershing's role being limited to 'all organisations in the rear.'[36]

Although this arrogant, not to mention insulting, proposal never saw the light of day, Smuts identified a chink in Pershing's armour. As the American presence grew in France, his myriad responsibilities threatened to overwhelm him, creating concern in some quarters in Washington. Colonel Edward House, who was in close contact with key Allied leaders, proposed to Wilson in June that Pershing's responsibilities be limited to the training and leading of American forces into battle. His frequently confrontational role at the conference table with the Allied leaders in particular should be eliminated.[37] With the anti-German coalition in peril, Wilson, too, began to have second thoughts about the virtual independence that he had given Pershing. At one point he informed the British that 'if PERSHING really stood in the way, he would be ordered to stand out of the way.'[38] If indeed the President ever expressed such sentiments to Pershing, it made no impression. Subsequently, when Allied leaders threatened to go over his head, he responded: 'Refer it to the President and be damned. I know what the President will do. He will simply refer it back to me for recommendation and I will make to him the same recommendation as I have made here today.'[39]

Another threat to Pershing's commanding position in Europe came from Peyton C. March and Tasker Bliss, the two generals who held the same rank as the AEF Commander-in-Chief. March, who was as strong-willed as Pershing, had been appointed Chief of the General Staff in March 1918. He saw himself, not without justification, as the government's advisor on all military questions. The general staff had been created as an instrument for the President and his Secretary of War to control the army. Its chief supervised both staff and line, and orders were issued over his signature to the army. When the AEF's logistical system broke down in the spring of 1918, March sought to delegate supply to one of his close friends, the able George W. Goethals, who had played the central role in constructing the Panama Canal. Opposed to Goethals, Pershing placed his loyal Chief-of-Staff, James G. Harbord, in charge of supply. 'I am his man,' Harbord once said of his relationship with Pershing; 'he can send me to Hell if he wants to.'[40] Pershing, who wanted no intermediary between himself and Wilson, thus prevailed, although he failed to convince Baker to replace March, who continued to resent being treated as a rubber stamp.[41] March had also been critical of Pershing's dual military and political role in France, deeming him 'peculiarly unfitted'[42] for diplomacy.

Bliss, a former Chief-of-Staff and an intellectual of the first rank, threatened to supplant Pershing at the conference table when the President, who refused to appoint a permanent political representative to the SWC, selected him as the US military representative on this newly formed inter-Allied body. Bliss, fearful that the British and French might be defeated, was inclined to accept the Allied point of view over Pershing's on several critical issues. A schism between America's two four-star generals in Europe, however, was averted when Bliss accepted a subordinate position. In disagreement over allocating US troops to British divisions, Pershing reacted sharply when Bliss suggested that they cable their opposing views to Washington and request a decision. This would place the decision directly in Wilson's hands, where the critical and essentially political issue of amalgamation belonged in the first place. Pershing, however, reached another conclusion. Fearing that the creation of an American army was in jeopardy, he wanted the army to speak with one voice – his. 'Well, Bliss,' he said, 'do you know what would happen if we should do that? We would both be relieved from further duty in France and that is exactly what we should deserve.'[43] Bliss deferred to Pershing. Having settled the amalgamation issue on his own terms, Pershing was content to allow Bliss to speak for US interests at the SWC during the last phase of the war, especially when that body began to focus on the peripheral question of Allied intervention in Russia. On issues that mattered to him, Pershing remained confident Bliss would loyally represent his views at the SWC. Moreover, as the German threat receded from July onwards, amalgamation became a much less critical issue.

After the fifth and last German offensive was checked in July, the strategical initiative passed to the Allies. US forces had been engaged in limited actions at Cantigny, Chateau-Thierry and Belleau Wood, and their commander began to focus on the day when they would dominate the battlefield. At a meeting with the Allied generals on 24 July, he scored a major success when he gained support for creating an independent force, the First Army, with its own theatre. In the following weeks he began to collect his scattered divisions for the first all-American offensive of the war.

On 30 August, however, Foch appeared at his headquarters with a most unwelcome plan, a co-ordinated Allied attack against the flanks of the German front where it bulged into France, with US and French troops advancing on the right flank or shoulder in the direction of Mezieres. Pershing was stunned. 'This virtually destroys the American Army that we have been trying so long to form,' he hotly protested. In truth, it was Pershing's desire to give America the leading role in the war, not the AEF, which was being undermined. Pershing, without foundation, suspected that the Allies did not 'wish America to find out her strength.' To the contrary, Allied generals usually had a high opinion of the quality, if not the training, of US troops, but they believed that the recently organized First Army, if it fought on its own, was no match for the experienced German army in its strong defences. Matters became very heated when Foch emotionally asked, 'Your French and English comrades are going into battle; are you coming with them?' Although Pershing was so angry that in an irrational moment he considered striking the generalissimo, a compromise was eventually effected, which allowed the First Army to remain an independent force while still participating in the converging Allied attacks. Pershing, it should be noted, was not the only national Commander-in-Chief who sought to highlight the role of his forces. Witness the bitter rivalry between Haig and Nivelle over a common strategy during the first half of 1917. But in his aversion to joint operations where the US role would be blurred, Pershing, as he had done over the issue of amalgamation, took a considerable gamble. To keep his forces intact, he agreed to disengage once the St Mihiel salient had been eliminated and transfer without delay the bulk of his forces some sixty miles to the north to a narrow sector where US forces would have to drive straight forward across rugged and easily defended terrain.[44]

On 12 September Pershing finally got his chance to launch an independent offensive (although the Allies provided artillery, tanks, planes and additional troops). The timing of his attack at St Mihiel could not have been more fortuitous. US troops caught the German defenders in the process of a staged withdrawal from their vulnerable position. Within thirty hours the battle had been decided in America's favour. Pershing had reason to be elated. Fighting some 3,000 miles from home, the AEF had made dramatic progress since a regiment-sized attack against Cantigny in May. Although Pershing later claimed that 'without doubt, an immediate continuation of the advance would have carried us well beyond the Hindenburg Line and possibly into Metz,'[45] this quick and easy victory ('the sector where the Americans relieved the Germans') revealed that the First Army was experiencing serious birth pains: a breakdown in supply, the failure to co-ordinate artillery and infantry, and serious command and control problems.

That the First Army was still in its formative phase was once again underlined when nine American divisions, five of which had never served in the line, began the Battle of Meuse-Argonne on 26 September. It was not an auspicious beginning for the largest battle yet fought by any American army. Staff work was amateurish, poorly trained dough-boys attacked in bunches and were mowed down, and logistics collapsed. 'It was as if someone had taken the army's intestines out,' Donald Smythe has noted, 'and dumped them all over the table.'[46] Although the First Army renewed its attack on 4–5 October, little progress was made.

Pershing now faced his greatest personal crisis of the war. 'I feel like I am carrying the whole world on my shoulders,' he exclaimed. On another occasion, while driving to the front, his head dropped to his hands and he cried out his dead wife's name: 'Frankie . . . Frankie . . . my God, sometimes I don't know how I can go on.'[47] But he did. Constantly on the move, he pushed his men forward, once reassuring a group of battle-weary soldiers, 'if you can stick this a little longer I'll have you out of here in a few weeks.'[48] Officers who did not match his tenacity were sacked; four infantry brigade commanders, three division commanders, and a corps commander lost their commands. Pershing, who made frequent visits to US wounded, was affected by the heavy casualties. But his indomitable will for victory remained unshaken. He told the commander of the 90th Division: 'We are not getting on as we should. But by God! Allen, I was never so much in earnest in my life and we are going to get through.'[49]

With the US offensive between the Meuse River and the Argonne Forest stymied, Germany sued for peace and Allied generals began to discuss armistice terms. Pershing did not want the war to end before America won a decisive victory. He had recently divided the AEF into two armies. The Second Army, activated on 12 October, had been positioned east of the Meuse River to strike at Metz. 'Our second army is ready and waiting to march on Metz,'[50] Pershing told Major Lloyd Griscom, his personal representative to the British War Office.

On 30 October Pershing shocked Washington when he suggested to the SWC that peace was premature and argued in favour of uncon-ditional surrender. 'I am of the opinion,' he wrote to House, 'that we shall not be able in case of an armistice to reap the benefits of a decided victory which has not yet altogether been accomplished.'[51] On this occasion Pershing overreached. His opinion on the peace question had not been requested or wanted. Yet he took a position in the SWC and informed the President afterwards. Wilson was infuriated, thinking him 'glory mad'.[52] Although Pershing beat a hasty retreat, he continued to believe that a great opportunity had been thrown away, especially after the First Army, on 1 November, launched a successful attack which forced a German withdrawal. During the next ten days, US forces advanced further than they had during the previous month. Characterizing his offensive as 'probably the most important operation that has been undertaken by the allies,'[53] Pershing's desire for a battle of annihilation seemed possible. Minutes before the Armistice went into effect, Pershing, surveying a map on his office wall, talked about his unrealized plans to take Metz. 'What an enormous difference a few days more would have made!'[54] he lamented.

Unable to end the war on his terms, Pershing was largely responsible for an embarrassing episode: the inept and unsuccessful attempt by US forces to beat the French to Sedan, a target of considerable emotional value to France. Pershing's motive, in all likelihood, was to silence his Allied critics by demonstrating that his army was superior to the French. His orders to take Sedan, although it was clearly in the French zone, seemed to prove the opposite. A chaotic situation developed when the 1st Division marched across the front and rear of the 77th and 42nd Divisions in the dead of night with confused US soldiers shooting at each other.

How is one to evaluate Pershing? No US field commander had ever been given such myriad responsibilities in both the political and military realms. As the American proconsul in Europe he was virtually independent. If anything the pressures on him were all the greater because of his exceptional powers. At critical moments the fate of the coalition appeared to depend upon his decisions. To the consternation of America's war partners, he took great risks in rejecting amalgamation and insisting on an independent army with its own front and strategic objectives. If the British and French had broken, his place in history would be that of the architect of defeat, the man who lost the war by placing US interests over the common interests of the coalition. He became a lightning rod for European anger and frustration, although in truth he could not have been a more loyal representative of the President's priorities. As late as 30 September, Lloyd George, who had hoped to intensify the war against Turkey by substituting US for British soldiers on the Western Front, angrily told Baker that in Britain's view, the AEF was 'perfectly useless, and the shipping devoted to bringing it over utterly wasted.'[55] This was quite unfair. If not for Pershing's escalating demands the arrival of US troops in Europe would not have surpassed all Allied expectations. Nor would an independent US Army, which was fast developing into a first-rate fighting force, have existed. If the war had lasted another year (as almost every Allied leader thought it would in the summer of 1918) the US Army almost certainly would have delivered the mortal blows to the Imperial German Army.

As a fighting commander, however, Pershing had serious flaws. His belief in the individual rifleman and his bayonet represented an unrealistic nineteenth-century image of warfare.

Pershing can be understood as a reflection of his country which had been forced out of its political isolationism and onto the world stage by the European conflict. Confident of American exceptionalism, he was self-righteous, visionary, and boldly optimistic about the role of American arms in Europe. Accepting the 'tremendous task' which had been given him by Wilson, whose crusading political objectives were even more ambitious than his own, he promised that he would 'try to realize to the utmost my obligations to you and to the American people.'[56] He was truly, in the words of Captain B. H. Liddell Hart, 'THE HUNDRED-PER-CENT AMERICAN,'[57] which to many French and British war leaders had a more negative than positive connotation in 1918.

Notes

1 Pride of place for Pershing biographers belongs to Donald Smythe, *Pershing General of the Armies* (Bloomington, 1986). See also Frank E. Vandiver, *Black Jack: The Life and Times of John J. Pershing.* 2 vols (College Station, 1977), Frederick Palmer, *John J. Pershing. General of the Armies: A Biography* (Harrisburg, 1948), Gene Smith, *Until the Last Trumpet Sounds: The Life of General of the Armies John J. Pershing* (New York, 1998), and Richard Goldhurst, *Pipe Clay and Drill. John J. Pershing: The Classic American Soldier* (New York, 1977).

2 Vandiver, *Black Jack*, 2:673.

3 Ibid., 676.

4 S. L. A. Marshall, *World War I* (New York, 1985), 279.

5 Interview with Colonel John Virden, 22 March 1961, quoted in Donald Smythe, 'John J. Pershing: A Study in Paradox,' *Military Review* 49 (September 1969): 66.

6 James G. Harbord, *The American Army in France, 1917–1919* (Boston, 1936), 40.

7 Palmer, *Pershing*, 84.

8 John J. Pershing, *My Experiences in the World War*, 2 vols (New York, 1931). Though accurate in detail, the entries, drawn from a variety of headquarter records as well as his diaries, were in fact fictionalized. See Smythe, *Pershing*, 290.

9 Ibid., 293.

10 Ibid., 6.

11 Italics are the author's. Baker to Pershing, 26 May 1917, Arthur Link, ed. *The Papers of Woodrow Wilson* (Princeton, 1983), 42: 404–5. There were actually two letters of instruction given to Pershing. This one, which was very precise on preserving the 'identity' of US forces, beginning with the

words, 'the President directs me to communicate to you the following,' was the one that mattered.

12 See David R. Woodward, *Trial by Friendship: Anglo-American Relations, 1917–1918* (Lexington, 1993), 17–65.

13 Bliss to Baker, 25 May 1917, confidential copy for Pershing, Pershing Papers, Box 123, Library of Congress Manuscript Division, Washington, D.C.

14 See Woodward, *Trial by Friendship*, 17–65.

15 For a discussion of the AEF's tactics and strategy during this campaign, see Paul F. Braim, *The Test of Battle: The American Expeditionary Forces in the Meuse-Argonne Campaign* (Newark, 1987).

16 Smythe, *Pershing*, 187.

17 Prepared by Fox Conner, LeRoy Eltinge, and Hugh Drum, G-3, GHQ, AEF, Secret General Correspondence, File 1003, No. 681, pt. 2, Box 3112, Record Group 120, National Archives, Washington, D.C.

18 Ibid.

19 Ibid.

20 David R. Woodward, 'World War I,' in *Encyclopedia of the American Military*, ed John J. Jessup and Louise B. Ketz (New York, 1994), 2:908.

21 Smythe, *Pershing*, 239.

22 'An Unpublished Prolegomenon to a Peace Note,' c. 25 November 1916, *Papers of Woodrow Wilson* (Princeton, 1982), 40:67–70.

23 Vandiver, *Black Jack*, 2:693.

24 Harbord, *American Army in France*, 185.

25 Pershing, *Experiences in the World War*, 1:152.

26 See Woodward, 'World War I,' 910, and AEF 'Combat Instructions,' 5 September 1918, quoted in John Whiteclay Chambers and G. Kurt Piehler, ed., *Major Problems in American Military History* (New York, 1999), 256–57.

27 Pershing, *Experiences*, 1:153.

28 James W. Rainey, 'The Questionable Training of the AEF in World War I,' *Parameters*, 22 (Winter, 1992–1993), 100. See also James J. Cooke, *Pershing and His Generals: Command and Staff in the AEF* (Westport, 1997), 139–52.

29 B. H. Liddell Hart, *Reputations: Ten Years After* (New York, 1928), 315.

30 Timothy K. Nenninger, 'American Military Effectiveness in the First World War,' in *Military Effectiveness*, vol 1: *The First World War*, ed Allan R. Millett and Williamson Murray (Boston, 1989), 130.

31 Pershing, *Experiences*, 1:150.

32 Ibid., 365.

33 War Cabinet (388 A), 10 April 1918, CAB 23/14, Public Record Office, Kew, Richmond.

34 Sackville-West to Sir Henry Wilson, 8 April 1918, H. Wilson Papers, File 12 B/14, Department of Documents, Imperial War Museum, London.

35 SWC, 1 May 1918, CAB 28/3/IC–57, Public Record Office, Kew, Richmond; and Smythe, *Pershing*, 113–15.

36 Cabinet Paper G.T. 1573 of 31 July 1917, CAB 24/21, Public Record Office, Kew, Richmond; and Smuts to Lloyd George, 8 June 1918, Lloyd George Papers F/45/9/18, House of Lords Record Office, London.

37 David F. Trask, *The AEF and Coalition Warmaking, 1917–1918* (Lawrence, 1993), 79.

38 Wilson also noted: 'It would, of course, distress him to have to override his Commander-in-Chief because he felt he ought to be loyal to him, and he did not like overriding a man so far from home and possibly only understanding part of his case.' Wiseman to Drummond, 30 May 1918, *Papers of Wilson Papers* (Princeton, 1985), 48:205.

39 Smythe, *Pershing*, 135.

40 Ibid., 163.

41 Edward M. Coffman, *The Hilt of the Sword: The Career of Peyton C. March* (Madison, 1966), 104–18.

42 Trask, *AEF and Coalition Warmaking*, 80 n 25.

43 Pershing, *Experiences in the World War*, 1:305.

44 Woodward, *Trial by Friendship*, 197–201, Smythe, *Pershing*, 169–178, and Trask, *AEF and Coalition Warmaking*, 102–106.

45 Pershing, *Experiences in the World War*, 2:270.

46 Smythe, *Pershing*, 200.

47 Ibid., 208.

48 Smith, *Until the Last Trumpet sounds*, 197.

49 Smythe, *Pershing.*, 208.

50 Lloyd C. Griscom, *Diplomatically Speaking* (Boston, 1940), 440.

51 Pershing to House, 30 October 1918, House Papers, Box 89, fol. 3073, Manuscripts and Archives Department, Sterling Memorial Library, Yale University, New Haven.

52 Arthur Walworth, *America's Moment: 1918. American Diplomacy at the End of World War I* (New York, 1977), 44.

53 Pershing to House, 6 November 1918, House Papers, Box 89, fol. 3074, Manuscripts and Archives Department, Sterling Memorial Library, Yale University, New Haven.

54 Griscom, *Diplomatically Speaking*, 446.

55 Woodward, *Trial by Friendship.* 204.

56 Pershing to Wilson, 27 June 1918, *Papers of Woodrow Wilson* (Princeton, 1985), 48–451.

57 Liddell Hart, *Reputation*, 289.

Chapter 8

James Watson Gerard: American Diplomat as Domestic Propagandist

Matthew S. Seligmann

The seventeenth-century traveller, diplomat, scholar and poet Sir Henry Wotton once pithily observed that 'an ambassador is an honest man sent to lie abroad for the good of his country.' Although this laconic *bon mot* quickly emerged as a favourite truism among all those cynical about international affairs, it would have been rejected out of hand by New York Supreme Court Justice James Watson Gerard, the man appointed in 1913 to represent American interests in the German Empire. But then Ambassador Gerard was not the archetypal diplomat. If he had a failing with the truth, it was not in its economical use, but in the regularity with which he told it. If he had a problem with discretion, it was not from a prevalence for dissembling, but rather from an unwillingness to hide his opinions. In short, James Watson Gerard was a very forthright man who told the truth as he saw it and who did not care how many people knew his views. These personality traits – considered by many to be far from ideal in an ambassador – were not the only undiplomatic sides to this character. As with many outspoken individuals, Gerard also possessed a formidable temper. This meant that, while blessed with considerable personal charm and a natural ability to win over those he encountered, he nevertheless frequently clashed with them instead. Not surprisingly, such talents for openness and argument did not go unnoticed by the career diplomats who served under him at the Berlin Embassy. One of them, Hugh Wilson, described Gerard as 'caustic' and noted that 'he had an impish delight in creating embarrassing situations.'[1] In a similar vein, Joseph Clark Grew, who was later to acquire fame as the American Ambassador in Tokyo at the time of the Japanese attack on Pearl Harbor, but who spent the early years of the First World War at a posting in Berlin, noted that Gerard's method of persuading someone to his point of view was 'to cow the wretched individual by volleys of curses.' Given this predilection for violent language, Grew sarcastically wrote: 'the Ambassador has picked out the two callings for which he is least fitted, Judge and Diplomat.'[2] Many others who encountered Gerard felt the same way. One such individual was the former American Ambassador to Italy and to France, Henry White. Writing to President Woodrow Wilson, he reported that 'Gerard's manners are unsympathetic, to use no stronger term' and later added that the root of this problem was that Gerard did not seem to understand 'that absolute firmness can be combined with perfect courtesy.'[3] Serious though this indictment was, it came as no surprise to President Wilson. Colonel Edward House, Wilson's closest friend and confidant, recorded in his diary that 'the President considers Gerard a reactionary of the worst sort, and has little confidence in his ability. . . .'[4] This assessment actually understated the case considerably. To his future second wife, Mrs Edith Bolling Galt, Woodrow Wilson described Gerard as an 'ass' and fervently expressed the wish that the Germans 'would hand this idiot his passport.'[5]

Although Woodrow Wilson, and many others, considered Gerard's natural forcefulness and honesty to be traits totally unsuitable for a man in his position, this judgement is open to some question. For one thing, these characteristics ensured that Gerard did nothing if not present the American point of view resolutely to his German hosts. As Hugh Wilson conceded in his memoirs:

> [Gerard] was young vigorous and forceful, his moral courage was of a high order, he spoke without intimidation to the highest in the land and urged the point of view of the United States with the same vigor on the Kaiser and on the lowliest member of the Foreign Office.'[6]

Given that the message thereby conveyed could never be misunderstood for reasons of ambiguity, this forthrightness was often a virtue, a point that even the critical Grew was forced to admit. As he recorded in his diary about a meeting with the German authorities at Charleville in 1916: '[Gerard] does not mince his words, he speaks with force and directness – which is sometimes the only method of talk that carries weight here . . .'[7]

Consequently, whether a man of Gerard's character was a liability or an asset to the American diplomatic service is, by no means, a clear-cut issue. As can be seen, the point can be argued both ways. What cannot so easily be disputed, however, irrespective of the conclusion one draws regarding Gerard's value as an ambassador, is that he was to prove extremely useful to the government in Washington when, in early 1917, relations between the United States and Germany broke down and the two nations went to war. At this juncture, the Wilson administration found itself in need of people who could explain the reason for the conflict to an often sceptical and unenthusiastic American public and thereby rally them to the national cause. In this capacity, Gerard's forcefulness and clarity, his ability to argue and cajole – features not always appreciated when he was a diplomat – were suddenly valuable qualities. His greatest strength as a champion for the American war effort, however, stemmed from one of his greatest weaknesses as a diplomat: his natural provocativeness. This had regularly engendered bitter confrontations between him and Germany's leaders and had proved troublesome when the goal of American diplomacy was to smooth relations with Berlin. However, once the United States found itself at war with Germany, this reservoir of previous diplomatic *contretemps* was to prove an unexpected asset. Through his tales of his own past quarrels with German officials, Gerard was able to personify his nation's quarrel with Germany in a manner that was not open to anybody else. His accounts of how he, the plain-speaking American, refused to be ridden over roughshod by the aristocrats, autocrats and militarists of the Kaiser's court – many of whose foibles are profiled in the chapters in this volume by Matthew Stibbe, Annika Mombauer and Robert Foley – were to bring alive the American cause to millions of his country's citizens. Consequently, by making public his past conflicts with the leading personalities of the German Empire and graphically disseminating his own experiences, Gerard made a major contribution to the mobilization of the American home front and thereby to his nation's ability to wage the First World War. It is this aspect of Gerard's career that will now be examined.

On 18 April 1917, twelve days after the American declaration of war against Germany, a banquet was held at Boston's South Armory. Entitled the 'National Defense Dinner', its purpose was to raise awareness of America's new role in the bitter conflict against the Central Alliance and, to this end, Gerard was invited to address this exclusive gathering. His selection as principal speaker reflected the celebrity status that the war with Germany had bestowed upon him, a point reinforced by the toast master's introduction to the assembled dignitaries:

> With us tonight as our honored guest is one who has been fighting alone
> – not on the battlefields but in the courts of diplomacy. He alone, bravely,
> courageously, patriotically, has represented the rights, the honor and the
> dignity of the United States of America. . . .[8]

This description, short though it is, nevertheless vividly illustrates the manner in which Gerard was perceived by many segments of the

American public. Regarded not as a failed diplomat, but rather as the longest-serving warrior in the now overt battle against Prussian autocracy, his reputation gave him the potential to make a considerable impact as a propagandist. Ironically, however, although he had evinced the desire to serve as a mouthpiece for the American case against Germany soon after the severing of diplomatic relations, the Wilson administration had, at first, been far from eager to see this happen. In the months between this diplomatic breakdown and the actual declaration of war, President Wilson had maintained the forlorn hope that he could still somehow avoid this irrevocable final step. As fiery words from Gerard were hardly suited to this outcome, they were naturally discouraged. Thus, even in the very week before Wilson went to Congress to ask for a declaration of war against Germany, the State Department could still be found writing to Gerard to suggest that he should be 'discreet in [his] utterances.'[9]

With the declaration of war, however, all of this changed. As can be seen by the establishment of a central propaganda agency, the Committee on Public Information (CPI), on 14 April 1917, a mere week after America's entry into the conflict, the Wilson administration quickly became alive to the necessity of arousing public passions behind the war effort. In this light, it is hardly surprising that they also recognized that their former attitude to Gerard was inappropriate and immediately reversed it. Thus, where once the government were counselling him to act with discretion, they were now enthusiastically encouraging Gerard to spread his message. Hence, President Wilson, urged by the Mayor of Oakland, on 28 May 1917, to send Gerard to address a mass meeting at the city's civic auditorium, wrote the very next day to Gerard to tell him that 'he would very much like to have you go.'[10] Although the former ambassador was unable to accept this particular invitation, he would take up with relish the opportunity provided by the government's demonstrable change of heart with respect to his activities to embark upon a major campaign of propaganda. Broadly speaking, his efforts can be divided into three different categories: public appearances, publishing, and the new medium of mass communication, the cinema.

Beginning with public appearances, Gerard undertook numerous speaking tours throughout the length and breadth of the United States in an attempt to promote support for the war effort. His suitability for this role rested in part on his celebrity status as the one American most intimately involved with German affairs. As a local newspaper from Norristown, Pennsylvania reported in April 1917:

Since the return of Mr Gerard from his official capacity in Germany, he has been in great demand as an orator and is being greeted with great enthusiasm in the largest cities in the country, as he is recognized as a man who is able to speak authoritatively of dealings with the country that has so flagrantly violated American rights.[11]

However, personal experience was not the only factor that contributed to Gerard's appeal. In addition to the expertise gained from four years inside Germany, he also happened to be a highly accomplished speaker with a very refined sense of how to mould his words to suit his audience. His grasp of the popular idiom, despite the unashamedly elitist nature of his background, meant that he was extremely proficient both at stirring the passions of those who heard him and at leaving a lasting impression upon them. Oratorical skills doubtless constituted a major part of this, but sadly are beyond historical reconstruction. However, it is apparent from the surviving evidence that no less a role was played by the carefully crafted content of his speeches, which were unashamedly populist. In marked contrast to President Wilson, who propounded lofty but abstract principles of justice, ethics and law, Gerard delivered instead chatty and anecdotal talks filled with short and memorable tales of his own experiences. Like biblical parables or Aesop's fables, they contained an unmistakable moral message: in this case, that the American people should participate to their utmost in the war because the rulers of the German Empire despised American values and wanted to destroy the American way of life, a fact that they did little to hide. As Gerard told a crowd in Kansas City, on one occasion the Kaiser even 'shook his finger in my face and said: "I will stand no nonsense from America after this war! America had better look out after this war!" . . .'[12] Providing an allegorical twist to this tale that effectively converted it into a parable was not a difficult task for Gerard. As he explained to a crowd in San Francisco in a version of this story that was subsequently printed for distribution to California schoolchildren.

> Well, now, suppose you saw a man across the street fighting with three or four other men, and he called out to you and said 'Look out, now; I won't take any nonsense. As soon as I finish with these people I am coming across the street and I am going for you.' Now, don't you think that it would be the part of the most ordinary elementary prudence to cross the street and take a hand at him while he is occupied with the others?[13]

If the applause reported by the *San Francisco Call* is anything to go by, his listeners agreed: the message contained in this inverted version of the parable of the good Samaritan had been received. Equally clear were Gerard's entreaties to support other wartime concerns. Thus, for example, asked to promote the government's food conservation programme, he told the guests at the National Democratic Club dinner in celebration of the 174th birthday of Thomas Jefferson: 'I have had a number of people treating me as an expert in war because I have come from Germany, and asking me what they could do at this time . . . There is one thing that the people can do, and you can do immediately, namely, cut down the food.'[14] In the context of a sumptuous banquet, this ironic point was well made and could not have been lost on the listeners. In a similar fashion, Gerard, like such Hollywood stars as Charlie Chaplin, Douglas Fairbanks, and Mary Pickford, regularly campaigned on behalf of the government's Liberty Loan programme. 'I do not consider,' he told one audience,

> I am doing anything patriotic in subscribing to the Liberty Loan. I consider it a sound investment and believe that in a short time the bonds will sell at a premium. It would, however, be unpatriotic for us to allow the loan to fail. The Germans always told me that in case of war between Germany and America, that we would undoubtedly furnish money, but could do nothing more. We must not disappoint them on the money question. And with the Liberty Loan and Universal Service we are giving the Central Empires a double wallop in the first round of the war.[15]

Once again, the moral message that it was the patriotic duty of Americans to undermine the hubris of the German Empire was ingeniously advanced, this time alongside a call to enlightened financial self-interest.

These public appearances had a considerable impact on the American people. For one thing, Gerard did his utmost to ensure that his words were heard by as widespread a segment of the populace as was conceivably possible by travelling widely to spread his message. As he informed his friend, the Associated Press journalist Seymour Conger, one of his tours involved 'a long trip through the west speaking in Minneapolis, Butte, Spokane, Takoma, Portland, San Francisco, Seattle, Los Angeles, Chicago, Cleveland, etc. In a number of places speaking several times, as for instance in Los Angeles where I spoke sixteen times. . . .'[16] Contemporary evaluations of the results of these efforts suggest that Gerard, who spoke himself hoarse and required an operation on his frontal sinus as a result of these oratorical exertions, had not wasted his breath. Typical of these is a letter written by E. S. Burke, Jr, the vice-chairman of the Liberty Loan committee for the Cleveland area:

> I am sure that you will be interested to know that the final total of subscriptions to the second Liberty Loan of 1917 in Cleveland reached

the very large amount of $100,450,000.00. I assure you that your splendid address on the night of Wednesday, October 24th, played a very important part in achieving this great success.[17]

In a similar fashion, George Creel, the former journalist and long-time Wilson supporter who became chairman of the CPI, wrote to Gerard in July 1918 to thank him for undertaking so many speaking tours, a task that he considered especially important given that 'I am not yet able to convince Congress that this work is a vital and necessary part of the war machinery.'[18] This, of course, was not strictly true. Like the White House, Congress was well aware of the value of propaganda, but as the House of Representatives had cut the CPI's funding request by 40 per cent in June 1918 to a 'mere' $1,250,000, one can understand both Creel's gratitude to Gerard and his irritation with Congress.

In addition to speaking tours, Gerard also produced written propaganda. In the first instance, this took the form of articles distributed in the country's major newspapers and periodicals. Their effectiveness can be gauged from a letter written to Gerard by J. J. Tobias, dedicated Freemason and chancellor of the Chicago Law School:

> Perhaps you will recall that in July and August of 1914, I arrived in Berlin as a special envoy of the Oriental Consistory of Chicago to the Grand Sovereign Lodge of the Masons in Germany. . . . On my return to Chicago, I published a small pamphlet on 'Why Germany is at war.' . . . After reading your articles which are profoundly philosophic and of great statesmanship, I am more and more convinced that I was fooled, like millions of others, with Prussian Military Diabolism.[19]

Hot on the heels of these contributions to the country's newspapers came two major bestselling books. The origins of these volumes is revealing both of Gerard's celebrity status and the way in which American wartime propaganda was formed. As early as the spring of 1916, when the Ambassador was still in post, he began to receive invitations from mainstream publishers eager to commit his experiences of wartime Germany to print. Naturally, the desire to make a quick return satisfying the insatiable demand of the American public for details of the conflict in Europe provided the main motive for these efforts to secure Gerard's imprimatur. However, underlying the profit motive, there was also an awareness that a book written by the American Ambassador could have broader uses. As Arthur Page – son of Walter Hines Page, the American Ambassador in London, and a manager of Doubleday, Page and Company – outlined while trying to entice Gerard to make a commitment to his firm:

In time to come the testimony of the American Ambassadors in the belligerent countries will be the most important source of information about the great struggle and its origins and it will especially be interesting to Americans. To the whole world and particularly the United States it is highly important that this testimony be published.[20]

This concern for the historical record as it related to the origins of a war being fought far away in Europe was clearly only a subsidiary issue for Americans when Arthur Page wrote this letter in May 1916. Titillating details were what the American public then sought. However, following the breach between Germany and America in February 1917, which left the United States teetering on the brink of war, the background to this calamitous deterioration in German-American relations became a matter of much more pressing and general interest. In deciding whether they should enter the fray against Germany, Americans wanted to know how they had come to this pass and who was responsible. In this context, the views of the American Ambassador, recently returned from Berlin, were of the utmost importance. A book by him could clarify to the American people, not just why the European nations were at war, but why it was that America needed to fight. As David Lawrence, one of the leading correspondents of the *New York Evening Post*, accurately stated: '[Gerard] has a marvellous chance with this book to create public opinion on the German controversy.'[21] It was a chance he was to seize eagerly. In March 1917, with invitations to publish well into double figures, Gerard signed a contract with George H. Doran and Company for his first book, an autobiographical account of his ambassadorship entitled *My Four Years in Germany*.

The usefulness of this book at rousing Americans out of their torpor and transforming them into partisans for more active involvement in the conflict has been called into question. Stewart Ross, author of *Propaganda for War* has described *My Four Years in Germany* as 'more an informative travelogue than a useful piece of anti-German propaganda.'[22] As Ross' book aims to show that, despite a predilection against so doing, the American public was 'conditioned to fight' by ceaseless pro-Allied and anti-German propaganda, this is an opinion that must be taken seriously. It is, after all, not like Ross to pass up an opportunity to show that Germany was unfairly maligned. Nevertheless, contemporary judgements do not back up his claim that *My Four Years in Germany* was ineffective as propaganda. On the contrary, all the evidence points exactly the other way. For one thing, the book was an instant bestseller and took Gerard's message directly to numerous members of the American public, most of whom were far from being unmoved by what he had to say, as this gushing letter from one reader illustrates:

> Permit me to express appreciation for the information given out by your book. . . . The words cannot of course express the width of your experiences which to an American must have had an almost uncontrollable blood-boiling effect, in view of the senseless arbitrary practice of German militarism.[23]

Moreover, it was not only in America that the book produced a positive propaganda effect. It also caused quite a sensation among readers in the Allied nations. In Britain, for instance, where the book was serialized in the *Daily Telegraph*, the American Ambassador, the distinguished ex-journalist Walter Hines Page, remarked that 'everybody has read it, everybody is grateful to you. . . .'[24] The publishers of the *Daily Telegraph* felt likewise, writing to Gerard that 'it is impossible to exaggerate [the book's] effect on public opinion here. . . .'[25] Similar results were noted in other Allied countries, leading Jean Jules Jusserand, fellow author and French Ambassador in America to send Gerard the eulogistic comment: 'Your book, which reached fame the day it came out and even before, which is very rare for a book, is already spoken of with due praise everywhere in Europe, and in more than one country translations will be printed to the advantage of the common cause.'[26] This was no exaggeration. As the American Ambassador in Madrid reported, British officials were eager to put out a Spanish edition of Gerard's book for propaganda purposes, a tactic the Americans would later adopt themselves in Mexico, where Ambassador Henry P. Fletcher used it 'as propaganda . . . to very good purpose, sending copies to President Carranza and the leading men of this government.'[27] Even more startlingly, John Buchan, the Scottish novelist who was put in charge of British propaganda at the Foreign Office's Department of Information in 1917, had high hopes of using the book to subvert the loyalty of German soldiers, writing that he was 'very anxious to get a short edition of Mr Gerard's "Four Years in Germany" in German for frontier distribution. It should only be about 100 pages and contain the passages most suitable for influencing German minds.'[28]

All of these endorsements make it evident that far from being a mere 'travelogue', *My Four Years in Germany* was actually an extremely robust piece of propaganda. As one American reader summed up its worth: 'I have recently finished your book "My Four Years in Germany", which I have read not only with great interest, but also with a sense of obligation for the much needed message you have brought to the American people.'[29] That the book was so proficient in delivering this 'much needed message' was a function of Gerard's skills as a writer of propaganda. While certainly no literary masterpiece, *My Four Years in Germany* contained, much like Gerard's speeches and articles, descriptions of his experiences dealing with German dignitaries that made it unambiguously clear just how hostile the German Reich was towards the United States. Among the better known of these encounters was a meeting between Gerard and Arthur Zimmermann, then Under-Secretary of State at the German Foreign Office:

> Zimmermann on one occasion said to me, 'The United States dare not do anything against Germany, because we have 500,000 German reservists in America, who will rise against your Government if your Government should dare to take any action against Germany.' As he said this he worked himself up to a passion, and repeatedly struck the table with his fist. I told him that we had 500,001 lamp-posts in America, and that was where the German reservists would find themselves if they tried any uprising. . . .[30]

What made this story so effective as propaganda was both the explicitly threatening position taken by the German diplomat and the pluck of the American response. In this one paragraph was both proof of the German menace and an example of how to deal with it. And the book reiterated this point over and over again, using other examples to make it plain that America was in the war solely in response to unprovoked German aggression. As an advertisement described the book's central message:

> It is this book which contains Germany's declaration of war upon America, a declaration which was made *years before* April 6th, 1917.
> For it was to Gerard, your ambassador and mine, that the Kaiser said, 'America had better look out after this war. I shall stand no nonsense from her.'[31]

This story, which Gerard had already used to good effect in his speeches and would later incorporate successfully in his film, proved just as rousing to Americans when disseminated through his book. Indeed, the version in *My Four Years in Germany* would even provide the basis for a song. Entitled 'Keep Your Eye on Uncle Sam' it was composed by an inspired reader, one Margaret Speik, and included the 'memorable' lyric:

> When they get across the Rhine
> They'll make the Kaiser toe the line
> And when they get to old Berlin
> They won't take any nonsense from him.

'Respectfully dedicated to Ambassador Gerard',[32], this patriotic jingle, written in 2/4 time and in the key of F major, shows the diverse fruits of Gerard's first book.

Yet, the greatest testimony to the success of *My Four Years in Germany* was the eagerness with which the publishers put a second book by Gerard into press. Entitled *Face to Face with Kaiserism*, it enjoyed a comparable success to the first book and for similar reasons. Starting from the premise that 'we are at war because Germany invaded the United States – an invasion insidiously conceived and vigorously prosecuted for years before hostilities began . . .'[33], it again exemplified this through Gerard's own personal experiences of German hostility. Where it differed from the earlier work, however, was in the care taken to fashion it into a piece of propaganda. *My Four Years in Germany* had been produced quickly. As Gerard explained to Walter Hines Page: 'speed in order to inform this country was so essential that the publishers would not even send me the proof sheets because of the hurry to print the book.'[34] By contrast, *Face to Face with Kaiserism* was subject to much more rigorous scrutiny and editing in the effort to ensure that it would have maximum impact. Among the measures taken to achieve this end was the employment of David Lawrence, a respected journalist with the *New York Evening Post*, to work with Gerard on the fine-tuning of the manuscript. Such efforts paid dividends. The new book was not merely a continuation of the narrative from the first publication, but contained several new means of spreading Gerard's message. The most important of these – comprising the centrepiece of the volume – consisted of sixty-six pages purporting to be a verbatim copy of Gerard's diary from June 1915 to January 1917. The decision to include a daily journal had been taken early on in the plans for the volume, much to the satisfaction of those involved in the production. They believed, as a letter from David Lawrence indicates, that it would cause a sensation. 'The more I think of it', he wrote, 'the more I believe that [the] diary is going to make a big hit and really show more of your trials and tribulations and your attitude towards them than was possible in your first book.'[35] This was undoubtedly so. The detailed and vivid descriptions of people and places, the records of conversations along with the dates on which they had taken place all lent an immediacy as well as an authenticity to the book that surpassed that of his memoirs. There was, however, one small problem. During his time in Berlin, Gerard had kept a small diary as an appointment book, but had never written a full daily journal. If an 'unpublished diary' were to be printed in *Face to Face with Kaiserism*, it would, thus, have to come from other sources. Fortunately for Gerard he had kept copies of the wartime letters that he had written to President Wilson, Colonel House and Secretary of State Robert Lansing. These he now collected and edited into a continuous monthly narrative. In the first instance, this involved altering the grammatical structure of the letters, removing greetings, as well as changing verbs and pronouns. Thereafter, more serious editing took place to remove all statements liable to cause Gerard embarrassment. Thus, the view that he had expressed to Lansing in November 1916 that 'there is no chance of starving Germany out'[36] was excised to reflect the fact that America now supported, and indeed participated in, the Allied blockade. Also struck out was a paragraph on the question of U-boats and armed merchant ships that showed Gerard in agreement with the German position on this sensitive issue:

> All my sympathies are with the Germans on this matter . . . It seems to me to be an absurd proposition that a submarine must come to the surface, give warning, offer to put passengers and crew in safety, and constitute itself a target for merchant ships, that not only make a practice of firing at submarines on sight but have undoubtedly received orders to do so.[37]

The 'diary' that was created by these means, as well as the book in which it was contained, proved to be a supremely efficacious propaganda vehicle. Once again letters of praise rolled in. Henry F. Burton, a member of the Department of Latin at the University of Rochester, was unusual in writing to correct 'two typographical errors in the Latin quotation on page 126.' However, his comment that 'you have done the country a great service, both in your former book and in this one, in exposing so vividly the unscrupulous hostility of the German Government to us and all free peoples'[38] was more of a piece with the other letters Gerard received. Many readers would express the view, succinctly recorded here by one from Paris, Texas, that 'it does not seem possible for anyone to read "Face to Face with Kaiserism" without fairly boiling.'[39] From Gerard's point of view, reactions like this made the book – and, indeed, all of his written propaganda – an unqualified triumph.

Finally, if Gerard enjoyed considerable success mobilizing American public opinion with such traditional tools as the spoken and written word, he was to prove even more adept at achieving this end when using the newest and most modern form of popular communications and mass entertainment, namely the cinema. At the time of the American declaration of war against Germany, Gerard was no stranger to the world of the motion picture. Indeed, as early as March 1915, he had realized the potential value of cinema as a means of self-promotion and, accordingly, had persuaded a movie company to produce a short film depicting him at work at his desk at the embassy in Berlin. As he had correctly anticipated the finished product, entitled 'Our Ambassador to

Germany Shown for the First Time', had proven highly effective at enhancing public awareness of his work when it was screened back in America; so much so, in fact, that it helped to turn Gerard into a household name.⁴⁰ Naturally, with this cinematic success behind him, Gerard proved very receptive when, in 1917, the first proposals reached him for turning his autobiographical writings into a picture for the big screen. The offer that he eventually accepted came from Jack Warner of Warner Brothers, who wrote to Gerard in July:

> Please advise us if there would be a possibility of arranging with you for the exclusive right to produce your articles in motion picture form. We are in a position to produce the subject on an elaborate scale, which, at this time, would create much thought and comment, and would have a telling effect on the American public.⁴¹

This letter, as Jack Warner would later admit in his autobiography, while 'without any outright falsehoods', was slightly disingenuous.⁴² Contrary to its vague implications of movie-making expertise, neither Jack Warner nor any of his brothers had as yet produced a single major feature. Indeed, at this stage in their career, their business had not progressed much beyond being a very small and largely unknown movie distribution company. As a result, the brothers Warner were not nearly as well placed as they implied to turn Gerard's writings into a blockbuster motion picture. Quite the contrary, in the business world almost nobody had heard of them, which meant that their name carried no influence and they could not easily secure credit or any of the other facilities necessary for making a movie. Indicative of their then level of anonymity and lack of business muscle is a letter that Gerard received in August 1918 from the Claridge Hotel: 'In establishing credit at this hotel, Mr H[arry] M. Warner . . . has given us your name as referee. We would greatly appreciate a confidential statement from you . . . regarding Mr Warner's responsibility. . . .' Gerard's reply, by return of post, that 'so far as I know Mr Warner's credit is good'⁴³, seems comical when viewed with the knowledge that Warner brothers was shortly to become a major studio. However, it accurately represented their status at the time: they were but small players in the world of the big screen.

If Jack Warner's letter was, thus, liberal with the truth in respect to Warner Brothers' status as film makers, it was, nevertheless, to prove completely accurate in its prediction of their ability to turn Gerard's story into a 'motion picture . . . which . . . would have a telling effect on the American public,' as their film of *My Four Years in Germany* turned out to be an enormous success in just about every possible respect. In financial terms, for example, it can only be described as a blockbuster. Having cost them $50,000 for the screen rights, it grossed approximately one and a half million and provided Warner Brothers with a net profit after the repayment of all loans and expenses of $130,000. As they themselves were more than happy to admit, both then and later, gaining the opportunity to produce Gerard's story was the break that turned them from just another small movie company into major players in the motion picture industry. As Harry Warner conceded to Gerard in 1924: 'We feel that you were the foundation of our success, and we know that when you put your confidence in us and gave us the rights to your book in preference to others, we were well started on our upward path.'[44]

Matching the film's success as a commercial venture was its success as a piece of propaganda. In part, the latter condition was a natural consequence of the former. As the takings reveal, the film was seen by a great many people. Although some modern cinema historians have been less than flattering about the picture – Kevin Brownlow, for example, describes it as 'primitive propaganda' and observes that 'the simple-mindedness of the film is beyond belief'[45] – this was not the re-action of contemporaries. With the notable exception of President Wilson, who was 'much distressed'[46] by its casual violence and extreme nationalism, reviewers and film critics vied with one another to heap praise on the production. The *Boston Herald*, for example, eulogized the film as 'one of the most remarkable screen productions ever seen' and went on to exclaim:

> Gerard's account of America's fight from inside Germany against the barbarities of the Hun as it appeared in book form was remarkable, but it takes visualization to bring home a full realization of some of the strange truths in the book. . . . One is almost sickened with the unfolding of Teuton perfidy and murderous calculation on the screen. . . .[47]

These sentiments were echoed in the *Boston Advertiser*, which described the film as 'an absorbingly interesting narrative from start to finish', before noting, without apparent consciousness of the exaggeration of the claim, that 'artistically, it is almost perfect.' As to the picture's ability to convince its audience of the justice of the American cause, this also received hyperbolic treatment. 'The havoc that militarism can wreak is illustrated in full,' it proclaimed and then added:

> . . . the film lends a realism and directness to the narrative that gives it a living, vivid appeal. There are thrills, horror, tragedy, in this remarkable film, but, above all, facts that everyone should know. . . . Ambassador Gerard's book was a revelation. The film will bring its message to thousands who have not had the time to read Gerard's story in his own words.[48]

As these reviews predicted, many individual cinema goers were, indeed, deeply affected by the film. Few letters, however, illustrate its extraordinary impact better than one that Gerard received in March 1918 from Arthur C. Train, an attorney-at-law:

> With some forebodings we took a party to see 'My Four Years in Germany' last night. I must confess to having had a good many misgivings about it from many points of view, but I want to tell you without delay that I believe that this is the most powerful and convincing argument for a finished fight with militarism that has or ever could be presented. If I tell you that a case-hardened old fan like myself left the theatre trembling with indignation and excitement so that I could think of nothing else and could not sleep for hours, you may believe that this note is not perfunctory. I cannot tell you how glad I am that you had this put on the screen.[49]

Wilson aside, the United States government felt likewise and, in the form of the CPI, both licensed and exported it for propaganda purposes, not unsuccessfully as a letter from Sydney, Australia, makes evident: '... the film surpasses all things we have ever had in Aus.... Wish you could have seen the outburst of applause at so many scens [sic] in that picture.'[50]

As with Gerard's speeches and writings, the Ambassador's proximity to the events described and his willingness to vouch for the veracity of what was depicted went a long way towards explaining both the popularity and the propaganda value of the film, which ceaselessly played on its supposed realism by flashing up the title card 'Fact, Not Fiction!' at every opportunity. This simple expedient worked. The reviewer in *Moving Picture World* (30/3/18) who observed that the film's 'chief merit is its authenticity'[51] was but one of many commentators who would make this point; Fred Dangerfield in *Pictures and Picturegoer* (11/4/18), for example, likewise praised the film on the grounds that 'this peep behind the scenes of German militarism is an actual record of history and not the fantastic story of some crazy and imaginary kingdom.'[52] In addition to the kudos gained from being an 'eyewitness' account, another important contribution to the film's success as propaganda was made by the anecdotal style adopted in the screenplay. The film presented a series of vignettes from Gerard's career as ambassador in Berlin. As with the stories he told in his speeches and articles, these tales presented an unambiguous message to the audience: German hostility towards America made it necessary for America to fight back. Once again, Gerard's own personal confrontations with the leading figures of Wilhelmine Germany provided the main means for conveying this. One scene, for example, adapted loosely from one of the better-known sections from his book, has the Kaiser, in bellicose mood, confronting Gerard with the taunt 'America will not dare to fight. I have 500,000 reserves in America.' To this, the screen Gerard, played by Halbert Brown, retorts in an obvious reference to the modern-day hanging tree, 'And we have 500,000 lampposts in America.' Similar signs of American strength in the face of German contempt are shown in the scene depicting Gerard's departure from Berlin following the resumption of unrestricted submarine warfare, during which Chancellor Bethmann Hollweg presented Gerard with his passports while remarking, 'we have decided that America won't fight anyway.' Gerard's riposte, 'Won't fight, eh?', is followed by footage of marching American soldiers. Bitter exchanges such as these were a regular feature of the movie. They were not, however, the film's only way of suggesting a German threat to the United States. In an obvious attempt to cast people's minds back to the infamous Zimmermann telegram, the film made much of German plans to divide America between Mexico, Japan and themselves, while a montage depicting the American flag under a German boot was used to reveal the true nature of German militarism's schemes for the American people. This may have been unsophisticated, but it left viewers in no doubt as to which side was in the right.

In conclusion, how can one evaluate Gerard's impact on the American home front? The former Ambassador was an audience-pulling public speaker, a bestselling author, and a successful writer for the big screen. All of these triumphs were achieved in the context of explaining to the American public how the First World War came about and generating support for the United States' participation in it. By regaling Americans with tales of how he had confronted German militarists in the diplomatic arena, which, by extension, illustrated how the United States could triumph over the German military machine, he helped to persuade numerous people that it was both necessary and possible to fight them on the battlefield. Given the strength of feeling that had once existed in America behind non-intervention and neutrality, this transformation, which can be attributed to, among others, Gerard, is all the more remarkable.

Notes

1   Hugh Wilson, *The Education of a Diplomat* (London: Longmans, 1938), p.171.
2   Rachel West, *The Department of State on the Eve of the First World War* (Athens, GA: University of Georgia Press, 1978), p.91.
3   James Lawrence Troisi, 'Ambassador Gerard and American-German Relations, 1913–1917' (D.Phil, Syracuse University, 1978), p.157.
4   Diary of Colonel House, 18 September 1914, Edward M. House papers, Manuscripts and Archives, Yale University Library.

5   Arthur S. Link, *Wilson: The Struggle for Neutrality, 1914–1915* (Princeton: Princeton UP, 1960), p.657.

6   Wilson, *Education*, p.171.

7   Joseph C. Grew, *Turbulent Era: A Diplomatic Record of Forty Years, 1904–1945* (Boston: Houghton Mifflin, 1952), I, p.240.

8   Transcript of National Defense Dinner, South Armory, Boston, 18 April, 1917. James Watson Gerard Collection, Mansfield Library, University of Montana (hereafter Gerard papers), box 425, folder 5.

9   Robert Lansing to Gerard, 29 March 1917. Gerard papers, box 422, folder 6.

10 Joseph Tummulty to Gerard, 29 May 1917. Gerard papers, box 417, folder 4.

11 Gerard papers, box 423, folder 3.

12 Address by Gerard at the Baltimore Hotel, Kansas City, Missouri, 7 October 1918. Gerard papers, box 425, folder 8.

13 'Address of James W. Gerard: Published by The San Francisco Call for California School Children' (undated). Gerard papers, box 426, folder 1.

14 Address by Gerard at the Hotel Astor, New York, 14 April 1917. Gerard papers, box 425, folder 5.

15 Address by Gerard for the liberty Loan Committee, 12 June 1917. Gerard papers, box 425, folder 5.

16 Gerard to Seymour B. Conger, 31 October 1917. Gerard papers, box 20, folder 3.

17 E.S. Burke, Jr to Gerard, 1 November 1917. Gerard papers, box 23, folder 3.

18 George Creel to Gerard, 12 July 1918. Gerard papers, box 28, folder 14.

19 J.J. Tobias to Gerard, 20 August 1917. Gerard papers, box 25, folder 12.

20 Arthur W. Page to Gerard, 29 May 1916. Gerard papers, box 17, folder 30.

21 David Lawrence to [unknown], 15 March 1917. Gerard papers, box 20, folder 4.

22 Stewart Halsey Ross, *Propaganda for War: How the United States was Conditioned to Fight the Great War of 1914–1918* (Jefferson, NC: McFarland and Company, 1996), p.253.

23 A.E. Anderson to Gerard, 24 October 1917. Gerard papers, box 19, folder 10.

24 Walter Hines Page to Gerard, 28 September 1917. Gerard papers, box 24, folder 6.

25 *Daily Telegraph* to Gerard, 23 August 1917. Gerard papers, box 19, folder 17.

26 Jean Jusserand to Gerard, 31 October 1917. Gerard papers, box 22, folder 17.

27 Henry P. Fletcher to Gerard, 5 August 1918. Gerard papers, box 29, folder 6.

28 Colonel John Buchan to Walter Hines Page, 27 September 1917. Gerard papers, box 24, folder 6. Buchan's central role in selecting those books that would be used in British propaganda is confirmed in a British government memorandum (probably from 1917) written by Robert Donald. See 'Report on the Purchase and Publication of Books', PRO: INF 4/10.

29 Ernest T. Carter to Gerard, 13 February 1918. Gerard papers, box 425, folder 18.

30 Many versions of this book were published. All citations in this essay come from the British edition. See James W. Gerard, *My Four Years in Germany* (London: Hodder & Stoughton, 1917), pp.167–8.

31 Advertisement by Grosset & Dunlap for *My Four Years in Germany*. Gerard papers, box 444, folder 5.

32 M. Margaret Speik, 'Keep Your Eye on Uncle Sam', (Music Score, Los Angeles, 1918). Gerard papers, box 488, folder 3.

33 James W. Gerard, *Face to Face with Kaiserism* (London: Hodder & Stoughton, 1918), p.vii.

34 Gerard to Walter Hines Page, 30 October 1917. Gerard papers, box 24, folder 6.

35 David Lawrence to Gerard, 16 December 1917. Gerard papers, box 22, folder 28.

36 Edited copy of Gerard to Robert Lansing, 16 November 1915. Gerard papers, box 13, folder 10.

37 Edited copy of Gerard to Colonel House, 23 February 1916. Gerard papers, box 16, folder 12.

38 Henry F. Burton to Gerard, 6 July 1918. Gerard papers, box 28, folder 9.

39 Reginald B. Leach to Gerard, 9 August 1918. Gerard papers, box 31, folder 5.

40 Timothy L. Lohof, 'The Berlin Embassy of James Watson Gerard: Reflections of a Diplomatic Paradigm Shift, 1913–1917' (Ph.d, University of Montana, 1997), pp.112–3.

41 J.L. Warner to Gerard, 23 July 1917. Gerard papers, box 26, folder 7.

42 Jack L. Warner, *My First Hundred Years in Hollywood* (New York: Random House, 1965), p.90.

43 Hotel Claridge to Gerard and Gerard to Hotel Claridge, 20 August 1918. Gerard papers, box 28, folder 3

44 Harry M. Warner to Gerard, 7 January 1924. Gerard papers, box 64, folder 20.

45 Kevin Brownlow, *The War, the West and the Wilderness* (New York: Knopf, 1972), pp.135 & 138.

46 Ray Stannard Baker, *Woodrow Wilson: Life and Letters* (Garden City, NY: Doubleday, Page & Company, 1927–39), VIII, p.213.

47 *Boston Herald*, 16 April 1918, Gerard papers, box 30, folder 4.

48 *Boston Advertiser*, 16 April 1918. Gerard papers, box 30, folder 4.

49 Arthur C. Train to Gerard, 18 March 1918. Gerard papers, box 34, folder 7.
50 Rev. C.T. Forseuth to Gerard, 15 June 1918. Gerard papers, box 29, folder 10.
51 Michael T. Isenberg, *War on Film: The American Cinema and World War I, 1914–1941* (Rutherford: Fairleigh Dickinson UP, 1981), p.152.
52 Brownlow, *The War*, p.135.

Part Four

The Italian Front

Chapter 9

General Luigi Cadorna:
Italy and the First World War

James F. Gentsch

The year 1866 was not an auspicious time to join the Italian Army. The service was still reeling from the disastrous influence of its constabulary duties during the *brigantaggio*, the period from the unification of Italy to the late 1860s, when the primary function of the army was maintaining law and order, and was not, therefore, organized to engage a major European opponent. Although theoretically reforms had been set in motion since the late 1850s[1], the Italian Army defeated at Custozza in June continued to be plagued by natural inertia, the causes of which were a rigid officers corps, a lack of operational precedents, and a dearth of natural resources and national cohesion. It was in this atmosphere that Luigi Cadorna began his military career.

When he joined the army, Cadorna, like his colleagues, faced slow advancement and poor salaries. However, certain ambitious and motivated officers were interested in the study of the art and science of war, forming a 'dedicated and compact' corps.[2] Luigi showed potential and an exceptional ability to organize, and in 1892 at forty-two years of age, he earned his colonelcy.[3] Nevertheless, he was overshadowed in many respects by his father. Raffaele Cadorna had enjoyed much success during his career, fighting in 1848–9, and serving in the Piedmontese Army in the Crimea. In 1866, his corps was one of the few noteworthy Italian success stories, which helped to distance him from Italy's dismal failures in the Seven Weeks' War. Raffaele's crowning achievement came in September 1870, when he completed the unification of Italy by capturing Rome during the *Porta Pia* while the French were fighting the Franco-Prussian War.

The years after the demise of France as Europe's chief land power was a monumental era in the evolution of warfare. It was in this climate that Luigi formulated the ideas that were to prevail later in his military tenure. He was quick to see that the Italian Army had to modernize in order to compete in European military circles. However, this was easier to conceptualize than it was to implement. The need for quick mobilization was readily apparent, but in Italy, with its mountainous terrain and regional population differences, the new standards of military rail organization proved difficult to realize.[4] Military modernization was expensive; and although Italy spent most of her national expenditure on the armed forces during this period, by August 1914 Italy was still considered in its military infancy. Cadorna was just reaching the higher command positions as the Italian Army grappled with these imposing dilemmas.[5]

Four years after being promoted to colonel, Luigi was appointed to the General Staff, and there had to wait fourteen years before obtaining corps command. When the Chief of Staff position became vacant around the same time, Cadorna was considered, but was passed over for the more pliant Alberto Pollio, although many believed that Cadorna was better suited to address many of the army's more urgent problems. However, Pollio was pro-German, and therefore seemed to be a safe choice in this era of diplomatic and military instability.[6] Pollio continued to plan military operations with Germany and Austria-Hungary, although the alliance had been deteriorating for some time. Indeed, the reason that Italy joined the *Triplice* in 1882 was the need to capitalize on German military prestige. The central difficulty with the alliance was that the national antagonism between Rome and Vienna hindered diplomatic and military co-operation, and by the turn of the century, many European commentators questioned its validity.[7] From 1902 to the beginning of the First World War, Italy negotiated with Great Britain and France, although the Italian government did not want to see the French continue to grow into a Mediterranean power.[8] This created an enormous rift between Italy's political and military leaders, for the politicians kept the negotiations secret, and continued to do so right until Italy declared war in May 1915. To operate in a diplomatic and military climate that was basically Clausewitzian in nature, communications between the heads of state and the military leaders were a necessity.[9] Correspondence between the Italian government and the military establishment was virtually non-existent, and when the representatives did talk about crucial matters, the meetings were normally strained and led to misunderstandings. Furthermore, the lines of communication between the army and the navy were worse than existed between the politicians and the generals.[10] These conditions so hampered Italian military operations that Cadorna must have felt that he was an island in a sea of confusion. With no reliable information coming from any quarter, Cadorna became isolated in his own theories. This made him appear like a hapless and disconnected commander, out of touch with reality, and unable to keep his finger on the pulse of contemporary diplomatic and military attitudes.

Just after assuming his country's highest military rank after Pollio's death in July 1914, it seems that many of Cadorna's characteristics became readily apparent. He was born of an aristocratic family in the northern Italian region of Piedmont, and therefore it was assumed that he inherited many 'Nordic' traits from his Germanic ancestors. He was a firm disciplinarian, who was often regarded as cold and indifferent to the conditions of his front-line soldiers.[11] However, Cadorna was preparing the Italian Army for the storm of the First World War from the time he was appointed Chief-of-Staff until Italian mobilization, for he needed to rectify numerous weaknesses before the army could become an effective force.[12] Cadorna was not a 'from the front' style of commander, choosing to lead by telephone and courier, staying behind the lines to perceive the front as a whole instead of becoming fixated on one particular sector. The truth of the matter was that most of his contemporaries could not produce solutions to the complexities of modern attritional warfare, and it was Cadorna's misfortune that many considered the Italian Army defeated by its reputation before it was ever engaged in military operations.[13]

In a conundrum rare in the annals of military-diplomatic history, Italy needed to align herself with the leading land and naval powers to achieve anything diplomatically.[14] Desiring to manoeuvre behind the shield of German military might, Italian diplomats also had to consider that the Italian peninsula presented over 4100 miles of indefensible coastline, therefore Great Britain and the spectre of the Royal Navy heavily influenced any Italian military venture.[15] Although this difficulty was not as severe just after 1871, due to the awe in which Germany was held after her impressive defeat of France, as the Royal Navy continued to assert its presence in world affairs, Italy's diplomatic bonds with Germany and Austria-Hungary weakened. At the time of the Sarajevo assassination, Italy was in a quandary about what she would do in case of a European war. When Cadorna assumed command, he fell straight into this abyss, for he was not kept abreast of the vicissitudes in Italian diplomacy. While Italian politicians wrangled with Allied and *Triplice* negotiators for territorial compensation, Cadorna remained dangerously unaware of the change in Italian foreign policy.[16] Just a few weeks before Italy was to announce that she was going to war with Austria-Hungary, Cadorna was informed to make the necessary plans for conducting an offensive against the Habsburg Empire. Cadorna, taken completely by surprise and astonished that he was kept in the dark for so long, rightfully exploded

'What? I knew nothing!'[17] Much of the military planning to this time had been directed against France. Although exigency plans had been created for a war with Vienna, many changes had to be implemented before the Italian high command could enact any effective strategy against Austria-Hungary.

No one was prepared for the tactical realities of the First World War. Not only did Cadorna have to contend with an army that was materially weak and engaged in a nasty little colonial war, but, in addition, his theatre of operations was arguably the most difficult of the entire war. Hemmed in along the northern frontier with mountains often reaching elevations over 10,000 feet, the Italians were at a severe topographic disadvantage. Any other avenue of approach to the Austro-Hungarian Empire would have to be by sea, an unlikely prospect considering the strained relations that existed between the army and navy. Selecting the extreme north-east sector of the Austro-Italian frontier just north of the Adriatic Sea for his main effort, Cadorna soon found himself in a slugging match with a skilled and determined enemy.[18] Since most of the writings about the influence of modern weapons on tactics were poorly received or simply ignored, Cadorna reacted to the stalemate in a typically First World War fashion: head-long assaults with massive concentrations of artillery and infantry.[19] Although the existing historiography does not cover the matter in detail, it was an Italian characteristic to make up for the deficiencies in weapons and tactics with the blood of the foot soldier. To assuage the popular myths created by the debacle at Caporetto, and by British and American veterans of the Second World War, the Italian infantryman between May 1915 and October 1917 displayed abundant courage and zeal when coming to grips with the Austro-Hungarians.[20] However, Cadorna failed to consider the wellbeing of his main instrument, for rest in the rear areas was almost unheard of in most Italian divisions. The morale of any soldier would be devastated by the rigours of combat without periods of recuperation.

Since Cadorna fought his war from behind the lines, the Italian high command was slow to develop tactical innovations that considered the hostile geography of the Italian front. More often than not, Italian infantrymen had to attack over rocky and rugged surfaces, up slopes averaging between thirty and forty-five degrees, against a well-equipped enemy protected by defences excavated out of solid rock. Much of what the Italians learned tactically was from the Austrians, who were refining tested German operational and tactical practices, or from the French, who were not known at this time to be a source of tactical innovation.[21] A good example of this was the Austrian offensive in the Trentino in May 1916. Using loose formations that used terrain features to open holes in the Italian lines after a tremendous artillery preparation, the

Austrians enjoyed some success before the weight of their attack caused the logistic apparatus to break down. Using this information to form infiltration units of his own, Cadorna shifted ample reserves and guns to the Isonzo while the Austrians were preoccupied with the Brusilov offensive on the Eastern Front to capture Gorizia in August 1916.[22] Proving adept at handling large bodies of men over Italy's less than adequate rail system, Cadorna shifted the brunt of his army and guns to the Isonzo after the abortive Austrian attack on the Asiago plateau. Massing one of the largest artillery concentrations ever to be used on the Italian front, and employing select infantry units at certain concentration points, the Italians captured Gorizia, Mount Sabotino, and carried the western section of the Carso plateau in two weeks, whereas before nearly six months of offensive action failed to secure any of these objectives.

At the beginning of the war, the Italian Army consisted of thirty-five divisions. When Cadorna started his eleventh battle on the Bainsizza plateau in September 1917, he had sixty-five divisions at his disposal.[23] The drain of attritional mountain warfare and rapid growth produced severe problems, such as an acute lack of munitions. Cadorna had to organize, arm, and train over one million men in two years – not an inconsiderable feat for an institution that was not known for its organizational capacity, especially considering that going into the conflict the Italians were still suffering substantial casualties in Africa.[24] It is in this realm where Cadorna did his best work, and if it were not for this progress, the results of the Austro-German offensive in October would have been far worse.

Nearly two years of continual action was not only sapping Italy's material ability to wage the war, it was also draining her morale. Cadorna, a strict disciplinarian far removed for the realities of trench warfare, failed to allow his soldiers to have any substantial periods of rest and relaxation, and therefore they lost much of their elan. Moreover, the offensive posture of Cadorna's military operations often forced Italian division and corps commanders to neglect their forward defences.[25] Just after the Italian successes in September on the Bainsizza, Cadorna ordered defences to be strengthened, for the near capitulation of Russia had freed Austrian formations from other duties, and he feared an enemy offensive. Although the Italians had fortified certain areas, mainly in the topographically favourable stretches of terrain around Gorizia and the Carso plateau, the Austro-German army struck on the upper Isonzo, along a lightly defended ridge just south of the small town of Caporetto. The Italians had planned to use a mobile defence, but the speed of the enemy advance caught them completely off guard, and soon the Italian Second Army was in flight, while the Third Army was forced to enact a strategic withdrawal across the Fruili Plains. The enemy offensive forced Cadorna to leave behind much of his heavy equipment and artillery – the accumulation of two years' hard work. These losses, and the capture of about 300,000 men severely crippled the Italian war effort.

Not having secured the defeat of the Austro-Hungarian Army after two years of extreme hardship and losses, Cadorna was sacked and replaced by one of his corps commanders, Armando Diaz.[26] Cadorna's cold and indifferent attitude toward not only his soldiers, but also toward the politicians had not ingratiated him with any power bloc that might have proved beneficial to him in case of a disaster. Therefore, Cadorna was supposedly kicked upstairs, and was sent to represent Italy on the Supreme Allied War Council. Soon thereafter, an investigation fixed the blame for the debacle squarely on his shoulders, and Cadorna retired in disgrace in December 1918. In all fairness, the Italian government needed a scapegoat, and since Cadorna was no longer the Chief of Staff and had directed the Italian armies since the beginning of the war, he was the logical choice. The government failed to pay attention to Cadorna when he warned that the front-line soldiers were being saturated with anti-war propaganda, which was growing vociferously all over Europe.[27] He should have expected a great deal of criticism for his lack of preparedness when the Central Powers struck; however, the government should have realized that by attaching most of the blame to Cadorna, they had negated a fair record of success along the Isonzo during the first two years of the war.

The reputation of the Italian Army and Cadorna continues to languish. Holger Herwig, for example, recently deprecated him and his Austrian counterpart General Franz Conrad von Hötzendorf in the following way: 'Both ignored terrain and weather. Both underestimated supply. Both stressed the will to fight. Both devised grandiose strategies that bore little relation to ready strength. And both insisted on their own infallibility.'[28] However, Cadorna should not be uncritically blamed for the apparent lack of Italian progress during the war. He took an army embroiled in a colonial venture and forged it, under the most trying conditions, into one comparable with other European armies of the era. It is easy to say the Italian Army was bad, and that Cadorna was unimaginative or, as John Keegan puts it, a 'château general'.[29] However, the Italian Army had to attack in the most inhospitable front of the entire war, and was capable of capturing many key objectives, often when their efforts were hampered by lack of artillery and ammunition.[30] The Austrian defences were exceedingly strong and set in mutually supporting positions across the front, providing Austrian machine gunners and artillery officers with strong positions for enfilade fire. Cadorna had conducted reconnaissance of the front before the war, and knew what his soldiers would have to face while fighting in the mountainous terrain.[31] He was aware that operations on the Italian front would take patience and technical innovation, and was quick to adopt new weapons, such as the trench mortar and the *teleferiche* railway. The latter was a cable anchored to a base and stretched to the summit of an elevation, on which a cart or basket moved supplies and men to areas where the altitude and slope prohibited road construction. The need for mechanical assistance played an important role in the development of Cadorna's army. Unfortunately, these gadgets were seen as the answers to tricky tactical and operational questions instead of being incorporated into existing doctrine, or being the catalysts for entirely new procedures. Often when certain divisions formulated new practices, the lack of communication on the administrative level prevented them from being disseminated. This is probably Cadorna's most glaring fault, and shows just how isolated he was from the various contingents of his own army.

Contending with the rocky rugged terrain and the Austrian positional supremacy should have been an ideal catalyst for tactical innovation. However, the topographical compartmentalization of the front prevented the Italian high command from forming a clear picture of what was working or failing. Still, the Italians implemented some astonishing tactical changes, which were generally a result of learning from the enemy, or from division commanders who assessed certain areas and formed their units according to specific geographic problems.[32] As the first four Isonzo offensives attempted to pierce the Austrian defences, the first just north of Mount Sabotino, the last three on the topographically more conducive Carso plateau, the Italians found it impossible to make any substantial progress against the enemy while using tactics that would not have been out of place on a battlefield during the Napoleonic era or during the American Civil War. This was not just an Italian problem – even the much vaunted Germans went to war in 1914 with tactical formations that were little changed since the victorious campaigns of 1866 and 1870–1. Realizing that they had to contend with perplexing terrain difficulties, and that their methods lacked the finesse to overcome and retain most defensive positions, the Italians began to search for solutions and, unfortunately, looked to the French for tactical answers.[33] Although not as inept as many historians portray it be, the French Army was not exactly the source from which any belligerent would want to borrow military instructions at this stage of the war. The French were also enamoured by the results of the Wars of German Unification, and thought the answer to their military conundrum was to emulate the German model on a larger, more efficient scale. Each nation is a separate and unique entity, and therefore should forge its military accordingly. Therefore the problem with Italy, and indeed much of Europe, was that she should have been trying to create a national force based on her own capabilities and limitations instead of copying a successful yet dated German model. The Italian Army needed to be Italian, not a mere imitation of the German Army whose strength was as much from economic and industrial power as it was from any radical advances in the military arts and sciences.[34]

By the time the Austrians struck in the Trentino, the Italians had received some tactical advice from the French, who were then going through the horrors of Verdun. However, the problem was not that they were receiving procedural assistance from the French, it was that they were usually receiving this help nearly six months after the tactics were first employed. Considering the rigid and ponderous methods prevalent in the Italian Army, it was usually several more months before any of this experience could be translated into military practice. Some procedures would take even longer to employ because of material deficiencies. The result was that the Italians were tactically and operationally behind most of the other major belligerents. A case in point was the massive artillery concentration used against Austrian defences on the Bainsizza. An overwhelming concentration of guns was nearly a constant goal of Allied and Central Power planners since the beginning of the war, the desire increasing after the German attack at Verdun. The attack on Verdun began in February 1916. The battle of the Bainsizza started in August 1917. This was just three months before the Central Powers introduced new tactical methods at Caporetto. Cadorna was methodical, but he often did not push tactical and operational changes fast enough, and hardly had time to use the old methods before he fell victim to a new set of offensive procedures.

Many historians wonder why Cadorna did not use the navy to land combat units in an area where geography would allow them to be employed more effectively.[35] The army and navy never enjoyed a convivial relationship, and therefore could not count on each other to be the most 'co-operative' partners.[36] Both were wary of enterprises that would waste resources and leave themselves in the lurch. Cadorna was hesitant to release any of his battalions to make a landing along the eastern coast of the Adriatic, and the navy did not want to risk its capital ships in the same enterprise, for they knew amphibious operations would force a major surface action with the Austrian Navy.[37] Although the Italians had landed approximately 40,000 troops along the north African coast during the war with Turkey in 1910-1, the aftershocks of this campaign still weighed upon the minds of military planners. Moreover, the areas where troops could be landed did not offer better geographic conditions than existed on the Isonzo Front. Italian formations were landed in Albania, and promptly suffered a reverse in the field and had to be evacuated with the loss of much equipment.[38] Another venture, where Italian forces were deployed in Salonika, did little more than isolate a sizeable force. The enterprise held little chance of tactical success, and did not make a strategic contribution until the collapse of the Austro-Hungarian and Bulgarian armies late in 1918.

In hindsight, Cadorna seems to be just another commander that falls into the stereotype of a First World War general, an indifferent man who sent his soldiers to die by the thousands, while staying safely behind the front, out of harm's way. This is only half true. Cadorna was conscious of the heavy losses the Italians were suffering – one and a half million casualties during the war, 460,000 of which were fatalities – if not from a humanitarian viewpoint, from operational realism.[39] He knew that the Italian nation could not go on indefinitely due to its lack of natural resources and economic reserves. He used the only commodity the Italians possessed, a sizeable population base, until better operational and tactical methods could be developed. It was his misfortune that the Central Powers were generally the first to introduce innovative tactical and operational procedures, and just happened to test them in the secondary theatres before employing them on the Western Front.

It is curious that the Italians have been castigated for their debacle at Caporetto, as Cadorna skilfully withdrew his Third Army across the congested Fruili Plains, and even managed to salvage certain portions of the Second Army. Although trying to establish defensive positions on the major waterways in the eastern sector of the plains, he was forced back to the Piave River before he could restore his front. Geography and distance prevented the British or the French from saving the Italians, for by the time Allied troops reached Italy, Cadorna had stabilized the front, but had been fired in the process.[40] Haig finally had to succumb to French pressure for overall direction of the war so that unity of command could re-establish Allied defences on the Western Front.

Cadorna was not totally forgotten after Caporetto. He went on to be the Italian representative on the Supreme Allied War Council, and exhibited an uncanny grasp of military problems. There are two reasons for this. The first is that Cadorna had invaluable experience in handling an army; the second was that he was a well-known theoretical writer about European military affairs, and had dealt academically with many problems concerning coalition warfare before the war. Cadorna's problem was that he undoubtedly held the wrong post, for he could not deal appropriately with the minutiae of war. His father, the general who had shown some promise in the Seven Weeks' War, realized his full potential as the Minister of War for the government of Tuscany in 1859. It was in this area where Cadorna showed his optimum potential. Once the politicians confided in him concerning Italy's diplomatic endeavours, Cadorna followed their policies and worked energetically toward their realization. His realistic mind, although restricting his creativity, never allowed him to entertain fantastic or unrealistic schemes. This aptitude for the diplomatic-military sphere was clearly seen at the Supreme War Council, for he could quickly equate objectives with available means and gauge probable outcomes, not only in a military sense, but in the diplomatic realm as well. This could be a result of having to contend with Italy's chronic lack of resources while trying to conduct a major war effort – something that he lost sight of during the offensives of 1915, but then addressed in future operations. Therefore, his organizational talents would have been better suited to the war ministry, and were not geared to the frustratingly complex phenomenon of a First World War army command. After the war, Cadorna busied himself with writing a book about the Italian front, much of which was in defence of his actions connected with Caporetto. Falling into relative obscurity, he was somewhat revitalized when Mussolini, ever the astute politician and consummate showman, made Cadorna a Field Marshal in 1924. This ceremony was an empty gesture, doing nothing to vindicate Cadorna's reputation, which still suffers today from a lack of scholarship and interest. He will never be known as one of the great captains of history, but considering what he did with what he had available, his story deserves better treatment.

Soon the Western Front would be embroiled in a chaotic retreat, and many of the divisions sent to Italy would be recalled. However, with Cadorna fading into the history of the First World War, a new phase of the war emerged in Italy, as British and French contingents arrived to bolster their crippled ally.

Notes

1   John Gooch, 'Clausewitz Disregarded: Italian Military Thought and Doctrine, 1815–1943' in Michael I. Handel (ed.), *Clausewitz and Modern Strategy* (London 1986) p.306.

2   John Gooch, *Army, State and Society in Italy, 1870–1915* (London 1989) p.xii.

3   Trevor N. Dupuy et al, *The Harper Encyclopedia of Military Biography* (New York 1992) p.120.

4   Gooch, *Army*, pp.21, 30, 104; B.R. Sullivan, 'The Strategy of the Decisive Weight: Italy, 1882–1922' in Murray, Knox and Bernstein (eds), *The Making of Strategy: Rulers, States and War* (Cambridge 1994) p.317.

5   Giorgio Rochat, 'L' Esercito Italiano Nell' Estate 1914', *Nuova Revista Storica*, 45, 1961, 297.

6   James Edmonds, *Military Operations, Italy. 1915–1919* (London 1949) p.3.

7   Ibid., pp.2–4.

8   J.C. King (ed), *The First World War* (London 1972) p.121.

9   Sullivan, 'Decisive Weight', p.310.

10   John Gooch, 'Italy during the First World War' in Allan Millett and Williamson Murray, *Military Effectiveness. Volume 1: The First World War* (London 1988) p.158; Paul G. Halpern, *A Naval History of World War I* (London 1994) p.167.

11   Arminius (pseud.), *From Serajevo to the Rhine: Generals of the Great War* (London 1933) pp.233-4.

12   Richard Bosworth, *Italy and the Approach of the First World War* (London 1983) p.125.

13   Charles à Court Repington, *The First World War* (Hampshire 1991) Vol.1, p.222-3.

14   John A. Thayer, *Italy and the Great War* (Wisconsin UP 1964) p.145.

15   Z.A.B. Zeman, *A Diplomatic History of the First World War* (London 1971) p.4.

16   Christopher Howard, 'The Treaty of London, 1915', *History*, 25, 1941, 351; James H. Burgwyn, *The Legend of the Mutilated Victory: Italy, the Great War and the Paris Peace Conference, 1915–1919*, (Westport CT 1993) p.221.

17   Sullivan, 'Decisive Weight', pp.331, 334.

18   See James F. Gentsch, 'Italy, Geography and the First World War' (London PhD 1999).

19   Gooch, 'Italy during the First World War', pp.170–1.

20   For Italian-Slavic enmity see Antonio Sema, *La Grande Guerra Sul Fronte Dell' Isonzo*, (2 vols Gorizia 1995–7).

21   Salvatore Pagano, *Evoluzione Della Tattica Durante La Grande Guerra* (Turin 1930) p.72.

22   Mario Caracciolo, *Italy in the World War* (Rome 1920) p.109.

23   Luigi Villari, *The War on the Italian Front* (London 1932) p.130.

24   Bosworth, *Italy*, pp.100, 125.

25   Ministero Della Guerra, Comando Del Corpo De Stato Maggiore – Ufficio Storico, *L'Esercito Italiano Nella Grande Guerra 1915–1918; Vol.4 – Le Operazioni Del 1917: Gli Avvenimenti dall' Ottobre al Dicemrbre, Tomo 3 (Narrazione)* (Rome 1967) pp.328-9.

26   R. Seth, *Caporetto: The Scapegoat Battle* (London 1965) p.190.

27   Ibid., p.178; G.L. McEntee, *Italy's Part in Winning the World War* (Princeton UP 1934) p.57.

28   Holger H. Herwig, *The First World War: Germany and Austria-Hungary 1914–1918* (London 1998) p.152.

29   John Keegan, *The Mask of Command* (New York 1987) p.330.

30   Douglas W. Johnson, *Topography and Strategy in the War* (New York 1917) p.131.

31   Helen Zimmern, *Italian Leaders of Today* (London 1915) p.181.

32   *49th Division, XI Corps, Third Army – Division Diary*, Vol.1,

Rec.no.1350 f. Pos.127/S, 3 June 1916–31 January 1917 in Military Archives, Rome, General Staff of the Army History Department.

33 French circulars became available to the Italians in late 1915 and were used until the end of the war: see Pagano, *Evoluzione*.

34 Gooch, 'Italy during the First World War', pp.162, 184.

35 Ibid., p.166.

36 Ibid., p.158.

37 Halpern, *Naval History*, pp.142, 167.

38 Gooch, 'Italy during the First World War', p.166.

39 G.M. Trevelyan, *Scenes from Italy's War* (London 1919) p.235.

40 Edmonds, *Italy*, p.91.

Chapter 10

Personalities in Conflict? Lloyd George, the Generals and the Italian Campaign, 1917–18

Matthew Hughes

Early in the morning of 24 October 1917, the Austro-German Fourteenth Army struck at the Italian front line in the Julian Alps by the town of Caporetto. After a six-hour hurricane bombardment with high explosive, smoke and gas shells, a shelling of 'unprecedented fury', the Italian Second Army collapsed.[1] The disintegration of the Second Army at the battle of Caporetto threatened the Italian Third Army to the south along the river Isonzo with encirclement and soon Italian units along almost the entire front with Austria-Hungary were in full retreat. As Austrian and German shock troops pushed west and south down the mountain valleys of the Julian Alps, the Italians withdrew from the hard-fought gains of 1915–17 along the Isonzo and on the limestone plateau of the Carso. The German assault troops included a young Württemberger mountain infantry company commander, Erwin Rommel, who won the coveted *Pour le Mérite* decoration for his actions at Caporetto, and who would rise to even greater fame twenty-five years later commanding Italian and German forces in the deserts of north Africa. The Austro-German assault threatened Italy with defeat, surrender and departure from the war. In many sectors of the front, the Italian withdrawal became a *sauve qui peut* as ragged mobs of leaderless soldiers fled rearwards. Many Italian soldiers took the opportunity to surrender. The Italian Prime Minister from 30 October 1917, Vittorio Orlando, was determined to fight on, in Sicily if necessary.[2] Fortunately for Italy and the Entente Alliance, the Italians avoided a final battle on Sicily and eventually they regrouped behind the river Piave to face an overstretched enemy. However, when the Italians reformed on the Piave, they had lost, besides a huge swath of north-eastern Italy, 10,000 dead, 275,000 taken prisoner and some 400,000 deserters.[3] The magnitude of the defeat at Caporetto forced Britain and France to rush divisions from the hard-pressed Western Front to stabilize the Italian line on the Piave. Commanded at different times by Lieutenant General the Earl of Cavan and General Sir Herbert Plumer, the British expeditionary force in Italy at its peak numbered five divisions. The French force peaked at six divisions.

As a case study, the British intervention in the Italian campaign, 1917–18, provides valuable insights into the personal conflicts between the forceful and astute individuals within the highest echelons of the British decision-making process at a moment of crisis when it looked as though another Entente power would be knocked out of the war. In addition, the British intervention in Italy sheds light on how senior British officers in the field responded to having to work away from home alongside an allied army with which they were unfamiliar. This civil-military dispute is discussed further in Ian Beckett's chapter within the context of an examination of the role of King George V during the First World War.

The commonly held theory is that the 'generals', headed by the Chief of the Imperial General Staff (CIGS), Sir William Robertson, and Commander-in-Chief of the British army in France, Sir Douglas Haig, opposed and obstructed any peripheral campaigns such as the one in Italy, while the 'politicians', led by the British Prime Minister, David Lloyd George, looked to 'sideshows' as a means of redirecting war strategy.[4] This conflict has variously been described as 'westerners' versus 'easterners' and 'brass hats' versus 'frock coats'.[5] It has been argued that to obstruct Lloyd George's efforts to control war planning, the 'generals' produced disingenuous military reports and these partisan appreciations from the military experts skewed and damaged Britain's war effort.[6] In addition, the adage that the only thing worse than fighting in an alliance is not fighting in an alliance suggests that relations between the British force in Italy and the recently defeated Italian army it came to rescue would be awkward, especially considering the negative view held by the average 'Tommy' towards an army considered to be effete, poorly trained, carelessly led and badly equipped. The suggestion is that the British military was unable to work with an army made up, in the parlance of the time, of 'dagoes' and who, notwithstanding the war, still took a daily siesta.[7]

At the highest levels of command, the British generals of the Great War, even though they ultimately won the war, have never had a good press. The war poetry of Wilfred Owen, the prose of Leon Wolff (*In Flanders Field*, 1958) and Alan Clark (*The Donkeys*, 1961), Joan Littlewood's musical and then film, *Oh! What a Lovely War* (1963, 1969), films such as *Gallipoli* (1981) and television comedy series such as 'Blackadder Goes Forth' (1989) confirmed what most people already knew: that the 'generals' were a heartless bunch of conniving, hidebound, indeed stupid, 'Blimps', unable or unwilling to adapt to modern warfare. As a consequence, an entire generation of young men was sent 'over the top' to be mown down by German machine guns. The appalling casualties of attritional battles such as the Somme and Passchendaele appeared to confirm this hostile perspective.

This chapter sets out to prove a contrary thesis: that Lloyd George's military advisors acted in good faith, and it was Lloyd George doing the duping and not the 'generals'. More than this, senior advisors and commanders such as Robertson and Haig were, in fact, amenable and more thoughtful than is generally acknowledged when it came to implementing the decisions of their political masters. The events surrounding the battle of Caporetto show that Lloyd George outmanoeuvred Robertson and used Caporetto as an excuse to set up an inter-Allied forum to co-ordinate overall strategy, the Supreme War Council (SWC), established on 7 November 1917 at a conference at the Italian town of Rapallo, an organization that Robertson opposed. The Prime Minister was able to do this not because the CIGS was an ingénue, but because Robertson subordinated his strategy to that of Britain's elected politicians. Robertson's willingness to work with, as opposed to against, the civil decision-makers helped Britain win the war and can be readily contrasted with Germany where an autocratic, undemocratic military caste led by Paul von Hindenburg and Erich Ludendorff took charge from 1916, united Germany's war effort, led the Central Alliance to defeat in 1918 and subsequently claimed it was not their fault.[8] The German military leaders of the Great War, despite later claims, were not stabbed in the back in 1918, but shot themselves in the foot by their unwillingness to allow the politicians and the military to work in tandem and bring to the struggle the best in both professions. It is now time to set the record straight about the personalities in conflict over the Italian campaign and show the British generals in London and in Italy in a more favourable light: products of their generation it is true, but at heart democratic, intelligent, able to deal with immensely difficult situations and, ultimately, part of the reason why Britain defeated the Central Alliance and won the war in November 1918.

Lloyd George and 'Wully' Robertson both came from disadvantaged backgrounds, yet had truly outstanding, meteoric careers that took them to the pinnacles of their chosen professions. They were remarkable individuals whose successes were the result of much intelligence and a great deal of hard work that overcame the prejudices of Victorian and Edwardian Britain. Robertson was the son of a village tailor and entered domestic service at the age of thirteen before joining the 16th (Queen's) Lancers as a trooper in 1877. 'I would rather bury you than see you in a red coat' was his mother's lament when he joined the army.[9] Meanwhile, Lloyd George's widowed mother struggled on limited means to bring up her family in rural Wales. Yet, as the military thinker Sir Basil Liddell Hart pointed out, this shared background did little to bring the two men together.[10] On 9 August 1917, some two months before Caporetto, Robertson wrote to Sir Launcelot Kiggell, Haig's Chief of Staff, how Lloyd George was 'an under-bred swine'.[11] Lloyd George felt the same antipathy towards Haig and Robertson. In 1932, talking to Liddell Hart, Lloyd George remarked: 'Robertson never attempted to guide [the] strategy of war. Merely backed Haig and would have backed a successor similarly.' Lloyd George added, with obvious anger, that Haig was 'utterly stupid' and 'was the man we made an earl. And I gave £100,000 to.'[12] In November 1917, Sir Henry Wilson, who replaced Robertson as CIGS in February 1918, recorded in his diary how Lloyd George referred to Robertson as a 'damned fool'.[13] Leopold Amery, the Assistant Secretary of the War Cabinet and someone close to the Prime Minister, supported Lloyd George's hostile summary, recalling that Robertson 'had no other conception of strategy than to back up Haig through thick and thin', adding that the CIGS obstructed all 'sideshows'.[14] (For their part, the Italians referred to Robertson as a 'sort of English peasant'.[15])

Lloyd George's hostility to Robertson's guidance of the British war effort was not without some foundation. In November 1917, discussing Plumer's posting to Italy, Robertson warned Plumer:

> You know my views on the general policy, namely, to fight the Germans on the West front. . . . I am also convinced that anything in the nature of a big offensive in Italy would not only be unsound for the above reasons but that communications render it impracticable. I will trust to you therefore not to send at any future date, at any rate officially in the first instance, anything tending to imply that you think that the war can easily and properly be won by sending troops from the West front to Italy.[16]

In December 1917, Robertson reiterated his fears to Plumer:

> The Supreme War Council as you know is formed entirely of politicians who naturally cannot have the educated military mind and I foresee that they will become very rattled when the Bosche gets on the move and will want to rush the troops about from one end of the front to the other. . . . I hope therefore that you will do what you can to assist me in this matter in the telegrams you send.[17]

Robertson's system of secret 'R' telegrams that allowed him to communicate with his commanders in the field without going through official channels seemed to confirm that there was a collusion to produce misleading reports that the CIGS could then use to manipulate British war strategy.

Plumer's response to Robertson's requests was, however, lukewarm and does not suggest a united military front against Lloyd George. On 4 December 1917, Plumer stressed to the CIGS the need to help the Italians and how, while he was 'fully convinced' that the correct strategy was to continue the offensive on the Western Front, he also felt that the 'Italians should be encouraged to make preparations to assume the offensive themselves in the spring'.[18] It is also vital to measure word with deed, and with Robertson's correspondence across the board. The suggestive missives to Plumer detailed above were the exception rather than the rule. All in all, the historian trawling through the archives finds little to support the notion of a deceitful CIGS, and much to substantiate the idea of an amenable CIGS responding quickly and efficiently to the crisis in Italy following the battle of Caporetto. As Cavan recalled, Robertson's instructions to him prior to departure for Italy were unambiguous (and it cannot have been many a tailor's son and ex-trooper who could address an earl and general as 'my lad'): 'He then said: "Look here Cavan my lad, you've got to go to Italy and put new heart into our Allies. I don't know what the situation may be when you get there, but make sure of your line of retreat if things are very bad."'[19] Cavan repeated this advice in a short sketch about the Italian campaign, where he wrote how Robertson told him that 'you've got to go to Italy and your job is to put new heart into the Italians'.[20] In Cavan's papers there is no sense whatsoever of trickery by Robertson. Cavan added that after the Rapallo Conference, in early November 1917, Robertson readily subordinated British strategy for the greater good of overall war strategy considering the range of Entente theatres of operation: 'my orders from Sir William Robertson, the CIGS, were to do what Cadorna wanted'.[21] Equally, Plumer's biographers, who went through his correspondence, show that while he was 'sick' and 'depressed' at the thought of leaving France and going to Italy there was no suggestion of any duplicity.[22] Ordered to go to Italy, Plumer grumbled, went and then made a good job of his new assignment.

Robertson's correspondence with Lloyd George was equally straightforward and proved that while the CIGS had inner conflicts about war policy he did not let these personal differences dictate his conduct of the war or in any way lead him astray. On 27 October, just three days after Caporetto, Robertson wrote to Lloyd George that: 'The great thing is to let the Italians know that we are coming to their help. This they will know by the time this letter reaches you and I hope it will help to pull them together.'²³ At the same time, Robertson wrote to Haig how Italy's collapse 'ought never to have arisen having regard to relative numbers and terrain, but it has arisen and it is of first military importance that it should be adequately dealt with so that Italy might be kept as effectively in the field as possible. Otherwise the result may be really disastrous to the Entente cause.'²⁴ It was also the case that when it came to liaising with the Italians in the field, Robertson made few objections to Italian control over British deployment. When Cavan arrived in Italy, there was some confusion over whether he should deploy his troops at Brescia to prevent a possible Austrian breakout from Trentino into the Lombardy plain, or along the new front line of the river Piave. While the politicians meeting at Rapallo wanted Cavan's men to deploy at Brescia, General Luigi Cadorna, the Italian supreme commander, replaced by General Armando Diaz on 7 November 1917, wanted Cavan's firepower along the Piave. When Cavan pointed out the discrepancy, Robertson told him to adhere to the wishes of Cadorna, the Italian commander.²⁵ Robertson knew that Cavan and Plumer needed to work with and not against the Italians, and instructed them accordingly. These were hardly the actions of a man in such conflict with the politicians he was willing to lie and deceive to further his own agenda.

Lord Esher, an *éminence grise* in the British decision-making process, recorded in his journal a conversation with Haig about the Supreme War Council that says much about the 'generals': 'D.H. [aig] spoke with no bitterness or even criticism of L.G., or of Henry Wilson, who, under the G. Staff would be the "Military member" representing Great Britain [in the SWC].'²⁶ On 10 November, Esher wrote to Haig and Robertson. These letters show not a secretive military cabal, but senior officers genuinely concerned about the direction of British war strategy. To Haig, Esher wrote the following about the CIGS: 'I think that Wully himself, however much he dislikes the Allied Committee, is too honest a man to endeavour to render its chances nugatory.' Writing to Robertson, Esher outlined the view held, one suspects, by many senior military figures during the First World War: 'But so long as he [Lloyd George] is chosen by "Democracy" (a rotten institution) he ought to be supported. Otherwise we shall sink to the level of the French and Boloism.'²⁷ Other senior government ministers felt the same. For Lord Derby, the Secretary of State for War, and someone close to the military leaders, Robertson was essentially 'honest'. A.J. Balfour, the British Foreign Secretary, concurred with Derby, writing how while the military were lacklustre on peripheral campaigns they were not dishonest.²⁸

Haig admitted in his diary that he was opposed to sending troops to Italy but, crucially, added in a letter to Robertson, on 28 October 1917, just after the collapse at Caporetto: 'I am doing my best to comply with your demands on this Army to supply a Field Force for Italy.'[29] If Haig and Robertson were being dishonest about meeting the wishes of their political masters on sending troops to Italy, one would expect them to send the poorest troops to support Italy. It would certainly not be difficult for Haig, in charge in France, to shift troops so that the worst were made available for Italy. In fact, Haig sent some of his best troops, men he could ill afford to lose considering the intensity of the fighting on the Western Front and the threat of a German offensive in 1918 looming. Watching a march past of the 23rd Division, prior to departure for Italy, Haig recorded in his diary: 'The regiments are from the north of England . . . and the men look hard bitten fellows. They certainly have gained a fine reputation for fighting and soldierly qualities. On that account I have selected the divisions to go to Italy. Babington and his brigadiers have had much experience of active fighting and the *moral* [sic] of the division is very high.'[30] As George H. Cassar writes in his recent history of the Italian campaign, Haig initially selected two of his better divisions, the 23rd and 41st for Italy.[31] In his choice of Cavan, Haig also sent one of his best corps commanders, a 'cool, quiet guardsman who had hardly put a foot wrong throughout the war.'[32] While Haig was hostile to Lloyd George's plans for a Supreme War Council to co-ordinate overall Allied strategy, and while he opposed the Prime Minister's support for peripheral campaigns, nonetheless he faithfully complied with the wishes of the elected Prime Minister. Haig's diary entry for 7 November, the day that the SWC was formally established, recorded how 'These politicians are certainly very ignorant and troublesome people!! I did not remonstrate on receipt of the order [to send more troops to Italy], but decided to comply and do my best to help the Expeditionary Force we are sending to Italy.'[33] Even the War Cabinet in London recognized the efforts of Haig and the military, minuting on 29 October 1917: 'The War Cabinet expressed their appreciation of the action of Field-Marshal Sir Douglas Haig in making this selection [of men and *matériel* for Italy] and in releasing first-rate divisions for service in Italy.'[34]

While Robertson and Haig struggled to meet the needs of the civilian decision-makers in London, the soldiers on the ground in Italy, from the men and the NCOs deploying in the field up to the senior officers at GHQ, did sterling work forging good relations with the Italians and helping to rebuild the shattered Italian army. This work paid off. In October 1918, the Italians counter-attacked at the battle of Vittorio Veneto, resoundingly defeated the Austro-Hungarian army and so revenged the humiliation of Caporetto. This victory was due, in part, to British officer and technical schools in Italy that had helped transform the Italian army into an effective fighting force able once again to take the offensive. Besides specialist training schools run by the British, the British troops along the Piave introduced new tactics common to the Western Front but novel for the Italians. As the British Official History records, the Italian defences on the Piave were of a 1914 type, unsuited to the changed tactics of 1917.[35] The British showed the Italians how to site machine guns so that they fired in enfilade rather than at right angles to the front; the Italians were introduced to the tactical doctrine of defence-in-depth with the front line held lightly, while strong forces in reserve were ready to counter-attack. To be fair, this was a process that the Italians initiated themselves after Caporetto, but it was a transformation that the British troops in the foothills of the Alps and along the Piave did their utmost to encourage. As a commander, Cavan consistently invited senior Italian officers to his section of the front so as to disseminate good military practice. And it worked: the Italian units alongside the British were soon relocating their machine guns and pulling the bulk of their troops out of the front line. By the power of example, the British accelerated the Italians' learning curve, helping to restore lost prestige and weld the men and officers of the Italian army into a confident fighting force.

Cavan also led the way with his command of the multi-national Italian Tenth Army, made up of one British corps and two Italian corps. Here was a British commander in charge of foreign troops; here were British troops under the overall supreme command of an Italian. The British in Italy showed that alliance warfare could work. It is also worth emphasizing that commanders such as Plumer and Cavan delegated responsibility and made their officers and men self-reliant. This was a valuable example for the Italians and a radical departure from the excessively hierarchical Italian army that, under Cadorna, had discouraged independent thinking. Cadorna, while competent in many ways, was intellectually arrogant, aloof and avoided contact with the ordinary soldier. His military thinking was rigid and autocratic, and his plans relied on fixed *a priori* assumptions that left little for the imaginations of junior officers. Cadorna mistrusted the common soldier and relied on a ferocious system of military discipline to motivate the Italian soldier. Cadorna's famous maxim, *Il superiore ha sempre ragione, specialmente quando ha torto* ('The superior is always right, especially when he is wrong'), fed down the line, lowering the morale and trust of the front-line soldier.[36] Into this staid atmosphere the British brought a breath of fresh air.

P.E. Longmore, on Plumer's staff in Italy, wrote to Brigadier General Sir James Edmonds, compiling the Official History in the 1940s, at how 'amazed' the Italians were by the British army. The care taken by individual officers for individual privates was something with which Italian soldiers were utterly unfamiliar. As Longmore rightly observed: 'The lack of this feeling in the Italian Army was, I believe, one of the caused [sic] of their disasters.'[37] Plumer also commented on the good example set by the British troops when he wired the CIGS in January 1918 about how the Italians had 'been much impressed by the frequent visits of British Commanders and Staffs' who were willing and able to get out into the field to visit front-line units.[38] As a GHQ Staff summary recorded, the Italian troops were 'keen and anxious to learn' but the lack of trust in the Italian army held back soldiers with initiative and verve. The training schools established by the British met this need for realistic, modern training, and provided an example for the Italians to set up similar training establishments.[39] As Cavan recalled, the Italian soldier was a formidable fighter *'if properly led and encouraged'*. The problem was the poor Italian officer-man relationship.[40] The infusion of British troops helped change this situation.

In addition to training Italian troops, at the highest levels of command in Italy, the British commanders proved themselves adept at developing inter-Allied co-operation. On 21 November 1917, Plumer wrote back to Robertson how 'Foch is still here – and in command of the French – I am getting on quite well with him and Diaz.'[41] Plumer's Chief of Staff recalled how Diaz liked Plumer and how the British worked well with Diaz, the Italians and the French.[42] This flexible attitude, based on trust, was vital for eventual success. Just before Vittorio Veneto, Cavan talked to two of his Italian generals and outlined their tasks in the coming battle. He then shook their hands and 'asked in bad [sic] French "Bien entendu?" was quite happy with "Oui mon general" and left them with the words – "Vous ne recevrez pas un seul mot d'ordre de plus! Agissez-vous." It was a gamble but it came off!'[43] While the different languages used were always a problem, the officers often resorted to French, a language many of them had picked up in school, while the men were helped by the large number of Italians who spoke English having spent time working in the United States. In Italy the disparate elements pulled together, as Cavan again recalled: 'Three generals up a tree discussing a coming battle in a language of which none of the three could be said to be the master, contains an element of risk – but the spirit was right and moral [sic] was high – and that was enough.'[44] In his biography of Plumer, Major General 'Tim' Harington (Harington was Plumer's Chief of Staff) pointed out how Plumer established 'the most friendly relations' with the Italian High Command.[45] The British Official History supports Harington, observing how Plumer's tact worked wonders:

When some progress had been made General Plumer invited General Diaz to visit the British sector on the plea that an inspection by him as Allied Commander-in-Chief would greatly please the troops and give them confidence. The Italian commander was highly flattered and agreed to come. After his visit it was noticed that the Italians on either side of the British set about improving their very simple defences, which previously they had never troubled about.[46]

The British also worked to establish good relations with the French expeditionary force in Italy. Major General J.F. Gathorne-Hardy wrote to his daughter in December 1917 how he had a 'delightful' time with his French counterpart who was an old friend from the Western Front. Gathorne-Hardy's main complaint was with Foch and the fact that he would never stop talking at meetings.[47] The experience of working together in France before Caporetto gave these two expeditionary forces a solid foundation on which to build good relations.

All in all, British attitudes to both the French and the Italians showed a maturity not always apparent in alliance warfare. The French, for example, had problematic relations with the Italians. The French, recalled one Italian, 'assumed occasionally a certain air of superiority as saviours of the Italian front'.[48] With this in mind, the British helped ease the bad relations between the French and the Italians. Cavan detailed how 'Sir Herbert Plumer was a greatly strengthening influence and he did much to soften the bitter feeling that occasionally manifested itself between the French and the Italians. I noticed that from the time of his arrival to the end of the war the British Corps was always interposed between the other Allies.'[49] Senior British officers and diplomats were acutely aware of the need to maintain good relations. Thus, the British ambassador in Rome, Sir James Rennel Rodd, wrote to Lord Hardinge at the Foreign Office how some junior officers on leave in Italy had called the Italian 'dagoes'. Rennel Rodd went on to complain:

There was one down here the other day, senior enough to know better, who in the presence of the Swiss minister . . . said the Italians were no good, their information was hopeless, and for his part he thought the Austrians would go straight into Milan. And when the offensive came as a matter of fact it was a bit of our small line which was taken by surprise! This kind of thing does not make our people liked, and we could be so popular here if only these ignorant young asses were not so full of self complacency and ignorance.[50]

Cavan took this report about gossiping officers seriously enough to cancel leave in Italian towns for all officers below the rank of major.[51] These efforts by the likes of Cavan to stamp out chauvinism by British officers worked. When the Italians attacked at Vittorio Veneto in October 1918 Cavan wrote to Wilson, the CIGS, how 'Liaison of British and Italians working well and smoothly – and no crabbing so far of anybody or anything.'[52] These positive reports compare favourably with the French experience in Italy. On 31 October 1918, Cavan wrote how 'Something must be done to allay the feeling between French and Italians – it is worse and worse.'[53] On 30 December 1918, in one of his last letters to Wilson, Cavan recalled how the Italians resented the way in which the French treated them as '"lover boys" and minimised their efforts in the war.'[54]

The Italians recognized and appreciated this effort by Cavan and his men to make the alliance work. In 1945, Gathorne-Hardy recalled how when the Italian commander, the Duke of Aosta, came to bid Cavan farewell after the war he said: '"Goodbye General. I am indeed sorry that you are leaving Italy. Without the presence of you and your troops there would have been no victory of Vittorio Veneto.'[55] While there was obviously an element of formal praise to this valedictory address, the evidence shows the British to have formed real friendships with the Italians besides providing a useful psychological and material addition to the Piave front. Cavan summed up the feelings of many British soldiers when he wrote: 'The memories are sweet and if Italy can enjoy a hundred years of peace in all those glorious uplands our efforts will not have been made in vain.'[56] Again, Cavan's account of his meeting with the Italian King, Victor Emmanuel III, when the war was over, and the award by the King to Cavan of the Italian Grand Cross of the Order of St Maurice and Lazarus for his war-time service, is touching. The actions of the King were more than just the token giving of a medal to a foreign general.[57]

It is interesting to compare the challenges of the British in Italy with a comparable scenario on the enemy side. From 1914, the Germans sent advisors and then troops to help their war-time ally, Turkey. These troops behaved in such an arrogant fashion that the Turks universally loathed the Germans fighting in Turkey. They even ended up fighting one another in the Trans-Caucasus in 1918.[58] The overbearing chauvinism of the average German serviceman, something not discouraged by senior German officers, coupled to Turkish *amour propre*, led to a fraught and troublesome relationship that hampered the war effort of the Central Alliance. By contrast the average British soldier in Italy made a genuine effort to get on with his Italian counterpart. Some of this was forced on them by senior officers eager to preserve good relations, but the response across the board showed a willingness to work together and pool common strengths regardless of nationality. These achievements in the field need to be acknowledged.

While the military struggled to prevent Italy's total collapse, Lloyd George used the crisis as an opportunity to further his grand strategy. From early in 1917, Lloyd George had looked with interest at Italy as a means of redirecting strategy by taking troops away from France. Lloyd George also wanted to establish a supreme council as a means of circumventing Robertson and the military. As Maurice Hankey, head of the War Cabinet secretariat, recalled, months before the battle of Caporetto, Lloyd George was attracted to the idea of a Supreme War Council to co-ordinate the Allied effort on all fronts.[59] This had been a theme of the Prime Minister's strategy: to reinforce peripheral fronts such as Italy to divert forces from the Western Front. As Robin Prior and Trevor Wilson show, Caporetto gave Lloyd George the 'opportunity to vent all his resentment' against what he saw as a flawed decision-making process.[60] While Robertson subordinated his personal feelings on British war strategy, Lloyd George saw the Italian collapse as a God-sent opportunity to change policy. As David Woodward has observed: 'The crafty Welshman seized upon a better opportunity to undermine Robertson: the Caporetto disaster.'[61] By managing the Caporetto crisis to best effect, Lloyd George hoped to take control of the war. Therefore, when the information about the Italian collapse reached London, Lloyd George began scheming. As Hankey recorded in his diary for 29 October: 'After lunch I saw the P.M. for a moment. He told me that he would not go on unless he obtained control of the war. He meant to take advantage of the present position to achieve this.'[62] Again, from Hankey's diaries: 'He [L.G.] was very gloomy owing to the loss of Udine by the Italians, but pleased at the hope of "dishing" the soldiers by establishing the allied council.'[63] At the conference at Rapallo, where the SWC was established, Hankey emphasized to Robertson the futility of resistance: 'I had promised LL.G. that I would make it quite clear to Robertson that the War Cabinet was absolutely committed to this scheme of a central council of allies, and that it was useless for him to kick against it.'[64] At the same time, Wilson recorded in his diary for 5 November 1917 how Lloyd George 'let himself go about Robertson's pig-headedness and narrowness of vision, and said he was going to expose, on Friday in his speech in Paris, all our gross strategical blunders.'[65] Caporetto was a useful opportunity for Lloyd George to manipulate a crisis to further a particular agenda. Therefore, for the Prime Minister, crisis management became another means of policy-making. The Prime Minister outmanoeuvred Robertson, leaving the CIGS angry and impotent. Balfour had a conversation with Robertson immediately before the CIGS's resignation where Robertson pointed out his dilemma: 'An objectionable object in the middle of a table (to use his own metaphor) was equally objectionable from whichever end of the table you looked at it.'[66] The CIGS was angry at what was going on but, to continue the metaphor, was not willing to move the object on the table without proper authority.

The events surrounding the British intervention in Italy show that personalities were in conflict, but that the 'generals' were only willing to engage in this conflict up to a point. Ultimately, they did their best carrying out the orders passed on to them by the civilian decision-makers. This was one of the reasons why Britain won the war. In the end, Lloyd George and his 'generals' found the successful mix of strategy. It is certainly time to dispel the notion that deceitful senior military figures duped Lloyd George. The opposite was true: the Prime Minister carefully manipulated the Caporetto crisis to pursue his strategy. There is not the space here to assess the correctness of Lloyd George's strategy, but it is time to state the case that Britain's 'generals' were honest and democratic during the First World War. At a moment in history when governments across Europe were collapsing, when violent revolutions were sweeping dictators to power, the closest that the British 'generals' came to a 'mutiny' was when one of their number, Major General Sir Frederick Maurice, wrote an angry letter to the national press in May 1918 about Lloyd George's supposed manipulation of reinforcements for the Western Front. Maurice got his letter published but as punishment the Army Council retired him from the army.

Notes

The author would like to thank the Trustees of the Liddell Hart Centre for Military Archives, the Clerk of the House of Lords Record Office, the Masters and Fellows of Churchill College Cambridge, the Trustees of the Public Record Office and the Trustees of the Imperial War Museum for permission to quote from material for which they hold the copyright.

1 George H. Cassar, *The Forgotten Front: The British Campaign in Italy, 1917–1918* (London & Rio Grande: Hambledon, 1998) p.64.

2 Cyril Falls, *The First World War* (London: Longmans, 1960) p.291.

3 John Keegan, *The First World War* (London: Hutchinson, 1998) p.375 and C.R.M.F. Cruttwell, *A History of the Great War, 1914–18* (London: Paladin, 1986) [1934] p.465.

4 Basil Liddell Hart, *History of the First World War* (London: Pan, 1972) [1930] p.365.

5 See David French, *The Strategy of the Lloyd George Coalition, 1916–18* (Oxford: Clarendon, 1995) p.1; also Keith Simpson, 'Frock Coats, Mandarins and Brasshats: The Relationship between Politicians, Civil Servants and the Military', *RUSI Journal*, February 1992, pp.57–63.

6 For disingenuous reports see David Woodward, *Lloyd George and the Generals* (Newark: University of Delaware Press, 1983) and *Field Marshal Sir William Robertson: Chief of the Imperial General Staff in the Great War* (Westport and London: Praeger, 1998); also Matthew Hughes, *Allenby and British Strategy in the Middle East, 1917–19* (London: Frank Cass, 1999).

7 For 'dagoes' see Imperial War Museum (IWM), Wilson papers, HHW2/28/A, Rennell Rodd to Hardinge, 2 July 1918 (also in House of Lords Record Office (HOL), Lloyd George papers, F/56/2/6); for siesta see

Public Record Office (PRO) London, CAB45/84, Reginald Buckle to Edmonds, 11 June 1943.

8   See Martin Kitchen, 'Civil-Military relations in Germany during the First World War' in R.J.Q. Adams (ed.), *The Great War, 1914–1918: Essays on the Military, Political and Social History of the First World War* (London: Macmillan/King's, 1990), pp.39–68 for a lucid discussion of the take-over by the military in Germany.

9   Quoted in Woodward, *Robertson*, p.1.

10 Basil Liddell Hart, *Through the Fog of War* (London: Faber & Faber, 1938) p.114

11 Liddell Hart Centre for Military Archives (LHCMA), King's College London, Kiggell papers, 3/9, Robertson to Kiggell, 9 August 1917.

12 LHCMA, Liddell Hart papers, 11/1932/42, 'Talk with Lloyd George – Generals in WW1', 24 September 1932

13 IWM, Wilson papers, Diaries, 6 November 1917.

14 L.S. Amery, *My Political Life* (London: Hutchinson, 1953) Vol.2, p.82.

15 Quoted in John Wilks and Eileen Wilks, *The British Army in Italy, 1917–1918* (Barnsley: Leo Cooper, 1998) p.63.

16 LHCMA, Robertson papers, 8/3/38, Robertson to Plumer, 26 November 1917.

17 LHCMA, Robertson papers, 8/3/43, Robertson to Plumer, 28 December 1917.

18 LHCMA, Robertson papers, 8/3/40, Plumer to Robertson, 4 December 1917.

19 Churchill College Cambridge (CCC), Cavan papers, 1/3 Part 1, Recollections Hazy but Happy by FM The Earl of Cavan.

20 PRO, WO79/70, Cavan papers, Handwritten Summary of Campaign, p.1.

21 CCC, Cavan papers, 1/3 Part 1, Recollections Hazy but Happy by FM The Earl of Cavan.

22 Quotes from Geoffrey Powell, *Plumer: The Soldiers' General* (London: Leo Cooper, 1990) p.235; also in Charles Harrington, *Plumer of Messines* (London: John Murray, 1935) p.134.

23 HOL, Lloyd George papers, F/44/3/29, Robertson to Lloyd George, 27 October 1917.

24 HOL, Lloyd George papers, F/163/1/3, CIGS to C-in-C France, 28 October 1917.

25 PRO, WO79/70, Cavan papers, Handwritten Summary of Campaign, p.5.

26 CCC, Esher papers, 2/20 Journal, 3 November 1917.

27 CCC, Esher papers, 2/10 Journal, 10 November 1917. 'Boloism' is a reference to a French scandal that suggested corruption in the highest echelons of government.

28 HOL, Lloyd George papers, F/14/4/83, Derby to Lloyd George, 11 December 1917; British Library (BL), Balfour papers, Add.Mss.49693, Balfour to Bonar Law, 10 September 1917.

29 PRO, WO256/23, Haig papers, Diary, 28 October 1917 and Haig to Robertson 28 October 1917.
30 PRO, WO256/23, Haig papers, Diary, 31 October 1917.
31 Cassar, *Forgotten Front*, p.71.
32 Cyril Falls, *Caporetto 1917* (London: Weidenfeld & Nicolson, 1966) p.73.
33 PRO, WO26/23, Haig papers, Diary, 7 November 1917.
34 PRO, CAB23/4, War Cabinet Minutes, WC 259, 29 October 1917.
35 James Edmonds, *History of the Great War, Military Operations Italy 1915–1919* (London: HMSO, 1949) p.104 (hereafter *British Official History*).
36 From Cruttwell, *Great War*, p.447.
37 PRO, CAB45/84, Longmore to Edmonds, 21 July 1943.
38 PRO, WO100/810, report by Plumer on the condition of the Italian army, 20 January 1918, wired to CIGS.
39 PRO, WO95/4194, GHQ Staff in Italy, Summary of events from 10/3/18–30/4/18, pp.5–6.
40 PRO, WO79/70, Cavan papers, Handwritten Summary of Campaign, p.16.
41 LHCMA, Robertson papers, 7/5/78, Plumer to Robertson, 21 November 1917.
42 LHCMA, Robertson papers, 8/3/37, Harington to Maurice, 24 November 1917.
43 CCC, Cavan papers, 1/3 Part 1, Recollections Hazy but Happy by FM The Earl of Cavan.
44 CCC, Cavan papers, 1/3 Part 1, Recollections Hazy but Happy by FM The Earl of Cavan.
45 Charles Harington, *Plumer of Messines* (London: John Murray, 1935) pp.137, 139.
46 *British Official History* p.107.
47 LHCMA, Gathorne-Hardy papers, 1/2/20, Gathorne-Hardy to daughter, 25 December 1917 and Ibid., 1/2/21 Gathorne-Hardy to daughter, 15 November [*sic*] 1917.
48 Luigi Villari, *The War on the Italian Front* (London: Cobden-Sanderson, 1932) p.190.
49 CCC, Cavan papers, 1/3 Part 1, Recollections Hazy but Happy by FM The Earl of Cavan.
50 IWM, Wilson papers, HHW2/28/A, Rennell Rodd to Hardinge, 2 July 1918 (also in HOL, Lloyd George papers, F/56/2/6).
51 IWM, Wilson papers, HHW2/28/A, Cavan to Wilson, 16 July 1918.
52 IWM, Wilson papers, HHW2/28/A, Cavan to Wilson, 23 October 1918.
53 IWM, Wilson papers, HHW2/28/A, Cavan to Wilson, 31 October 1918.
54 IWM, Wilson papers, HH2/28/A, Cavan to Wilson, 30 December 1918.
55 PRO, CAB45/84, Gathorne-Hardy to Edmonds, 1945 [day and month obliterated].

56 PRO, WO79/70, Cavan papers, Handwritten Summary of Campaign, p.17.

57 CCC, Cavan papers, 1/3 Part 1, Recollections Hazy but Happy by FM The Earl of Cavan.

58 W.E.D. Allen and Paul Muratov, *Caucasian Battlefields: A History of the War on the Turco-Caucasian Border, 1828–1921* (Cambridge: CUP, 1953) pp.477–8.

59 Maurice Hankey, *The Supreme Command* (London: George Allen & Unwin, 1961) Vol.2, p.695.

60 Robin Prior and Trevor Wilson, *Passchendaele: The Untold Story* (New Haven and London: Yale UP, 1996) p.188.

61 David Woodward, *Robertson*, p.191.

62 CCC, Hankey papers, 1/3 Diaries, 29 October 1917.

63 CCC, Hankey papers, 1/3 Diaries, 30 October 1917.

64 CCC, Hankey papers, 1/4 Diaries, 6 November 1917.

65 IWM, Wilson papers, Diaries, 5 November 1917.

66 BL, Balfour paper, Add.Mss.49726 ff.90–2, Notes of a conversation which I had with the CIGS on 14 February 1918, dated 15 February 1918.

Part Five

The Home Front

Chapter 11

National Party Spirits:
Backing into the Future

Keith M. Wilson

The 'National Party Spirits' who are the subject of this chapter were at
odds, during the war, with those responsible, at the highest levels, for
the conduct of the war. They were also at odds, in varying degrees, with
the British political system itself, and with the way in which it had operated even in peacetime. The sharing of these outlooks gave them
something in common. It did not, however, eliminate differences in
temperament, tactics, and commitment as between the advocates of a
new political party and of a revised political system.

The National Party, which was launched on the troubled waters of
British politics at the end of August 1917, went on to secure, at the
General Election held in December 1918, proportionally the highest
poll by a minor party in the first half of the twentieth century. The
concept of a new party, into which existing parties would merge and
lose their previous separate identities, was not new. Lord Randolph
Churchill had considered something in the nature of a 'central party' in
the late 1880s; between 1895 and 1905 it was a cause embraced by the
former Liberal Prime Minister, Lord Rosebery. Its most recent mani-
festation was in a plan devised by David Lloyd George, then Chancellor
of the Exchequer, in August 1910, under the heading 'Coalition against
Party Government for dealing with social reform'. Arguing the merits
of this plan with the leadership of the Conservative Party, F.E. Smith
claimed that if it was adopted it would mean 'a National Party and
a well-directed power for ten years'.[1] The First World War delivered a
fresh impetus to thinking of this kind.

In May 1915 Walter Long, who became President of the Local
Government Board in Herbert Asquith's coalition government of that

month, expressed the view that 'the formation of *National* Government, not a coalition, would be the best thing'.[2] At the same time Austen Chamberlain, who became Secretary of State for India, volunteered to make way for Lord Milner, the former British High Commissioner at Cape Town. As he put it to Andrew Bonar Law, the Leader of the Conservative Party, 'I am confident that the inclusion of [Milner's] name would give confidence both to the country and the Army that this was a *national* Government and not merely a two-party or three-party Government and that it meant business'.[3]

Later that year, in August, Milner's name came up again. Leopold Amery, Conservative MP for Birmingham and a disciple and admirer of Milner, put pressure on the former Proconsul to assert himself, writing:

> You want to proclaim the outline of a complete policy, in which N[ational] S[ervice] fits in as an essential lever, but which also deals with all the other problems, munitions, finance, food and so on, not least relations with Dominions. The Milner policy or National policy as distinct from the Party or Mandarin Policies, must be something clear and definite in the public mind.[4]

Amery wanted Milner to announce such a programme through a speech in Birmingham. He believed that a nucleus of support might come from members of the British Covenant, the movement developed in the first six months of 1914 with a view to resisting Home Rule for Ireland. He thought that Sir Edward Carson, Unionist MP for Dublin University, who had led the resistance to Home Rule, would be almost certain to co-operate with Milner, and that the same applied to Lloyd George, provided the latter was convinced that he had no chance of becoming Prime Minister. Amery went on to list others who might co-operate. These included Geoffrey Robinson, editor of *The Times* and a former editor of the *Johannesburg Star*, H.A. Gwynne, editor of the *Morning Post*, and General Sir Henry Wilson, who 'could do a lot in the way of talking seriously to people who might want converting to the gravity of the situation'.[5]

At some point before the war Milner had noted privately, 'I am sick to death of party. What we want is Clean Government on national lines'.[6] In the autumn of 1915, although he had not responded to Amery's invitation, Milner wrote to another member of his South African Kindergarten, Lionel Curtis, editor of *The Round Table*:

> The root mischief is that while we talk of democracy and government by the people there is no such thing. We are just as often and think [sic] oftener governed by small minorities than we are in accordance with general public feeling and the despotism of the machine is in *no* way better . . . than the

despotism of the Kaiser. We are putting all our money on Democracy. Well, Democracy is going to fail and the British Empire with it, unless we can emancipate ourselves *to some extent* from machine-made caucus ridden politics and give men of independence and character more of a chance . . .

He went on to say that he saw only madness in the present method of appointing what passed for 'our Supreme Imperial authority'. He wanted a method found of producing

something more like a Council of Statesmen cooperating for a common end and less like a crowd of competing cheap-jacks, always trying to trip one another up and devoting all their energies to deluding the people, whom they flatter . . . into the belief that it is a matter of vital importance to be governed by Tweedledum and not by Tweedledee – and vice versa.[7]

Whilst Milner was proving himself less of a man of action than Amery had hoped, others did come forward. On the evening of Wednesday 12 January 1916, a meeting was held at the Constitutional Club, the purpose of which was to discuss 'Suggestions for a National Policy'. Gwynne was the main speaker. He was introduced by Sir Edward Carson, who presided over the meeting, and who took the opportunity to state:

If a national policy meant a policy of the Empire and nothing but the Empire and its interests, and if it meant putting aside all the sordid bicker-ings of party politicians, and having before us the one ideal of the happiness of the people as a whole, then [I] welcome it.[8]

Three days later, at a recruiting meeting in Liverpool on 15 January, Lord Derby, then Director General of Recruiting, said:

As to the future of parties, there is little that one can say. Many old politi-cal associations will be broken up by the events of the last eighteen months. For my own part, I shall only look forward to supporting and supporting with all my power, that party, whether composed of those who have been up to now Unionists or those who have been Liberals or have represented the Labour Party – if they can fuse in one great national party – a party that, having secured victory on land over the enemy and peace for ourselves and succeeding generations, will also take care that the fruits of our labours are not lost, and that the influence of foreign nations and the hold that they have got on the commerce of this country shall be destroyed for all time . . .[9]

Gwynne immediately tried to recruit Derby, much as Amery had Milner in 1915. On 19 January 1916 he sent Derby a note headed 'Some

Suggestions for a National Policy'. He followed this up by writing: 'I had hoped that this war would have thrown up a man in whom the public would have faith and confidence, not only in regard to his honesty, but also in regard to his statesmanship. So far nobody but Carson and yourself have appeared.' Gwynne suggested that Derby should set up and preside over a meeting that Gwynne would address. If it went well, Derby could then consider whether or not to put himself 'at the head of the movement'. Gwynne was to be as disappointed with Derby, who described his 'Suggestions' as utopian, as Amery had been with Milner. He went on, in the course of the next three months, to try to groom Carson for the role he had in mind.[10]

Meanwhile, at the end of March 1916, Arthur Lee, Conservative MP for Hampshire and Lloyd George's Private Secretary at the Ministry of Munitions, had written a letter arguing strongly for a 'National' Government and the bringing in to a new Cabinet of 'distinguished, non-Party' figures. This letter was sent to Lloyd George, Carson, Austen Chamberlain, Milner, the newspaper magnate Lord Northcliffe, and Geoffrey Dawson.[11]

In the services, and especially in the Army, which many members of Parliament had joined, there were stirrings along the same, or similar lines. General Sir Douglas Haig, for instance, appointed General Officer Commanding the British Expeditionary Force in France in December 1915, was urging on Derby in March 1916 'the necessity of *you* taking on yourself the complete control of the Government as long as war lasts'.[12] General Sir Henry Wilson, who was on the staff at GHQ when, in August 1915, Amery first mentioned his name as one who might be able to convert people 'to the gravity of the situation', had been given command of the Fourth Army Corps by the time Gwynne confided to him his plan 'to get the Tory National Party in the House [of Commons] and the Radical ditto to coalesce'.[13] In March 1916 Wilson advised Bonar Law to pull the Conservatives out of the Coalition Government.[14] In the following month Wilson wrote to Milner to say that he wanted Milner, Lloyd George, Carson, plus one Labour and one other as the Cabinet.[15]

＊   ＊   ＊

The resignation of Asquith in December 1916, and the creation by Lloyd George of a new administration, appeared to advance somewhat the 'national' cause. Certainly the *Morning Post* greeted the new government as if it were a National Ministry. Enthusiasm was displayed for the small War Cabinet, which consisted of Lloyd George, Milner, Lord Curzon, Arthur Henderson, and Bonar Law, of whom only the latter, at the Treasury, had departmental duties. Also welcome was the fact that all three political parties were represented, together with 'a sensible number' of men without strong party ties, and some from altogether outside the political fold. All things considered, the *Morning Post* allowed itself to say that 'the Cabinet as a whole, formed as it is upon broad national lines, not only gives hope of permanence but of a national policy founded not on political catchwords but on the interest of England and the British Empire'.[16] That Carson had been appointed First Lord of the Admiralty and Derby Secretary of State for War was also encouraging.

Within a few months, however, it became clear that Lloyd George's determination to prosecute the war vigorously was not enough to stop the advocates of a 'national' policy from seeing him in what was from their point of view the most damning of lights, as just another 'politician'. This was one factor in the background against which, in the summer of 1917, the National Party finally emerged. Other factors included food shortages, strikes and manpower problems in Britain, the progress of revolution in Russia and the falling away of Russia's participation in the war, the failure of the French offensive of April–May and the consequent war weariness in France and mutinies in the French Army, and the prospect of an International Socialist Congress at Stockholm later in the year. Once under way, the momentum of the movement towards a new party was increased by reports of the disposition of members of the War Cabinet to consider an early peace, and by rumours of overtures from Lloyd George to former ministers, and the speculation these rumours produced about a general election and the creation by Lloyd George of some sort of 'Centre' or 'National' party of his own. The momentum was further increased by the news of Matthias Erzberger's Reichstag speech of 6 July against annexations and in favour of a negotiated peace, by the pressing of certain French newspapers for a revision of the constitution in favour of open diplomacy, by the Special Labour Party Conference of 10 August at which Henderson spoke in favour of Stockholm, and by his resignation from the War Cabinet on 13 August.

✳   ✳   ✳

The game was started by an inadvertent remark on the part of Gwynne. The play was developed by Lord Esher, and then taken over by Viscount Duncannon, Conservative MP for Dover and ADC to General Wilson.

On 1 June 1917 Esher wrote to Gwynne from Paris:

> I don't like the outlook. Henry Wilson, who is not allowed by our idiotic government to pull his real weight may perhaps have written to you. If not, come over and have a talk. What with strikes, socialists, *small*

politicians, want of 'directions', and ingrained peace mentality, the Allies show signs of disintegration . . .

It is a mere thread of suggestion, but keep your eye on government changes of personnel. There is a touch of something sinister in wanting to link up with the old gang. No strong and self-possessed ruler of our country would desire this. The mental currents of even our best men are unfathomable . . . Watch it.[17]

Esher had from an early date in the war been one of the main channels of liaison between the British and French armies, and between British GHQ in France and the War Office. He operated in Paris from the offices of British Intelligence, in the Boulevard des Invalides. In mid-May he had been paid a visit by Derby, who had brought news of the state of affairs in England so bad as to cause him to record in his diary: 'The spectre of revolution stands behind his chair.'[18] Esher had been in correspondence with Gwynne throughout the war. He may well have selected Gwynne to write to on this occasion because in a leading article on 1 June the *Morning Post* had claimed that Ramsay MacDonald, the leader of the Independent Labour Party, represented 'the anti-British and pro-German party in this country'.

What Esher meant by 'keep your eye on government changes of personnel . . . Watch it', was derived from the lunch he had had on 29 May with Wilson, Duncannon, and an itinerant Winston Churchill. Wilson recorded in his diary that 'Winston was evidently in high favour with Lloyd George', and on the following day Esher anticipated, with mixed feelings, Churchill's re-employment as a minister in a letter to Haig. Esher also made a note of Churchill's idea that Lloyd George should leave the present Foreign Secretary, Arthur James Balfour, in the United States as Ambassador to Washington, and replace him with the former Prime Minister, Asquith.[19]

It was in Gwynne's reply to Esher's letter of 1 June that the seminal words were transmitted. Gwynne wrote, on 4 June:

I agree with nearly all you say about the outlook . . . I am quite certain that this country is solid for the war to the bitter end but they are frightened of the talkers. One of the remedies seems to me to be a League of Patriots, who would number I feel sure nine-tenths of the population. It is the small men who are losing the war.[20]

Whether Gwynne, who was due to depart for GHQ in France the following day, actually met Esher on this occasion, as he expressed the desire to do, cannot be ascertained. Whether he did so or not, his resurrection of his League of Patriots came at a crucial time. Derby's visit to Esher of mid-May was made in response to Esher's letters of

9 May to Derby and to Lloyd George urgently recommending drastic changes in the organization and personnel of the British representation in France. To the Prime Minister, Esher had suggested separating the ordinary work of the British Embassy from the war work; giving leave to the Ambassador, Lord Bertie, placing the Embassy under a *chargé d'affaires*, and putting the Military Attaché LeRoy Lewis and his Liaison Officer Spiers in charge of a Secretariat, which would be responsible to Lloyd George personally, for all business connected with the war.[21] Esher pressed this idea on Lloyd George again at the end of May: there should be in Paris a British War Mission in direct communication with the War Cabinet; in the Mission, Lewis and Spiers could liaise between the War Councils of the two countries, and General Wilson, as the Military Envoy of the British Government, could liaise between the General Staffs of the two countries.[22] Although Esher mentioned this scheme to Sir William Robertson, the CIGS, on 20 June, it was not really 'on' after 5 June.[23]

For, on 1 June, Wilson, who was becoming determined to leave Compiègne, because of the coldness towards him displayed by Paul Painlevé and Philippe Pétain, the successor to Robert Nivelle, had sent Duncannon to London to investigate his prospects with Milner. On 3 June he received a letter from Duncannon in which Milner was reported as considering Esher's plan 'rather difficult'. Milner preferred Wilson to return home and remain *disponible*. This is what Wilson decided to do. He informed Esher of his decision on 5 June, inducing the reaction 'All the links in the chain are breaking', and travelled to London on the 6th, the day on which Esher was told by Murray of Elibank that Lloyd George was seeking 'a very moderate peace, and at an early date'.[24]

The new circumstance of Wilson's availability gelled, for both Wilson and Esher, with Gwynne's enthusiasm for a League of Patriots. In letters to Milner over a year before, Wilson had stated that he wanted Milner, Lloyd George, Carson, plus one Labour and one other as the Cabinet. Under Esher's influence, Wilson now began to see himself as the 'one other'. After a few days in London Wilson returned to France to tell Haig of his decision. On 12 June he lunched with Gwynne, who was still in France, and put to him what he now called his 'polo match'.[25] This was followed by a long talk with Esher and Duncannon on Wednesday 13 June in Compiègne. As Wilson recorded it

They want me to go into the House [of Commons] and form a small party of 20–30 men who will work together and force the Government along the right path. They said all sorts of flattering things about me of which I am entirely sceptical but they insisted that I have the brains, knowledge and character to do all that they proposed. Esher said he would come over also and work under me and work the Press. It is all rather tempting.

Wilson had some reservations – it would mean a final parting from soldiering, and there was also 'the great practical difficulty of money'. He nevertheless undertook to 'think it over'. Esher, who was now anticipating the arrival of Austen Chamberlain as Ambassador, speculating that under a new and vigorous ambassadorial regime he would not be required in Paris, and regretting the 'pushing out' of Wilson, this representative of war à outrance, encouraged Wilson to do so, suggested that an Ulster member should at once vacate a seat for him, and finally saw him off from Paris on 25 June, undertaking for his part to stay on there until he knew what Wilson's plans were going to be.[26]

On arriving in London, Wilson immediately sought out Sir Edward Carson, and was assured that if he decided to stand for Parliament, Carson would secure an Ulster seat for him. (This assurance lasted for five days, for on 5 July Carson told Wilson that it might be better if he sat for an English constituency.[27]) Duncannon, meanwhile, had been mobilizing support. He told Wilson on 2 July that he wanted him to dine at the House of Commons on Monday, 9 July, with 'about a dozen of the pushing younger fellows'. This was confirmed on 4 July, and Duncannon made further preparations by seeing Walter Guinness, Conservative MP for Bury St Edmunds, and Leo Maxse, editor of the *National Review*.[28] On 5 July he told Milner of the scheme, and reported a favourable response. Wilson himself saw Leo Amery the following day; found out at lunch with Lord Percy that he was in favour of Wilson leading what he described as 'our party'; and went on to be flattered at the Marlborough Club by Duncannon and Edward Goulding, Conservative MP for Worcester City, who were 'very busy to get me on the War Committee [sic]'. It emerged at this meeting that Duncannon had also involved Sir Henry Page Croft, Conservative MP for Christchurch, who had given the vote of thanks to Carson and Gwynne at the Constitutional Club in January 1916.[29]

On 7 July Wilson asked Bonar Law about the possibility of his going onto the War Cabinet, only to be told that this was 'quite impossible'. Bonar Law also said that Wilson could do 'no possible good' if he went into the House of Commons.[30] There was another setback in that the dinner planned for 9 July had to be cancelled as a result of Lloyd George calling a secret session of the House of Commons. The next day, Tuesday 10 July, was more mixed. Wilson met Duncannon and David Davies, Liberal MP for Montgomeryshire, whose resignation as his Military Private Secretary Lloyd George had called for on 24 June. They agreed to form 'a combined meeting of Tories and Radicals to push the claims of the war'.[31] On 11 July Wilson met and so enthused F.S. Oliver, of the Tariff Reform League, that the latter said he would go into Parliament himself if Wilson would. Duncannon announced that £1,000 had already been collected 'for our crusade'.[32] Esher subscribed a note of encouragement, writing on 12 July:

> I hope that the Lord [Duncannon] is progressing with his Committee of Public Safety. Tell him from me that I shall think very little of his organising power if he fails to form a Joint Committee of both Houses, with you as Chairman (and a seat in the House of Commons) together with the backing of the M[orning] Post, P[all] M[all] Gazette and Evening Standard.[33]

In the course of the next few days, Henry Wilson visited Ireland, and developed his platform of conscription in Ireland through letters to Milner, Lord Bessborough, and others, and had conversations with Ulster politicians concerning the prospect of a Belfast seat.[34] Whilst Wilson was away, Duncannon made a formal offer to Oliver on 17 July:

> A few of us, accustomed to work together at the Tariff Reform League feel that we ought to help in trying to combat this [Labour] unrest. We are anxious to start a movement with that object. Would you care to meet Leconfield, Page Croft and me one morning at the Tariff Reform League offices?[35]

What Duncannon put to Oliver at their subsequent meeting was that Oliver should draft a manifesto for the new movement. Oliver accepted with alacrity, and by 28 July both Duncannon and Page Croft were offering comments on the draft.[36] Wilson, who on 23 July had written to Esher, 'My inclination for the House of Commons increases', was finally brought together by Duncannon with Oliver on 29 July.[37]

On 1 August Wilson dined with Gwynne. Gwynne expressed himself as now entirely favourable to Wilson's going into the House of Commons, offered to pay for his election expenses, and announced that he was joining Duncannon's new party.[38] A few days later Gwynne received Duncannon, whom he had met following Wilson's visit to Russia earlier in the year, at his country cottage in Essex. Duncannon brought with him two letters from Esher to Wilson.[39] Following a long discussion on 7 August between Wilson, Duncannon, Oliver and Page Croft of what Wilson called 'the Lord's new National Party', Duncannon suggested to Oliver that he have a talk with Geoffrey Robinson.[40] Duncannon's expectations that the editor of The Times 'would be a great help' were not fulfilled. A week later a rather disheartened Duncannon called Gwynne over to the Tariff Reform Offices in King Street to discuss tactics. Gwynne brought with him Dr Leander

Starr Jameson, the former Prime Minister of Cape Colony, and the chief leader writer on the *Morning Post*, Ian Colvin.[41] On 20 August it was decided to launch the National Party at the end of the month. Page Croft was to be the nominal leader. General Wilson took over Eastern Command on 1 September.

*　　*　　*

For Wilson the formation of the National Party was essentially a *divertissement*. It filled in the time whilst he was kicking his heels whilst angling for an acceptable military appointment. Though there is nothing, either in the version of his diaries published by General C.E. Callwell, or in the biography *The Lost Dictator* by Bernard Ash, to indicate even this passing interest in a new political party or movement, it is clear that the lure of soldiering was always the stronger. So far as the devising of any sort of political programme was concerned, he could think of nothing beyond the introduction of conscription in Ireland, which was something that Milner, for one, would not hear of.[42] The danger of Wilson at this time was aptly stated by Esher when asking Haig to try to keep him 'straight'. It was that 'of any loose gun in a ship'.[43]

For Sir Edward Carson the formation of the National Party was something of an embarrassment. Whilst the prospect of Henry Wilson's leadership or involvement was alive, Carson was prepared to offer him every help short of actual assistance, perhaps appreciating that the presence in the House of Commons of an Ulsterman every bit as charismatic as himself but much younger and fitter, would only weaken his hold over his own particular following. Even when that prospect had faded, Carson was decidedly hostile to the new party, as was Robinson of *The Times*.[44]

For Lord Milner, who was much more generous than Carson towards Wilson's efforts to get into Parliament, the National Party was a welcome complement to the British National Workers League.[45] Milner had circulated to the Cabinet in August 1917 a paper from Professor E.V. Arnold of Bangor University called 'Labour in Revolt'. This paper was an attempt to describe the progress of a movement which could be distinguished from the Labour Party and which Arnold held responsible for bringing recruiting almost to a standstill over the previous six months, for making a dead letter of the Munitions Act through strikes or threats of strikes, and for engineering the overwhelming welcome given at the Special Labour Conference of 10 August to the Stockholm proposal. Arnold supplemented his paper with a digest of a letter from Lord Sydenham, a former Secretary of the Committee of Imperial Defence, which had appeared in the *Weekly Despatch* of Sunday 12 August. Arnold agreed with Sydenham that 'during the last twelve months there has been a regular landslide in the attitude of unionist working men. Then they were working for victory over the Germans, now it is for victory over "society"'. Milner was no doubt pleased to see, on the *Morning Post's* leader page of 30 August, opposite the leading article on 'A National Party', a letter from Victor Fisher, the Honorary Secretary of the British Workers' League, including a resolution from the Pemberton Miners' Association which was used to demonstrate 'how little' such Labour Caucuses as the Conference of Allied Socialists, which was opened in London on 28 August by a speech from Arthur Henderson, 'represent the sentiments and opinions of the rank and file of British Working men'. Both Milner and Amery were in favour of the National Party itself.[46]

For Esher the National Party was not simply a compensation for the failure of his other plans for Wilson. Esher in the course of his career turned down many responsible positions – Permanent Under Secretary at the Colonial Office, Permanent Under Secretary at the War Office, Governor of Cape Colony, Secretary of State for War, Viceroy of India, Ambassador to Paris. He was not, however, an irresponsible individual. He was emphatic about the necessity of defeating what the German Empire represented, and, through victory, avoiding social unrest. At the end of May 1917 he was concerned not simply about the disposition of Lloyd George to link up with certain members of the 'old gang', and the implications of this – a less thorough-going and less well-directed war effort. He was also concerned lest 'the monumental error of Russian disorder' extend to France, whose Army's mutinies he knew as much about as anyone[47], and ultimately to Britain too. 'We shall all go down before the new forces that are coming into the war', he wrote to Derby on 31 May, 'Thrones (beginning with Greece), aristocrats, plutocrats and all. Peace – a thoroughly dangerous peace – is clearly in sight.' To Lloyd George on the same day he wrote that the governing forces of France were losing control: 'We are on the high road to a peace such as no one has ever dreamed of, arranged over the heads of statesmen, parliaments and Armies'. Two more letters, both to General Sir William Robertson, complete the picture. In the first, of 6 June, Esher wrote that 'the subtlest phase' of the war had arrived:

> The published telegrams of the Kaiser; the Russian appeal to inter-nationalism; the crystallisation of French parliamentary opinion upon the restitution of Alsace and Lorraine, together with 'reparation' for the wastage in Northern France, are of strange pregnancy, when compared with the bolder and equally dangerous conception of no annexations and no indemnities. It is the pure materialism of France in the ascendant, the

materialism of Painlevé and Pétain, reflected in the procedure of the Chamber . . .

In the second, of 20 June, Esher wrote:

By admitting the right of organised Labour to settle national questions by sectional wrangling, the King's Government has abrogated its functions . . . The attitude of the Army and the physical condition of the civil population have led to the narrowing of the war aims of France to the restitution by Germany of Alsace and Lorraine. Nothing else greatly matters to the people of France . . .

In short, 'Here [in France] and in England the war seems to be crumbling at the Labour fringe. Powerful social forces appear to be getting beyond control'.[48] In Esher's view, Lloyd George was losing his grip, and not only of the Anglo-French relations. The purpose of Esher's proposed reorganization of the British representation in France had been to erect 'a moral barrier between the disintegrating Russian mysticism and the "Défaitism" always sub-conscious in the soul of a Frenchman'.[49] Over and above this, as Esher put it to Gwynne on 28 June, Lloyd George's Government 'is far from fulfilling the hopes of all of us who acclaimed its advent to power. The interpolation of political issues between the successive decisions required of the War Cabinet if the war is speedily to be won, is a lamentable exhibition of weakness'. Esher continued:

Why do the English people stand the deflection of their rulers from the great issue they were put into office to settle?
Here in the army zones . . . no one understands any man or woman forgetting the all-absorbing issue of the war. Nothing else seems to matter. Yet there you are discussing methods of governing Ireland, Franchise, Reform of the House of Lords, and whether Party funds shall be swollen by bestowing peerages upon plutocrats that ought to go to the leaders of our armies in the Field. Then comes the shock of hearing that [Lord] Newton and others are sticking their legs under a table at the Hague with German colleagues . . .[50]

He wrote to Gwynne in similar vein a week before the launch of the National Party:

I believe D[ouglas] H[aig] is the only man in a high position in England or out of it, who believes in his heart of hearts that the Boche can be beaten . . . People who come over here, and who move in what is called society, say that fatigue and discouragement and above all scepticism as to the attainment of a military success are prevalent in those circles as well as among the industrial population.

When in profound peace all men speak of war there is great risk that war is imminent. When in the throes of war, all men talk of peace, there is a probability that Peace is not far off.[51]

To keep 'Peace' at bay until the war was won was Esher's interest in the National Party.

Those who left the Conservative Party to form the National Party were dubbed by Walter Long 'Tooley Street Tailors'.[52] For Duncannon, who did so much of the leg-work, the National Party served two purposes. It was a means of pre-empting a reunion between Lloyd George and Asquith, or a National Party at which Lloyd George was rumoured to be working at in August, and which might include Churchill and F.E. Smith.[53] Duncannon was increasingly convinced that the Government was dead and that Lloyd George knew it.[54] Quite as important as this was the combating of industrial unrest, with which the Government did not seem to know how to deal. By the end of July, Duncannon was reporting to Wilson 'an alarming spread of Revolutionary feeling'.[55] It was to Duncannon's appeal of 17 July that 'from one cause or another Labour unrest in the country continues to develop' that F.S. Oliver had responded.[56] Reassured that the new party would co-operate with his existing interests, the Tariff Reform League and the British Empire Union, Oliver saw an opportunity to use his proselytizing flair to put forward once more his ideas for a truly alternative government, which Lloyd George's replacement of Asquith's Coalition had turned out not to be.[57] For Page Croft, who stepped into the breach vacated by Henry Wilson, the National Party was an opportunity to work for 'victory in the war and victory for a "happier" England after the war'.[58] Page Croft made his personal position clear to Lady Bathurst, who owned the *Morning Post*, in a letter of 16 October:

> I too am pro-Tariff Reform, for strong government in Ireland, for a free hand to Ulster. I am pro-Turk and anti-Boche. I do not love the Jews. I am anti-democratic if that means mob rule but I am for leading the people and letting them share in influencing our National life because I think if *kept informed* they are more sound than so-called leaders. I am for a small Regular Army and Universal service on a two-year basis . . . I hate the idea of women being enfranchised but as they are now part and a large part of our economic and industrial life I think the National Party should welcome women into our organisation . . .[59]

After the formation of the Coalition Government in May 1915, Ian D. Colvin of the *Morning Post* had written to Lady Bathurst: 'I wish we had a good Aristocrat to lead a National Party.'[60] On 28 March 1916 he had written to Lord Milner, hoping the latter would agree with the *Morning Post*'s leader of that day, entitled 'The Need for a Man': 'Your Lordship realises that a National Party must be found itself upon the National Interest, which is the producers.' Colvin had been trying to convince Carson of this point, in the rightness of which he was confirmed by 'the revolution in Manchester, the National Programme of the Chambers of Commerce, the recognition given to the speeches of Hughes [the Prime Minister of Australia]'. He went on to say:

> There can be little enthusiasm in the popular mind for turning the German out of Flanders, if he is to be left in this country: by German I mean the importer of German manufacturers. And the only real way to get him out is by a policy of production. The manufacturers are now very touchy and very sore. Carson will have to woo them very frankly. As to the working men, I think the best of them believe in Fair Trade and might be won over to a national policy without bribes . . .

Colvin concluded by telling Milner that he was writing a book on the National Policy, tracing it from where his last book, *The Germans in England*, left off. *The Unseen Hand in English History* was published early in 1917, and its introduction was printed in the *National Review* of January 1917 under the title 'A National Policy'.[61] The message of this was that commercial penetration was the most dangerous of all attacks upon the integrity of a state. On the same day that Gwynne dispatched to Esher his letter containing the seminal words 'a League of Patriots', the writer of *The Unseen Hand in English History* was telling Milner that he had been reading Bacon on sedition. Colvin, who was clearly concerned about current labour unrest and the German influences that might be behind it, noted that Bacon put 'strangers as foreigners' as one cause of revolutions and that he proposed protection of manufacturers as one of the remedies.[62] For Colvin, the formation of the National Party represented the culmination of a cause which he had been advocating since the early summer of 1915.

The same applied to Colvin's chief, the editor of the *Morning Post*, Gwynne. He was caught off-balance, in July 1917, by the use to which Esher put his idea for a League of Patriots. He was not enthusiastic, initially, about Wilson's running for Parliament.[63] What reconciled him to this was the announcement, on 18 July, that Churchill was to be appointed Minister for Munitions, and Edwin Montagu Secretary of State for India. Gwynne's first instinct was to oppose Churchill's re-election at Dundee, if necessary by standing himself. He found the prospect of Churchill 'sickening'; it increased 'what is still more dangerous – the unrest of the country'.[64] These priorities were reversed in the presence of Wilson on 1 August.[65] To them, on 23 August, was added another factor: Lloyd George was perceived as 'making the fatal mistake of trying to carry on the war and at the same time to create a party'. The Churchillian dimension to this, in Gwynne's view, was that his appointment was designed 'to deprive the Asquithian lot of the advantages of a man of energy and authority'.[66] In these circumstances Gwynne swung round to active participation in and promotion of something the groundwork for which he had in no small degree been prepared by himself and through the *Morning Post* over the last two years. As he wrote to Lady Bathurst on 27 August 1917:

> As they are putting into practice what we have been preaching for the last two years, I think that we can do nothing also but support them .... The programme of reconstruction is nothing new as far as you and I are concerned, for we have been preaching it for the last two years. Tariff Reform ... prevent Labour and Capital quarrelling ... great productivity ... faith in the soldiers who are coming home ...

Gwynne acknowledged that they were quite a small party, that they wanted a leader, and that he did not see where a leader was to come from. Nevertheless, it seemed to him 'that the only way out of the present impasse was to try and create a new Party that would play a straight game with the people and would not always pander to them'. The creation of a new party was the only way he could see 'of trying to instil wisdom into people, and of getting rid of the money-making politician'.[67] In October 1917 Gwynne sought to be put on the Provisional Council of the National Party in order to try to take it in hand.[68]

✳   ✳   ✳

Despite the precise circumstances of its creation, the National Party of August 1917 was in direct line of descent from the 'non-party governments' and 'parties above politics' which were discussed at the turn of the century and during the constitutional crisis of 1910. The pamphlet written by F.S. Oliver to accompany the manifesto was entitled 'A National Party to promote Reform, Union, and Defence'. 'Reform' was defined as reform of the British constitution; 'Union' was understood as the union of classes, of capital and labour; 'Defence' meant economic defence against Germany, protection of home markets and Imperial understanding, together with the continuation of the present alliances after the war. The smallness of the size of the National Party – initially composed of seven Members of Parliament and seventeen members of the House of Lords – was a tribute to a fact recognized by Gwynne on

1 May 1916, namely that 'With some men, party is so much part of their blood, that not even a European war of this magnitude can shake them out of it . . .'.[69]

Notes

1   R.B. Scally, *The Origins of the Lloyd George Coalition: The Politics of Social-Imperialism 1900–1918* (Princeton 1975) pp.189, 204.

2   Long to Gwynne, 18 May 1915, MS Gwynne 20, Bodleian Library Oxford.

3   A. Gollin, *Proconsul in Politics* (London, 1964), p.265.

4   Amery to Milner, 15 August 1915, MS Milner 350, Bodleian Library Oxford.

5   Ibid.; and see Gollin Proconsul, pp.184–188.

6   Note by Milner, undated, MS Milner 124.

7   MS Curtis 2, Bodleian Library Oxford.

8   *The Liberal Magazine* vol.24 (269) p.4, February 1916.

9   *Ibid.*

10   Note by Gwynne, 'Some Suggestions for a National Policy', no.111 in K. Wilson (ed.) *The Rasp of War: The Letters of H.A. Gwynne to the Countess Bathurst 1914–1918* (London, 1988), p.161; Gwynne to Derby 20 and 21 January 1916, nos 110 pp.159–160 and 113 p.162 in Ibid; Gwynne to Wilson, 17 February 1916, no.114 p.163 in Ibid; Gwynne to Carson, 16 March 1916, MS Gwynne 17; Gwynne to Lady Bathurst, 20 March 1916, no.119 pp.167–8 in *Rasp of War*; Gwynne to Lady Carson, 24 March 1916, no.121 pp.168–9 in Ibid.; Gwynne to Wilson, 27 March 1916, no.122 p.169 in ibid.

11   A. Clark (ed.) *A Good Innings: The Private Papers of Viscount Lee of Fareham* (London, 1974), pp.147–8.

12   Haig to Derby, 21 March 1916, Derby MSS 920 Der 26/3, Liverpool City Libraries.

13   Gwynne to Wilson, 16 January 1916, no.109 pp.157–8 in *Rasp of War*.

14   Wilson to Bonar Law, 21 March, Bonar Law to Wilson, 31 March 1916, in R.Blake (ed.) *The Unknown Prime Minister* (London, 1955), pp.280–1.

15   Wilson to Milner, 11 and 20 April 1916, MS Milner 352.

16   *Morning Post*, 11 December 1916.

17   Esher to Gwynne, 1 June 1917, no.168 p.218 in *Rasp of War*.

18   P. Fraser, *Lord Esher: a Political Biography* (London 1973) pp.25, 364; note by Esher, 19 May 1917, Esher MSS 2/19, Churchill College Cambridge.

19   Henry Wilson Diary, 29 May 1917, Imperial War Museum; note by Esher and Esher to Haig, 29 May 1917, Esher MSS 2/19.

20   Gwynne to Esher, 4 June 1917, no.169 p.219 in *Rasp of War*

21   Esher to Lloyd George and Derby, 9 May 1917, Esher MSS 2/19.

22   Esher to Lloyd George, 31 May 1917, ibid.

23 Esher to Robertson, 20 June 1917, Balfour MSS, British Library Add. MSS 49719 f.285.

24 Wilson Diary, 1, 3 and 6 June 1917; M.V. Brett and Esher, *Journals and Letters of Reginald Viscount Esher* (London, 1934–38), iv.123; Fraser, *Lord Esher*, p.366; note by, Esher 4 June 1917, Esher MSS 2/19.

25 Wilson Diary, 12 June 1917.

26 Wilson Diary, 13 and 25 June 1917; Esher to Haig, 7 June and notes by Esher 12 and 13 June 1917, Esher MSS 2/19.

27 Wilson Diary, 29 June and 5 July 1917.

28 Ibid., 4 July 1917.

29 Ibid., 6 July 1917.

30 Ibid., 7 July 1917.

31 Ibid., 10 July 1917.

32 Ibid., 11 July 1917.

33 Esher to Wilson, 12 July 1917, Wilson MSS 73/1/21.

34 Wilson Diary 15 and 18 July 1917.

35 Duncannon to Oliver, 17 July 1917, F.S. Oliver MSS, Acc.7726/97, National Library of Scotland, Edinburgh.

36 Duncannon to Oliver, 28 July, Page Croft to Oliver, undated but late July 1917, ibid.

37 Wilson to Esher, 23 July 1917, Esher MSS 5/55; Wilson Diary, 29 July 1917.

38 Wilson Diary, 1 August 1917.

39 Wilson to Esher, 5 August 1917, Esher MSS 5/55; Gwynne to Lady Bathurst, 13 August 1917, no.175 pp.223–4 in *Rasp of War*.

40 Wilson Diary, 7 August 1917; Duncannon to Oliver, 8 August 1917, Oliver MSS Acc. 7726/97.

41 Duncannon to Oliver, 16 August 1917 Ibid.; Wilson Diary 14, 16 August 1917.

42 Wilson Diary, 20 July and 15 August 1917.

43 Esher to Haig, 25 June 1917, Esher MSS 2/19.

44 Wilson Diary, 7 August and 3 September 1917.

45 See J.O. Stubbs, 'Lord Milner and Patriotic Labour, 1914–1918', *English Historical Review* 87 (1972) pp.717–754.

46 War Cabinet G.T. 1849, CAB 24/24; *Morning Post*, 30 August 1917.

47 See memo by D. Davies, 'International Situation in France', 11 June 1917, Davies MSS C2/28, National Library of Wales, Aberystwyth.

48 Esher to Derby and Lloyd George, 31 May, to Robertson 6 and 20 June 1917, Esher MSS 2/19.

49 Esher to Robertson, 6 June 1917, ibid.

50 Esher to Gwynne, 28 June 1917, Ibid. 5/52. The last sentence was omitted from the version published in Brett and Esher Journals iv. 128–9, as were all the passages quoted here from letters to Haig, Robertson, Lloyd George, and Derby. There is no mention of the National Party in either

Fraser's biography or the more recent work by J. Lees-Milne, *The Enigmatic Edwardian* (London 1986).

51 Esher to Gwynne, 23 August 1917, no.177 p.225 in *Rasp of War*.

52 Long to Bonar Law, 4 September 1917, Bonar Law MSS 82/4/120, House of Lords Record Office.

53 Wilson Diary, 4 July and 14 August 1917; Duncannon to Oliver, 16 August 1917, Oliver MSS Acc.7726/98.

54 Wilson Diary, 20, 24 and 30 July 1917.

55 Ibid., 29 July 1917.

56 Duncannon to Oliver, 17 July 1917, Oliver MSS cc.7726/97.

57 Duncannon to Oliver, 25 July 1917, Ibid.; Gollin Proconsul, p.329.

58 Page Croft to Oliver, undated but 28 July 1917, Oliver MSS Acc.7726/97.

59 Page Croft to Lady Bathurst, 16 October 1917, Glenesk-Bathurst MSS 2978, Brotherton Library, University of Leeds. See also Page Croft's article, 'Why I left my Party' in National opinion, October 1917, quoted in W.D. Rubinstein, 'Henry Page Croft and the National Party, 1917–22', *Journal of Contemporary History* vol.9 no.1 (1947) p.140.

60 Colvin to Lady Bathurst, 10 July 1915, Glenesk-Bathurst MSS 2948a.

61 Colvin to Milner, 28 March 1916, MS Milner 44/105; *National Review* no.407, pp.605–16.

62 Colvin to Milner, 4 June 1917, MS Milner 354.

63 Wilson Diary, 10 July 1917.

64 Gwynne to Lady Bathurst, 20 and 27 July 1917, nos 172 and 173, pp.221–2 in *Rasp of War*.

65 Wilson Diary, 1 August 1917.

66 Gwynne to Rawlinson, 23 August 1917, no.178 pp.225–6 in *Rasp of War*.

67 Gwynne to Lady Bathurst, 27 and 29 August 1917, nos 179 and 180 pp.227–31 in ibid.

68 Gwynne to Lady Bathurst, 4 October 1917, no.182 pp.233–4 in ibid.

69 Gwynne to Wilson, 1 May 1916, no.124 p.170 in ibid.

Chapter 12

'Regeneration' Revisited: W.H.R. Rivers and Shell Shock during the Great War.

Denise J. Poynter

It is largely due to the work of Pat Barker[1] that the name of W.H.R. Rivers has achieved such great recognition as a doctor who treated shell-shocked soldiers during the Great War. Again, in 1985, Elaine Showalter, viewing the 1914–1918 war as one of three periods of 'psychiatric revolution', equally ennobled Rivers by stating that he was one of those 'individual physicians who not only dominated their generation's thinking but also transformed the social role of the psychiatrist in line with the age's cultural ideals'.[2] That his notoriety seems to have arisen mainly from his treatment of a very untypical patient, Siegfried Sassoon, who recorded with much veneration his encounter with the now famous doctor, or that the hospital where Rivers worked, Craiglockhart, was unique and only housed officers, is largely overlooked. Granted, Rivers helped to make a controversial method of treatment, psychoanalysis, more acceptable to both the medical profession and the public, and he is reputed as offering a more sympathetic method of treatment compared to other more direct approaches often associated and practised by Lewis Yealland. Yet he lived and worked during a period of great change in the fields of psychiatry and psychology and, however 'distinguished' he may have been, he was but one of a number of equally influential physicians. The years preceding 1914 saw a struggle to adapt to and incorporate a 'new psychiatry' which drew upon the concept that the 'mind' was equally as capable as the brain of producing symptoms of mental illness. With the outbreak of the Great War came industrialized warfare capable of inflicting greater horrors to the bodies and minds of soldiers who presented, in increasing numbers, an apparently mysterious new malady – shell shock. As a result, previous concepts of insanity and Victorian values concerning masculinity were thrown into disarray. Medical practitioners struggled to incorporate both old and new ideas in an effort to treat the various disorders amongst men and women incurred through being on or near the front lines.[3] This essay attempts to re-examine Rivers and his work but in the context of his being one of a number of equally qualified physicians who also made notable contributions in the fields of psychiatry and psychology.

William Halse Rivers was born on the 12 March 1864 in Chatham, Kent, the first of four children to the Rev. H.F. Rivers and Elizabeth née Hunt. He was educated at Tonbridge as a dayboy and, in accordance with both family and school tradition, he was to sit a scholarship exam in his final year for entry to Cambridge. Such hopes were dashed by a severe illness, typhoid fever, which left him almost continually convalescing. He 'tired rather easily and could not sustain effort for many hours at a stretch . . .'.[4] Following the illness, he also restricted his diet to milky drinks, did not smoke and took little or no alcohol. There is evidence, according to his biographer Richard Slobodin, that Rivers 'always had to fight against ill-health: heat and blood vessels' and there are frequent references to his 'weariness and need of rest'.[5] It is possible, therefore, that Rivers developed, or could perhaps be described as having, the fashionable disorder 'Neurasthenia'.[6] As a consequence, he may have been able to exercise a degree of empathy with those he was later to treat.

Compelled to abandon thoughts of going to Cambridge he turned his attention to studying medicine with the aim of going into the Army Medical Department. In 1882 he entered the University of London and St Bartholomew's (Barts') Hospital where, in 1886, at the age of twenty-two he achieved the Bachelor of Medicine degree, the youngest medical graduate in the hospital's history at that time. By 1888 Rivers had been awarded an M.D. (London) and also elected Fellow of the Royal College of Physicians. Reports and papers given by Rivers at the Abernathian Society, Barts', suggest an increasing interest in matters relating to neurology and psychiatry, including two entitled 'Hysteria' (1891) and 'Neurasthenia' (1893).[7] In 1892, he spent some time employed at the National Hospital for the Paralysed and Epileptic. Rivers appeared to be following a trend, for the topics of most interest to psychiatrists at this time were hysteria, epilepsy and general paralysis. However, in his paper 'Delirium and its Allied Conditions' (1889), he argued against the use of harmful narcotics as a treatment and condemned the '. . . wide separation at present existing between mental and bodily diseases', urging instead '. . . that more attention should be paid to the mental symptoms of general diseases'.[8] Full of youthful

enthusiasm for new ideas it was perhaps inevitable that he would identify with the novel approaches to insanity offered by the Continent.

Continental medicine, especially in Germany, 'contained a significant
element of the school of Romantic medicine, strongly combating the
materialism and rationalism of the 19th Century. The development of
psychoanalysis in Germany and Austria can be seen as a confluence
of the streams of scientific rationalism and Romanticism.'[9] The same
could not be said of English psychiatry where the brain was simply
viewed as the organ of the mind. John Hughlings Jackson summarized
this idea by stating: 'Physical symptoms are to medical men only signs
of what is wrong in a material system'.[10] Equally, Henry Maudsley,
eminent psychiatrist of the late nineteenth century wrote: 'It is not our
business, it is not in our power to explain *psychologically* the origin and
nature of any of the depraved instincts manifest in typical cases of
insanity. . . .'[11] Thus, British psychiatry in comparison with that
promoted in Germany was concerned only with the diagnosis of mental
disorders and, consequently, the patient's confinement within an institution. As an innovation the ideas emanating from the Continent
proved a strong attraction for many young doctors and students, Rivers
included, and he resigned his post at the National Hospital to attend
lectures in Jena, Germany in 1892. He was not alone in making this
decision, for Charles S. Sherrington and Henry Head, two medical
researchers who were to influence Rivers' thinking, also travelled to the
Continent around this time. After only four months there Rivers
decided that, '. . . I should go in for insanity when I return to England
and work as much as possible at psychology.'[12] Rivers was to remain
in touch with his German contacts, returning to Heidelberg in 1893
to work with Emil Krapelin and he continued his visits occasionally
thereafter.

The field of psychiatry had begun to gain some ascendancy at this
time, even though it still did not hold much credibility in the eyes of the
rest of the medical profession. Yet from the evidence of pioneering
woman psychiatrist and psychotherapist Isabel Sutton,[13] the state of
Scottish psychiatry was seemingly well advanced in its management
of asylum patients. Also progressive was the experience of Dr Helen
Boyle, practising in the East End of London at the end of the last
century, who visualized the idea of a hospital where patients suffering
from 'nervous breakdown' could be treated. She, too, had visited the
Continental clinics, and had worked at the Claybury Asylum. In 1905
she established the Lady Chichester Hospital at Hove where she set up
a small outpatient clinic and by 1911 it boasted thirty-eight patients.[14]

By the end of this same year (1892) Rivers, back in England, had been
appointed Clinical Assistant at the Bethlem Royal Hospital and in 1893
he assisted G. H. Savage in his lectures on mental diseases at Guy's

Hospital. In so doing he was able to express his ideas by placing particular emphasis on the psychological features of such disorders. Around the same time he began to pursue his interest in experimental psychology, again another popular innovation, and he lectured on this subject at University College, London. It was his interest in this area which was to take him from London to Cambridge, and Rivers now had the opportunity previously denied him when young, that of taking a position at Cambridge where he was made University Lecturer of Physiology and Experimental Psychology.

Personal testimonies to Rivers revere him as a man with exceptional qualities. Frederick Bartlett, a psychologist, recalls his first encounter with Rivers as a student:

> My course of lectures was quickly settled, and there, I suppose the interview should have ended. But I ventured to say that I had read a certain amount of sociology, and found most of it interesting but indefinite. At once the whole atmosphere of the visit changed. . . . When, eventually, I came away I realised I had not been treated at all as the raw student I really was. In the following years I was to realise more fully that this was the main secret of Rivers' success and power with people. Every new person he met he treated at once as a potential success. So his power did not lie in what he said or wrote though there was a lot of both especially as time went on but in himself.[15]

Rivers took up residency in Chapel Court, St John's College in October 1893 and was also admitted to the Fellows' Commons. Apart from the occasional room change, his anthropological excursions and a spell in the Army, he was to consider this home for the next twenty-nine years until his death in 1922.[16]

Having established a leaning towards matters psychological and an awareness that symptoms of illness could be related to the cause or result of mental pathology, Rivers became part of a small, but growing, psycho-dynamic movement. This controversial and slowly advancing movement arose out of the 'new psychiatry' whereby the concepts of evolution, selection, inheritance and the influence of the environment provided reasons for insanity and, consequently, the condemnation of asylum care. The care of the insane, previously an occupation for charlatans, was now placed under government supervision and new boundaries were established between sanity and madness. The insane became the 'mentally ill' necessitating a field of medicine to assume responsibility for them.

The teachings of Freud did little to improve psychiatry's early marginalized position. Formulating a theory of hysterical neurosis with his colleague Joseph Breuer, Freud argued that 'neurosis' was created because of a 'conflict' between mutually exclusive ideas.[17] Freud placed great emphasis on this conflict as existing between self-preservation on the one hand and sexual instincts and desires on the other. Neurosis developed, he proposed, when the libidinous wish was repressed by anxiety leaving its only outlet via dreams, slips of the tongue or neurotic symptoms. Treatment, he felt, could be pursued along the lines of revealing these unconscious wishes via 'free association' and this formed the basis of his psychoanalytical methods.

Freud's teachings did find some support. George Robertson, first Professor at the Morningside Hospital (later the Royal Edinburgh) invited, in 1914, Dr William Stoddart to the Scottish Branch of the Royal Medico-Psychological Association to give three lectures on the 'new psychiatry'. This was to receive a mixed reception:

> Many of the senior psychiatrists heard about Freud's researches for the first time and could hardly believe their ears. One learned doctor stumped out during the first lecture and many were heard to bark 'utter rubbish', 'preposterous', 'filthy', 'vile', 'nothing but sex' . . .[18]

Robertson, however, was greatly interested and apparently introduced it into his lectures immediately. The speaker, William Henry Butter Stoddart, a pupil of Hughlings Jackson, and former Superintendent of Bethlem and Lecturer in Psychiatry at St Thomas's, Lecturer in the Faculty of Medicine, London University and Professor of Psychological Medicine to the Royal Army Medical College is described as 'a man of courage, of good nature, of great clinical gifts, and of utter common sense (and) in many respects, . . . not the kind of person to be associated with a pioneering spirit . . .'[19] However, in the third edition of his highly regarded textbook of psychiatry, entitled *Mind and its Disorders*, Stoddart declared his allegiance to psychoanalysis.

Other figures supporting the pre-war psychodynamic movement include Bernard Hart, Hugh Crighton-Miller and David Eder. Hart was Consultant in Psychological Medicine at University College Hospital in 1913. His book, *The Psychology of Insanity* (1912) 'was probably the most widely read and influential work on a psychoanalytic approach to psychiatry for more than two decades'.[20] Aubrey Lewis wrote 'Bernard Hart blended to an uncommon degree shrewd practical judgement with a philosophical approach to the problems of psychological medicine'.[21] While still a young man he recognized the forceful implications of Freud's ideas. His 1910[22] article about the unconscious was described by Freud in a letter to Ernest Jones as the, '. . . first clever word on the matter' and 'the best paper on the damned topic of the unconscious I have read in the last years'.[23] Hart's 'elegant but critical description of Freud's work' is reputed to have 'greatly helped to establish the serious nature of analytical theory in the minds of British psychiatrists'.[24]

Hugh Crichton-Miller, one of the founders of the Tavistock Clinic after the First World War, practised as a psychotherapist before 1914. He worked in Scotland before moving to Harrow-on-the-Hill in 1911 and opened Bowden House, a nursing home for functional disorders. Similarly, David Eder (1866–1936) who graduated from St Bartholomew's in 1895 began his career as a General Practitioner in Johannesburg. Like Rivers, he was a fervent traveller and worked in Colombia, also making three journeys to the Andes. He became embroiled in the South American revolutions as a surgeon in the field, falling ill amongst the cannibals at one point. From 1908 to 1914 he was a founder member of the London Labour Party (Rivers was also to become an active Socialist after the war) and was Medical Officer to the Margaret MacMillan Clinic for Children.[25] In 1911 he presented a paper to the Neorological Section of the British Medical Association on hysteria and obsessional neurosis. When he had finished speaking, '. . . the Chairman and the entire audience, numbering about 9 rose and stalked out without a word.'[26] Eder went on to serve in the Royal Army Medical Corps (as Rivers did) in Malta and wrote *War Shock*. In it he opposed the use of the term 'shell shock' because of its pseudo-organic connotations.

The above sequence of events is important in the history of shell shock as both medical opinion and official policy fluctuated throughout the war. Accordingly, the first year of the war witnessed a major debate as to the condition's aetiology. The question of 'whether or not repeated exposure to high explosives without external injury produced a syndrome of emotional or 'nervous' change from organic disturbance',[27] was a major source of contention within the medical sphere. F.W. Mott, the main proponent of this theory, 'was then attempting to show, that the (symptoms of hysteria) arose from the effects of minute cerebral haemorrhages or other microscopically visible lesions' incurred by the blast of the shell and its noxious fumes.[28] Dr Charles Myers, who treated some of the first cases in 1914 and continued until the end of 1917 when he became inspector of army neurological hospitals, was never convinced. Writing in the Lancet in 1915 he described the cases of three soldiers who had been 'blown up' and who displayed symptoms of amnesia.[29] The following year he wrote again in the same journal having seen hundreds of cases from which he chronicled a multiplicity of disorders, including blindness, paralysis and hearing and speech disorders.[30] Yet he felt there were inconsistencies in the cases he treated which did not fit with the bio-medical approach. The senses of taste, smell and sight were often damaged but not the hearing. Questions inevitably arose in view of the fact that explosions were always accompanied by enormous productions of noise along with the release of gases that were odourless. As early as 1914/15 he had opened his mind to the idea of a psychologically oriented approach. Myers is credited with 'play[ing] an important role in rejecting the connection of battle neurosis with organic 'molecular' commotion in the brain' and similarly as doing 'magnificent work in recognising the psychological nature of the physical representation of war stress and was responsible almost single-handedly for setting up a modern system of diagnosis and treatment.'[31]

The belief in an underlying physical cause also found its origins in the understanding of the term concussion or 'commotion'. In 1880, Charles Bland Radcliffe had suggested: 'Concussion of the spinal cord, like concussion of the brain, is the result of a fall or some other accident, and its symptoms vary with the intensity of the shock . . .'[32] Furthermore, in 1866 Erichson had noted a correlation between the supposed symptoms of concussion and the increasing incidence of railway accidents.[33] Millais Culpin, writing after the war, confirmed that for a long time the symptoms of railway accidents were generally regarded as due to organic or physical injury, and it took, Culpin states, '. . . the controversial efforts of the late Furneaux Jordan and of Mr Herbert Page to demonstrate its emotional nature.[34]

> The incidents of a railway accident contribute to form a combination of the most terrible circumstances, which it is possible for the mind to conceive. The vastness of the destructive forces, the magnitude of the results, the imminent danger to the lives of numbers of human beings, and the hopelessness of escape from the danger, give rise to emotions which in themselves are quite sufficient to produce shock, or even death itself.[35]

Modern warfare, Culpin claimed, produced even more 'terrible circumstances than those of the railway accident'[36] and it should not be surprising to find '. . . all the symptoms of shell shock described in Mr Page's book on *Railway Injuries*, which was written in 1890.'[37]

The idea of an inner molecular disturbance or concussion helped to make emotional symptoms more respectable and acceptable to the Great War soldier, the military and society. As more and more men became 'emotional wrecks', it was inevitable that a popular term would emerge that encapsulated and preserved masculine and heroic ideals. Shell shock was a singularly appropriate phrase in that it implied close proximity to the front lines and therefore exploding shells, the experience of which could produce a traumatic and emotional response with little or no responsibility. However, the idea of there being emotional and psychological consequences to warfare was not unique to the First World War:

Medical officers of various countries noted an excessive prevalence of mental disease in military personnel, particularly in time of war. An increase in mental cases was reported during the Franco-Prussian War, the Spanish-American War, the Boer War, and the Russo-Japanese War.[38]

Indeed, during the Russo-Japanese War of 1904–5, Russian doctors described a condition '. . . amounting to traumatic neurosis, marked by confusional states and brief hysterical excitement, leading to irritability, fearfulness and emotional instability'.[39]

With this great influx of patients, evacuated back to England, the term 'shell shock' had become more generally recognized, and treated as if it were a new disease. A combination of the facts that certain members of the medical profession 'lectured and wrote on the subject as if it were some kind of mysterious new malady', along with the understanding that '. . . some patients with hysterical symptoms were psychoanalysed, others with mental conflicts were hypnotised;' then treatment on these lines '. . . could not fail to impress on the soldier's mind the mysteriousness of his malady'.[40] To the soldier's mind it was as much an entity as scarlet fever, with the further addition that, being incurable, shell shock was more to be dreaded.[41]

Nevertheless, the military was faced with the difficult position of providing care for its ill because of the need to maintain manpower, high morale and discipline, the very characteristics which were threatened by the increase in shell shock cases. Inevitably the question arose as to whether certain men were succumbing to the horrors of a mysterious mental illness or being compelled to run presented a very real problem to the military and one, which they felt, required strict measures. The position taken by the military authorities, according to the *Medical History*, was that

> The psychoneuroses cannot be ignored. Certain cases required medical care. The subject is, however, so bound up with the maintenance of morale in the army that every soldier who is non-effective owing to nervous break-down must be made the subject of careful enquiry. In no case is he to be evacuated to the base unless his condition warrants such a procedure.[42]

In previous wars the main concern had been infection but advances in medical science saw this problem largely overcome. Advances of a technological nature, however, produced a type of warfare hitherto unseen in the form of high explosives and rapid firing machine guns capable of inflicting terrible injuries. This, combined with the static participation of the soldier, the horrors of the trenches, along with the relative inexperience of recruits taken from civilian life, was slowly recognized as factors behind the increase in physical and emotional breakdowns. Put simply:

> The literature in all languages soon emphasised that the symptoms were frequently hysterical and that almost all the chronic symptoms after shell shock were also psychological in origin.[43]

It was in this context that, in July 1915, Rivers joined the staff at the newly requisitioned Maghull Military Hospital in Lancashire, formerly Moss Side Asylum, where the 'identification, understanding, and treatment of severe emotional disturbance due to war trauma was the order of the day'.[44] Under the supervision of Major R.G. Rows, Maghull Hospital, like that at Netley under C. Stanford Read, cared for hundreds of the worst mental war casualties, and attracted psychotherapeutically minded RAMC doctors. Between 1917 and 1919 three month courses of instruction in psychotherapy were organized at Maghull and offered to groups of fifty RAMC officers. 'The psychotherapists at Maghull (and Netley) developed an approach to the treatment of shell shock based on various abreactive or cathartic techniques designed to get patients to re-live and re-experience painful "emotional memories" which had been buried from consciousness.'[45] This was the approach adopted by Rivers.

In charge at Maghull was Richard Gundry Rose. Born in 1867, Rose had trained at University College Hospital and later worked in various asylums in Lancashire. He published in the *Journal of Mental Science* and attended many of the Medico-Psychological Association's meetings. Reminiscent of Rivers, Rose thought that the barriers between sanity and madness were too distinct. He also believed that clinics providing treatment for 'borderline' patients would prevent the need for and haste of committal. (An idea earlier advanced by Dr Helen Boyle). More importantly, his contribution to the understanding of shell shock was that

> The breakdown follows from some incidents which disturb the patients so that they could not carry on in the line and had to come down; not merely the bursting of a shell, but a scene of horror or a period of exhaustion . . . Long service, which must lead to exhaustion, would be quite sufficient to so unnerve a man that he would have to retire from the line . . . They were in an emotional state which had been produced by a series of causes, some of them not connected with the war at all; maybe a letter from home with bad news . . . which so upset the control of the man that he can stand the line no longer . . .[46]

Amongst other notable psychologists to train at Maghull, were William McDougal and William Brown, who made contributions to the psychodynamic approach in the war period. McDougal went on to achieve fame both in England and America where he became Professor of Psychology at Harvard. His book *An Outline of Abnormal Psychology* was based on over thirty volumes of case notes collected whilst working in army hospitals. He, like Rivers, renounced Freud's theories believing instead that the 'instincts' resulted in behaviour that was goal directed and purposive. William Brown, again like Rivers, had worked in Germany and became a pioneer in experimental psychology. He became head of the psychological department at King's College, London in 1908 and also worked at Maghull and Craiglockhart during the war years. After declaring his support of Freudian principles he then '. . . revolted against their over-emphasis on materialism'.[47]

When Rivers, newly commissioned Captain in the Royal Army Medical Corps, was sent to Craiglockhart War Hospital in Edinburgh, theories as to the causes of shell shock were becoming clearer. Exposure to exploding shells was not thought to be the sole reason for break-down. The majority of doctors, seeing associations with diseases familiar to them in peacetime, applied traditional diagnoses when it was felt that the effects of prolonged responsibility and long service was responsible. Thomas Lumsden stated:

> . . . shell shock is a misleading and bungling term, covering several different disorders which were familiar before the war, viz. Neurasthenia. Patients should recognise that they are not suffering from some new and wonderful disorder, but from common and curable diseases with which every physician has long been familiar.[48]

In 1916, Wiltshire, assistant physician at King's College Hospital and temporary Captain (Royal Army Medical Corps), rejected the term shell shock in favour of functional nervous disease. He further emphasized that the many cases of so-called shell shock were '. . . invaluable for the purpose of disproving the universal application of the "sex" theory of Freud and his followers'.[49] Indeed, the War Office Commission of Inquiry conducted in 1922 under Lord Southborough concluded from the testimonies of various doctors that the term 'shell shock'

> . . . was born of the necessity for finding at the moment some designation thought to be suitable for the number of cases of functional nervous incapacity which were continually occurring among the fighting units. Undoubtedly 'shell-shock' signified in the popular mind that the patient had been exposed to, and had suffered from, the physical effects of explosion of projectiles. Had this explanation of the various conditions held good, no fundamental fault could have been found with the term.[50]

At Craiglockhart, where he was to meet Sassoon, Rivers began formulating his theories for the understanding and treatment of shell shock. Rivers' methods received a mixed reception, not least by the military for being both time-consuming and too sympathetic to the individual. Yet the military was not completely hostile to ideas of a psychological aetiology for the condition of shell shock. The Army Medical Services had sent William Aldren Turner out to France to investigate shell shock, who concluded that '. . . whatever the special symptoms may be, the patients have been subjected in most instances to prolonged and often serious general nervous strain'.[51] The Army's acceptance of a psychological origin was one that drew on the ideas of the French neurologist, Babinski:

> Their approach to treatment centred on the use of suggestion – and what Babinski referred to as 'Persuasion' – to remove symptoms. Sometimes this was carried out using hypnosis or 're-education'. Other methods included painful lumbar punctures and retinal examinations. However, more often than not the preferred treatment was electrical faradisation.[52]

Lewis Yealland is the name perhaps most associated with this form of treatment. In treating those patients with aphonia, or mutism, his patients would be '. . . made to queue in the treatment room and watch the first in line receive painful electric shocks to his larynx'. Likewise, in his testimony to the War Office Commission of Enquiry into shell shock, 1922, Gordon Holmes stated:

> It was found in most centres that the quickest method was to tell the patient that we should give him electricity to help him along and almost invariably he got his speech back within half an hour.[53]

While much attention has been focused on the barbarity of this technique, faradization or electrical therapy was sometimes given in lower doses prompting an unresponsive muscle into action.

It is a generally held opinion that the First World War and the experience of shell shock influenced the evolution of psychiatry and helped to promote and establish Freudian notions of neurosis. More recent research doubts this view.[54] Similarly, Rivers is credited with making Freudian theory and psychoanalytical thinking '. . . more acceptable to a wide circle of influential persons'.[55] In his article Freud's Psychology of the Unconscious, Rivers argued that

> It is a wonderful turn of fate that just as Freud's theory of the unconscious and the method of psychoanalysis founded upon it should be so hotly discussed, there should have occurred events which have produced on an

enormous scale just those conditions of paralysis and contracture, phobia and obsession, which the theory was especially designed to explain.[56]

But, he continued:

> We now have abundant evidence that those forms of paralysis and contracture, phobia and obsession, which are regarded by Freud and his disciples as pre-eminently the result of repressed sexual tendencies occur freely in persons whose sexual life appears to be wholly normal and commonplace, . . . there is in my experience, singularly little evidence to show that, even indirectly and as a subsidiary factor, any part has been taken in the process of causation by conflicts arising out of the activity of repressed sexual complexes.[57]

Yet, Rivers was not alone in advocating that 'sex' had very little to do with shell shock. Many of his contemporaries had reached the same conclusions. As a revisionist Freudian, Rivers made clear his views on the unconscious defence mechanisms in his work *Instinct and the Unconscious*, (1920) and in *Conflict and Dream* (1923). He argued that

> . . . the neuroses of war depend upon a conflict between the instinct of self-preservation and certain social standards of thought and conduct, according to which fear and its expression are regarded as reprehensible.[58]

Rivers believed that the psychoses and psychoneuroses were 'attempts, successful or unsuccessful, so far as the patient's comfort is concerned, to solve conflicts which are disturbing the normal course of life.' In the situation of war, a 'conflict' arose out of an unconscious desire for self-preservation on the one hand, with 'duty' on the other. The physical and mental symptoms that arose because of this conflict served a purpose in that they 'incapacitate the patient from further participation in warfare'.[59] He believed that treatment was possible through the analysis of dreams because, '. . . dreams are attempts to solve in sleep conflicts which are disturbing the waking life.'[60]

Rivers' theories evolved from his understanding that as infants we all have an innate tendency to express fear. This fear is repressed through the influence of teachers and parents and because civilized society presents no greater demands for its expression. Only in the presence of danger such as war does it surface. Rivers also believed that one of the main reasons for the high incidence in cases of war neurosis was due to large numbers of men being called upon to endure '. . . hardships and dangers of unprecedented severity with a quite insufficient training.'[61] In this Rivers distinguished certain neurotic conditions and symptoms as being specific to war and not necessarily being due to soldiers being 'unstable' in mental health or character before enlistment.

As a military psychiatrist Rivers was required to address himself to relieving the condition of war neurosis, as well as adhering to the need to preserve manpower. This of course meant not only returning the 'recovered' and fit man back to the front line with the possibility that he might be injured again or worse, but the connection between shell shock and cowardice meant that as doctors they were also required to identify possible malingerers. The War Office Committee of Enquiry into Shell Shock (1922) identified the role of the doctor very clearly:

> The doctor must get the full confidence of the patient. The persistence of symptoms often resolves itself into a tour de force in the struggle for ascendancy between the patient's selfish and social tendencies . . . In no type of case is there more need to maintain firm disciplinary control . . . there should be not too many inducements to prolong the stay in hospital . . . it should be avoided that any general impression that the disorder is one for which invaliding from the service is bound to take place if the symptoms prove intractable.[62]

This role caused Rivers some concern; nevertheless, he performed his military duties as was required of him.

It may be that his medical qualifications combined with his personal attributes enabled him to become a much admired and respected figure. His approach to treatment was apparently effective, largely because it professed to explain a mysterious and frightening condition and hence returned a degree of self-respect to the sufferer. Furthermore, with an increased understanding of their condition, victims of war neurosis seemed less likely to succumb again. Rivers' methods are outlined in his publication 'Psychotherapeutics' where he states:

> . . . If the patient learns that his disease is only the expression of an exaggeration of a widespread trend of feeling, thought, or action, his condition will no longer appear mysterious, terrifying, or horrible, but will assume proportions which can be faced rationally and dispassionately.[63]

It has to be agreed that Rivers was worthy of praise for his contribution to the understanding of the war neuroses in that he was amongst the first to offer an articulate and consistent scheme for their psychopathology, and his personable qualities, evident from the many personal testimonies, appear to elevate him above many others. However, crediting him alone with making psychoanalytical methods acceptable to a wider audience undervalues the contributions made by his contemporaries. Many psychologists embraced the concepts of psychoanalysis, both in their writing and in their work. Furthermore, they, like Rivers, did not agree with a number of Freud's claims, the major criticism being that Freud had been wrong in emphasizing that sexual factors were all important to the aetiology of neurotic disorders. Focus is placed upon the wide distinction between the methods practised by Rivers and those of Lewis Yealland. Electrical therapy was not always administered in high, potentially life threatening doses. Likewise, many methods of psychoanalysis, practised as they were in their infancy, might have been equally as painful. Practised as it was in its early infancy and in some cases with only three months of training, psychoanalysis could confront soldiers with memories and problems they might not really have had. Medical practitioners were at the mercy of the rapidly changing cultural ideals and advances in scientific and medical knowledge. Their decisions, policies and subsequent methods reflected this. Many had claimed that what they were witnessing in their patients with so called shell shock was nothing they had not seen before and their traditional skills in the techniques of treatment were applied. Others were more willing to embrace the new theories. Shell shock remains the Great War's emblematic psychiatric disorder. As a clinical term, it was made redundant almost as quickly as it was conceived. As a cultural phenomenon it embodied (and still does) all that the Great War represented. It was an essential element of a narrative that contemporaries used to encompass the sheer scale, character and horror of the war. As a term of mediation it stood between those at home and those at the front, offering a shred of understanding to those incapable of comprehending the plight of the other. The haunting legacy of the war and the suffering it caused persist and so it is that we prefer to think of its victims being treated sympathetically, humanely and successfully rather than with what appeared to be barbaric and painful procedures. Rivers' story satisfies that need within us, and is perhaps why we choose to remember him above many others.

Notes

1   P. Barker, *Regeneration* (London: Viking, 1991); *The Eye in the Door* (London: Viking, 1993) and *The Ghost Road* (London: Viking, 1995), constitute the 'Regeneration' Trilogy.

2   E. Showalter, *The Female Malady: Women, Madness and English Culture, 1830–1980* (London: Virago, 1985) p.19.

3   D.J. Poynter, 'Shell Shocked Women: A Study of the Incidence and Experience of War Neurosis and Other Psychological Disorders Occuring Amongst British Women who Served Alongside the British Expeditionary Forces during the First World War.' (University of Luton: PhD in Progress).

4   R. Slobodin, *W.H.R.Rivers* (New York: Columbia University Press, 1978) p.11.

5   Ibid., p.82.

6   S. Wessely, 'Neurasthenia and Fatigue Syndromes' in German Berrios and Roy Porter (eds), *A History of Clinical Psychiatry: The Origins and History of Psychiatric Diseases* (London: Athlone Press, 1995). 'Neurasthenia' was a common, and 'fashionable' ailment and frequently diagnosed by medical practitioners of the time for disorders thought to be of a 'nervous' origin.

7   W.H.R. Rivers, 'Hysteria'. Abstract of paper read before the Abernathian Society St Bartholomew's Hospital Reports, 27, 1891, pp.285–6. Interestingly Rivers believed the symptoms of hysteria to be 'due to molecular change and not merely a functional disease'. Also Rivers, 'Neurasthenia'. Abstract of paper read before the Abernathian Soc. St Bartholomew's Hospital Reports, 29, 1893, p.350. Neurasthenia he states is 'more common than is supposed' and related to 'hysteria, hypochondriasis and melancholia'.

8   Rivers. Abstract of paper on 'Delirium and its allied conditions', read before Abernathian Society St Bartholomew's Hospital Reports, 25, 1889, pp.279–80.

9   M. Pines, 'The Development of the Psycho-dynamic Movement' in Berrios and Freeman (eds), *150 Years of British Psychiatry 1841–1991* (London: Gaskell, 1991) p.207.

10 M.J. Clarke, 'The Rejection of Psychological Approaches to Mental Disorders in Late 19th Century British Psychiatry' in A. Scull (ed.), *Madhouses, Mad-Doctors and Madmen*. (London: Athlone Press, 1981) p.283. Cited in Pines, p.217.

11 Ibid p.207.

12 Slobodin, op.cit., p.13.

13 I. Hutton, *Memories of a Doctor in War and Peace* (London: Heineman, 1960) As an Edinburgh graduate working at the Morningside Hospital (later the Royal Edinburgh) under George Robertson, Professor of Psychiatry, Hutton reports a humane and considerate form of custodial psychiatry was practised.

14 H.A. Boyle, 'The Ideal Clinic for the Treatment of Nervous and Borderline Cases', *Proceedings of the Royal Society of Medicine*, 15, 1922, pp.39–48.

15 F.C. Bartlett, 'W.H.R. Rivers.' *The Eagle*. 62, 269, 1968, p.157.

16 Rivers died on 4 June 1922. Being a Whitsuntide weekend Rivers had told his servant not to come in and that he would get his own breakfast. During the night he developed acute intestinal pain believed to be a strangulated hernia. When he was eventually found, having spent the night alone and in pain, it was too late. He died after an emergency operation at the St Evelyn Nursing Home. Slobodin, op.cit., p.82.

17 Joseph Breuer and Sigmund Freud, *The Standard Edition of the Complete*

Psychological Works of Sigmund Freud. Vol. 2: Studies on Hysteria (London: Hogarth, 1955).

18 Pines, 'The Development of the Psycho-dynamic Movement' in Berrios and Freeman op.cit., p.209.

19 J. Rickman, 'Obituary of W.H.B. Stoddart'. *International Journal of Psychoanalysis*, 31, 1950, pp.286–7.

20 Pines, op.cit., p.209.

21 A.J. Lewis, 'Obituary of Bernard Hart'. *British Medical Journal*, 2, 1966, p.806. Cited in Pines, op.cit., p.210.

22 Ibid.

23 Ibid., p.210.

24 Ibid., p.210.

25 Ibid., p.211.

26 J.B. Hobman, *David Eder, Memoirs of a Modern Pioneer* (London: Gollanz, 1945). Cited in Pines, op.cit., p.211.

27 H. Merskey in Berrios and Freeman, op.cit., p.245.

28 F.W. Mott, *War Neurosis and Shell Shock* (London: Henry Frowde and Hodder and Stoughton, 1919) Cited in Merskey, op.cit., p.251.

29 C.S. Myers, 'A Contribution to the Study of Shell Shock', *The Lancet*, 1, 1915, pp.316–20.

30 C.S. Myers, 'Contributions to the Study of Shell Shock', *The Lancet*, 1, 1916, pp.65–9.

31 Pines, op.cit., p.214.

32 Merskey, op.cit., p.246.

33 Ibid.

34 M. Culpin, 'The Problems of the Neurasthenic Pensioner', in *British Journal of Medical Psychology*, 1, 1920–21, p.317.

35 Ibid.

36 Ibid., p.318.

37 Ibid.

38 A.J. Glass, 'Army Psychiatry Before World War Two' in R.S. Anderson (ed.), *Neuropsychiatry in World War II. Zone of the Interior* (Washington DC: Medical Department of US Army. Office of the Surgeon General, 1966) p.3.

39 Merskey, op.cit., p.247.

40 Ibid.

41 Ibid.

42 W.G. Macpherson et al, *Official History of the War: Medical Services: Diseases of the War* (London: HMSO, 1923) Vol.2, p.11.

43 Merskey, op.cit., p.253.

44 Slobodin, op.cit., p.55.

45 Stone, op.cit., p.255.

46 R.G. Rows, *Testimony to the War Office Commission of Inquiry into Shell Shock. Headed by Lord Southborough*, 1922, pp.70–1.

47 Pines, op.cit., p.218.

48 T. Lumsden, *The Lancet*, January 1917, p.34.

49 H. Wiltshire, 'A Contribution to the Etiology of Shell Shock', *The Lancet*. I, 1916, pp.1207–1212. Cited in Merskey, op.cit., p.254.

50 *War Office Commission of Inquiry into Shell Shock*, p.4.

51 Stone, op.cit., p.254.

52 Ibid., p.253.

53 *The Report of the War Office Commission of Enquiry into Shell Shock*. See the testimony of G. Holmes, P.39.

54 See E. Jones and S. Wessely, 'The Impact of Total War on the Practice of psychiatry', in Forster and Chickering (eds), *Shadows of Total War 1919–1939*. (Cambridge: CUP, 2000), who write 'conflict of 1939–1945 was more "total" than that of 1914–1918, expos[ing] large numbers of civilians to hazardous situations. They were subject to air-raids, rationing and the tight controls of labour and production. As a result, psychiatrists found themselves working key posts not just in military hospitals but in civilian practice and in the selection, training and management of personnel. Important foundations had been laid for psychological medicine during the First World War but it was not until the Second War that fundamental changes in treatment and the ways mental disorders were conceptualized became widely accepted'.

55 Pines, op.cit., p.217.

56 Rivers, 'Freud's Psychology of the Unconscious', *The Lancet*, June 1917, p.913

57 Ibid.

58 Rivers, *Instinct and the Unconscious* (Cambridge: CUP, 1924) p.208.

59 Ibid.

60 Rivers, *Conflict and Dream* (London: Kegan Paul, 1923) p.v.

61 Ibid.

62 *The Report of the War Office Commission of Enquiry into Shell Shock*, pp.130–2.

63 Rivers, 'Psycho-therapeutics' in James Hastings (ed.), *The Encyclopaedia of Religion and Ethics* (Edinburgh: T & T Clarke, 1918) Vol.10, p.437.

Part Six

Royalty at War

Chapter 13

King George V and His Generals

Ian F. W. Beckett

During the Great War, a number of European monarchs nominally exercised supreme command of their armed forces. Kaiser Wilhelm II, for example, as the next chapter will show, was theoretically Supreme Warlord and head of High Command (OHL) although, in practice, his generals increasingly drew an unconstitutional distinction between the Kaiser and OHL. Similarly, King Victor Emmanuel was the Italian Commander-in-Chief but, for all practical purposes, the Chief of the General Staff, General Count Luigi Cadorna, was *de facto* Commander-in-Chief.

In some cases, military command was eventually assumed by the monarch. In Russia, it had been intended that Tsar Nicholas II should be Commander-in-Chief, but he was persuaded in August 1914 to appoint instead Grand Duke Nicholas. In the event, and with disastrous results, the Tsar chose to take over as Commander-in-Chief himself in September 1915, relegating the Grand Duke to the Caucasus command. In the case of Austria-Hungary, the role of a royal Commander-in-Chief, Archduke Friedrich, was usurped by the Chief of the General Staff, Conrad von Hötzendorf. On the death of Emperor Franz Joseph in November 1916, the new Emperor, Karl, assumed the role of Commander-in-Chief himself and subsequently dismissed Conrad. The best example of a monarch exercising actual field command, however, was that of King Albert I of the Belgians. Subsequently, Albert also acted as Allied northern army group commander in Flanders in 1918.

The constitutional powers of most of these monarchs greatly exceeded those of a genuinely constitutional monarchy such as the British Crown. Famously, indeed, it was Walter Bagehot's contention in *The English Constitution*, published in 1867, that a constitutional monarch enjoyed but three rights: the right to be consulted, the right to encourage, and the right to warn. As has been pointed out recently, however, neither Queen Victoria (reigned, 1837–1901) nor King Edward VII (1901–1910) subscribed to Bagehot, other than in the most general terms. Indeed, Edward was anxious to extend his exercise of the royal prerogative in certain areas and remained something of a bulwark against democratization of the political system. Consequently, it was only during the reign of King George V (1910–1935), who had been instructed in Bagehot's theories by Professor J. R. Tanner in 1894, that Bagehot's constitutional vision was fully realized.[1]

One significant remaining part of the royal prerogative was the monarch's role as titular Commander-in-Chief of the armed forces. It was a role which was of immense importance for monarchy and armed forces alike. For most soldiers, the Crown represented a higher form of authority than that of government. By posing, first and foremost, as servants of the Crown, soldiers could distance themselves from what was perceived as the squalid nature of politics. Potentially, indeed, the army could play off the royal prerogative against parliamentary authority. Thus, given the conflict that emerged between British soldiers and politicians over the direction of strategic policy during the First World War, there was a considerable danger that the King would be drawn into a damaging confrontation with government.

＊　　＊　　＊

In some respects, George V's ready submission to perceived constitutional proprieties reflected his comparative lack of interest in politics, but it was also the case that his relative inexperience of affairs of state upon his accession provided politicians with an opportunity to constrain further the exercise of the prerogative. In this, they were assisted by the advice tendered to the new King by his father's liberally inclined principal private secretary, Lord Knollys, to accede to the request of the Prime Minister, Herbert Asquith, to create sufficient Liberal peers to ensure the passage of the Parliament Bill through the House of Lords should the peers reject legislation which radically curtailed their political powers.

It was by no means clear that Edward VII would have given such a guarantee and Knollys concealed from the King the willingness of the Unionist leader, A.J. Balfour, to attempt to form an administration if Asquith resigned. By contrast, Sir Arthur Bigge, the former principal private secretary to Queen Victoria, George's own principal private secretary since 1901, and now joint principal private secretary to the new King with Knollys, recognized how far the guarantee had weakened the monarchy's long-term position.[2]

There is little doubt that, in public, George V was a model of scrupulous rectitude, whatever his personal views. In private, however, his language could have 'about it the tang and exuberance of the salt sea waves'. Moreover, he was conservative by nature. Thus, while prepared to accept 'the larger transformations', George V acted to preserve the royal prerogative where smaller encroachments 'appeared to him to detract from the repute of the Crown' such as ecclesiastical appointments and the conferment of honours and appointments.[3]

Just as executive government was carried on in the monarch's name, so honours and appointments were also made in the monarch's name, though generally bestowed upon the advice of ministers. With regard to the armed forces, the monarch was represented respectively by the Secretary of State for War and the Lords Commissioners of the Admiralty. In the case of the army, the officer Commanding-in-Chief, as the service's professional head, had been formally subordinated to the Secretary of State since 1870. In fact, a kind of duality had survived until 1895, but the professional appointment of Commander-in-Chief had been abolished in 1904. This was replaced by that of Chief of the General (Imperial from 1909) Staff acting as *primus inter pares* among his professional colleagues on an Army Council chaired by the Secretary of State.

The monarch, however, remained titular Commander-in-Chief. It would also appear that the architect of the changes in War Office administration effected in 1904, Lord Esher, contemplated Edward VII, who had a keen interest in military affairs, becoming a much more active, Commander-in-Chief. Moreover, the new post of Inspector General of the Forces, enjoying effective control over military patronage through the simultaneous presidency of the army appointments board, was vested in the King's younger brother, the Duke of Connaught.[4] Equally, Queen Victoria had never made any secret of her view that the army was decidedly 'not the property of Parliament' and she had pressed strongly for her son, Connaught, to succeed her cousin, the Duke of Cambridge, who had been officer Commanding-in-Chief from 1856 to 1895.[5]

Even before the Great War, the dangers of the army involving the monarchy in political affairs were fully demonstrated by the Curragh incident in March 1914. Through a series of misunderstandings, officers of the 3rd Cavalry Brigade at the Curragh camp near Dublin, and many others serving in and beyond Ireland, threatened to resign if called upon to coerce Ulster into accepting the imposition of Irish Home Rule. It was the unauthorized use of the King's name which did much to induce obedience, since it was suggested that he had personally approved what were perceived to be highly distasteful orders. Major General Sir Charles Fergusson, commanding the 5th Division, shouldered the blame for spreading this mistaken impression through the Irish Command but, in fact, it was the wholly bogus fabrication of the GOC in Dublin, Lieutenant General Sir Arthur Paget. The King was perturbed by events of which he had not known in advance and secured a pledge from Asquith that no military movements would be ordered in Ulster without him being consulted.[6]

In terms of the damage done to civil-military relations and its continuing repercussions well into July 1914, the Curragh affair was the worst possible basis from which to embark upon a major war. Moreover, the contest between the soldiers and the politicians for the control of strategic policy exacerbated mutual hostility. Indeed, Sir William Robertson, CIGS between December 1915 and February 1918, was not beyond veiled hints at the benefits of military dictatorship. Such talk alarmed the King's assistant private secretary, Lieutenant Colonel Clive 'Wug' Wigram, when it was suggested that the King should turn out the politicians and install a military government. As Wigram wrote to Lieutenant General Sir Henry Rawlinson on one occasion, 'The people, the press and Parliament would not for one moment stand such an unconstitutional act, and it is asking for disaster.'[7]

Wigram also believed that it was the long-term intention of David Lloyd George, who became Prime Minister in December 1916, to destroy the monarchy. Thus, Lloyd George's attempt to subordinate the Commander-in-Chief of the British Expeditionary Force (BEF) on the Western Front, Field Marshal Sir Douglas Haig, to the French general, Robert Nivelle, in February 1917 was portrayed as weakening the army in order, in turn, to undermine the monarchy. Characterized by Lord Beaverbrook as the 'keeper of the Palace gates', Haig was urged not to resign, lest Lloyd George appeal to the country and 'possibly come back as a Dictator'. The King concurred with Wigram's analysis and believed that his own position 'would then be very difficult. He would be blamed for causing a General Election which would cost the country a million, and stop munitions work etc.'[8]

George V himself had been a career naval officer for fifteen years when the death of his elder brother, the Duke of Clarence, made him the heir to his father in 1892, forcing him to abandon his chosen profession. Understandably, he often took a more favourable view of the Royal Navy than of the army. Indeed, at the time of the Curragh, he remarked that 'such a thing could never have happened in the Navy' though, in reality, the senior service was equally riven by political dissension on the issue of Home Rule. Similarly, in July 1915, the King remarked to Haig, somewhat improbably, that, in the Grand Fleet, unlike the army, 'all the Admirals were on the most friendly terms with one another'.[9]

Nonetheless, the King was extremely well informed of events and attitudes within the army. Asquith, for example, complained that the

King needed 'a really good *civilian* among his Secretaries, instead of always drawing them from his (mostly less) instructed soldiers'.[10] Bigge, who had been raised to the peerage as Lord Stamfordham in 1911 and had become once more sole principal private secretary when Knollys retired in 1913, had been an officer in the Royal Artillery until appointed to Victoria's household in 1880. Wigram was an officer in the 18th Bengal Lancers when he joined the then Prince of Wales's staff in 1905. Both Stamfordham and Wigram nominally remained on the active list after joining the royal household and both continued to correspond with old military friends. The King himself also directly solicited reports from a number of officers.

Those from whom letters were received in response to specific royal invitations to correspond, either directly or through Stamfordham and Wigram, included, in 1914, Field Marshal Sir John French, commanding the BEF, Haig, then commanding I Corps, and Lieutenant General Sir Horace Smith-Dorrien, commanding II Corps. In 1915 invitations were extended to Major General Edward Montagu Stuart-Wortley, commanding 46th Division and Major General Lord Loch, commanding 28th Division. In 1916 a similar invitation was extended to Major General Sir Harold Ruggles-Brise, commanding 40th Division. Similarly, invitations were extended in 1917 to General Sir Hubert Gough, commanding Fifth Army; and Lieutenant General the Earl of Cavan, commanding XIV Corps, although Cavan had earlier sent reports relating to the Guards Brigade and the Guards Division. As we have seen in the earlier chapter by Matthew Hughes, Cavan later went on to command British forces in Italy. Regular correspondents of Wigram also included Rawlinson, commanding IV Corps from 1915–16 and Fourth Army from 1916–18; and Major General Sir Robert Whigham, Deputy CIGS from 1915–18.

In the case of Haig and Smith-Dorrien, the King also received their daily journals in batches. French was a lazy correspondent and delegated the task of communicating with the King to his military secretary, Colonel the Hon. (later Major General Sir) William Lambton. Lambton continued to communicate with the King once he was promoted to command 4th Division in September 1915, while his successor on French's staff, Henry Lowther, took on the task of reporting from General Headquarters (GHQ).[11]

In fact, the King had known Smith-Dorrien for many years, and had asked for similar regular reports when Smith-Dorrien held Southern Command in 1911. Haig was also well known to the King, although Haig had enjoyed a closer relationship with Edward VII, having married a lady-in-waiting to Queen Alexandra. George V had also become well acquainted with Robertson when the latter was Assistant Quartermaster General at Aldershot in 1907. Robertson was to be a regular wartime correspondent. So, too, were a number of the King's close relatives serving with the army in one capacity or another, including his brothers-in-law, the Duke of Teck (later Marquis of Cambridge) and Prince Alexander of Teck (later Earl of Athlone); and his cousins, Prince Alexander of Battenberg (later Marquis of Carisbrooke) and Prince Arthur of Connaught. Prince Alexander, for example, served with the British military mission to the Belgian army while, at one point, the Duke of Teck was Haig's military secretary.

A more distant relative was Major General Lord Edward Gleichen, commanding 37th Division, who was a grandson of Queen Victoria's half-sister, Princess Feodore of Hohenlohe-Langenburg. Like some others, Gleichen was sent game from the Sandringham estate during the war. The King also took a special interest in the 4th (Guards) Brigade and the later Guards Division, to which the Prince of Wales was attached at one time; and the Household regiments serving with Brigadier General Charles Kavanagh's 7th Cavalry Brigade. It was, indeed, at the King's suggestion that the Welsh Guards were formed in 1915.[12]

Much of the correspondence reaching the King and his secretaries emanated from the Western Front, but they were also informed of events elsewhere, particularly at the Dardanelles. Mediterranean Expeditionary Force (MEF) correspondents included General Sir Ian Hamilton; Lieutenant General Sir William Birdwood, commanding the Anzac Corps and an old friend of Wigram, who continued to correspond throughout the war; Major General Alexander Godley, commanding the New Zealand Division; Lieutenant-Colonel G. H. Pollen, the assistant military secretary to the MEF; the Earl of Granard, serving with the 10th Division at Gallipoli and then Salonika; and Lord Lovat, serving with the Highland Mounted Brigade. As is well known, the King also enquired into the fate of the Sandringham Company of the 1/5th Royal Norfolk's, lost while serving in Major General Francis Inglefield's 54th Division.[13]

While Hamilton at one point counselled against the reliability of Granard's views, the correspondence from the Dardanelles was at least a useful counterpoint to the 'westerner' proclivities of correspondents like Haig and Robertson. Haig thus characterized the campaign as 'almost like the canker of the Peninsula to Napoleon's Armies!' and Robertson as 'the blackest spot of all'. By contrast, Birdwood complained that those sent out from England to assess progress 'seem only capable of saying "Every man is wanted in France to kill Germans." I on the other hand, who has been through everything here, and am perhaps incapable of seeing beyond the Dardanelles, say – "Here we are! For goodness sake let us do all we possibly can to get through".'[14]

Elsewhere in the Middle East, correspondents included General Sir

Edmund Allenby, commanding in Palestine from 1917–19; Brigadier General Gilbert Clayton, head of the Military Intelligence Department in Cairo, who forwarded several of the reports of T. E. Lawrence; Major General J. S. M. Shea, commanding 60th Division in Palestine; and General Sir John Nixon, commanding in Mesopotamia from 1915 to 1916 and another of Wigram's Indian Army friends. In addition to correspondents, the King regularly saw officers while they were on leave in London. Haig, for example, undertook to notify the Palace of officers on leave whom the King might wish to see. Similarly, Birdwood, who was also favoured with game from Sandringham, arranged for a series of Australian officers to see the King.[15]

*   *   *

According to the King's official biographer, military and naval commanders were relieved 'to be able, without incurring the reproach of professional disloyalty or political intrigue, thus to confide in the Head of their own Services, whose experience was akin to their own, whose judgement dependable, whose discretion absolute, and whose influence great.' It is the last of those advantages attributed to the King's position that is most relevant. Many of the correspondents confined themselves to descriptions of military operations. This was frequently of interest to the King where it filled gaps in the official despatches. Rawlinson's letters to Wigram, for example, gave very full descriptions of the tactical innovations of the operations of his army during the 'Hundred Days' in 1918. The more prominent correspondents, however, also felt free to give full rein to their personal views on the conduct of the war. Of course, such views were always presented as being absolutely necessary in the interests of the country.[16]

The most obvious use of this rationale was by Haig and Robertson in their conscious undermining of French's position as Commander-in-Chief of the BEF. As is well known, Haig made use of the royal visit to Aldershot on 11 August 1914 to impress on the King his doubts whether French's 'temper was sufficiently even or his military knowledge sufficiently thorough to enable him to discharge properly the very difficult duties which will devolve upon him during the coming operations with Allies on the continent.' Tellingly, Haig prefaced his remarks by emphasizing that he raised these doubts 'as I felt it my duty to do so'.

By the spring of 1915, attacks by Haig and Robertson, then Quartermaster General GHQ, on French's reputation were increasingly common. In May 1915 Haig told Wigram that French 'is of very jealous disposition, and is at the same time not quite sure in *his own mind* as to his fitness for his present position'. The following month, Robertson opined to Wigram, 'What is needed here as C. in C. is a high-principled honourable man of fine character, not necessarily a great soldier. Is he here? I leave you to answer the question.' Equally, Robertson told Stamfordham the same month that, if, as it appeared, the government felt French 'a discredited nonentity', then he should be replaced. His replacement should be 'a man who is trusted, absolutely', with high principles and standards. In forwarding these views, together with his suggestions on the reconstitution of the General Staff in the War Office and various documents on the current shells shortage in France, Robertson asked that he should not be quoted, but Stamfordham could 'make such use of my views as you deem best in the good of the cause and as far as they seem to merit attention'.[17]

French did not help his own position by attempting to discredit the Secretary of State for War, Field Marshal Lord Kitchener, over the so-called 'shells scandal' in May 1915, the King being a personal friend and firm supporter of Kitchener. Indeed, the King was adamant that Kitchener should not resign from the War Office. The situation was exacerbated by the press activities on French's behalf by his private secretary, Brinsley Fitzgerald, and a dubious American railway magnate, George Moore, whose house French shared in London. Robertson was especially critical of Fitzgerald's role at GHQ and Lambton, too, was increasingly alarmed at his influence.[18]

The King's confidence in French may also have been shaken by the removal of Smith-Dorrien from command of First Army in May 1915. French and Smith-Dorrien had been on poor terms ever since 1909 and French had asked for Sir Herbert Plumer rather than Smith-Dorrien to take over II Corps when Lieutenant General Sir James Grierson died of a heart attack on his way to the front on 17 August 1914. French's attitude had not been improved by the knowledge that the King had asked Smith-Dorrien to write to him. This had been made known to French by Smith-Dorrien as soon as he met French on 20 August, the King having specifically instructed Smith-Dorrien to seek French's permission. Smith-Dorrien invariably circulated letters received from Stamfordham or Wigram among his staff and, in addition, also appears to have made his journal available to Kitchener and the War Office.

Initially, French praised Smith-Dorrien's decision to stand at Le Cateau on 26 August 1914 during the retreat from Mons and Smith-Dorrien believed French's former hostility had been dissipated. In reality, however, French remained cool towards Smith-Dorrien and took the opportunity of his alleged pessimism during the second battle of Ypres in April 1915, first, to remove all troops from his command and, then, to force his resignation. Within a few days of his return to England, Smith-Dorrien had received a gift of a box of mangoes from the King.[19]

The dispute between French and Haig over the deployment of the reserves at Loos in September 1915 brought the issue of French's future to a head, especially as Haig ensured that documents contradicting French's official despatch reached the King through Lady Haig and Stamfordham. Significantly, the King had expressed his own dissatisfaction with French to the Duke of Connaught in May 1915, a few weeks after Smith-Dorrien's dismissal and during the shells scandal: 'French may be a good soldier, but I don't think he is particularly clever & he has an awful temper. Whether he is now suffering from the strain of the campaign or from swollen head I don't know, but he is behaving in a very odd way, which adds to my many anxieties.'

The King had been critical of French's relations with the press when he saw Haig in London in July 1915, indicating that he had now lost confidence in him. In October, while Robertson, bolstered by Haig, impressed the lack of confidence in French on Stamfordham in London, the King visited the Western Front and, during his tour, took further soundings on French. Absent in London for a crucial two days, French tried to curtail the royal visit, but the King's blunt reply was that French could 'go to hell'.

It was the second of five trips that the King made to the Western Front during the war. In private interviews, Hubert Gough, then commanding I Corps, and Lieutenant General Richard Haking, commanding XI Corps, expressed their dissatisfaction with French. Gough's corps had been directly involved at Loos, while Haking's recently arrived corps had formed the crucial reserve. Gough recalled, 'I could only say what I knew. I would not pretend that Sir John was fitted for the responsibility he had and the King was surprised by the examples I gave him of the C-in-C's failings.' According to Haig, who saw the King the same day, Gough and Haking told the King 'startling truths of French's unfitness for command'. Naturally, Haig's own view of French's incapacity was offered 'for the sake of empire'. He was 'ready to do my duty in any capacity, and of course, would serve under anyone who was chosen for his military skill to be C. in C.'.[20]

The King had made soundings concerning possible army commanders in the summer of 1915 since, theoretically, all command appointments were made only after he had been consulted. Asquith remarked that this represented 'a sort of "divine right of King's prerogative"'. When, in June 1915, it was rumoured that Paget might be appointed to the new Third Army, both Haig and Robertson had immediately expressed their opposition. Haig characteristically informed Wigram that the situation was 'so serious that it is my duty to tell you my opinion of this appointment'. Both Haig and Robertson suggested instead either Lieutenant General Sir Charles Monro or Lieutenant General Sir John Keir, while Haig also suggested Robertson. In the same month, Lambton made an extensive report on the suitability of various general officers for divisional, corps or army commands. Paget had clearly been considered seriously, but, in Lambton's view, it came down again to Monro or Keir, with the addition of Lieutenant General Sir William Pulteney. Lambton preferred Pulteney and believed this view generally shared. In the event, it was Monro who was appointed though he was soon despatched to succeed Hamilton in the MEF.[21]

While Haig and Robertson were undoubtedly correct, in the light of the Curragh, in believing that Paget would have been a disastrous choice for army command, it should also be noted, as Robertson pointed out to Wigram, that Paget was senior to Haig. It was Robertson's view that Haig should succeed French and he expressed this, not only to Wigram, but also in a personal interview with the King during the latter's visit to France. Much to Haig's chagrin, the King fractured his pelvis in falling from a horse lent him by Haig on 28 October 1915 and had to curtail his visit. The message from the army, however, had already struck home, the King writing to Stamfordham three days before his accident, 'I find that several of the most important Generals have entirely lost confidence in the C. in C. And they assured me that it was universal & that he must go, otherwise we shall never win this war. This has been my opinion for some time.'[22]

It is clear that, upon his return to England, the King played a pivotal role in pressing Asquith and Kitchener to remove French. French resigned on 6 December 1915 and Haig formally succeeded to the command of the BEF on 19 December. Esher, indeed, was despatched as a special emissary to ease French out of his command. Equally, through Stamfordham, the King pressed upon Asquith the need to re-organize the War Office in the absence of Kitchener, who had gone to assess the situation at Gallipoli. Robertson had long advocated restoring the primacy of the General Staff, submitting to Stamfordham in June 1915 the suggested outline of a new War Council. Kitchener, whom the King still supported, remained Secretary of State but, on 23 December 1915, Robertson became CIGS and sole military advisor to the War Council.[23]

Meeting the secretary to the War Council, Colonel Maurice Hankey, on 14 December 1915, the King 'told me all about the forthcoming changes, Haig for French in France and Robertson as Chief of Staff, and rather hinted that he had done the whole thing'. The King sent a special personal message to Haig pledging his support and 'expressing the great satisfaction with which I approved of your succeeding Sir J. F. as C. in C. of my troops in France' and reiterating the invitation for Haig to continue to communicate with the Palace. Haig equally recognized the significance of royal support, sending Wigram 'a thousand thanks for all you have done in this matter'.[24]

Thereafter, Haig was careful to continue to cultivate the King. Prior to December 1915 all but one of Haig's letters had been communicated through Wigram or Stamfordham. Now, Haig wrote direct to the King. In particular, Haig was assiduous in discussing appointments and dismissals, especially as the King regarded himself as the proper authority to deal with injustices to officers. The command of the Guards Division following Cavan's promotion to corps command was of particular interest to the King, both Lambton and Major General Geoffrey Feilding being considered in January 1916.

Similarly, Haig was at pains to explain in October 1916 that he had requested the appointment of Sir Eric Geddes as Director General of Transportation at GHQ, and that the removal of the Inspector General of Communications, General Sir Frederick Clayton, had been neither unjust nor a plot by "subversive" influences' to put civilians over soldiers. In the event, Geddes still encountered difficulties with the Director of Movements at the War Office, Brigadier General Richard Montagu Stuart-Wortley, whose position was supported by the King. Subsequently, Stuart-Wortley was moved to a brigade command in January 1917. Haig also trod carefully in November 1916 with regard to J.E.B. Seely, the former Secretary of State for War at the time of the Curragh, who was now commanding the Canadian Cavalry Brigade, since the King favoured his retention while Kavanagh, now commanding the Cavalry Corps, wanted Seely removed.[25]

*   *   *

In many respects, the events of December 1915 represented the apogee of the King's real influence over military affairs. Ironically, this was partly because of the new appointments of Haig and Robertson, in whom the King had implicit trust. At the same time, Robertson's appointment in particular also marked the end of the former primacy of 'strategic entrepreneurs' like Churchill within the War Council in the policy vacuum which had opened with the despatch of most of the General Staff to France in August 1914. The King regarded the renewed grip of the soldiers upon the formulation of strategy as quite proper since they were the experts. It posed, however, an increasing threat to his own position when his concern to retain Haig and Robertson clashed with the determination of Lloyd George to remove them.[26]

The King's support was certainly one of a number of potential advantages favouring Haig and Robertson against Lloyd George, who became Secretary of State for War on Kitchener's death in June 1916 and, subsequently, of course, Prime Minister. Other crucial props for Haig and Robertson were the support of the Unionists and, until early 1918, of the Northcliffe press. Yet, while Lloyd George could not find a realistic alternative to Haig as C-in-C in France and Flanders, he derived considerable leverage from the difficulty of his opponents in finding any realistic alternative to himself as Prime Minister. Hence the fears of the royal household with regard to an election being fought on Lloyd George's terms in February 1917, to which reference has already been made.

In real terms, therefore, there were distinct limitations as to how far the King could support his generals. In September 1916, for example, Robertson sought the King's support to prevent Lloyd George diverting British troops from the Western Front to Salonika. Equally, the King supported Robertson's refusal to go to report on events in Russia in the following month, remarking, 'I will not hear of it.' Having warned Haig of the damaging criticism of his strategy by French and his circle in the summer of 1916, the King saw French himself in November 1916 to caution him to moderate his conduct. The King's public support for Haig was also demonstrated by the granting of honours within his personal gift, the GCVO in October 1916 and the Thistle in July 1917. He also made Haig a field marshal in January 1917.[27]

The parameters of the King's influence, however, were better illustrated by the events surrounding the Calais conference in February 1917 and Robertson's resignation as CIGS in February 1918. In the case of the former, the conference was ostensibly assembled on 26 February 1917 to discuss transportation problems on the Western Front. Lloyd George then presented Haig and Robertson with a *fait accompli* in announcing the War Cabinet's agreement two days earlier to the BEF being subordinated to Nivelle for the forthcoming Allied offensive. Not only was this highly disagreeable to Haig and Robertson, but it also directly challenged the King's own prerogative in subordinating his army to a foreign power without his consent.

The institution of the War Cabinet by Lloyd George in December 1916 and, especially, of a permanent secretariat under the direction of Hankey, had greatly improved upon the information reaching the King. He now received the minutes rather than the previous, often hastily written, long-hand letter from the Prime Minister. Significantly, on this occasion, the minutes of the War Cabinet meeting, at which neither the Secretary of State for War, Lord Derby, nor Robertson had been present, did not reach the King until 28 February. As Stamfordham later wrote to Haig, 'Had the ordinary procedure been followed and the King informed of this momentous change in the conduct of the Campaign His Majesty would have unquestionably demanded further explanation before giving consent to the proposal.'[28]

Meanwhile, Haig had written to the King from Calais with a full account of the proceedings. A compromise had been reached on 27 February, by which Haig agreed to conform to Nivelle's directives during the offensive while reserving the freedom to choose the means by which his forces would be employed in 'that sector of operations allotted' by Nivelle. In the end, this was not especially restrictive, but Haig informed the King of all that had ensued so that 'Your Majesty may be watchful and prevent any steps being taken which will result in our Army being broken up and incorporated in a French corps'. Moreover, while it had been Lloyd George's hope that Haig would simply resign, Haig declined to do so, writing to the King that 'with full confidence I leave myself in Your Majesty's hands to decide what is best for me to do at this juncture'. The reply through Stamfordham expressed the view, first, that it would now be better not to discuss the terms of the compromise any further, and, second, that there must be no thought of resignation.

As indicated earlier, the fear was that Haig's resignation would enable Lloyd George to call a general election with potentially danger-ous consequences for the monarchy. Stamfordham's closing remark was, 'I am to say from His Majesty you are not to worry: you may be certain that he will do his utmost to protect your interests . . .'. Similarly, when seeing Haig himself shortly afterwards, the King promised to support him 'through thick and thin'. Such declarations did not neces-sarily offer much real protection should Lloyd George choose to press the issue. On this occasion, however, the man characterized by Hubert Gough in the light of the Calais affair as 'an unscrupulous & dirty intriguer' backed down.[29]

The limitation of the King's influence was even clearer when Lloyd George's machinations led to Robertson falling into a carefully prepared trap in February 1918. Essentially, Lloyd George, who had been using both French and Sir Henry Wilson as unofficial strategic advisors, conceived in November 1917 of the establishment of a Supreme War Council at Versailles with Wilson as British military representative. In February 1918 he proposed that the Council control an Allied general reserve. As CIGS, Robertson objected to such an arrangement, at which point Lloyd George offered him the opportunity of remaining CIGS with more limited powers or going to Versailles and being replaced as CIGS by Wilson. Robertson refused Versailles and was replaced on 19 February 1918. Derby then resigned as Secretary of State for War.

Sensing the corner into which Robertson was backing himself, the King attempted to persuade him to accept the Versailles post. This having failed, Stamfordham was despatched on 13 February 1918 to inform Lloyd George that the King 'strongly deprecated the idea of Robertson being removed'. Meeting Stamfordham again on 16 February, Lloyd George countered that, if the King insisted on retaining Robertson as CIGS with his former powers, 'the Government could not carry on and His Majesty must find other Ministers. The Government *must* govern, and this was practically military dictatorship'. Stamfordham was immediately forced to state that the King 'had no idea of making any such insistence'.

Subsequently, when the King also objected to the removal of Trenchard as Chief of the Air Staff in April 1918, a process described in more detail in David Jordan's chapter in this volume, Lloyd George suggested to Stamfordham that the King 'was encouraging mutiny by taking up the cause of those officers (e.g., Trenchard and Robertson) whom the Government had decided to get rid of'. A final chance to remain CIGS with restricted powers or of going to Versailles was made to Robertson at the King's insistence, but Robertson remained unmoved. Subsequently, the King also sought the possible re-employment of Robertson with the BEF, but Haig could not find anything suitable for so senior a soldier.[30]

With Robertson's resignation, the King complained that he received far less information from the War Office and there was clearly deep suspicion of Wilson. In November 1918 the King sent his personal congratulations to Haig on the achievement of victory, but, when Haig wished to publish the telegram, publication was denied in case Lloyd George regarded it as unconstitutional.[31]

*   *   *

During the war, Smith-Dorrien had shown a keener sense than most of the necessities of posterity, urging Wigram to persuade the King to use his influence to have an official history compiled before memories faded. In fact, the King appears to have been most concerned that the postwar 'battle of the memoirs' should not unnecessarily stir up former animosities within the army or, indeed, among politicians.[32]

Understandably, it was also certainly the King's wish that much of his own role in events should remain concealed. Thus, George V appears, if at all, in the major postwar memoirs very much on the periphery, visiting munitions factories, making an occasional national appeal, or setting an example by his pledge of wartime abstinence. In reality, however, even had the King's wartime role in relation to the army become known earlier, it would merely have demonstrated the increasing limitations of the royal prerogative in the face of the machinations of a Prime Minister such as Lloyd George who knew that he was virtually irreplaceable.

Notes

Quotations from the Royal Archives appear by gracious permission of Her Majesty the Queen. Grateful acknowledgement is also given for permission to consult and quote from archives in the possession and/or copyright of the

1   Simon Heffer, *Power and Place: The Political Consequences of King Edward VII* (London, Weidenfeld & Nicolson, 1998), pp.86–97.

2   Ibid., pp.303–6; Harold Nicholson, *King George V: His Life and Times* (London: Constable & Co, 1952), pp.61–3, 106–22, 129, 136-9.

3   Ibid., pp.249–50, 510–11.

4   New Strachan, *The Politics of the British Army* (Oxford: The Clarendon Press, 1997), pp.66–8; John Gooch, 'Adversarial Attitudes: Servicemen, Politicians and Strategic Policy in Edwardian England, 1899–1914' in Paul Smith, ed., *Government and the Armed Forces in Britain, 1856–1990* (London: Hambledon Press, 1996), pp.53–74; Noble Frankland, *Witness of a Century: The Life and Times of Prince Arthur, Duke of Connaught* (London: Shepheard-Walwyn, 1993), pp.229–32; David Cannadine, 'The Last Hanoverian Sovereign?: The Victorian Monarchy in Historical Perspective, 1688–1988' in A. L. Beier, D. Cannadine, and J. R. Rosenheim, eds., *Essays in English History in Honour of Lawrence Stone* (Cambridge: Cambridge University Press, 1989), pp.127–65.

5   British Library, Lansdowne Mss, L(5)42, Bigge to Lansdowne, 26 August 1895; Frank Hardie, *The Political Influence of Queen Victoria, 1861–1901* 2nd edn. (Oxford: The Clarendon Press, 1938), pp.178–82.

6   Strachan, *Politics of British Army*, p.73; David French, '"A One-Man Show?": Civil-Military Relations during the First World War' in Smith, *Government and Armed Forces*, pp.90–91; Ian F. W. Beckett, ed., *The Army and the Curragh Incident, 1914* (London: Bodley Head for Army Records Society, 1986), pp.15, 25, 88, 106, 132–5, 154–5, 226–7, 317–8, 323, 326; Richard Holmes, *The Little Field Marshal: Sir John French* (London: Leo Cooper, 1981), p.184.

7   David Woodward, ed., *The Military Correspondence of Field Marshal Sir William Robertson, CIGS, 1915–18* (London: Bodley Head for Army Records Society, 1989), pp.40–41, 315, n. 23; National Army Museum (hereafter NAM), Rawlinson Mss, 5201–22–73, Wigram to Rawlinson, 18 April 1918.

8   National Library of Scotland (hereafter NLS), Haig Mss, Ms 3155, Haig diary, 9 and 11 March 1917; Churchill College, Cambridge (hereafter CCC), Rawlinson Mss, RAWL 1/7, Rawlinson diary, 12 March 1917; David Woodward, *Lloyd George and the Generals* (Newark: University of Delaware Press, 1983), p.150; Gerard De Groot, *Douglas Haig, 1861–1928* (London: Unwin Hyman, 1988), pp.308–9; Robert Blake, ed., *The Private Papers of Douglas Haig, 1914–19* (London: Eyre &

Spottiswoode, 1952), p.209; Lord Beaverbrook, *Men and Power,
1917–18* (London, Hutchinson, 1956), p.165.

9   Ian F. W. Beckett and Keith Jeffery, 'The Royal Navy and the Curragh
Incident', *Historical Research* 62, 147, 1989, pp.54–69; De Groot, *Haig*,
p.196.

10   Michael and Eleanor Brook, eds., *H. H. Asquith: Letters to Venetia
Stanley* (Oxford: Oxford University Press, 1982), p.432.

11   Royal Archives (hereafter RA), Geo V. Q. 2522/9/166, Loch to Wigram,
19 April 1915; Geo V. Q. 832/72, French to King, 5 September 1914;
832/111, Haig to King, 21 September 1914; 832/200, Lambton to King,
23 August 1914; 832/259, Lowther to King, 28 September 1915; 832/294,
Gough to Wigram, 7 January 1917; 832/324, Ruggles-Brise to Ponsonby,
28 September 1916; 832/328, Smith-Dorrien to Wigram, 5 September
1914; 832/355, Stuart-Wortley to Wigram, 13 March 1915. For
Whigham, see Q. 2522/6; and, for Rawlinson, NAM, Rawlinson Mss,
5201–33–66–73. A typed and bound version of Smith-Dorrien's journal
is to be found in both RA, Geo V. Q. 832/365 and Imperial War Museum
(hereafter IWM), Smith-Dorrien Mss, 87/47/10. Some extracts appeared
in Appendix A of Smith-Dorrien's own 'statement with regard to the first
edition of Lord French's book, 1914', reproduced in Ian F. W. Beckett,
ed., *The Judgement of History: Sir Horace Smith-Dorrien, Lord French
and 1914* (London: Tom Donovan, 1993).

12   Beckett, *Judgement of History*, p.xiv; Woodward, *Lloyd George and
Generals*, p.77; RA, Geo V. Q. 832, Box 1 for correspondence with
Alexander, Teck, Maurice, Arthur and Gleichen; 832/87–110 on the
Guards; 832/71, 195–9, 286–7 on the 7th Cavalry Brigade; Brook and
Brook, *Asquith*, p.418.

13   RA, Geo V. Q. 2521/2, 4 for correspondence with Birdwood and Godley;
2522/1 for Pollen; Q. 832/79–86 for Granard; 832/152–79 for Hamilton;
832/192–3 for Inglefield; Field Marshal Lord Birdwood, *Khaki and
Gown: An Autobiography* (London: Ward Lock & Co, 1941), pp.167,
426.

14   RA, Geo V. Q. 832/173, Hamilton to Wigram, 19 August 1915; Q.
2521/2/43 Birdwood to Wigram, 13 December 1915; 2521/5/131, Haig
to Wigram, 12 June 1915.

15   RA, Geo V. Q. 2521/1 for Allenby; 2521/3 for Clayton; 2522/4 for Shea;
Q. 832/305–23 for Nixon; Q. 2521/5/144, Haig to Wigram, 16 May
1916; Q. 832/363 Wilson to Wigram, 16 May 1915; Q. 2521/2/62, 78,
Birdwood to Wigram, 4 October 1916 and 19 October 1917.

16   Nicholson, *George V*, p.254; NAM Rawlinson Mss, 5201–33–66 Wigram
to Rawlinson, 26 April 1915; 5201–33–73, Rawlinson to Wigram, 7 and
17 July, 20 September, 2 and 16 October 1918; RA, Geo V. Q. 832/310,
Nixon to Wigram, 23 April 1915.

17   NLS, Haig Mss, Ms 3155, Haig diary, 11 August 1914; RA. Geo V. Q.

2521/5/129, Haig to Wigram, 27 May 1915; Q. 2522/3/180 Robertson to Wigram, 17 June 1915; Q. 832/276, Robertson to Stamfordham, 23 June 1915.

18 Cameron Hazlehurst, *Politicians at War, July 1914–May 1915: A Prologue to the Triumph of Lloyd George* (London: Cape, 1971), p.281; Woodward *Lloyd George and Generals*, p.70-1, n. 27; RA. Geo V. Q. 2522/3/176, 178, Robertson to Wigram, 17 and 23 May 1915; Q. 832/229, 230, Lambton to King, 3 and 8 June 1915.

19 IWM, Smith-Dorrien Mss, p.365, Smith-Dorrien diary entries for 12 and 26 September 1914; RA, Geo V. Q. 832/329, 330, 339, 354, Smith-Dorrien to Wigram, 12 and 20 September 1914, 9 November 1914, and 13 May 1915.

20 Nicholson, *George V*, pp.252, 266-7; NLS, Haig Mss, Ms 3155, Haig diary entries, 1 and 14 July and 14 and 23 October 1915; Holmes, *Little Field Marshal*, pp.298-9, 307-10; Anthony Farrar-Hockley, Goughie: *The Life of General Sir Hubert Gough* (London: Hart-Davis, MacGibbon, 1975), p.174; Blake, *Private Papers*, p.138. On the question of the reserves at Loos, see Peter Bryant, 'The Recall of Sir John French' *Stand To* 22/23/24, 1988, pp.24-9, 32-8, 22-6.

21 Brook and Brook, *Asquith*, p.297; RA. Geo V. Q. 2521/5/132, Haig to Wigram, 18 and 28 June 1915; 2521/9/181, 182, 183, Robertson to Wigram, 18, 19, 23 June 1915; Q. 832/230, 233, Lambton to King, 8 June and 12 July 1915; Q. 832/276, Robertson to Stamfordham, 23 June 1915.

22 RA, Geo V. Q. 2522/3/182, 185, Robertson to Wigram, 19 June and 13 July 1915; Nicholson, *George V*, p.276.

23 Holmes, *Little Field Marshal*, pp.309-10; French, 'One-Man Show', p.81; RA, Geo V. Q. 832/276, 279, Robertson to Stamfordham, 23 June 1915, and 'Notes on the Machinery of Government for Conducting the War', 30 June 1915; Woodward, *Lloyd George and Generals*, pp.79-80; Paul Guinn, *British Strategy and Politics, 1914-18* (Oxford: Clarendon Press, 1965), p.113.

24 CCC, Hankey Mss, HNKY 1/1, Hankey diary, 14 December 1915; RA Geo V. Q. 832/112, King to Haig, 17 December 1915; Q. 2521/5/135, Haig to Wigram, 19 December 1915.

25 RA, Geo V. Q. 2521/5, 137, 145, Haig to Wigram, 3 January and 24 October 1916; Q. 832/114 Haig to King, 24 December 1915; Nicholson, *George V*, p.255; Blake, *Private Papers*, pp.121, 159, 181-2; Keith Grieves, 'The Transportation Mission to GHQ, 1916' in Brian Bond, ed., *Look to Your Front: Studies in the First World War* (Staplehurst: Spellmount, 1999), pp.63-78. For similar correspondence on other appointments or dismissals, see also RA, Geo V. Q. 832/122, 123, 126, Haig to King, 2 June, 28 July, and 5 October 1916.

26 Nicholson, *George V*, p.319.

27 John Turner, *British Politics and the Great War: Coalition and Conflict,*

1915–18 (New Haven: Yale University Press, 1992), p.123; Guinn, *British Strategy and Politics*, p.158; Woodward, *Military Correspondence of Robertson*, pp.93, 104–5, 110, 112; Ibid., *Lloyd George and Generals*, p.111; Holmes, *Little Field Marshal*, p.328; Blake, *Private Papers*, pp.158, 161, 182, 188, 243; RA, Geo V. Q. 2521/5/153, Haig to Wigram, 4 July 1917.

28 Strachan, *Politics of British Army*, pp.70–3; Stephen Roskill, *Hankey: Man of Secrets* (London: Collins, 1970), pp.233–4, 340–1; Nicholson, *George V*, pp.302–6; RA, Geo V. Q. 832/134, Stamfordham to Haig, 5 March 1917.

29 RA, Geo V. Q. 832/130 Haig to King, 28 February 1917; 832/134, Stamfordham to Haig, 5 March 1917; Blake, *Private Papers*, p.209; RA, Geo V. Q. 832/296, Gough to Wigram, 3 March 1917.

30 Nicholson, *George V*, pp.321–2; Woodward, *Lloyd George and Generals*, pp.262–75; Ibid., *Military Correspondence of Robertson*, pp.247, 284, 289, 295–6; Beaverbrook, *Men and Power*, pp.408–14 reproduces Stamfordham's notes of 13, 14 and 16 February 1918; Roskill, *Hankey*, pp.497, 519, 546; Keith Jeffery, ed., *The Military Correspondence of Field Marshal Sir Henry Wilson, 1918–22* (London: Bodley Head for Army Records Society, 1985), pp.36–8; NAM, Rawlinson Mss, 5201-33-73, Wigram to Rawlinson, 18 April 1918.

31 NAM, Rawlinson Mss, 5201-33-73, Wigram to Rawlinson 18 April, 13 May and 4 September 1918; Blake, *Private Papers* pp.293, 343–4.

32 RA, Geo V. Q. 832/347, 348, Smith-Dorrien to Wigram, 8 and 18 January 1915; Beckett, *Judgement of History*, p.xv. See also Ian F. W. Beckett, 'Frocks and Brasshats' and Richard Holmes, 'Sir John French and Lord Kitchener' in Brian Bond, ed., *The First World War and British Military History* (Oxford: Clarendon Press, 1991), pp.89–112, 113–41.

Chapter 14

Kaiser Wilhelm II:
The Hohenzollerns at War

Matthew Stibbe

He was no war criminal, but he was also no prince of peace; no villain but also no hero; not a great man but then again by no means a nonentity. One can never really feel malevolent towards him; but at the same time one can never really take him seriously, because throughout his life he was no more than a big child, egotistical like a child, easily interested and quickly bored like a child, easily hurt and easily appeased; easily crushed and easily consoled, needy and treacherous like a child; a gifted, bright child, almost an infant prodigy; but incapable of real seriousness, a perpetual stranger to the murky, terrifyingly real world of men, the world in which history – or what we call history – is acted out.[1]

To say that Kaiser Wilhelm II was a man of contradictions, a personality quite literally in conflict with himself, would be to simplify a life of enormous complexity. He could shock and dazzle, be sadistic and cruel with a terrifying gaze, play the autocrat with devastating consequences, rubbish his country's neutral stance during the Boer war and yet survive a motion of censure in the Reichstag at the height of the *Daily Telegraph* affair (1908). During his reign a joke passed round in Viennese circles that Wilhelm wanted to be the stag at every hunt, the bride at every wedding, and the corpse at every funeral.[2] Others referred to him as the *Reise-Kaiser* – the 'emperor on the move' – for much the same reasons. Even his closest advisors were prone to express alarm at his impulsiveness and unpredictable behaviour, leading them at times to question his sanity. And indeed, in 1927 – almost a decade after the Kaiser's abdication and exile to Holland – the Crown Princess of Prussia was still wondering how it was that a man could lose all sense of proportion and say the most fantastic things and even believe them. At a certain moment there is absolutely nothing more to be done with the Kaiser, he closes his eyes to every reality and then believes in the most impossible connections. He is and remains a riddle.[3]

Not surprisingly, historians as well as contemporaries have frequently asked themselves whether so unstable and volatile a personality could really have exerted a decisive influence on the government of the German Reich.[4] This applies as much to the period of the First World War as to his earlier attempts to establish 'personal rule'. Here, however, a general consensus has emerged that Wilhelm had little or no say in military and political affairs during the final years of his reign, that he was in effect marginalized and pushed to the sidelines by more important figures, especially the supreme military commanders in the East, Hindenburg and Ludendorff. The East German Willibald Gutsche, for instance, writes that 'Wilhelm II's role as Supreme War Lord was from the very outset a formal one only. Once the war had started the extremely complex and varied demands of decision-making could not tolerate an autocratic leadership, the more so as the Kaiser increasingly lost control of events and was simply overtaxed'.[5] Likewise, Wilhelm Deist, a leading specialist in German military history, asserts that Wilhelm was 'not up to the demands of his position as Supreme Warlord', a fact with far-reaching and mainly negative consequences, especially 'in regard to the mobilization of all resources for the war effort'.[6] And finally even John Röhl, the Sussex-based historian who has done more than any other scholar to re-open the debate on the Kaiser's significance, agrees that Wilhelm was reduced to a 'mere shadow' under the impact of the war.[7]

Having said this, our understanding of Wilhelm II's reign as a whole owes a great debt to the work of John Röhl, in particular to his development of the idea of a 'kingship mechanism' operating at the centre of German politics in the decade after 1897.[8] This was a new system and style of government which based itself on what Bernhard von Bülow, one of its chief architects, described as 'personal rule in the good sense'. Its main feature was an assertion of the Kaiser's exclusive power of command (*Kommandogewalt*) over all areas of military policy, and of his right to appoint, promote and dismiss all senior officials in both Prussia and the Reich. As a result, responsible decision-making bodies were automatically conditioned to anticipate an Imperial veto on their proposals, and to adjust their behaviour and expectations accordingly. In this way, the 'kingship mechanism' could act as a block or barrier to certain policy initiatives, even if it failed to produce a coherent or stable form of government in its own right.[9]

So far, Röhl has confined his discussion of the 'kingship mechanism' and its effects to the period before 1914. To date, there has been no comprehensive attempt to apply his ideas to the era of the First World War itself. Nonetheless, as Holger Afflerbach has suggested in a recent journal article, newly-available archival evidence and eye-witness accounts from the war years can be used to demonstrate a much higher degree of involvement of the Kaiser in the overall management of the war effort than has previously been suspected. In spite of his notorious mood swings, his recurrent highs and lows, he was not entirely a shadow and was able – within the area of personnel policy in particular – to make a number of indirect and direct contributions to major strategic issues.[10] This is not to say that the Kaiser was in any way successful in translating the fiction of personal command into reality. Ultimately, the responsibility for the failure to develop a co-ordinated strategy for winning the war was his and his alone.[11] But this failure in turn opens up a whole host of further questions. Did Wilhelm really believe that he was destined to lead his armies to a magnificent victory on the continent, and was it this which led him to prevent others from pursuing a constructive peace policy, as suggested, for example, by the Reichstag Peace Resolution of 1917? How far had he personally absorbed the war aims, the demand for a victorious peace settlement and the hostility towards internal political reform which were characteristic of those who surrounded him on a daily basis at Great Headquarters? And finally, what role did he play in the abandonment of all pretence at responsible constitutional government in the final years of the war, and in its sudden resurrection in October 1918, at the moment of defeat? These are the questions to which we will now turn.

THE JULY CRISIS AND THE OUTBREAK OF WAR

Any investigation of the role played by Wilhelm II in the years 1914 to 1918 must begin with an analysis of the outbreak of the war itself. The documentary evidence painstakingly pieced together by Fritz Fischer and Imanuel Geiss, among others, has established beyond reasonable doubt that (a) Austria received full backing from Germany for an aggressive response to the Sarajevo assassination (the 'blank cheque' of 5 July 1914), and (b) Germany put extensive pressure on her ally to settle accounts with Serbia through use of military force.[12] The risk that such a war would escalate into a conflict involving all the Great Powers was consciously taken by the rulers in Berlin and Vienna, although many of Germany's leaders continued to hope for British neutrality until the very last minute. As the German ambassador in

London, Prince Lichnowsky, later wrote in a secret memorandum in January 1915:

> The Austro-Hungarian attack on Serbia, supported by us, was bound to be taken by Russia as a challenge, and replied to accordingly, since Tsardom . . . would otherwise have been deprived of the ground it stands on. It was therefore incomprehensible from the outset how anyone could seriously believe in a 'localization of the conflict'. *Unfortunately my urgent and repeated warnings went unheeded.*[13]

Such comments nonetheless leave open the question as to who exactly had been responsible for making this calculated response to the Sarajevo crisis on Germany's behalf, in other words who was ultimately to blame for the outbreak of war.

In the aftermath of the 'Fischer controversy' of 1961, most accounts of German decision-making during the July crisis have focused on the actions of the Reich Chancellor, Bethmann Hollweg, and of his foreign secretary, Gottlieb von Jagow.[14] More recently, and as previous chapters have detailed, new evidence has emerged on the role played by Germany's military leaders, and by two figures in particular: the Minister of War, Erich von Falkenhayn, and the Chief of the General Staff, Helmuth von Moltke, both of whom are known to have been pushing for war from at least 1911 onwards.[15] But where does this leave the Kaiser himself? Could it be that he, too, wished to provoke a European-wide conflict? Or did he simply lose control of the situation, forcing him to give way at the last minute to the demand of his generals for 'war, the sooner the better'?

According to the American historian Isabel Hull, Wilhelm was ultimately 'shamed' into approving the decision for war by virtue of his underlying lack of self-confidence and endless desire for recognition. This in turn reflected some of the deep-seated flaws in his own personality.[16] He feared that as a champion of peace he would risk losing face with his last remaining ally in Europe, Austria-Hungary. He also feared the growing strength of the Russian armies, which might stand in the way of a German-dominated Europe in the future. But above all he feared the reaction of his own military leaders and 'inner circle' if he was seen, once again, to engage in a humiliating and 'unmanly' climb down in the face of the 'encircling' enemy. This latter fear was indeed not entirely unjustified. On 28 July 1914, the Prussian War Minister, Erich von Falkenhayn, noted somewhat scathingly in his diary after a conversation with the Kaiser at the Neues Palais in Potsdam: 'He makes confused speeches. The only thing that emerges clearly is that he no longer wants war, even if it means letting Austria down. I point out that he no longer has control over the situation.'[17]

Two further factors also need to be taken into account in explaining the Kaiser's wavering and uncertain behaviour at the end of July 1914. The first of these was his naive conviction that the monarchs of Europe would stand together against the threat posed by Serbian terrorists and thus could be persuaded to accept a limited military response by Austria as justified. This was the motive behind his famous 'Halt in Belgrade' proposal of 28 July.[18] The second factor was his belief, which he shared with the Chancellor, Bethmann Hollweg, that it might still be possible to keep Britain out of a continental war. As Annika Mombauer has outlined in some detail in her chapter in this volume, on 1 August he therefore reacted to an apparent promise of British neutrality if Germany refrained from attacking France by ordering his Chief of Staff, Moltke, not to put the Schlieffen plan into operation but instead to begin preparations for a deployment against Russia only. It was only after it had been established that the offer from Britain had been based on a 'misunderstanding' that Moltke was again permitted to proceed with his mobilization orders in the west. 'Now do as you please', the Kaiser told Moltke, 'I don't care either way'.[19]

When the last hopes for peace had broken down, Wilhelm appeared on the balcony of the Imperial palace in Berlin to deliver his famous address to the crowds gathered below: 'I no longer see parties, I see only Germans'. The success of this speech, which inaugurated a short period of domestic peace between the warring political factions in the Reichstag, must nonetheless be measured against the knowledge that he (Wilhelm) was now responsible for having led the German nation into a war which it could not possibly hope to win.

THE KAISER AND GERMAN WAR AIMS, 1914–1916

On the outbreak of war, Wilhelm II became both Commander-in-Chief of the 'Reich's entire land powers' and the ultimate symbol of the unity of 'fighting nation'.[20] In him were placed the hopes of millions for a German victory over her enemies, for the transformation of the German Reich into a fully-fledged world empire, a *Weltreich*. In order to give full weight to his position as Supreme War Lord, he decided not to stay in the Imperial capital, Berlin. Instead, he spent most of the war at Great Headquarters, moving with his entourage first to Koblenz, then to Luxembourg, Charleville, Pless, Kreuznach and finally, in the last months of the war, to the Belgian town of Spa. From here he could be on hand to co-ordinate the strategic and operational plans of his army and navy staffs and uphold the Hohenzollern tradition of the 'soldier-king', fighting alongside his armies in the field. The glorious precedents set by Frederick the Great and by his more immediate ancestor, Kaiser Wilhelm I, cannot have been far from his mind.

In reality, however, Wilhelm soon found himself out of his depth, and began to retreat more and more from the burden of his duties, leaving military functions to the military authorities and political questions in the hands of Bethmann Hollweg. Undoubtedly the outbreak of war placed a huge strain on his nerves, which had already taken a harsh battering during the various scandals associated with his reign over the previous decade. As if to add to his misery, by the beginning of 1916 he was faced with the ever-growing possibility of a breach with the United States over submarine warfare, a 'terrible ordeal' which kept him awake at night and prone to feelings of depression and despair.[21] Already in August 1914 he had instructed the army high command (the *Oberste Heeresleitung* or OHL) that the responsibility for managing the war effort was theirs and not his; and although he sometimes complained that he was being left out of decisions, for the most part he was quite happy with this arrangement.[22]

The first chief of the OHL was General von Moltke. This was until 14 September 1914, when he suffered a breakdown under the impact of the events of 1 August and the failure of the Schlieffen plan.[23] He was replaced by the Minister of War, General Erich von Falkenhayn, who held this post until the late summer of 1916 and managed, by various means, to persuade Wilhelm to support his costly strategy of attrition on the Western Front. In spite of the growing power of the OHL, however, the supreme command still lay in the hands of the Kaiser, who at any time and without explanation could dismiss the Chief of the General Staff and indeed all army officers except those in the Bavarian, Württemberg and Saxon contingents.[24] Legally, Falkenhayn could only issue operational orders to the field armies by delegation from the Kaiser; he had no power of command except that exercised through the Supreme War Lord. Wilhelm's continued support for Falkenhayn was therefore crucial, not only on a day-to-day basis, but also for the overall direction of the war effort.[25] Indeed, until 1916 Hindenburg and Ludendorff, the supreme commanders in the East (*Oberost*), were still subordinate to the OHL, and were therefore obliged to accept Falkenhayn's orders as if they had come directly from the Kaiser's own person. Admittedly, this was a source of much conflict in the early part of the war, a conflict which ultimately Hindenburg and Ludendorff were able to win.[26]

Meanwhile, the Kaiser's main contribution to events on the home front was to back the efforts of the Chancellor, Bethmann Hollweg, to create a united war effort on the basis of the *Burgfriede* or wartime political truce. This was no mean feat, particularly given the ferocity of right-wing attacks on the Chancellor coming not only from the Pan-

Germans and their industrial-agrarian allies, but also from advisors within the Kaiser's own entourage and even from members of his own family.[27] Bethmann had aroused the anger of such groups because of his belief in the necessity of a 'new orientation' in domestic affairs as the fundamental precondition for a German victory. Crucially, this meant pursuing policies designed to persuade patriotic elements within the SPD (the Social Democratic Party) to support the war effort in return for the vague promise of political reforms at home once the war had been won. Once again, the success or failure of this project was in the hands, ultimately, of the Kaiser. Until 1917 Wilhelm remained determined to protect 'his' Chancellor from unwanted interference from the military and Pan-German groups, although his motives for doing so may well have had more to do with protecting his own image and authority than a genuine enthusiasm for reform.[28] Reform, at any rate, would have to come through the person of the Kaiser and at a pace acceptable to him, as his Easter message of April 1917, announcing his intention to permit limited changes in the outdated Prussian electoral system, was to show.[29]

The Kaiser also approved in principle the strategy developed by Bethmann for defeating the enemy coalition. This involved some flexibility with regard to war aims on the continent (provided, of course, that this did not conflict with the 'general aim' of 'security for the German Reich in west and east for all imaginable time') and the retention of the High Seas Fleet as a bargaining counter to force England to accede to Germany's terms. Some form of permanent control over Belgium was paramount, as was the driving back of Russia's border in the east and the reduction of France to the rank of a second class power. The ultimate goal, as Fritz Fischer has argued, was international recognition of Germany's claim to world power status. But this did not necessarily rule out the option of early peace negotiations with either England or Russia as a part-way stage towards achieving this aim.[30]

In recognition of the strategy worked out by Bethmann, Wilhelm was prepared, at least in the first two years of the war, to exercise caution when voicing war aims in public. This was essential in order to avoid embarrassing the government or doing damage to its *Burgfriede* strategy. After all, the Social Democrats, the largest party in the Reichstag, had only approved the war budget because they believed that Germany was fighting to defend her borders against unprovoked Russian aggression. In his public address on 31 July 1915, the first anniversary of the outbreak of the war, the Kaiser dutifully maintained this fiction for the benefit of his subjects. Germany, he said, was aiming for a peace 'which provides us with the necessary military, political and economic guarantees for the future and allows us an unhindered development of our creative forces at home and on the free seas'.[31]

There were, however, occasional signs that Wilhelm was prepared to go much further than Bethmann in his own war aims programme. At the end of December 1914, for instance, he told the former Chancellor, Bernhard von Bülow, that there would be 'no peace before England is defeated and destroyed. Only amidst the ruins of London will I forgive Georgy'.[32] Such views would, of course, have caused considerable alarm among 'responsible' officials in the Foreign Office, who were concerned to impose a restraint on the number of Zeppelin raids in order to uphold good relations with neutral countries, especially Italy and the United States. They were nonetheless entirely consistent with attitudes among some of the Kaiser's industrialist friends, such as Walther Rathenau, who had likewise urged that Britain should be brought to its knees through the destruction of London and other cities by air.[33]

Unlike Rathenau, however, and indeed unlike almost everybody else in Europe at this time, Wilhelm continued to view the war in traditional, nineteenth-century dynastic terms. Whilst he regarded the Serbs as 'Orientals, liars and tricksters'[34] and Sir Edward Grey as a 'common cheat',[35] fellow monarchs (and cousins) 'Georgy' and 'Nicky' still held an exalted place in his view of the world. For this reason he was willing, after the final collapse of the original German war plan at the end of 1914, to consider an unofficial offer of mediation made through various private channels by Christian X of Denmark. 'He really believes in a tacit understanding between monarchs to spare one another', wrote Admiral von Tirpitz, the State Secretary at the Naval Office, in April 1915, 'a quaint sort of notion!'.[36] The same kind of sentimental considerations may also have determined his stance on unrestricted submarine warfare, which he opposed on the grounds that he would never torpedo a ship if he knew women and children were aboard.[37] Indeed, such were his feelings on this subject that he was even prepared to accept Tirpitz's resignation in March 1916, rather than go back on his order restricting submarine warfare to 'armed merchantmen' only.

On the other hand, Wilhelm remained strongly opposed to the repeated offers of mediation coming from the United States. 'I and my cousins George and Nicholas shall make peace when the proper time has come', he told President Wilson's special envoy, Colonel House, who twice travelled to Europe in order to negotiate an end to the fighting.[38] On another occasion he told the American ambassador, James Gerard, that 'mere democracies', such as France and the United States, were unfit to be represented at peace conferences. This was because, in his view, war was a 'royal sport, to be indulged in by hereditary monarchs and concluded at their will'.[39] As Matthew Seligmann has shown in a previous chapter, Gerard would return this slight to his country in full once America entered the war.

In the meantime, Wilhelm's failure to recognize the new political and military realities of modern warfare, and his insistence on keeping Falkenhayn as Chief of the General Staff, began to have a negative effect on morale in the senior ranks of the army, especially given the repeated failure of Falkenhayn's strategy of attrition in the west. Numerous testimonies by army and navy officers give weight to this fact. Wilhelm's reaction to the naval battle of Jutland (1 June 1916) would be a case in point. Instead of rushing to Wilhelmshaven to congratulate his admirals on their apparent victory over the British, Wilhelm slunk off to his estate at Cadinen in East Prussia, forcing the chief of the naval cabinet, Admiral von Müller, to conclude that: '[His Majesty's] thoughts are no longer with the war'.[40]

Another example comes from the diary of Major Albrecht von Thaer of the IX Reserve Corps, who noted his impressions of a troop inspection on the Western Front in mid-June 1916 as follows:

His Majesty looked well, was gracious and spoke generally of world affairs. What he said about the war should better not be repeated . . . I wonder if His Majesty has any idea what is at stake for him in this war, that it is about sceptre and throne, even for the Hohenzollerns?!'[41]

Such was the situation when the Allies launched their long-planned offensive on the Somme on 1 July 1916, forcing the German army to defend its positions on the Western Front for the first time since the beginning of the war.

THE APPOINTMENT OF HINDENBURG AND LUDENDORFF

In fact, soon after the beginning of the Somme offensive, Germany's leaders were suddenly obliged to take real stock of the war situation. Following the entry of Romania into the war on the Allied side in August 1916, Wilhelm was forced to swallow his pride and appoint Hindenburg and Ludendorff to the OHL in place of the hapless Falkenhayn. This was a very real turning point, for the two eastern generals were not only determined to assert themselves as commanders in the field, but also to extend their influence into the German domestic sphere, thus encroaching directly on Wilhelm's prerogatives as supreme co-ordinator of military and political affairs. An example here would be the forced resignation on 5 November 1916 of the Foreign Secretary von Jagow, who was regarded as too keen an advocate of a compromise peace. This was followed a few weeks later by the lifting of the official ban on public discussion of war aims, a move which threatened the position of the Chancellor himself.[42]

The appointment of Hindenburg and Ludendorff was also significant because it meant an immediate resumption of the battle over unrestricted submarine warfare, which Bethmann believed he had won back in the spring of 1916. Now the arguments started all over again, with Hindenburg and Ludendorff placing themselves firmly on the side of the pro-submarine campaigners. In the end, Bethmann was given one last chance: with the Kaiser's approval, he was allowed to make a limited peace offer to the Allies at the end of 1916. Accordingly, on 12 December Bethmann informed the Reichstag that Germany was prepared to enter into preliminary negotiations with the enemy, but stopped short of setting out any concrete conditions. At the same time, Wilhelm himself explained the true purpose of the peace offer in a private conversation with his American dentist, Arthur Davis: 'We've got the English and French governments in a nice predicament, trying to explain to their people why they don't make peace. They're wild with rage at us for surprising them in this way.'[43] Given the circumstances of the German offer there was never much prospect of the Allies accepting it, and the Germans for their part turned down a renewed set of peace proposals from Wilson. 'If the President wants to end the war', Wilhelm wrote on 22 December, 'all he need do is make good a threat of denying the English pirates any more munitions, block their access to the loan market and institute reprisals against letter-snatching and black lists. That would quickly end the war without the need for notes, conferences etc.! I shall not be attending any conference. Especially not one chaired by him!'[44]

The Allied rejection of the German peace offer in turn strengthened the hand of those who advocated an all-out submarine warfare. By the beginning of 1917 the Kaiser himself was beginning to move away from the moderate position he had previously held on this issue, first and foremost because Hindenburg threatened to resign unless restrictions against sinking unarmed or neutral merchant ships were lifted. On 9 January, at a crown council held at Schloß Pless in Silesia, Wilhelm now expressed his support for this type of warfare which all his military and naval advisors had declared would lead to England 'being forced to her knees' within four to six months.[45] Even Bethmann no longer had the energy to counter the arguments of the generals. Although he decided to remain in office, his days were now clearly numbered and he was eventually forced to go in July 1917. In the meantime, war was declared by the United States on 6 April.

In the weeks and months after the decision on U-boat warfare, the Kaiser's image and prestige among the German people began to fall considerably, whilst that of Hindenburg rose still further.[46] Part of the problem, as Admiral von Müller recognized was Wilhelm's refusal to take up residence at the new military headquarters at Kreuznach. Instead, he preferred to remain at Homburg with the Empress, where he lived in a luxurious manner which was 'hardly distinguishable from peacetime Court life'. In fact, the Kaiser now saw it 'as a major achievement if he occasionally spends two or three days at Kreuznach to hear the military reports'.[47] This was a trend, moreover, which increased as the war went on. 'I cannot abandon my wife who suffers so much anxiety on account of the war and her sons', he told Müller on one occasion towards the end of 1917.[48]

In spite of Wilhelm's increasing failure to fulfil his duties as Supreme War Lord, however, his influence on events did not entirely disappear. We have already mentioned, for instance, his Easter message announcing postwar electoral reform in Prussia, a move which was opposed by many at court, including the Empress herself.[49] He was also responsible, ultimately, for all questions relating to Germany's foreign policy and the conclusion of new alliances and treaties. Here, admittedly, his influence was of a more negative nature, in that he successfully blocked any further efforts towards a negotiated peace without developing a consistent strategy of his own for winning the war.

At the beginning of April 1917, for instance, upon hearing of the American declaration of war, he intervened directly to demand that the following three points be emphasized by the Foreign Office in its briefings to the German and foreign press:

1. England was behind the Russian revolution and the abdication of the Tsar, whom she has also let down personally. England must now be held responsible for guaranteeing the personal safety of the Tsar and his wife.
2. In reality America has only entered the war against Germany because she needs a cover for creating a large standing army which she otherwise would not have been able to do and which she intends to use in order to protect the big capitalists against the proletariat.
3. Wilson claims that the war was started by the German government and dynasty for its own selfish interests, although he must know that in 1914 the entire German people stood behind its leaders. By contrast,

the American war effort is being conducted in the interests of a small group of big capitalists. It is contrary to the real interests of the American people and serves merely as a pretext for strengthening the rule of the big capitalists over the proletariat.[50]

A few months earlier, in January 1917, he had already expressed his inner feelings about the true nature of the war in a letter to the English-born racist philosopher Houston Stewart Chamberlain:

> The war is a struggle between two *Weltanschauungen*, the Teutonic-German for morality, right, loyalty and faith, genuine humanity, truth and real freedom, against the Anglo-Saxon [*Weltanschauung*], the worship of Mammon, the power of money, pleasure, land-hunger, lies, betrayal, deceit and – last but not least – treacherous assassination!

There could be no compromise between the two systems, he continued: 'one must be *victorious*, the other go *under*!'[51]

On the other hand, when informed by Admiral Paul von Hintze, the German ambassador in Christiania (Oslo), that the Norwegian Prime Minister favoured a return to the pre-war balance of power rather than a clear-cut military victory by one side, he noted in a moment of fury: 'That is just what *we do not want*! Balance of power must cease! It was the cause of the war!'[52] And in the autumn of 1917 he balked against a suggestion made by the new Chancellor Georg Michaelis to abandon non-essential war aims such as the coast of Flanders on the grounds that possession of the latter was a crucial precondition for a German victory in the 'second Punic war' against Britain.

> No cessation of the U-boat war until George has submitted. England has ... *not won* and therefore has *lost* the first Punic War; we, however, have *not* been able to defeat her ... For this reason we must begin immediate preparations for the second Punic War – this time with better alliance provisions and better chances. Since it will happen. Until one of us *alone* is victorious, there can be no peace in the world! *Great Britain* will never agree to a condominium, and so she must be thrown out.[53]

Thus it would seem that in 1917 the Kaiser was still determined to pursue the war with England and her allies to the bitter end. Undoubtedly this made it all the more difficult for advocates of a compromise peace, such as the new Foreign Secretary, Richard von Kühlmann, to make their voices heard.[54]

As the year 1917 merged into the year 1918 Wilhelm II allowed his position as Supreme War Lord to be further and further eroded by the growing power of his generals. He could not even save his most trusted civilian advisors, who were forced to resign at various intervals after losing the confidence of the army leadership or the Reichstag or both: the Chancellor, Bethmann Hollweg (in July 1917), his successor Michaelis (in October 1917), the head of the civil cabinet, Rudolf von Valentini (in January 1918) and the Foreign Secretary, Richard von Kühlmann (in June 1918). The high command, for their part, were quite happy to keep the Kaiser as ignorant and isolated as possible, allowing Hindenburg to emerge as a more credible *Ersatz-Kaiser* or substitute monarch in the hearts and minds of the ordinary German people. The former War Minister and commander of the Third Army, General von Einem, for instance, noted with disgust how, at the celebration of Hindenburg's birthday in October 1917, 'the Kaiser's behaviour was positively deferential throughout!'[55] Likewise, in December 1917 Crown Prince Rupprecht of Bavaria was disturbed and shocked when he witnessed a troop inspection on the Western Front in which the Kaiser brought greetings and a message of support 'from the Field Marshal' (i.e. Hindenburg). Surely it was wrong, in Rupprecht's view, that a reigning monarch should appear before his soldiers as a mere spokesman for one of his senior officers.[56]

In the field of foreign affairs, too, the Kaiser's views were now too unsteady and incoherent to be of any significance in the overall direction of strategy. The peace negotiations with the new Bolshevik government in Russia, for instance, were conducted largely through Ludendorff's representative at Brest Litovsk, General Max Hoffmann, with Wilhelm giving only scant and half-hearted support to the more moderate position adopted by Kühlmann and the Foreign Office.[57] At one stage in the negotiations, during a meeting of the war council held at Homburg on 13 February 1918, he demanded that the army march on Petrograd to destroy Bolshevism before it brought revolution to Germany. 'Had not Wilson', he declared, 'ordered the removal of the House of Hohenzollern as a war aim and did he not now support the Bolsheviks with the whole of international Jewry?'[58] On another occasion, a few weeks earlier, he had dubbed Ludendorff a 'malefactor' with whom he would never shake hands again. This was because he held the latter responsible for the forced dismissal of Valentini, his loyal civil cabinet chief for the past ten years.[59]

This latest run-in with the generals indeed illustrated, once again, the dangerous political and social isolation which Wilhelm had manoeuvred himself into. Now he absented himself from afternoon sessions of the war council, leaving operational matters entirely in the hands of the high command.[60] True, when things were going well for Germany, he was capable of returning to his old bombastic style. On 23 March 1918, for instance, he celebrated the first successes of the new German campaign on the Western Front with the words: 'The battle is won, the English have been utterly defeated'. Three days later champagne was ordered at headquarters and he declared: 'if an English delegation comes to sue for peace it must kneel before the German standard, for it is a question here of the victory of monarchy over democracy'.[61]

But as the prospect of victory faded, the mood of the Kaiser changed yet again. 'I am a defeated War Lord to whom you must show consideration', he told a small group of advisors on the evening of 22 July 1918, after receiving the first of Hindenburg's reports on the failure of the Avesnes offensive. Later that night he had a terrible dream in which he saw 'visions of all my English and Russian relatives and all the ministers and generals of my own reign marching past and mocking me. Only the little Queen of Norway [George V's sister] was friendly to me'.[62] The final blow was delivered when the Allied counter-offensive liberated Amiens on 8 August 1918, the 'black day' for the German army. Now Wilhelm accepted that there was no longer any hope of victory in the west. 'We have reached the limits of our capacity', he told Ludendorff. 'The war must be ended'.[63] But ended how?

In the early autumn of 1918 Germany's political and military leaders remained confident that peace could still be achieved on reasonably favourable terms. This illusion was shattered in October when the new government of Max von Baden understood, via an exchange of notes with President Wilson, that the Allies regarded the Kaiser's very presence as the chief obstacle in the way of immediate negotiations for an armistice. As a starting point the new government managed to persuade Wilhelm to dismiss Ludendorff, although Hindenburg remained as overall commander. A change in the constitution also made the Chancellor responsible to parliament for the first time in the history of the German empire. Max von Baden himself now hoped that the Kaiser would have the good sense to go quietly and of his own volition. By abdicating and making one of his grandchildren successor to the Hohenzollern throne, he could increase the dynasty's own chances of survival. Even the new Social Democrat ministers seemed to agree that a constitutional monarchy would be an acceptable alternative to a republic. But although he had threatened to abdicate on several previous occasions during his reign, Wilhelm now refused to countenance such a move. 'Who would replace me?', he asked on 3 November. 'The marvellous Max von Baden, for example?'[64]

In the end it was left to the generals at Headquarters to tell Wilhelm that his troops would march home in good order, but not in his name or under his command. It was best, they said, that he abdicate and go into exile; above all he must avoid the fate of the Tsar and his family in Russia.[65] But whilst Wilhelm temporized, the Majority Socialists declared a republic in Berlin on the morning of 9 November 1918. After 300 years, the Hohenzollern dynasty was finished. On the following day, Wilhelm fled to Holland, where he lived a comfortable existence as the 'squire of Doorn' until his death in 1941 at the age of 82. During this time he remained an unrepentant German nationalist and never once gave up the hope that he might be restored to the throne.[66]

CONCLUSION

Let us return, finally, to the question of the role of personalities in the First World War. Central to this discussion must be an analysis of the power structures at work in the different warring nations. In the case of Germany, Wilhelm II stood at the pinnacle of a leadership elite which embraced the army, the officer corps, the upper bureaucracy, the imperial entourage and the cabinet chiefs. Already by the end of 1916 he had dismissed both Moltke and Falkenhayn, thus demonstrating – if only indirectly – his continued importance as Commander-in-Chief. Admittedly, other factors intervened in the final years of the war, in particular the rise of Hindenburg and Ludendorff in what is known as the third army high command. Nonetheless, even then it would be wrong to dismiss him as a mere shadow. Through his unequivocal support for the war aims of German industry and agriculture, through his power of command over the German army and navy and through his final decision in favour of unrestricted submarine warfare in 1917 he placed a succession of obstacles in the way of a negotiated peace settlement. At the same time his restless and volatile personality mirrored exactly the paralysis in Germany's leadership structures as the war continued. As Admiral Albert Hopman, a close associate of Alfred von Tirpitz and somewhat belated critic of personal rule, wrote in his diary on 6 October 1918:

> Everything which I predicted, not just in the last few weeks but for much, much longer, has come true. What Germany has sinned in the last three decades it must pay for. It was politically paralyzed through its blind faith in, [and] its slavish submission to, the will of a puffed-up, vainglorious and self-overestimating fool.[67]

Indeed, Wilhelm's abdication only a few weeks later led directly to the downfall of the monarchical system in both Prussia and the rest of the Reich, and the dawn of a new, less certain, era in German history.

Notes

1 Sebastian Haffner, 'Wilhelm der Zweite', in: Sebastian Haffner and Wolfgang Venohr, *Preußische Profile*, Frankfurt am Main, 1986, p.261.

2 See John C.G. Röhl, 'Kaiser Wilhelm II. A Suitable Case For Treatment', in: idem., *The Kaiser and His Court. Wilhelm II and the Government of Germany*, Cambridge, 1994, p.13.

3 Ibid.

4 For a useful summary of the historiographical debate on this issue see Isabel V. Hull, '"Persönliches Regiment"', in: John C.G. Röhl (ed.), *Der Ort Kaiser Wilhelms II. in der deutschen Geschichte*, Munich, 1991, pp.3–23.

5 Willibald Gutsche, *Wilhelm II. Der letzte Kaiser des Deutschen Reiches. Eine Biographie*, Berlin, 1991, p.174.

6 Wilhelm Deist, 'Censorship and Propaganda in Germany During the First World War', in: Jean-Jacques Becker and Stéphane Audoin-Rouzeau (eds), *Les sociétés européennes et la guerre de 1914–1918*, Paris-Nanterre, 1990, p.200. See also Deist, 'Kaiser Wilhelm II als Oberster Kriegsherr', in: Röhl (ed.), *Der Ort Kaiser Wilhelms II.*, pp.25–42.

7 See Röhl's introduction in: John C.G. Röhl and Nicholaus Sombart (eds.), *Kaiser Wilhelm II. New Interpretations*, Cambridge, 1982, p.15.

8 See Röhl's essay, 'Der "Köingsmechanismus" im Kaiserreich', in: *Historische Zeitschrift*, 236 (1983), pp. 539–77. English translation in: Röhl, *The Kaiser and His Court*, pp. 107–130.

9 See also Katharine A. Lerman, *The Chancellor as Courtier. Bernhard von Bülow and the Governance of Germany, 1900–1909*, Cambridge, 1988, for a development of this theme.

10 Holger Afflerbach, 'Wilhelm II as Supreme War Lord in the First World War', in: *War in History*, 5 (1998), pp. 427–49. This article is based in part on Afflerbach's research for his book *Falkenhayn. Politisches Denken und Handeln im Kaiserreich*, Munich, 1994, and is buttressed by new archival finds, including the diaries of the Imperial Adjutant General, Hans von Plessen, and the war letters of the Chief of the Imperial Military Cabinet, Mortiz Freiherr von Lyncker.

11 Cf. Deist, 'Kaiser Wilhelm II als Oberster Kriegsherr', p.27.

12 The literature on the July crisis is too voluminous to be included here. Readers are referred to the volume by John W. Landon, *July 1914. The Long Debate, 1918–1990*, Oxford, 1991, and the references to other works contained therein.

13 Quoted in John C.G. Röhl, *1914: Delusion or Design? The Testimony of Two German Diplomats*, London, 1973, p.83.

14 For an overview of the Fischer controversy see John A. Moses, *The Politics of Illusion. The Fischer Controversy in German Historiography*, London, 1975. Among the more useful works on Bethmann Hollweg himself are Konrad Jarausch, *The Enigmatic Chancellor. Bethmann Hollweg and the*

Hubris of Imperial Germany, London, 1973; and Willibald Gutsche, *Aufstieg und Verfall eines kaiserlichen Reichskanzlers*, Berlin (East), 1973.

15 See eg Afflerbach, *Falkenhayn*, pp. 147 ff.; and Annika Mombauer, 'A Reluctant Military Leader? Helmuth von Moltke and the July Crisis of 1914', in: *War in History*, 6 (1999), pp. 417–46. Also Mombauer's forthcoming monograph, *Helmuth von Moltke and the Origins of the First World War*, Cambridge, 2001.

16 Isabel Hull, *The Entourage of Kaiser Wilhelm II, 1888–1918*, Cambridge, 1982, p.265.

17 Quoted in Afflerbach, 'Wilhelm II as Supreme War Lord', p.432.

18 See Wilhelm II to Jagow, 28 July 1914, in: Imanuel Geiss (ed.), *July 1914. Selected Documents*, London, 1967, pp.256–7.

19 The full story surrounding the events of 1 August 1914 is told in Mombauer, 'A Reluctant Military Leader?', pp.440–6. See also Barbara Tuchman, *August 1914*, London, 1962, pp. 84–8.

20 Afflerbach, 'Wilhelm II as Supreme War Lord', p. 433.

21 See Walter Görlitz (ed.), *The Kaiser and His Court. The Diaries, Note Books and Letters of Admiral Georg Alexander von Müller, Chief of the Naval Cabinet, 1914–1918*, London, 1961, p. 131. Müller's diary entry for 1 February 1916.

22 Hull, *Entourage*, p.268.

23 Mombauer, 'A Reluctant Military Leader', p. 445.

24 Robert B. Asprey, *The German High Command at War. Hindenburg, Ludendorff and the First World War*, London, 1991, p. 147.

25 Cf. Afflerbach, 'Wilhelm II as Supreme War Lord', p. 448.

26 On the conflict between Falkenhayn on the one hand and Hindenburg and Ludendorff (supported by Bethmann Hollweg) on the other see John Wheeler-Bennett, *Hindenburg. The Wooden Titan*, London, 1967 [1936], pp. 34–73; and Holger Herwig, *The First World War. Germany and Austria, 1914–1918*, London, 1997, pp. 130–5.

27 Among those who disliked Bethmann and his style of domestic political leadership were the Crown Prince Wilhelm and the Empress Auguste Victoria ('Dona'). See Hull, *Entourage*, p. 271.

28 See for instance the Kaiser's angry comments to Admiral von Müller in February 1917 regarding the participation of one of his admirals à la suite, Admiral von Knorr, in an anti-Bethmann meeting at the Hotel Adlon, reproduced in: Görlitz (ed.), *The Kaiser and His Court*, P. 244.

29 On the question of Prussian electoral reform see Hellmuth Weber, 'Zum Problem der Wahlrechtsreform in Preußen während der Jahre 1917–1918', in: Fritz Klein et al (eds), *Polittik im Krieg. Studien zur Polittik der deutschen herrschenden Klassen in Ersten Weltkrieg*, Berlin (East), 1964, pp. 189–203.

30 Limitations of space prohibit here any broader discussion of German war aims. The major monographs on this subject include Hans Gatzke,

Germany's Drive to the West (Drang nach Westen). *A Study of Germany's Western War Aims During the First World War*, Baltimore, 1950; Fritz Fischer, *Germany's Aims in the First World War*, London, 1967; Gerhard Ritter, *The Sword and the Sceptre: The Problem of Militarism in Germany*, 4 Vols, Coral Gables, FL, 1972; Fritz Klein et al (eds), *Deutschland im Ersten Weltkrieg*, 3 Vols, Berlin (East), 1968–9; and, more peripherally, Fritz Fischer, *War of Illusions: German Policies from 1911 to 1914*, London, 1975.

31 Quoted in Gutsche, *Wilhelm II*, p.179.

32 Hull, *Entourage*, p. 266.

33 See Bundesarchiv (BA) Potsdam, Reichskanzlei, No. 2465, Bl. 27, Rathenau to Mutius, 16 October 1914. Also Hartmut Pogge von Strandmann (ed.), *Walther Rathenau. Notes and Diaries, 1907–1922*, Oxford, 1985, p. 186.

34 Wilhelm II to Jagow, 28 July 1914, in: Geiss (ed.), *July 1914*, p. 256.

35 Wilhelm II's marginal comments on a telegram from Lichnowsky to Jagow, 29 July 1914, in: ibid., p. 289.

36 Alfred von Tirpitz, *Erinnerungen*, Leipzig, 1919, p. 471. Letter to his wife, 15 April 1915.

37 Görlitz (ed.), *The Kaiser and His Court*, p. 138, Müller's diary entry for 23 February 1916.

38 Palmer, *The Kaiser*, p. 183.

39 Quoted in Röhl, *The Kaiser and His Court*, p. 207.

40 Görlitz (ed.), *The Kaiser and His Court*, p. 169. Müller's diary entry for 2 June 1916.

41 Quoted in Herwig, *The First World War*, p. 215.

42 See Wilhelm Deist (ed.), *Militär und Innenpolittik*, Düsseldorf, 1970, Vol. I, No. 182, pp. 431 ff. (Schreiben der Oberzensurstelle an sämtliche Zensurstellen betr. die in der Berliner Presse gegebene Erläuterung zur Freigabe der Kriegszieleröterungen in der Öffentlichkeit, 25 November 1916).

43 Arthur N. Davis, *The Kaiser I Knew*, London, 1918, p. 52.

44 Quoted in Karl E. Birnbaum, *Peace Moves and U-Boat Warfare. A Study of Imperial Germany's Policy Towards the United States, April 18 1916–9 January 1917*, Stockholm, 1958, pp. 368–9.

45 For the minutes of this council see Helmut Otto and Karl Schmiedel (eds.), *Der Erste Weltkrieg. Dokumente*, Berlin (East), 1977, pp. 222–4.

46 See eg Bernd Sösemann, 'Der Verfall des Kaisergedankens im Ersten Weltkrieg', in: Röhl (ed.), *Der Ort Kaiser Wilhelms II.*, pp. 145–70. Also Müller's comments in his diary on 25 March 1917, in: Görlitz (ed.), *The Kaiser and His Court*, p. 250. Here Müller writes: 'In my opinion the Kaiser is losing face to an ever-increasing extent. He has allowed himself to be ousted by the High Command and a certain section of the press has "ousted him" too . . .'.

47 Ibid., p. 251.

48 Ibid., p. 313. Müller's diary entry for 11 November 1917.

49 Ibid., p. 249. Müller's diary entry for 18 March 1917.

50 See Politisches Archiv des Auswärtigen Amtes (PA-AA), R 22252, Grünau to the AA, 5 April 1917. With regard to the Kaiser's first point, it is now a well-known fact that George V ignored pleas from his cousin Tsar Nicholas II to allow him and his family to come to England. They were all later murdered by the Bolsheviks in the summer of 1918.

51 Quoted in Röhl, *The Kaiser and His Court*, p. 208. This quotation is taken from the original version of the letter, rediscovered in the Chamberlain *Nachlaß* in the Richard Wagner Museum in Bayreuth, which also contains a reference to Lloyd George and Briand as being 'under the spell of Satan'. The version in Chamberlain, *Briefe, 1882–1924*, Munich, 1928, Vol. II, p. 250, has been heavily edited. Cf. Chamberlain's reply to Wilhelm on 20 January 1917, which expresses complete agreement with these sentiments – published version in ibid., pp. 251 ff.

52 Quoted in Holger H. Herwig, 'Admirals *versus* Generals. The War Aims of the Imperial German Navy, 1914–1918', in: *Central European History*, 5 (1972), p. 221.

53 Quoted in Gutsche, *Wilhelm II*, p. 183.

54 Cf. Richard von Kühlmann, *Erinnerungen*, Heidelberg, 1948.

55 Quoted in Deist (ed.), *Militär und Innenpolittik*, Vol. II, No. 425, p. 1137 n. 5.

56 Cf. Palmer, *The Kaiser*, p. 200.

57 For a detailed analysis of the peace of Brest Litovsk see Fischer, *Germany's Aims*, pp. 475–509.

58 Görlitz (ed.), *The Kaiser and His Court*, p. 333. Müller's diary entry for 13 February 1918.

59 Ibid., p. 325, Müller's diary entry for 17 January 1918.

60 Palmer, *The Kaiser*, p. 201.

61 Görlitz (ed.), *The Kaiser and his Court*, p. 344–5. Müller's diary entries for 23 and 26 March 1918.

62 Ibid., p. 374, Müller's diary entries for 22 and 23 July 1918.

63 Palmer, *The Kaiser*, p. 205.

64 Michael Balfour, *The Kaiser and His Times*, London, 1964, p. 403.

65 Ibid., p. 405.

66 Cf. Willibald Gutsche, *Ein Kaiser im Exil. Der letzte deutsche Kaiser Wilhelm II. in Holland*, Berlin, 1991; and idem., 'Monarchistitsche Retaurationsstrategie und Faschismus. Zur Rolle Wilhelms II. im Kampf der nationalistischen und revanchistischen Kräfte um die Beseitigung der Weimarer Republik', in: Röhl (ed.), *Der Ort Kaiser Kaiser Wilhelms II.*, pp. 287–96.

67 Quoted in Röhl, *The Kaiser and his Court*, p. 27.

Index